JOE STRUMMER

and the legend of
The Clash

JOE STRUMMER

and the legend of
The Clash

KRIS NEEDS

Plexus, London

Dedication

For Mick, Topper, Robin, Johnny, Norro, Don, Jock, Colin, and Michelle.

Dedicated to the memory of Joe Strummer, Guy Stevens, St. Ledger Letts and John Peel.

There was an enormous freedom to the band's sound. It was complex, because freedom is complex; wild and anarchic, like the wish for freedom; sympathetic, affectionate and coherent, like the reality of freedom. And it was all celebration, all affirmation, a music of endless humour and delight, like a fantasy of freedom.
Greil Marcus, *Mystery Train*

Published by Plexus Publishing Limited
55a Clapham Common Southside
London SW4 9BX
www.plexusbooks.com
First Printing 2005

British Library Cataloguing In Publication Data

Needs, Kris
Joe Strummer and the legend of the clash
1. Biography
I. Title
782.4'2166'092

ISBN 0 85965 348 X

Printed and bound in Great Britain by Biddles Ltd
Cover design by Phil Gambrill
Book design by Rebecca Martin

Contents

Preface

Strummer and the band perfectly understood 'Needsy'. He was the real thing. As the affectionate nickname denotes, he was regarded as a friend and was privy to even the most intimate moments. Permanent 'Access All Areas'.

The reasons for this were both simple and complex - somewhat like Kris himself. One one level, he was always great fun to have around. Yet he also intuitively understood the semi-realistic behaviour and long running surreal comedy that was the necessary counter-balance to the burdens that The Clash inevitably came to bear.

But above all, Kris was a genuine fan and his motives were pure. There was an almost Zen-like lack of ego, which enabled him to take stick as well as dish it out. He fitted perfectly. I've lost count of the number of times Joe would turn to me and ask, 'When's Needsy comin' over?'

His musical pedigree was rather good too. As the former president of the Mott The Hoople fan club and a keen Keef devotee, his rapport with Mick was more than solid. He could talk Billy Cobham with Topper and chat ska with Paul. Even the colossus Johnny Green had a very real soft spot for him. As for animal noises, his knowledge was simply exhaustive.

So, all in all, he was - and still is - a good egg. Or, at the very least, an okapi omelette.

Love, Robin Banks, 2004

A Fore-Warning

I could always tell when Kris Needs was around. He brought vivacity, merri-ment and a delicious sense of the ridiculous with him. He would bounce into the dressing room as if his brothel-creepers were soled with magic rubber. His arms would flay with enthusiasm. Even his black spiky barnet would explode like Johnny Thunders meets Ken Dodd.

Kris was always welcome in The Clash's dressing room. He was close to all four of the band. Like our pal, Robin Banks, he could play the court jester *par excellence*. His juggling act with sandwiches was renowned and got him banned from a well-known hotel chain. He, like The Clash, did not tolerate authority gladly.

Kris Needs is a player, not a spectator. His value, particularly to Joe Strummer, was that he didn't bullshit. He has a serious, thoughtful side that comes out in his writing and conversation. He ain't no sap.

His knowledge of the zoological world is formidable. Joe, Mick, Paul and Topper were devotees of Needsy's animal and bird noises. You can hear his musi-cal influence across *London Calling*.

I know. I was there too. Check this . . .

Johnny Green, Road Manager, The Clash, 2004

CHAPTER ONE

GLOBAL A-GO-GO

All transmitters to pull. All receivers to boost.
This is London calling . . . This is London calling . . .
– Joe Strummer, introducing his 1998 BBC World Service broadcast.

In 1977, you had to be careful what you said. Despite its anarchistic manifesto, punk rock had its own unwritten list of qualifications for acceptance, especially within the ranks of its originators and elements of the media.

If you were a working class teenager from a council estate – preferably from a broken home with an alcoholic mother – and survived on a crap job or the dole, you were considered okay. The shittier your circumstances, the better. But if your background was comfortably middle-class, you'd attended a good school and were maybe tipping the scales in terms of age, there might be credibility problems. It was like you had *no right* to be a punk. Strange but true.

The fact that punk rock's two main management movers – Malcolm McLaren and Bernie Rhodes – were older and reasonably off didn't matter. The Sex Pistols were working class lads from London's dodgier areas, even if many of their original followers were drawn from middle class suburbia.

As The Clash sprang to prominence in 1977, the Pistols weren't looking at more than another year in existence. It was going to be down to The Clash to pick up the baton. But their singer, Joe Strummer, was already fielding jibes about his public school background, his father's career in the Foreign Office, and even the shocking revelation that he was twenty-four years old.

It didn't matter that Joe had worked for several years at menial jobs like cleaning toilets and digging graves while he tried to kick-start his musical career. The fact that he was one of the most charismatic front men to emerge in years, a brilliant wordsmith and a ferociously riveting performer should've been enough. When Joe died in 2002, it was these qualities that he was remembered for. An avalanche of tributes described Joe as the ultimate punk, a spokesman for a generation, and an icon comparable with John Lennon and Bob Marley.

A quarter of a century earlier, as punk was picking up amphetamine fuelled momentum, Joe was more of a target than an icon. One music paper writer who knew about Joe's background acted like he was in possession of classified information.

When I was getting involved with The Clash and reporting on the punk scene in 1976, I started to feel slightly guilty of the fact that I was twenty-two, married, with a job and came from a stable home with a reasonable education. Later, I didn't let it worry me, and it didn't most other people I befriended. If you heard certain individuals reciting from their personal arbitrary punk rulebooks, it paid to just say 'Bollocks! I'm like this – take it or leave it'.

Recalling the *zeitgeist*, Clash bassist Paul Simonon told *GQ*, 'This was something that we had to deal with internally insofar as Joe went to boarding school but then again, at the end of the day, does it really matter? By the time I met Joe, he was as broke as I was. OK, he had a better education than me but so what? What you're doing with your life now is more important. I don't really buy that – whether you're middle class or not – it's what you do with your life that's important. That's the thing about punk. It changed their lives and it changed ours too.'

Now see what those griping old punks are doing. Most of them are settled into exactly the kind of life they were railing against a quarter of a century ago. Married with kids in a normal job in a nice house. Meanwhile, Joe Strummer lived his last years exactly how he wanted to – making music, performing it wherever he wanted, then going home to his Somerset farmhouse to see his wife and kids.

Streetcore, Joe's final album, demonstrates that he never lost his edge and his enthusiasm to top everything he'd done before. One of his last gigs was in aid of striking firemen. Joe was a true punk rocker all his life.

In 2004 I can write about how the man who came to be called Joe Strummer grew up without feeling like I'm contravening the Official Secrets Act. But in April 1977, Joe felt it necessary to explain his background in an interview with *Melody Maker*'s Caroline Coon. 'I'm not working class at all. My father was born in India. His father died when he was eight and so he was an orphan and he went to an orphan school. Then, because he was so smart, they gave him a scholarship and he went to university, and he was really proud that he had come from nothing, with no chance, to have a degree – even though it was from the poxy University of Lucknow.'

Joe's father, Ronald Ralph Mellor, came to London after serving in the Second World War and joined the foreign office as a clerk – or 'junior bum', as Joe told Caroline. Over the next few years, Ron worked his way up to diplomat status.

One of nine children, Joe's mother Anna certainly came from working class roots. Her father, David Mackenzie, was a struggling farmer with a croft on the North East coast of Scotland. Jane, his wife, was born on the Isle of Raasay, next door to Skye, where there is now a whole forest planted in Joe's memory. Anna moved to London when her first marriage failed and became a nurse. Here she met Ron and the couple married, settling in Paddington, London.

The couple had their first son, David, in 1951 – the year that Ronald got his first overseas posting to Ankara, Turkey. The family remained in Ankara after David's birth and a second son, John Graham Mellor, arrived on 21 August 1952. The Mellors moved another three times before 1957 – to Cairo, Mexico City and Bonn. John Mellor's first five years in this world were a whirl of diversity, the bombardment of images and languages providing the basis for his later global outlook on music and life in general.

It must have been something of a culture shock when Ronald returned to Whitehall in 1959 and the family bought a bungalow in the suburb of Warlingham, Surrey. 15 Court Farm Road is situated firmly in the commuter belt, between Croydon and Caterham, with the Biggin Hill airbase nearby. It would be the Mellors' UK residence for the next twenty years.

The decision to send young John to the City Of London Freemen School, near

Epsom, Surrey, was not a sign of parental affluence. The school fees were paid for by the Foreign Office, in order to provide the children of diplomatic staff with a stable education. Later, under the tenets of the Year Zero fundamentalism peculiar to the nascent British punk scene, the fact that 'Joe Strummer went to public school' verged on heresy.

Joe first publicly opened up about his childhood in a November 1976 interview with *Melody Maker*. He told Caroline Coon that the school wasn't exactly top of the range, being a place where 'thick rich people sent their thick rich kids.' Ron had indeed wanted something a bit more upmarket for his youngest son, but he failed all the entrance exams. Joe told Caroline that he gained entrance to CLFS because they had an arrangement where, if one brother was already a pupil, subsequent siblings could get in too. So Joe followed in David's footsteps at the age of nine, and would stay there for the next eight years.

The large, mixed boarding school followed the traditional layout of an isolated manor house set in extensive grounds, which seemed to be the norm for such establishments. It certainly sounded pretty grim from the way Joe described it to *NME*'s Lucy O'Brien in 1986. 'I went on my ninth birthday into a weird Dickensian Victorian world with sub-corridors under sub-basements, one light bulb every hundred yards, and people coming down 'em beating wooden coat hangers on our heads.'

Joe also talked about his background in Don Letts' *Westway To The World* documentary. 'My father pulled himself up by his own intelligence. He had a very big ethos of, "You study". I often think about my parents and how I last felt about it because it was like being sent away. I just subconsciously went to the heart of the matter, which was "Forget about your parents", and did all of this.'

Joe later revealed that he was subject to merciless bullying on account of his diminutive stature. In December 1979, he told *Melody Maker*'s Chris Bohn, 'I was a dwarf when I was younger, grew to my normal size later on, but before then I had to fight my way through school.'

Unlike his classmates, the peripatetic nature of his father's posting meant that there was no guarantee that he'd see his parents during the holidays. His dad was posted to Tehran in 1962, then Malawi in 1966, by which time he had been promoted to Second Secretary of Information and awarded the MBE for his endeavours. For most of his school years, Joe often only saw his parents during the six-week summer break.

He had plenty of time to get into the books of TE Lawrence and George Orwell, along with watching old Hollywood gangster and cowboy films that got shown. These movies played a major part in stirring Joe's interest in Americana, and planted the seeds of rebellion that would fully bloom in The Clash.

The strictly regimented public school enviroment further inspired Joe toward discovering any means of sedition – and the best one has constantly been proven to be rock 'n' roll. 'I remember hearing 'Not Fade Away' by the Rolling Stones coming out of this huge, wooden radio,' recalled Joe. 'The Beatles, the Stones, the Yardbirds, the Kinks.'

Joe quickly discovered originators like Chuck Berry, Bo Diddley and the whole spectrum of rock 'n' roll, blues and R&B. 'In sixty-eight the whole world was exploding. Paris, Grosvenor Square, the counter culture. [The Rolling Stones'] 'Street Fighting Man' we just accepted as a fantastic song. I don't think we had the faculty to take on board what it was saying.'

One of Joe's major early influences at boarding school was eccentric psychedelic blues exponent Don Van Vliet – alias Captain Beefheart. Beefheart is one of the few artists who actually merit the much-abused accolade of genius. Beefheart came from California with his Magic Band and unleashed a torrent of earthy, surrealistic blues in 1966 with his debut album, *Safe As Milk*. Adopted by Radio One's tireless John Peel, Beefheart grew into a massive cult hero and pushed the boundaries with a multi-octave voice reminiscent of Howlin' Wolf's raw blues power, a band directed into genre demolishing alien structures and a way with words that dripped with surrealistic insight.

Joe got into Beefheart during his last year at school, and cited 1969's startling *Trout Mask Replica* double album as his favourite. 'That's when I became a weirdo', he recalled. Joe was particularly interested when I was granted an audience with Captain Beefheart at a West End hotel in late 1977. 'I love Beefheart' he whispered. Bearing in mind this was the precise point at which The Clash were at their punk peak, this was a side of Strummer that had yet to emerge. At the same time, John Lydon raved about the Captain's merits on Capital Radio. Punk's two figureheads were enthralled by the guy.

It's not hard to see why Joe rated Beefheart so highly. The Captain could spout a single nonsensical line and make it the point of the whole song, or simply go out there in a mind-boggling barrage of free association. Beefheart's streams of cerebral psycho-banter can be heard rustling in the undergrowth of many of Joe's rants and lyrical adventures – particularly his often-inscrutable stage announcements. Beefheart seemed to teach Joe that, when dealing with musical structures and lyrical traditions, there simply aren't any rules. The phrase 'Vacuum cleaner sucks up budgie' from The Clash's 'Magnificent Seven' is a slice of pure Beefheart logic that suddenly pops up in the middle of a rap about the drudgery of work. Beefheart was also fond of giving people nicknames, like 'Drumbo' and 'The Mascara Snake' – another trait that Joe assimilated.

When I met the remarkable Captain, who sat and expounded while constantly sketching and firing out one-liners, I mentioned punk and semi-jokingly referred to him as one too. But he agreed. 'It's very honest. Isn't it more honest than when the Beatles sang, "I wanna hold your hand." Who held their hand?'

With his musical tastes, rebel attitude and a loner mentality now firmly coalescing, Joe was more than happy to face the outside world when he left school in July 1970 – just after his parents had returned to this country for good. Joe was often vague about the qualifications he gained, giving different numbers of 'O' and 'A' levels. In a very forthright interview with *NME*'s Paul Rambali in 1981, he said he ended up with 'O' levels in English, Art and History.

After spending the summer at Warlingham with his parents, Joe realised that the conditioning of the previous eight years made it impossible for him to slot into instant happy families. Joe planned to leave home in September to go to art school. He would soon after lose contact with his parents for several years, disowning them in interviews and changing his name to 'Woody'.

This new identity paid homage to one of Joe's early musical heroes – Woody Guthrie, the massively influential American folk singer. Guthrie was another rebel, who sung stark, politically loaded, folk songs that were like the white man's version of the blues. He upset the establishment with Great Depression narratives like 'I Ain't Got No Home' and 'This Land Is Your Land', which rewrote the US constitution and got him branded a communist. He was the major influence on the young Bob Dylan, who became another of Joe's inspirations.

On 31 July 1970, a devastating blow was dealt to the Mellor family when David, who'd become increasingly depressed, committed suicide by taking an overdose of aspirin in Regent's Park. 'He was a Nazi,' Joe admitted to Caroline Coon. 'He was a member of the National Front. He was into the occult and he used to have these death heads and crossbones all over everything. He didn't like to talk to anybody and I think suicide was the only way out for him. What else could he have done?'

In 1999, Joe told *Uncut's* Gavin Martin – 'I still think about him a lot. He was withdrawn. It was a different world back then, no counselling or people to help you through. You just had to deal with it yourself.' Nowadays, Joe would've had the opportunity to get counselling after such a traumatic event. Instead, he kept it locked away with his other personal demons. Although Joe would reconcile with his parents after The Clash's peak, (he later told *Q* magazine that Ron was 'a right crazy lunatic' and credited his mother's Celtic roots for his musical leanings) when David died, he'd practically disowned his parents for abandoning him. Now the one person in his family that he had seen regularly was gone too.

Alone and reborn, 'Woody' Mellor started at London's Central School Of Art, in September 1970. When he first came to London he lived near the river – at the Ralph West Hall of Residence, near Albert Bridge Road, Battersea. Suddenly, Joe found himself in reach of a world he'd only heard about on the radio.

Almost immediately, on 7 October, Joe went to his first live gig – Mott The Hoople at a pub called The Castle, just a 77 bus ride away in Tooting. 'It was magnificent,' Joe admitted in *Q* in 2000. It's sheer coincidence that this was Mick's favourite group at the time, although Joe never admitted to liking Mott during the whole time I knew him.

After settling in at college, Joe moved into a room at a typically chaotic student house in Ash Grove, Palmers Green, which he named 'Vomit Heights' by placing a suitably inscribed sign above the front door. 'Woody' immediately set about immersing himself in the films, music and literature he'd missed out on during his adolescence.

By now the summer of love was well and truly over, with progressive rock gaining prominence among the college crowds. The majority of true rock 'n' roll danger still came courtesy of the Stones, then at the height of their Satanic majesty. The bloodbath of the Altamont festival was a recent memory and the band were firmly established as rock 'n' roll bogeymen. Hendrix had just died, pub-rock was yet to come and by far the most exciting music seemed to be coming from American underground bands like the Stooges and MC5. Joe didn't care though. He had a lot of catching up to do.

Rock 'n' roll became Joe's consuming passion and he soon started to get pissed off with the formalities of education. As he told Caroline Coon in April 1977, 'I went to art school like everybody else. I wanted to be an artist. But when I got there, pheew! What a lousy set-up. It just fucked me up completely.' Joe later described art school as, 'The last resort of malingerers, bluffers and people who don't wanna work, basically. They weren't telling us how to draw an object. They were teaching us how to do a drawing that looked like we knew how to draw an object.'

When *Rolling Stone* did a big Clash feature in 1980, Joe told James Henke that acid was responsible for him dropping out after the first year. 'I was really shattered from this LSD pill, and I suddenly realised what a big joke it was. The professor was standing there telling everybody to make these little poofy marks, and they were all going, "Yeah", making the same little marks. And I just realised what a load of bollocks it was. It wasn't actually a drawing, but it looked like a drawing, and suddenly I could see the difference between those two things. After that I began to drop right off.'

At 'Vomit Heights', Joe met two musicians he would be seeing quite a lot of over the next few years. Clive Timperley – a non-student who played guitar – moved in, bringing with him a young musician called Tymon Dogg. Tymon wrote his own quirky, folk-influenced songs, providing his own backing on acoustic guitar, violin and harmonium. He'd had an abortive stay on the Beatles' short-lived Apple label, but nothing was released, and had ended up busking on the London Underground. Joe rapidly struck up a firm and enduring friendship with Tymon.

Joe's departure from art school coincided with him leaving his student digs. He moved on to a place in Ridley Road, Harlesden – until the following year, when he was forcibly evicted. In 1980 he told *Sounds'* Alan Lewis, 'I've been fucked up the arse by the capitalist system. Me, personally. I've had the police teaming up with landlords, beating me up, kicking me downstairs, all illegally, while I've been waving Section 22 of the Rent Act 1965 at them. I've watched 'em smash all my records up, just because there was a black man in the house. And that's your lovely capitalist way of life: "I own this, and you fuck off out of it!"'

By 1971, Joe was not only carrying around anger at his parents, grief about his brother and disappointment with the failure of his art college education, but was also having his face rubbed in the cruel reality of urban life. He spent two years 'just bumming around', while helping collect money for Tymon on his busking expeditions.

'It was like, I found out later, the apprenticeship of a blues musician,' Joe told *NME*'s Paul Rambali.' I got a real kick out of that. All the great blues players started out collecting the money for some master, to learn the licks. [Tymon] would play the violin, and eventually, whenever there was a guitar lying around from some other busker, I would borrow it and he would teach me how to accompany. Just simple little country and western and Chuck Berry.'

Joe invested three pounds in a ukulele from a West End music shop and played his first solo set at Green Park tube station during the rush hour.

He chose the instrument most commonly associated with forties star George 'I'm Leaning On A Lampost' Formby because, 'I figured it must be easier having four strings,' he told *Unpop*'s Shawna Kenney in October, 2001. 'I figured the ukelele couldn't be as complicated as Eric Clapton . . . it was much more complicated than guitar . . . different tuning, the chord-shapes were different. Thankfully it spurred me on to move onto the guitar. That's the only instrument I can play and I can only play that very basically. To me the guitar has only got one string . . . So I played all six strings, or none. I only played chords, if you like. That's the way it was played, I thought.'

Busking suited Joe as a way of learning the ropes, and he was soon playing regularly. His repertoire encompassed blues, rock 'n' roll and folk standards, bashed out with considerable force in order to be heard.

Shortly after, Joe and Tymon went on a short-lived busking tour around France and Holland, but were nabbed by police and deported. As increasing pressure was exacted on buskers in the early seventies, Joe packed it in after being threatened with the Railway Police over a station tannoy. 'This is 1984' announced Joe to his audience of bemused commuters.

Convinced he'd missed the boat by not learning the guitar properly at an earlier age, Joe started practicing on an old drum kit he'd acquired. Around this time, he hitched up with a girl he'd previously met at the Central School Of Art, who was moving off to Cardiff College Of Art. Joe went too, and discovered that there was a happening rock 'n' roll scene amongst the students at the art college in nearby Newport. Here he struck up a friendship with a girl called Gillian Calvert, whose boyfriend was a quietish chap called Micky Foote.

Newport would become Joe's base until 1974 – especially the local art college. Like most colleges, it had a number of bands in operation. Joe hooked up with a rock 'n' roll revival outfit born out of the Rip Off Park All Stars, who had followed one of the current sub-trends of attempting to revive the pioneer spirit of early rock 'n' roll. America had bands like Sha Na Na, who made a big impression at Woodstock, while Wales threw up such gig circuit faves as Crazy Cavan & The Rhythm Rockers and Shakin' Stevens & The Sunsets. The Rip Offs had become quite well established locally before grinding to a halt. Two of the members – bassist 'Jiving' Al Jones and guitarist Rob Haymer – set about forming a new outfit with drummer Jeff Cooper – who didn't even have a kit! They were contemplating asking the magnetic 'Woody' Mellor to become lead singer. His drum kit clinched the deal.

Having moved into the spare room at Al's flat in Newport, Joe found himself poverty stricken and beset by Rob Haymer's dictatorial control of the group. By all accounts, Haymer was very much the leader and decreed what songs they played. He also named his band The Vultures. They played a handful of college gigs, with Joe recalling that the set always started with a cover of the Nashville Teens' big sixties hit 'Tobacco Road' and ended up with 'Johnny B. Goode'. At the time, Joe was still sporting shoulder-length curls but was already developing quite a forceful stage demeanour.

Melody Maker's Allan Jones (no relation to 'Jiving' Al) hailed from Newport and was still at the local college. He caught a Vultures gig and recalled that they were 'an erratic but occasionally stunning formation'.

The Vultures' only big gig was at Bristol's Granary club. It was packed but the band was beset by a series of technical problems. Although the audience chanted for The Vultures to get off, Joe was struck by the intense reaction that could be generated by an appropriately incited crowd. Afterwards, the band felt a bit deflated and drifted apart. Joe spent the winter of 1973 working in a Newport cemetery.

No band, no money, no fun. But Joe's next move would change his life forever.

CHAPTER TWO

ELGIN AVENUE BREAKDOWN

Until they become conscious they will never rebel, and until they have rebelled they cannot become conscious. – George Orwell, 1984

In May 1974, Joe decided that the time was right to return to London. He was now sporting his hair cut into the rocker style he would retain for much of his life. Joe made straight for Tymon's squat in Maida Hill and through him, was soon set up just around the corner, in a spare room at 101 Walterton Road.

Throughout the seventies, the Maida Hill/Ladbroke Grove area was full of squats, ranging from the luxurious to the decrepit, in houses that stood empty and neglected. As the decade wore on, people used these abandoned buildings to solve their housing problems. By the time Joe arrived in London, squatting had turned into a well-organised network. People were coming to London from poorer areas in the rest of the country, with no hope of paying the rents that were already spiralling throughout the capital. It was a relatively simple matter to locate an empty property, break in and start doing it up.

'In 1974 there didn't seem to be any colour', recalled Joe in *Westway To The World*. 'There were rows and rows of buildings, all abandoned but bought up by the council and just left to rot. For what reason I don't know. But there were hordes of people in London who couldn't afford to pay rent . . . The only thing to do was to kick in these abandoned buildings and then live in them.

'Thank God that happened because if that hadn't happened I would never have been able to get a group together . . . We were absolutely penniless. If we hadn't had the squats . . . (a) for a place to live, and (b), we could set up a rock 'n' roll group and practice in 'em.

'No-one would have lived where we lived – an abandoned bombsite. I had a guy come in. He was an expert at connecting us to the company head. I'll never forget this. He came in with overalls on, a welders mask and huge gauntlets. He advanced up the basement corridor and he thrust this power cable into the company head. He reconnected the house into the national grid. I'll never forget the shower of sparks, like twenty foot long blue sparks that flew down the corridor and blew him backwards. But he jammed the bloody leads into the company head, then we could plug in and start playing. It was that kind of situation.'

Joe quickly made new friends – such as Richard Nother, a zoology student who lived in one of the adjoining squats. Richard would later become the drummer of the band that came out of the Walterton Road squat.

Five star rock 'n' roll petrol – Joe with Richard Dudanski in the 101'ers, early 1976.

During the summer, Joe decided that he wanted to form a band to play the local pubs. He roped together a disparate bunch of locals from the house and surrounding area, who collectively boasted little musical expertise. They would bash away quite happily in the basement of 101.

'We started the 101'ers with one amplifier and one speaker', remembered Joe. 'We built our equipment . . . We got some drawers out of a skip and we used to buy cheap speakers down the Edgware Road and we'd just drop them into these drawers and put a facing board on them and turn them up. That would be a cabinet . . . I used to go to gigs with two bricks in a shoulder bag and these bricks were to sit in the deck of a record player upturned with a broom handle screwed in it, which was the microphone stand. The microphone was taped on the top and the bricks were there to drop in the record player and keep the thing steady so the mic didn't fall over.'

This merry band was forced on an unsuspecting outside world when 101 resident Alvaro Pena-Rojas, a saxophone player who'd enjoyed success in his native Chile, put them forward to play a benefit concert for the Chilean Solidarity Campaign. The CSC supported victims of the 1973 military coup that had overthrown the country's democratically elected socialist government. *The Evening For The Chilean Resistance* was to take place at the Brixton Telegraph, an early pub rock venue, on 14 September 1974.

Alvaro, whose housemate Antonio Narvaez was the new band's drummer, joined in as the group tried to work up a short set. It would have to be comprised of rudimentary standards that everyone knew. Much in the manner of the sixties garage bands, they turned to the Chuck Berry songbook and staples like Them's 'Gloria'.

With rehearsal time running short after the gig was brought forward to 6 September, disaster struck when Antonio announced that he was going on holiday. Enter Richard Nother, who had little previous experience but was prepared to give it a go. Aside from Joe, Alvaro and Richard, the group also consisted of the latter's brother Pat on bass and a guy called Simon Cassell joining in on vocals. They called themselves El Huavo and the 101 All Stars – putting Alvaro out as leader under the Chilean for 'countryman'.

On the night of the gig the All Stars were forced to ask the headliners – reggae band Matumbi – if they could borrow their equipment. Fortunately, they agreed. Despite the band's inexperience, their enthusiasm and energy saw them through a shambolic live debut in front of the Brixton reggae crowd.

The following weeks saw the new band's line-up subject to daily fluctuations, while Joe persevered in trying to get the necessary equipment and chops together to fulfil his new dream. To raise money for a new amp, he took a job cleaning toilets and caretaking at the London Coliseum in St Martins Lane.

The Coliseum was home to the English National Opera. During the course of his duties, Joe noticed a microphone, which was used to issue instructions to the spotlight operators, positioned at the very top of the building. On a particularly quiet day, he climbed a ladder and, using a pair of wire cutters, snaffled the mic, which he stuffed down his trousers. He then returned to the basement to stash it. On the way back he passed the manager, sweating buckets in case he'd get caught.

Maybe the guy just thought he was pleased to see him, but he got away with it and used the mic until the early days of The Clash.

Joe got the sack at the end of September when the same manager discovered him secretly practising his guitar in the basement. But by then he'd made enough money to buy a Vox AC-30 amplifier, so Joe returned to Newport to round up his guitars and any other equipment he could muster.

In addition to rent-free digs, squatting brought the possibility of being evicted at any moment. When the GLC decided to clear the Chippenham Road/Elgin Avenue area that September, the Maida Hill Squatters and Tenants Association organised a large demonstration in Notting Hill. The two hundred or so participants had to face the inevitable heavy-handed police tactics but won themselves more time.

Moving into a house with the number 101 was an amusing coincidence for Joe, who was a big fan of George Orwell's books. Orwell's grim predictions in *1984* of a cold, oppressive future where individuality was stifled sparked a chord that resonated through to The Clash. Room 101 was the feared torture chamber where unfortunate victims were sent to be de-personalised. He included 1984 references in his stage announcements and The Clash used a still from the film of another Orwell book, *Animal Farm*, on the sleeve of their single, 'The English Civil War'.

After shortening their name to the 101 All Stars, the band became the 101'ers when they were given the opportunity to start their own weekly club in a small room above The Chippenham pub, on the corner of Malvern and Shirland Roads. They'd been offered the room to rehearse their set into a suitable state for getting more gigs. The weekly club meant that they could rehearse in front of a crowd and make it pay.

'We booked our own club', recalled Joe. 'No-one was gonna book us into a pub. Can you imagine what we looked like? A bunch of crazed squatters . . . That's how we learned to play, by doing it for ourselves. It's like a punk ethos. You've got to be able to go out there and do it for yourself because no-one's gonna give it to you.'

The first 101'ers gig at The Chippenham took place on Wednesday, 4 December 1974, with the new venture called the Charlie Pigdog Club – after the squat's dog. These informal weekly parties saw the band blossom from a ramshackle free-for-all into a leaner, meaner rock 'n' roll outfit with plenty of attitude and a captivating powerhouse of a frontman. When Pat Nother left the band, he was replaced by a guy known as Mole – due to the hours he kept. Joe's old Vomit Heights mate Clive Timperley started turning up with his guitar.

At the time, Joe was the only axe-man in the line-up and was still mastering his basic, rhythm-dominated style. Clive joined the group as lead guitarist in early 1975 – Woody reversed his name so he became Evil C. A guy called Jules Yewdall was helping out on vocals and harmonica, so Joe could concentrate on his guitar playing. Simon Cassell – now known as 'Big John' – and Alvaro were still there on saxophones. Richard Nother saw his title changed to Richard 'Snakehips' Dudanski and has kept it ever since. In February, despite the return of Antonio, he became a full-time member. That month saw the band raise fifty pounds to acquire their own transport in the shape of a hearse. It was cheap and looked cool.

Also around this time, Joe hitched up with a Spanish girl – Paloma Romano, who was the sister of Richard's girlfriend Esperanza. She was promptly re-christened Palmolive and remained with Joe until The Clash's initial rise, by which time she was drumming in legendary female proto-punks The Slits.

In March, Alvaro – disgruntled with the way that Joe was taking charge of the band he had helped get off the ground – left the 101'ers to do his own thing. One of his outings found its way through my letterbox in 1977. By then he was calling himself Alvaro The Chilean With The Singing Nose. Of course, I laughed. When I saw that the (amusingly appalling) album was called *Drinkin' My Own Sperm*, I laughed even more.

The following month would see Jules Yewdall depart too. He wasn't totally committed and, it was becoming apparent that there was no way that Joe could share a microphone with anybody.

The Charlie Pigdog club closed its doors on 24 April. Allan Jones' July *Melody Maker* piece would later report carnage, bloodshed and police raids at the pub. By the following year those nights had become the stuff of legend – and the first of many times that Joe would see his name linked to something that would later be deemed worth mythologizing.

 In May, Joe was still working on getting a proper guitar – so to raise £100 he got married to a South African girl named Pam. Once Pam's British citizenship was established the marriage was dissolved. Joe now had the funds to buy the black Fender Telecaster he would sport like an extra limb for the rest of his life.

These marriages of convenience were rife at the time being a quick and easy way to raise cash. Sid Vicious was going to marry Chrissie Hynde to allow her to stay in the UK after her visa ran out. Sid got cold feet at the last moment and didn't show up. The only problem was now Joe couldn't marry Palmolive, who needed similar UK legitimisation for a visa. Richard had married Esperanza, so Palmolive married Pat Nother.

Also that month, with eviction imminent, the quartet abandoned 101 and relocated to nearby St Luke's Road, where they were joined by Joe's old Newport pal, Micky Foote.

In May, the 101'ers played their first gig at the Elgin pub – and commenced a Thursday night residency, which would run for the rest of 1975. The Elgin was situated on Ladbroke Grove, practically in the shadow of the Westway, and epitomised the type of rundown boozer where the normal clientele were seasoned drinkers, a few locals and wideboys.

'Woody Mellor' then decided to change his name to Joe Strummer – much to the confusion of his old mates, who were used to calling him Woody. Allan Jones recalls sitting around a pub table about to commence his long-planned *Melody Maker* interview. The band introduced themselves but, when it got to Woody's turn, he passed over a list of prospective names, asking Allan to pick one. The only name that Allan can remember off the list is 'Joe Strummer'.

The name suited his guitar style. Joe was left-handed and had learned to deal with right-hand guitars in a basic, manically thrashing style. When The Clash were on the road he would have to wear what he called a 'Strum Guard' on his forearm – a mixture of gaffer tape and bandages to stop his flailing limb getting sliced to ribbons.

The 'Joe' came from him plumping for the most ordinary name on the planet.

I mainly became aware of the 101'ers through Allan's *Melody Maker* piece, but had already heard that they were the wildest of the new breed of pub rock bands, that were reacting against the tedious indulgences of progressive rock. Their growing reputation seemed to stem from the human dynamo performances of their lead singer.

From accounts of the time, Joe was already exhibiting some of the trademarks that would show up in his supercharged Clash performances. That way he had of plugging into the rhythm and pumping it up with his strumming right hand while his left leg twitched like crazy. Whatever he lacked in technique, he made up with sheer hot-wired energy.

In less than nine months, the 101'ers had developed from a makeshift jamming unit thrashing out an unholy racket, into a truly exciting part of the developing pub rock movement. In 1975 the biggest pub-rock group were Dr Feelgood – four shady characters from Canvey Island, Essex, who blasted through R&B standards with amphetamined recklessness. 'It's a feeling of people wanting to get back to basic roots,' explained their guitarist Wilko Johnson.

Other prominent exponents included Kilburn & The High Roads – fronted by a charismatic Essex wordsmith named Ian Dury – Chill Willi & The Red Hot Peppers, The Kursaal Flyers and Eddie & The Hot Rods. These bands inhabited a twilight circuit of seedy basements and back rooms where you could get pissed and cavort around to raw rock 'n' roll. These included the Kensington in Shepherds Bush, Brixton Telegraph, the Windsor Castle in Harrow Road, Islington's Hope & Anchor, the Nashville next to West Kensington tube, and Fulham's Golden Lion. Landlords saw that takings could skyrocket by opening up to the new wave of groups who had no pretences about topping the bill at Earls Court.

It is probably fair to say that pub rock paved the way for punk rock. At the time I remember going to the gigs simply because there was no attractive alternative. I loved Dr Feelgood, mainly because of their speed-fuelled guitarist Wilko Johnson, who'd tear off solos while careering around the stage like a clockwork bunny on whiz. It was an exciting, no frills alternative to all the other musical trends. 'Punk rock' before the term had been lifted from the American sixties garage bands.

In New York City, the Ramones were already starting to hone their own brand of teenage blastoff. Pub rock was its London equivalent, but it was more retrospective, as groups trawled through the traditional bar band repertoire of Chuck Berry and company.

Likewise, Joe's biggest early influence, apart from Woody Guthrie, seems to have been Chuck Berry. Berry's *Rock And Roll Music* EP had been his favourite record for years, and the 101'ers' set was splattered with Chuck classics like 'Johnny B Goode', 'Carol' and 'Roll Over Beethoven'. Bo Diddley, the innovative voodoo-rhythm warrior, whose 'Who Do You Love?' and 'Six Gun Blues' were also covered by the 101'ers, was another favourite.

Joe's rudimentary guitar technique was reminiscent of a young Keith Richards, as it was similarly based on thrashing out the rhythm Berry-style. Joe had no desire to go any further than hammering his guitar until his hands bled and the strings hung broken off its neck. The 101'ers saw their cover versions shot through with their frontman's manic energy, until the material performed seemed to become almost a vehicle for his charisma.

Their set, after kicking off with their version of Larry Williams' 'Bony Maronie', took in covers ranging from Eddie Cochran's 'Summertime Blues' and Elvis's 'Heartbreak Hotel' to the Beatles' 'Back In The USSR' and 'Daytripper'. It always finished up with a lengthy trawl through 'Gloria'. The band also did a version of Louis Jordan's 'Choo Choo Ch' Boogie', which was also favoured by Western swing pub-rockers Chilli Willi & The Red Hot Peppers, plus an old New Orleans nugget called 'Junco Partner', which Joe would later revive with The Clash.

The group also started adding Joe's originals like 'Keys To Your Heart', 'Motor Boys Motor', 'Steamgauge 99', 'Letsagetabitarockin'', 'Silent Telephone' and 'Hideaway'.

Cover or original, the 101'ers became distinctive largely on account of the manic Strummer stamp. In his interview with Allan Jones, Joe was almost outlining a punk manifesto; 'I mean if you go and see a rock group, you want to see someone tearing their soul apart at thirty-six bars a second, not listen to some instrumental slush. Since '67, music has been chasing itself up a blind alley with all that shit.'

As the Elgin residency got under way Simon 'Big John' Cassell left the group by mutual agreement, leaving a four-piece consisting of Joe, Richard, Clive and Mole. The nature of their increasing gig-load said something about Joe's social orientation, as the 101'ers played benefits for local causes like squatting associations and the local Law Centre. In July, they played a free concert at the local Harlequin record shop (In the seventies Harlequin was a chain along the lines of HMV).

Between June and August the 101'ers also played some gigs at the St Moritz club in Wardour Street, which was a favourite haunt of men-about-town like Lemmy Kilminster of emerging rock behemoths Motorhead. The band's first forays into the West End weren't that successful, as crowds often showed the same kind of indifference that would greet early punk shows. Punk or not, full-on rock 'n' roll mania seemed to be looked down upon in that year's soporific calm-before-the-storm climate of drippy singer-songwriters and ponderous prog.

Joe was stirred enough by these Soho experiences to write a song called 'Sweety Of The St Moritz' – in which Joe recounts the difficulties he experienced in persuading the venue's owner to hand over the band's fee. As with The Clash later, Joe needed to get shat on periodically to stir his muse into action.

During the summer, the 101'ers also played Upstairs at Ronnie Scott's, the venerable Frith Street jazz club – plus festivals at Stonehenge and Watchfield. Their invasion of the London pub scene expanded to take in Islington's Hope & Anchor and Dingwalls, an increasingly popular venue in the railway warehouse complex that extended to the Roundhouse and would subsequently house The Clash's HQ, Rehearsals Rehearsals. Micky Foote now worked for the band full-time – as roadie, sound-mixer and general dogsbody/organiser.

In August, *NME* sent Chas De Whalley to check out what their rival paper had been raving about at the Hope & Anchor. De Whalley's review seemed to predate what they'd be saying about the Sex Pistols a few months later. ' . . . they start out of time, finish out of time, and play out of tune,' but he conceded that, 'They also churn out some very fine rock 'n' roll with no pretence at all towards music, let alone art.' Chas concluded that, with Dr Feelgood now seen as big business, the 101'ers 'are definite contenders for London's rock 'n' roll crown.'

The 101'ers were a punk rock group, and the Sex Pistols' first gig was still four months away. By that I mean 'punk' in the sense of the bands that sprung out of America's garages in the mid-sixties. Motley outfits like The Standells and Shadows Of Knight started out with sneering, noisy versions of rock 'n' roll standards and Stones songs, before developing their own identities. They made up for their musical shortcomings with attitude and energy, and were labelled with that somewhat derogatory generic term.

Zigzag – the UK fanzine which I would join the following year – was familiar with the sixties US groups and started labelling some of the pub bands 'punk rock' around this time. In early 1976, it was the first UK rock magazine to put the word on a front cover, with 'Punk Rock Comes To Town' heralding an Eddie and the Hot Rods feature. Many overlooked the fact that the word 'Punk' had originated as a derogatory term in American jails for someone who gets fucked up the arse. It was reserved for lowest of the low, and was a term that was constantly flung at mid-sixties US garage bands on account of their loud music and long hair.

By October 1975, the welcome at St Luke's Road had worn thin, as hassle from the locals and skirmishes with thieves became regular occurances. Luckily, a whole house with rehearsal-friendly basement was found nearby at 42 Orsett Terrace. The 101'ers continued to gig – including a residency at the Nashville with Eddie and the Hot Rods – and recorded some less-than-successful demos at Jackson's studio with Dr Feelgood producer Vic Maille, who was looking to set up a label venture which never came off.

The foundations of London's music scene started to shake on 6 November when the Sex Pistols played their first ever gig, supporting a band called Bazooka Joe (which included Stuart Goddard, the pre-Ant Adam). Short, chaotic and confrontational, the Pistols started a new ball rolling, which would take mere months for its irreparable impact to be felt.

In January 1976 the 101'ers replaced bass-man Mole with Clive's mate Dan Kelleher, with a view to buffing up the band's musical muscle. 'Desperate' Dan, as he was named, had been getting up and jamming with the band on guitar for some months and seemed to click with Joe. The pair cooked up some songs together, including 'Jail Guitar Doors', the title and chorus of which survived into The Clash repertoire. There was also the storming 'Five Star Rock 'n' Roll Petrol', 'Sweet Revenge' – the nearest they got to a ballad – and 'Rabies (From The Dogs Of Love)', an ode to the much-frequented Praed Street clap clinic.

The new year saw the 101'ers break out of the pub circuit, which they were beginning to outgrow. The band undertook a hectic schedule of one-nighters – the proverbial Transit van marathons just to play some toilet up north. Having taken up with the Albion agency, the band found themselves playing the college and university circuit. A fellow squatter named John Tiberi, who went by the nickname of Boogie, came in to help Micky.

On 15 February, the 101'ers played the most unusual gig of their career – Sunday lunchtime in the chapel at Wandsworth Prison, South London. This had come about after the group had played one of the all-dayers at the Roundhouse, and the event's promoter, John Curd, arranged the booking. The event was recalled by Richard Dudanski when he paid tribute to his old band-mate in *Uncut*'s 2003 Joe special, 'there was no doubting the major force in the ensemble. A certain Joe Strummer, a man with a mouth full of bad teeth, a voice that howled as if from Hades, and a heart as big as the domed prison chapel.' Richard also described how the band walked on and tore into their set with the usual fervour. The 400 or so lags present loved it, but were under heavy manners from the screws not to over-react. Shades of Johnny Cash were evident, as Joe took delight in singing warden-unfriendly ditties like 'Jailhouse Rock' and 'Riot In Cell Block Number 9'.

'Joe was in great form, and making the most of a continual battle with an unstable mic stand, he quickly established a rapport with the audience,' recalled Richard. 'I'll never forget the expressions on the faces in front of us. It's no exaggeration to describe most of them as ecstatic.'

The following month, the band were approached to record a single for a new label being started by Ted Carroll and Roger Armstrong, who ran the Rock On record stalls in Soho and Golborne Road, West London. Joe frequented their stalls, and the 101'ers were desperate to appear on vinyl. On 4 March, the band went into Pathway Studios, Canonbury, and laid down their own 'Keys To Your Heart', 'Sweet Revenge' and 'Five Star Rock 'n' Roll Petrol', returning within days for a second attempt at these songs, and also tackling 'Rabies'. A few weeks later, they went into the BBC's Maida Vale studios and had another bash at 'Petrol', 'Keys' and 'Rabies'. Eventually, they selected a Pathway version of 'Keys To Your Heart' and BBC take of 'Five Star Rock 'n' Roll Petrol' for the two sides of the single.

By early 1976, Joe and the 101'ers were winning new fans by the week. Two years later, Pete Silverton – writing about The Clash in American fanzine *Trouser Press* – talked about pub-rock, which he felt had been lacking something. He'd checked out the 101'ers at a college benefit gig. ' . . . it wasn't till I saw Joe that night that I realised just what was lacking – full-blooded desperation to become a star and communicate with your audience and the sense to realise that not only is that a far from easy task but that, if you don't find your own way of doing it, you might just as well junk the idea there and then. The 101'ers were an immensely lovable but generally pretty ramshackle bunch who'd rip through Chuck Berry and R&B numbers with not a trace of genuflection at the altar of the greats.'

Despite the 101'ers growing reputation, Joe had still been feeling increasingly more frustrated, as he later told *NME*'s Paul Morley. 'It was six gigs a week for maybe eighteen months . . . It was just a slog. It seemed after eighteen months of doing that we were just invisible. I started to lose my mind. I would go around the squat saying, "We're invisible. We should change our name to the Invisibles." You'd get back to London about 5am, unload the gear, put on a kettle and go, "What the fuck's that about?" . . . We were just shambling from one gig to the next banging our heads against the wall.'

CHAPTER THREE

CRASH STREET KIDS

If someone locks me out I kick my way back in – Mick Jones – 'Hate and War'

Joe needed some kind of musical partner to bounce ideas off and assist in turning his volcanic ideas into actual songs. To some extent, this had happened with the 101'ers, but he thought that Desperate Dan was too much of a muso. Joe was also becoming disenchanted with the ongoing refinement of the band's original sonic maelstrom. Joe felt that he needed the right foil to focus his untamed stage persona, individual style of lyrics and rough musical ideas.

Joe also needed the right band to realise his musical vision. What he ended up with would surpass anything he might have imagined.

Enter Mick Jones.

During those years I spent around The Clash, Mick was the member of the group I became closest to. He was a kindred spirit from when I first got to know him in the early days through to his later adventures in Big Audio Dynamite. We kind of drifted apart in the nineties but, when I do see him, it's still a massive buzz.

Having been born only a year apart, we'd both grown up with uncannily similar musical obsessions. It turned out that I'd actually met and talked to Mick a few years before I spoke to him properly at my first Clash gig, in October 1976. I'd seen him hanging out around Portobello Road and Camden throughout that year, as well as at important London gigs like Patti Smith, Ramones, etc. With his black jacket, leather strides, plus the spiked hair and chalk white gauntness of Keith Richards, I could tell that rock 'n' roll lived in this character. But I also wondered where else I'd seen him. Sometimes our eyes would catch and there'd be a glimmer of recognition between us. Like, 'I *know* this bloke'.

Then it all fell into place – Mott The Hoople! I'd spoken to Mick several times as we both religiously followed Ian Hunter and his hugely influential rock 'n' roll roadshow during the early seventies. Maybe the reason that there hadn't been instant recognition later was that back then we'd both been glammed up. I looked pretty stupid in my green satin flares. Mick looked like a junior member of the band.

It's a cliché, but Mick was born for rock 'n' roll. He'd grown up with it, and from the earliest age had dreamed of nothing else but being in a band of his own. It took hitching up with Joe Strummer to realise that dream.

Michael Geoffrey Jones was born on 26 June 1955 at the South London Hospital for Women in Clapham. His father Thomas was a taxi driver and his mother, Renee, was a fancy jewellery saleswoman. At that time, his parents lived in Mitcham, Surrey, but in 1957 they moved into the block of council flats in Streatham, South London – where Renee's mother Stella lived. This end of Brixton

Hill was where Mick would live for the next ten years.

Mick was an only child and, when he was six, the family moved in to Stella's flat after her second husband Harry died. Shortly afterwards, Mick's parents split up. Renee emigrated to America while Mick's dad stuck to driving cabs in South London. Young Mick was left in Stella's care, who he would be with until 1977. Such domestic instability was traumatic for Mick and had parellels with Joe's abandonment to public school.

'Maybe music became an escape for me,' Mick observed in *Westway To The World*, 'I think it did to a certain extent. My parents used to fight a lot . . . I definitely got a built-in self-preservation thing.' Luckily, his grandmother doted on Mick, accompanied by her sister and sister-in-law. Stella was also into Elvis and – 'surrounded by three old ladies' – Mick had little to divert his growing obsession with music.

In September 1966, Mick started at the nearby Strand School for boys. His boyhood musical tastes centred around the mid-sixties UK explosion, which included the Stones, The Kinks and The Animals. He checked out the obligatory blues club at school and by the following year, was getting into the psychedelic trailblazing of Hendrix and Cream – whose *Disraeli Gears* was the first album he bought.

Like many, a lot of Mick's musical mind expansion came courtesy of John Peel on his *Perfumed Garden* show on pirate station Radio London, which Joe had also listened to while at boarding school. The inestimably saintly and perceptive Peel was responsible for turning on a nation to anyone from Captain Beefheart to the young Marc Bolan's John's Children. He instilled in both Mick and Joe the power of radio to change lives. Mick's musical education was rounded off by buying the *NME* every week.

In 1968, Mick and Stella moved to a flat on Edgware Road, near Hyde Park – very convenient for the pioneering free rock festivals organised by future Clash managers Peter Jenner and Andrew King. The first gigs Mick went to were held there – including the massive Stones event of 1969, where he made it up to the front – close enough to have the Brian Jones memorial butterflies flutter down on his head.

1969 also saw Mick get a new neighbour in class: Robin Crocker, who was being forced to re-sit his fourth year. Robin was the class hoodlum, joker and troublemaker. Paradoxically, as well as being a complete nutter, Robin was well read and clever, especially adept at English. He was also an intensely friendly and likeable geezer.

In 2004, Mick leaned over to me as Robin was up at the bar ordering a round, and semi-whispered, 'You know what happens, you get in trouble with him when you're out.'

That seemed like a good moment to ask how the pair of lifelong friends met. Unsurprisingly, it's a rock 'n' roll story. They had an argument about who was better – Bo Diddley or Chuck Berry. This developed into a fight. 'We were on the floor in the maths lesson punching the shit out of each other,' laughs Robin.

'It was like, "Who's better? Chuck or Bo?" recalls Mick. 'And we were like fighting over it. Who was Bo and who was Chuck? He was Chuck and I was Bo.'

Mick affectionately remembers Robin as the class joker. 'Once he was making me laugh so much when we were in detention. He just made me laugh. I can't remember what it was. And the headmaster went berserk because we weren't taking our punishment seriously. He was so furious he was spitting, and the spit was going all over the desk. The more this spit come out, the more I was in hysterics. In the end he did a lunge for me and I fell over backwards on my chair. I put my hand up and said, "Please sir can I be excused?" As I fell off he lunged across the desk to try and throttle me.'

Mick lights up as he gets into telling his school stories, 'Hofler was the first headmaster, he used to be in a caliper!' he cackles, getting up to illustrate his point. 'Every day in assembly, you'd hear, click . . . click. It was so funny! We used to be in detention every week. Robin used to run a protection racket at school and when it got found it was on the *Tonight* programme or something, and all the pupils were like blacked out like professionals because they didn't want to be seen. When it all came out Robin had to take this walk of shame. We were caned and everything. I think all the teachers were tortured in the war.'

'We had so much in common. We liked all the same stuff. The Stones...Rod Stewart and the Faces . . . Mott the Hoople.'

After Mick introduced me to Robin in 1977, he told me how he'd look after Mick at school. Mick wasn't the biggest guy in the class and was always wrapped up in that week's *NME*. I know from experience that could be a gift for class bullies. Robin was the bloke who 'never took no shit from no-one' in 'Stay Free' – the song Mick wrote for The Clash about his adolescence. Mick and Robin soon started hanging out and going to gigs.

In 1969, Mott The Hoople emerged. They were the punk rockers of their time as, amidst a sea of post-hippy self-indulgence, they welded the wildness of Jerry Lee Lewis to the raunch of the Stones with a stage act that could drive their faithful followers to seat smashing riot levels. As I wrote at the time, 'They had the loudest amps, the longest hair, the hardest rock and the baddest attitude, although their ballads could have a hall in tears'. Instead of making the kind of whimsical album about pixies that was all the rage, Ian Hunter's songs tackled issues that the kid on the street could understand – like sex and the pressures of modern living.

Mott had been put together by Guy Stevens, a lunatic figure who would have great influence on the lives of The Clash for the next ten years, as well as sorely trying their patience.

Guy first became noticed in 1963, DJ-ing at a sweaty Soho basement club called The Scene. He played upfront R&B to a hip, mod-leaning crowd, who would later include the Beatles and Rolling Stones. He'd run the Chuck Berry fan club and was a leading authority on Jerry Lee Lewis. As a DJ, he broke R&B and soul records and got them released in the UK.

Joe already knew Guy's name from his long-time favourite record, as he told *Mojo*: 'I had a Chuck Berry EP on the Pye label and the sleeve notes were by Guy. And you know the way when you're listening to records, you pore over the sleeve, you want to suck every bit of information out of it? I used to listen to this EP a lot and stare at this sleeve, so I knew his name from very early on.'

When Island Records decided to start an R&B offshoot in 1964, Guy was roped in to start the newly minted Sue Records and released material by the likes of Ike &

Tina Turner, Bobby Bland and Rufus Thomas. In 1967, he moved over to A&R and subsequently began producing for the mothership label. He became renowned as a madman fond of waving his arms in the air and leaping about shouting to instil fervour in the studio. Guy worked with Free, Spooky Tooth and the ultra-psychedelic Hapshash And The Coloured Coat Featuring The Heavy Metal Kids. This got him in the Sunday papers as being at the forefront of the hippy movement. Soon after, he was sentenced to nine months imprisonment for possessing cannabis.

Once he was released, Guy set about creating his dream band. Wanting to splice the sensitive lyricism of Bob Dylan to the raging energy of Jerry Lee Lewis, Guy found an unknown group from Herefordshire called The Silence, auditioned a singer called Ian Hunter and re-named them Mott The Hoople, after a Willard Manus book. Mott rapidly rose to become the wildest, most exciting rock 'n' roll band in the country. Often their responses recalled the smashed-seat teddy boy era as the band hammered out their twenty minute version of the Kinks' 'You Really Got Me'.

Guy produced three Mott albums, which involved ingesting much speed and smashing up the studio furniture to fire up the group. Once, he even set the studio alight in order to get a reaction.

Mott enjoyed a fervent cult following among the older boys at Mick's school, which drew Mick and Robin to sixth-form fans like Kelvin Blacklock and John Brown. They started following the group about, bunking trains and striking up a rapport with the group to the point where they regularly let them into gigs for free. Mott valued their fans and Ian Hunter even paid tribute to them in songs like the 'Ballad Of Mott Of Hoople' and 'Saturday Gigs'. It was Mick's first taste of rock 'n' roll adrenalin, being a proper fan and feeling part of a scene. He told his school careers officer that he wanted to be in a group when he left.

I felt the same way after Mott played my school dance in December 1969. I'd met them in the pub and bemoaned the fact that I couldn't get in because I was too young, so they sneaked me in as a roadie and I watched their set from under the PA stack. As I left before the end to meet my parents' curfew, Hunter announced, 'This one's for Kris, who's got to go'. From then on I was hooked.

Like Mick, I saw Mott wherever I could. They'd let me hang out and such was my devotion I ended up running their fan club in 1972. The band had just had their career rescued by David Bowie, who had given them a guaranteed hit called 'All The Young Dudes'.

Running the club meant that I saw even more of the band, and would often notice the same faces backstage. Ian Hunter introduced me to Mick and Kelvin one night. Mick was the quieter of the pair, with long hair, platform shoes and a pleasant manner. Kelvin fancied himself as a kind of flash hybrid of Hunter and Jagger, and would sometimes leap on stage to pose and holler along to Mott's insertion of 'Jumping Jack Flash' into their own 'Walking With A Mountain'. 'We called him Jagger back then,' recalls Mick.

It was inevitable that Kelvin and his Mott-loving pals would try and form a group. This they did, coming up with the New York Dolls inspired name of Schoolgirl. Mick had yet to pick up a guitar but wanted to be part of it, so helped out as drum roadie. Meanwhile, he failed his 'O' levels, re-sat them again in 1972 and then passed with five – which would be enough to get him into art school the following year.

In the meantime, he got a job in a warehouse and made enough money to buy his first guitar – a Hofner. Despite trying his hand at drums, bass and erm, stylophone, Mick was drawn toward the guitar. 'The coolest place was the guitar player, because of Keith Richards and Mick Ronson,' he later observed. The line from Mick's later Clash song 'Stay Free' – 'I practiced daily in my room' – was true. 'I spent a year in the bedroom playing along to records. That's how I learnt.'

After being thrown out of school, Robin remained in touch with Mick. They saw less of each other as Mick became immersed in playing and Robin followed pursuits that ultimately led to him being handed a three-year prison sentence for armed robbery in 1975.

Back in 1972, Mick was into the glam rock explosion that had been detonated by Bowie and taken into the streets by Mott. As he was a year too young for art school, Mick took a temporary job – as a clerk for the Department of Health and Social Security in Paddington. This was during a period of IRA letter bombings, and one of Mick's jobs was to open the mail. Hence the line 'I won't open letter bombs for you' in The Clash's 'Career Opportunities'.

Early the following year, Mick and Stella were re-housed by the council to a flat on the eighteenth floor of Wilmcote House, a sixties tower block on the Warwick estate off Harrow Road. After I got to know Mick, I went there a few times, either to crash or play records in his room. The block was a dump – already rotting from the inside with piss stained lifts and graffiti. You can still see those edifices as the tube passes Royal Oak station, jutting through the skyline like a row of decaying teeth. Also if you happen to be negotiating London via the nearby A40 – better known as the Westway.

I also got to meet Stella, the quintessential kindly gran who always made you a cup of tea. Mick obviously felt a lot for the lady who'd effectively brought him up. I couldn't imagine how she coped with living in that hellhole, but she kept the flat immaculate. Apart from Mick's room, which was plastered in posters and littered with records.

By this time, Schoolgirl had split, but Mick and John Brown had become close mates, discovering and investigating music like the Flamin' Groovies, the MC5, Iggy & The Stooges and the New York Dolls. Each week's *NME* revealed new delights to track down and devour. John also taught Mick how to play bass.

That September, Mick started at Hammersmith School Of Art, in Lime Grove, Shepherds Bush. Apart from the grant being handy to buy equipment with, he saw this as his passport to being in a real group, keenly aware of how Keith Richards had learned his chops off guys he'd met jamming in the college toilets.

In Spring '74, Mick and John made the logical decision to form a group. In came fellow ex-Strand pupil Phil Wayman on lead guitar and drummer Mike Dowling. They called themselves The Delinquents, and via the usual path of dodgy gigs and personnel changes, arrived at a line-up that featured Mick on rhythm guitar while making his first stabs at songwriting. Apart from John, the band now featured Norwegian drummer Geir Waade, a guitarist called simply 'Brady' and – after some prevarication – Kelvin Blacklock on vocals. Pretty soon, Kelvin's massive ego would take over the band.

Now Mick finally had something resembling a proper group, who were developing the necessary gang mentality and looked a bit like the New York Dolls. The influence of the Dolls at that time was huge among the rock 'n' roll cognoscenti, largely thanks to Nick Kent's ravings in *NME*. They had the look, the high-energy licks and a mystique that was pure trash, drugs and sleaze – and were immediately alluring to Mick and his mates.

'The New York Dolls came along and they were like everything,' recalled Mick. 'They were incredible and blew my mind. The way that they looked, their whole kind of attitude. They didn't care about anything. They were a group who were all about style.'

Hip to the Dolls kitsch/camp aesthetic, The Delinquents became Little Queenie – the name by which they were known when Kelvin persuaded Guy Stevens to come and see them play. By June 1975, Guy's drunken madness – which had accelerated when he lost Mott three years earlier – had proved too much for Island and he was freelancing.

This must have seemed like a dream come true for Mick, who was now playing alongside his old school's original Mott fan club for the man who'd steered their heroes to success. But things swiftly turned sour for Mick when Guy decided that he wasn't good enough and should be replaced by a Mott-style keyboards player – This was a bit silly when you consider that Mick was writing most of the songs.

Understandably, Mick was devastated. He'd formed the band and these were supposed to be his mates. In August – by which time Guy had changed the group's name to Violent Luck – they recorded some demos at AIR studios. I remember going along that day – not to see them, but to check on what was happening in the next studio with the now Hunter-less Hoople. It was odd bumping into Guy and Kelvin – especially as their session keyboard player was Verden Allen from the original Mott.

Showing the determination that would serve him well when the same thing happened with The Clash in 1983, Mick resolved to improve his chops and form a better band. As a statement of intent, he bought the classy black Les Paul Junior that he would favour for the next few years. Nothing resulted from Violent Luck's sessions and without Mick the band fizzled out.

Ironically, through the complex network of auditioning that was going on in London back then, it was Kelvin who introduced Mick to a bass player called Tony James. Whereas Kelvin's ruthless ambition came to nought, Mick and Tony's careers blossomed and they remain close mates today. They started off by trying to build a group under the name of The London SS, placing a string of ads in *Melody Maker*, which always mentioned their key influences. First recruit was a guitarist called Brian James, who was suitably keen on the Stooges and MC5 and fitted the band's required image. He was about the nearest the group got to a permanent member, although a drummer called Roland Hot joined for a while.

The enduring legend of the London SS comes from the fact that so many of punk's later participants auditioned for the band. These included Rat Scabies, who would go on to form The Damned with Brian James, and Matt Dangerfield and Casino Steel, who subsequently formed The Boys. 'It wasn't a proper group,' recalled Mick. 'It was just a bunch of people. We used to hold weekly auditions. All we did was hold auditions!'

Throughout, Mick continued going to gigs and striking up conversations with likely looking individuals. An acquaintance he made in the late summer at the Nashville would change his life and become as responsible as anyone for the eventual formation of The Clash the following year: Bernard Rhodes.

The bespectacled Londoner was not a musician. He was more concerned with the broader aspects of youth culture, such as image, as well as the social repercussions of youth movements. He'd started as one of the original beach fighting mods, worked in Kings Road boutiques during the Swinging Sixties and 'knew everybody.'

During the hippy explosion Rhodes became attracted to the revolutionary possibilities the movement could realise – as was the case with organisations like Jerry Rubin's Yippie Party and MC5 manager John Sinclair's White Panthers. In the seventies, he invested in a Camden Town garage, and also got involved with Malcolm McLaren, an accquaintance from his mod days.

At the time, McLaren was already causing a stir with his Kings Road boutique *Sex*. Situated at the seedier end of the famous thoroughfare, *Sex* became known for selling fetish gear and confrontational t-shirts. Bernie started designing and printing the shirts himself.

Popular lines included two cowboys with their knobs hanging out and Bernie's pride and joy, which listed reams of prominent personalities and organisations under the banner, 'You're gonna wake up one morning and know what side of the bed you've been lying on!' Later designs would feature Christ on a swastika and the Cambridge Rapist. Once I could boast nearly a full set – and I kick myself daily for not having kept them in a bank vault somewhere!

Disenchanted teenagers found themselves drawn to *Sex*, which became a hip place to hang out. Out of this loose scene, a band emerged in 1974 when guitarist Steve Jones and drummer Paul Cook hooked up with Saturday shop assistant Glen Matlock, who played bass. Malcolm called them the Sex Pistols and Bernie fired them up with the notion that they could become 'a potential h-bomb' in the midst of the dreary music scene.

This duly happened when Bernie found them a singer in the shape of the terrifyingly charismatic John Lydon from Finsbury Park. This well documented collision starts with John – renamed Johnny Rotten after the state of his teeth – auditioning by cavorting about to Alice Cooper's 'Eighteen' in front of the shop's jukebox. The inimitable Lydon confirmed Bernie's early involvement with the Pistols in one of several interviews I did with him later.

Bernie was probably right to assume that he deserved an equal partnership with Malcolm. But McLaren wasn't having it, so Bernie looked around for a group to mould in his own image.

Mick had already visited *Sex* when he met Bernie at a Deaf School gig at the

Nashville, West Kensington. Both Mick and Tony were sporting t-shirts bearing Rhodes' designs, which led to a conversation. As they got talking, Bernie insinuated that he remained partners with McLaren. Maybe if he could get his own band, he still would be. First, he bombarded Mick and Tony with his political theories and merciless dogmatic rants about the importance of grand gestures and ideas.

By now, the London SS had Mick's old drummer Geir Waade back in the group and Matt Dangerfield took over on lead guitar while Brian James was abroad. The constant auditioning ensured that the line-up was in a state of perpetual change. Every week they placed an ad in *Melody Maker* for fresh blood. At one point Mick was being considered as a second guitarist for the infant Sex Pistols, but he was determined to put together his own band.

Bernie hired a basement for rehearsals below a cafe in Paddington's seedy Praed Street and Brian James returned to the fold. But by the end of the year, the SS still didn't have a vocalist or drummer. Future Clash stickman Topper Headon auditioned, but despite being offered the job, opted to stay with his current group. Another future Clash drummer, Terry Chimes, was turned down. When a guy called Steven Morrissey, got in touch from Manchester, Mick and Tony didn't bother to reply. The future Smith had been in my Mott fan club too.

In the midst of all this, Mick, Tony, Brian and Roland Hot put a few songs down on tape. This is the only London SS material I've ever heard, which Mick played me once at Wilmcote House. It was high energy Detroit-style rock 'n' roll – they tackled the MC5's 'Ramblin' Rose', Jonathan Richman's 'Roadrunner' and The Strangeloves' sixties garage classic, 'Night Time'. The fierce revolutionary stance of the MC5 was definitely a major influence on the early Clash and also Bernie, who saw his role as similar to the Detroit demons' own guru John Sinclair.

During this period, New York was throwing up its own post-Dolls explosion with acts like Patti Smith, Television, Blondie and the Ramones creating a whole new scene centred around small clubs like CBGB's and Max's Kansas City. This new music had already been labelled 'Punk' and was being well covered in the *NME* and *Creem*.

As the London SS continued to rehearse, Mick – who was filling in on most of the vocals – wrote some of the songs that would later feature in early Clash sets. 'Protex Blue' was named after the brand of condom on sale in the toilets of the local Windsor Castle pub. Another was called 'I'm So Bored With You'. This would become known as the first Clash song to be tackled by Joe Strummer, who changed it to 'I'm So Bored With The USA'.

For a few rehearsals, it looked like the London SS would settle upon a line-up consisting of Mick and Tony, Brian James and one Chris Miller, a Keith Moon-style powerhouse on the drums. But he wasn't considered to have the right look and – after being re-christened Rat Scabies due to a freakish alignment of rodents congregating around the drum kit and his skin complaint – took off with a disgruntled James to form The Damned once Bernie's dominant nature proved too much.

In January 1976, Mick and Tony reluctantly called it a day, and the London SS became a footnote in punk history books. Mick would always remain friends with Tony, with the pair sharing flats together as they followed their respective paths.

While Mick rose with The Clash, Tony formed Generation X with Billy Idol before ending up spearheading techno-billy future-shockers Sigue Sigue Sputnik in the mid-eighties. Nearly thirty years on, Mick and Tony reunited for a new venture they've called Carbon/Silicon. I saw them play their third gig and haven't felt so excited by a band for years. Creation Records supremo Alan McGee described the new band as 'the Stones jamming with a laptop.'

The first few months of 1976 saw the exciting rise of the Sex Pistols. If the London SS were a catalyst for The Clash and the Damned, the Pistols were the motivating force for the whole UK punk rock movement that made those groups possible. Riotous gigs, proud musical ineptness, a shocking wardrobe from *Sex* and nihilistic re-workings of mod teen anthems, made the band press darlings who attracted either the ultra-trendy or simply bored teenagers who loved the racket, attitude and DIY approach to rock 'n' roll.

During this period, Mick began jamming with the Pistols contingent – largely on account of his growing friendship with bass player Glen Matlock. There were so few people into this kind of high energy, no-frills rock 'n' roll that it was inevitable that those that were would hang out and play together. Mick, who was still techni-cally attending art college but on an ever-diminishing basis, was now going out with Viv Albertine, who he'd met at a Roxy Music concert.

He was also jamming with Chrissie Hynde, a rock and soul fanatic from Ohio who wrote for *NME* and had gone out with Nick Kent. Chrissie had also worked at *Sex* for a while. At Wilmcote House, Mick and Chrissie collaborated on songs that both would carry on to their respective later groups including Mick's 'Protex Blue' and Chrissie's 'Tattooed Love Boys'. She subsequently moved on to the Pretenders – who proved to be one of the biggest and certainly most enduring by-products of the punk explosion.

Paul Simonon was to be the third figure in The Clash's tripod frontline. I have an enduring mental image of Mick marching and flaying on the left, hot-wired Joe cajoling and hollering in the middle and Paul smouldering and laying into his low-slung bass on the right. Paul was always portrayed as the quiet one, setting up the bottom rumble in the archetypal fashion of The Who's John Entwistle. As time went by, in addition to becoming the band's pin up, Paul established a fearsome stage presence. He made his singing debut on 'Guns Of Brixton' and provided the classic image of bass-smashing frustration that adorns the sleeve of *London Calling*.

Paul Gustave Simonon was born on 15 December 1955, in Thornton Heath, South London where, apart from a few years in Kent, he grew up. Like Mick, Paul's parents – Anthony and Elaine – split up when he was eight. Paul and his younger brother Nick moved with their mum to Brixton, where he attended William Penn – a comprehensive school where white pupils were in the minority. The early sev-enties saw the start of the inner city decay that seems to have become so hopeless today. Overcrowded schools combined with ineffective teaching meant that the kids from poor backgrounds, and often broken homes, had nothing else to do but get into trouble. Vandalism, theft and fights were part of everyday life. Paul went with the flow and became a skinhead.

This could've worked out badly – in the early seventies, skins were a much-maligned tribe. They were the terror of the hippies, as I once found out to my cost (and I wasn't even a proper hippy!) Their pre-occupation with fighting and football made skinheads easy recruits to the burgeoning racist groups that flourished as the sixties dream turned sour. But, although he went to football, nicked things from shops and got into fights, Paul never took the fascist route. In fact, most of the guys he hung out with were black, and he rapidly developed a real passion for reggae and dub.

During his early teens, Paul and his brother relocated to their dad's place in Notting Hill, where he was subjected to a more structured daily routine, doing chores and odd jobs. His dad was an artist, which rubbed off on Paul – especially as his bedroom was in his father's studio. He also moved schools, switching to Sir Isaac Newton School, another grim inner London establishment.

Paul's reggae fixation grew, stoked by *The Harder They Come*, the movie about Jamaica's ruthless music business that, when it appeared in 1972, (alongside the emergence of Bob Marley and the Wailers) played a huge part in awakening mainstream interest in reggae. Paul's love of this type of music, was later mated with Joe's passion for pure rock 'n' roll and folk, and allied to Mick's grounding in more modern forms of high energy flash, to provide the basic Clash recipe.

'I'd walk past all these houses with West Indian music playing late at night and get pulled into parties when I should have been going home,' recalled Paul. But, 'Like most sons I wanted to do what my dad did.'

For Paul, this meant art. After leaving school in 1973, he was accepted at the Byam Shaw School Of Art in Holland Park. He would later tell interviewers that he nicked artists' materials from the 'rich kids' and painted urban landscapes like tower blocks and car dumps.

In late 1975, a chance meeting in the street with Mick Jones led to Paul auditioning for the London SS. He certainly looked the part, but had absolutely no knowledge of rock 'n' roll. Initially, he wasn't playing bass but was considered as a possible singer. 'Because he looked so stunning,' said Mick. After he'd belted out Jonathan Richman's 'Roadrunner' and the Standells' 'Barracuda', Mick and Tony decided that Paul 'didn't have enough stage presence'.

Paul and Mick kept in touch. In March 1976, Mick suggested that Paul learn to play an instrument so he could join the new band he was forming. Again it was Paul's look that drew Mick and Bernie. Some unrefined star quality. He certainly had the street credibility. Following an unsuccessful guitar lesson with Mick at Wilmcote House, Paul opted to take up the bass. His choice of instrument was rooted in pragmatism – it looked like the easiest. All you had to do was play one riff on fewer strings than a guitar. Later that year, Sid Vicious would arrive at the same conclusion.

But Paul needed a motivating force to get him to dive into the unfamiliar world of the rock band. This came on 3 April when Mick took him to see the 101'ers at the Nashville. The attitude and impact of the supporting Sex Pistols proved to be right up Paul's street. To help master his instrument, he painted guide dots on the

Fender copy he borrowed off Tony James. Paul practiced alone by playing along to reggae records – an influence that would become vital to the Clash sound.

For Paul, Sid, Joe and many more, the first Ramones album – released in April – was an invaluable reference point for picking up on punk's velocity and attack. I'd read about them in the music papers – these four guys in leather jackets who fired out instant rock 'n' roll classics that lasted for about two minutes. The Ramones were the first of the new American wave of groups to produce an inspirationally manageable blueprint for the new English bands.

'It can't be stressed how great the Ramones' first album was to the scene in London,' explained Joe. 'It was simple enough to be able to play. Me and Paul would definitely spend hours, days, weeks, playing along to the record.'

Paul lasted two years at Byam Shaw. This gave him enough time to decide, 'I can't see myself in a room doing this stuff' . . . I've got to do something more exciting.' By the time he was due to start the third year in October 1976, The Clash were up and running.

Meanwhile, Mick had started hanging out at another Clash landmark, 22 Davis Road – off the Uxbridge Road as you head towards Acton. Viv Albertine shared the squat with a guy called Alan Drake. The list of Davis Road houseguests would quickly swell to include Sid Vicious, a young guitarist called Keith Levene, journalist Steve Walsh and, increasingly, Mick as his relationship with Viv developed. Within a few months, Viv, Keith, Steve and Sid would be trying to get a band called Flowers Of Romance off the ground. The following year, Viv would join Joe's girlfriend Palmolive in the startlingly brilliant Slits. By the time Mick took me round Davis Road in October, it had become one of the focal points of London's nascent punk scene.

Like most of the early London punks, Keith Levene was a huge Bowie fan. This fact seemed to bring people together at the time (which made it quite unusual that Mick should end up fronting a band with two individuals who *hadn't* been that touched by the hand of Ziggy Stardust). Keith originated from East London and had taught himself to play guitar. I first met him at Davis Road, when we stayed up all night doing speed with Sid. Keith was sharp and wired, with an apparent penchant for wheeling and dealing.

Keith called his new mate 'Rock And Roll Mick'. They began playing together at Davis Road, and Paul started coming round too. By May, Paul had moved in and become a fully-fledged member. Mick already had some songs and Keith would often play along with them, as well as providing much of the basis for a new one called 'What's My Name?' A singer from High Wycombe called Billy Watts also started trying out at rehearsals.

Davis Road became band HQ, with Mick, Keith and Paul rehearsing either there or at Wilmcote House, while Bernie used Paul's bedroom as an office – even if he wasn't yet their official manager.

They all knew about this guy Joe Strummer from the 101'ers.

CHAPTER FOUR

THE CALL UP

We knew it was going to be good. You know that certainty when you don't even bother to think, that certainty was with us and I'm glad of it. We knew that this was it. – Mick Jones

At the start of 1976, being a thrill-seeker in your early twenties wasn't much fun. The charts were inundated by irrelevancies like the Brotherhood of Man and the New Seekers. 'Serious' music was ruled by bland singer-songwriters or prog-rock dinosaurs like Yes, Rick Wakeman and their naval-gazing ilk. Even the likes of the Stones and Bowie had become inaccessibly aloof.

Whereas black music, particularly reggae, offered a genuine sense of uncontrived energy, white youth had no new music of any worth to feel part of – unlike the mods or hippies during the previous decade. With the brief fun-rush of glam-rock now dissipated – even Mott had called it a day in 1974 – only pub-rock gave some light relief from the wallpaper soundscape.

However, despite its rawness, pub-rock was simply reheated R&B. Disco was one easy escape outlet, but it lacked social relevance and was quickly sanitised for mass consumption. Disco had originated in New York, which was simultaneously giving rise to the Stateside strain of punk rock. When the UK's disenchanted youth got their first whiff of this via Patti Smith and the Ramones it only stoked the craving for a scene of their own.

Socially and politically, things weren't getting any better. The global fuel crisis hiked up prices, resulting in the wage freeze, strikes and power cuts. With music in the doldrums, an evening's entertainment didn't go much beyond drab local pubs, tacky nightclubs or the three TV channels that generally went off-air before midnight. Sheer boredom was rampant and the summer of 1976 would be one of the hottest on record – further stoking the pressure cooker atmosphere.

Something had to happen. It took only the actions of a few militant music movers to bring the whole stagnant scene to boiling point.

In April 1976, the Sex Pistols had only been heard by a fortunate handful, but this included a number of influential rock critics who were firing up the imaginations of malcontents and ne'er-do-wells everywhere. The Pistols still wouldn't be beamed into the public's front rooms until the end of the year, but their presence was already sowing the seeds for one of the biggest youth cults of all time.

The Pistols were booked to support the 101'ers on 3 and 23 April at the Nashville. The gigs had been arranged to celebrate the deal between the 101'ers and Chiswick Records, which was actually signed the following month. The first of these shows would provide a significant turning point for the men that would become

The Clash. Apart from being Paul Simonon's punk epiphany, it was the night that Joe Strummer saw the Sex Pistols – and never looked back.

Although I wasn't there – unlike half of London, or so they claimed – this became the first time that I became aware of what this new thing called punk rock could do to people. What I'd read about the Pistols was fascinating, but their full impact had escaped me because I didn't live in London and hadn't seen them. However, my best mate Colin Keinch, who also played guitar in our band The Aylesbury Bucks, made the trek to check out the 101'ers who were being supported by the Sex Pistols.

Colin came back fizzing with enthusiasm and burbling about seeing the future of rock 'n' roll. He thought the 101'ers were great – 'Joe was so lively, totally going for it' – but it was obvious that the Pistols had blown his head clean off. Immediately, our band's take on American garage-punk gained a distinctly edgier sound.

'I think everyone there had a life changing experience that night', recalls Colin. 'The Pistols were totally challenging and the 101'ers weren't. I think that's what changed Joe's whole outlook on things.'

'It was only when I saw the Pistols that I realised how retro it was, not only the material but the concept of it,' Joe told *Uncut* in 2002. 'Like playing in pubs, the same old blues numbers. That kind of nowheresville . . . Suddenly the boot was on the other foot. A cog in the universe had shifted there. They were the only new thing that had been seen in London since living memory.'

Despite Joe's feelings about the 101'ers' shortcomings, his performance totally won Mick and Paul over. 'Joe was just fantastic,' said Paul. 'He was really exciting to watch. The only reason to see them, really.'

'I think that moment we realised that Joe was the best guy out there,' added Mick. 'I think we needed the fresh input and, seeing Joe, it crossed all our minds about nicking him.'

Allan Jones covered the gig for *Melody Maker* and finished his full-bore slagging of the Pistols' 'retarded spectacle' with a dismissive, 'I hope we shall hear no more of them.' He then praised the 101'ers as 'perfectly glorious', writing that Strummer – 'one of the most vivid and exciting figures currently treading the boards . . . projects himself onstage with the intention of solving, single-handed, the world's energy crisis.'

Shortly after the Nashville gig, Mick and Paul went to Lisson Grove dole office to sign on. There for the same purpose was Joe Strummer, 'I was in the queue and I could see them looking at me,' he recalled, 'I didn't know that they'd seen the 101'ers the previous weekend.' 'He caught us looking at him,' said Paul. 'I think he was a bit worried he was going to be done over . . . For that moment he looked really timid and in terror.' 'We were looking on in awe really, not at what he was getting,' added Mick. 'I just ignored them and got my dole,' said Joe.' I was expecting them to tangle me when I got to the door or out on the street. I thought I'd smack Mick first because he looked thinner. Paul looked a bit tasty. I thought I'd smack Mick first and leg it.'

When I spoke to them that October the band told me that after the Nashville, Paul and Mick ran into Joe in the street and told him, 'You're great, but your band's shit'.

In the meantime, the 101'ers had their second Nashville gig on 23 April, which erupted in the much-publicised fight between the Pistols contingent and punters. It was reported as a kind of variation on the 'You nicked my pint' scenario – 'Just a load of people falling all over the place . . . nonsense really', observed John Lydon in *Q*. The incident was considered newsworthy enough to make the front page of *Melody Maker* – maybe that was the idea. Joe's fascination with the Pistols grew, and he checked them out again during their May residency at the 100 Club in Oxford Street.

I first set eyes on Joe Strummer at the Roundhouse on 16 May when Patti Smith made her auspicious UK debut. It was attended by several of The Clash-Pistols circle. Swaying around them was a very pissed up Joe, who I only noticed when Colin recognised him from the Nashville show.

Joe was mentally wavering by then, but at least knew what direction he wanted to take. He even tried in vain to steer the still-gigging 101'ers down a punkier route. Fate seemed to be taking its time.

After a gig in Camberwell, South London, on 21 May, Joe's mood of frustrated discontent continued to cast a shadow of the group and matters were made worse when Clive Timperley quit. For the couple of 101'ers bookings that needed honouring, they were joined by guitarist Martin Stone, who'd started his career in prog-rockers Mighty Baby before landing up in pub-rockers Chilli Willi & The Red Hot Peppers.

Further fuel was thrown onto the fires of rebellion that month, when members of the Pistols and Clash attended the Rolling Stones' extravaganza at Earls Court. This was when both bands knew they had a solid enemy, as the Stones flaunted their lifestyle in the press – they were pictured hob-nobbing with Princess Margaret. The Stones put on an overblown show with appalling sound. Keith Richards was the most fucked up on heroin he would ever be on a British stage. They just seemed so untouchable and removed from what was really going on in their home country. When Joe was prompted to write, 'No Elvis, Beatles or the Rolling Stones' in '1977' he was talking about this lack of relevance. The Stones had always been one of Joe's prime musical inspirations. The same went for Mick Jones. Earls Court became known as the night the bubble burst. How could Joe now aspire to something like that?

The crunch came on 31 May, which also happened to be the day that 'Keys To Your Heart' was released. Bernie and Keith caught the 101'ers at the Golden Lion in Fulham and felt compelled to make their move. They went to see Joe in the dressing room and asked him if he'd like to come and meet the rest of their band with a view to joining them. Bernie took Joe to Davis Road to meet Mick and Paul, and he 'realised that it was the same two geezers who'd been staring at me!'

'We were nervous . . . I was anyway,' recalled Mick. 'He came in and we went into this little tiny room. It was really small. We all sat round with our guitars and said, "This is one of ours".' The song was 'I'm So Bored With You', which Joe promptly changed to 'I'm So Bored With the USA'. Later, he re-wrote the entire lyric to rail against the shallow influence of American culture on the UK. After playing through each other's songs, with Joe whipping out 'Keys To Your Heart', they asked him if he'd like to join their group. He was given forty-eight hours to make up his mind, rang back in twenty-four. His answer – 'Okay, I'm in.'

It might have seemed like a hasty decision to blow out two years' graft but this was obviously a marriage made in heaven. The Pistols had made Joe realise that his pub-rock group – good though they were – 'were yesterday's papers', and the Davis Road guys had a spark that pointed to the future.

'They were kind of already doing it: Simmo, Levene and Mick Jones, and what they lacked was someone to give them a front,' Joe told *Uncut*'s Sean Egan. 'A front guy and a lyric writer. They were a jigsaw waiting for the piece to fall in.'

'Keys To Your Heart' was a strong slice of R&B, in the mould of pub bands like Dr Feelgood. There was no mistaking Joe's punchy vocal delivery. The flip's '5 Star Rock 'n' Roll Petrol' was wilder. The 101'ers were a good band but the man on the back striking an Elvis pose in a baggy suit was already onto something else. On 6 June, the 101'ers played their last gig at Clare Hall, Haywards Heath.

The other 101'ers were understandably gutted. Joe actually gave Richard Dudanski the chance to try out for The Clash, but he declined after meeting Bernie. He went on to form a band with Tymon Dogg called The Fools, then his own Bank Of Dresden, had stints with girl band the Raincoats, John Lydon's Public Image Limited, the Vincent Units with former 101'er Mole, and ended up in punk-reggae pioneers Basement 5 during 1980.

Richard was an easy going kind of bloke who was proud of what his old friend Joe had achieved but also harboured regrets for what-could've-been. He'd open up during late night drinking sessions as I was thrashing the newly recorded *Sandinista!* on the Basement 5 tour bus. He didn't regret not joining Joe in The Clash and had nothing but happy memories of the 101'ers. I learned not to get him on the subject of Bernie, though.

After Basement 5 dissolved, Richard relocated to Spain with Esperanza, and still lives there. Apart from Tymon Dogg, he was one of the few figures from the 101'ers era that Joe kept in touch with until his death.

Joe approached anything he got involved in wholeheartedly, with a ferocious passion. This he would do for the rest of his life. He had already discarded his public school background to become a vital figure on the squat/pub rock scene. To fit into the punk rock ethic he jettisoned his entire previous life, including the 101'ers.

When I first met Joe in October 1976, I mentioned his former group. 'Who's the 101'ers?', came the growling reply. 'The day I joined The Clash it was very much back to square one, back to year zero,' said Joe in *Westway To The World*. 'We were almost Stalinist in our approach. Part of punk was shedding all your friends, everything you knew, everything you'd played before, all in a frenzied attempt to create something new – which isn't easy at the best of times.'

Paul talked about this new start when The Clash were given an Outstanding Achievement in *GQ* magazine's 2003 Men Of The Year awards. 'Me and Joe had pretty much cut away our lives completely and started from day one with this new ideal: we're in The Clash. I mean . . . I arrived from nowhere: I had no friends, no baggage and the same with Joe.'

As I was to soon discover, Bernie Rhodes was good at firing people up. 'They'll change your old-fashioned way of dealing with music,' was one of the deluge of polemics he threw at me when I first encountered him. And he was right too. Bernie could put people off, but he could also turn them on and, suitably primed, you did come out thinking you'd just seen the future. Which you had. It certainly worked on Joe. Even in 1991 he was telling MTV that 'The Clash wouldn't exist without Bernie's imagination.'

Bernie encouraged Joe to look around, encounter the harsh realities of city life and establish a better kind of lifestyle based on awareness and creativity. 'Bernie Rhodes made me realise it could be sung about, which is something I was kind of groping towards, singing about VD and squatting,' Joe told *NME*'s Paul Rambali.

Bernie explained his role when *NME* profiled him in mid-1977. 'I have no say about what goes, musically. My job is to co-ordinate, understand and clarify exactly what they are trying to express. It works on a basis of respect and team-work, although of course we argue like fuck a lot of the time, almost to the point of fights.'

'Bernie's been maybe over-praised for saying, "Write about things that effect you"', reflected Joe in *Uncut*. 'We've been careful to give him his due, but as for the actual songs, it was strictly down to me and Mick.'

Joe and Mick's songwriting partnership sparked immediately. In The Clash, Joe had found the perfect vehicle for developing his lyrics. Similarly, after all the setbacks and disappointments, Mick had found someone who could provide the words to compliment his musical ideas. The pair quickly developed the kind of to-and-fro' chemistry that is associated with Lennon/McCartney and Jagger/Richards.

'We used to write very fast in those days,' explained Mick, recalling how he'd come up with a tune, hand it to Joe and they'd have a song in about half an hour. A lot of the first Clash album was conceived in that fashion. 'Who couldn't write great tunes with such great lyrics?'

'I would consider myself mainly a lyric guy,' said Joe in *Uncut*. 'There really is a specialised area. You do spend your whole life thinking about lyrics. The lyrics would give us something to go with or build from. But we could swap over pretty seamlessly. Some songs – like 'London's Burning' – were more or less all me, and some songs – like 'Complete Control' – were more or less all him. But we always helped each other in the end.'

The five-piece Clash line-up was completed in June, with the addition of Terry Chimes on drums. Terry, from Mile End in East London, had auditioned for Violent Luck and the London SS and been turned down – probably because he didn't look right. But now it was obvious that the new group would be presenting such a formidable front line, it was no good plumping for a novice who couldn't keep time – especially as Paul was learning to play bass from scratch. Joe was fond of saying, 'You're only as good as your drummer,' and Terry, influenced by Led Zep's John Bonham, was a good drummer.

Terry would always have difficulties with The Clash's political stance – or 'lunatic overboard Stalinist behaviour,' as Joe put it – especially as his own aspirations went no further than owning a flash car. The Clash demanded total commitment, which a regular bloke like Terry couldn't pledge. That said, he never had any trouble propelling the proto-bombast of the early Clash. The following year he would be considered good enough to sit in for the mighty Jerry Nolan in Johnny Thunders' Heartbreakers.

'When I met these guys, I remember them being hell-bent on success and very focussed,' recalled Terry in *Mojo*. 'I never knew what the hell to make of Joe. He was very distant. You'd never know what he was thinking.' Terry added that Bernie, 'seemed like he was trying to harden everyone up.'

From my initial meetings with The Clash it was obvious that Joe took his new role as punk rock prophet very seriously – which often meant being quiet and stern. His innate sense of humour became apparent as time went on, and made his dogma more palatable. Even then, some could take his absolute dedication to the cause as aloofness. He didn't just disown his past, he trashed it by spraying slogans like 'Chuck Berry Is Dead' on his clothes. Strong stuff when you consider who his all-time favourite EP was by. Joe's motto at the time was, THE CLASH ARE THE ONLY BAND THAT MATTERS (his capitals).

The Clash derived their name from Paul leafing through a copy of the London *Evening Standard*, and noticing how many times the term 'Clash' was used. They just thought it sounded suitable – 'It describes our sound' – and stressed that it had to be written as *The* Clash. Other candidates included The Phones, The Mirrors, The Psychotic Negatives and, runner-up, the Heartdrops – after the Big Youth tune 'Lightning Flash (Weak Heart Drop)', which was doing the rounds on pre-release 45.

In June, the group started working up their set at a new HQ, which Bernie had found for them. It was called Rehearsals Rehearsals (which Mick thought was some kind of Jewish expression) and situated in a near-derelict complex of railway warehouses that led up as far as Chalk Farm's famous Roundhouse. Here the group kept their gear and rehearsed in the pink draped downstairs room, complete with a row of dentists' chairs for spectators. There was no heating, and I'd rather not mention the state of the toilet.

For a while, Rehearsals served as Paul's home, while all the band and road crew would end up crashing there at some time or other. In the larger room upstairs Paul had painted a giant wall mural of a car dump in the shadow of the Westway. They had a great jukebox (when it was working), which was packed with reggae faves like Desmond Dekker's 'Israelites' and Tapper Zukie's 'MPLA'. The building is still there, except now it forms part of the Camden Market redevelopment.

The first Clash gig was a low-key affair supporting the Sex Pistols on 4 July at the Black Swan, Sheffield (aka the Mucky Duck). 'It was great', recalled Joe in *Uncut*'s February 2003 feature. 'We made a few screw-ups. That was the first time Simmo was on stage and so forth. We actually managed to play the tunes. It was highly entertaining.'

The following night, the group were back in town to catch that week's hot ticket at Dingwalls, which was almost next to Rehearsals. The combination of the Flamin' Groovies and the Ramones was a much more street-level prospect for the

Mick, Joe and temporary drummer Rob Harper on the Anarchy Tour, December 1976

Pistols-Clash crew than the Stones had been.

I was there for *Zigzag* to do one of the Ramones' first UK interviews and, perched on a wall in the courtyard with 'Da Brudders', spotted those same guys I'd seen at Patti Smith in May. Hanging together, looking totally different to anyone else and, in my eyes, totally cool.

This time I didn't need any help in recognising that Strummer guy – despite the fact that he'd had a complete punk makeover. By now, The Clash were starting to customise their clothes with paint. Joe had dyed his hair black and, instead of staggering about drunk, exuded a suitably quite aggressive new assertiveness.

The Clash's second gig, on 13 August, was meant to be their official unveiling to the world – an invite-only set at Rehearsals for some twenty-five invited guests. These included sundry pressmen, booking agents and mates. Journalists Jonh Ingham, Caroline Coon and Giovanni Dadomo were present, with the latter giving The Clash an effusive write-up. 'I think they're the first band to come along who'll really frighten the Sex Pistols senseless'. His review mentioned that 'Strummer finally seems to have found his niche, his always manic deliveries finally finding their place in a compelling tapestry of sound and colour.' I remember this being the first review that really got me interested in The Clash. Giovanni praised the group's look, assimilation of musical styles and attack to a point where you felt like you were reading about the band you'd always dreamed of. Who could resist a group that made you feel like you've been 'hit by a runaway fire engine. Not once, but again and again and again?'

The band's first major public show was the *Midnight Special* on 29 August at Islington's five hundred capacity Screen On The Green cinema. The Clash again supported the Pistols. This event would later go down as the night when UK punk rock went public. The night had been modelled on the kind of sixties multi-media happening where films would be shown between the live attractions. I'd gone up to *Sex* that day to add to my t-shirt collection, and spotted the flyer. It was an all-nighter and I didn't know anybody, so I didn't go. Maybe I was still a bit scared of turning up in the flares I had on.

The Clash had only been allowed to play on condition that they built the stage. However knackered they may have been, the band's set – which has been preserved on a rather muddy bootleg – was delivered with plenty of energy. It kicked off with 'Deny', before Joe's curious (and short-lived) song about his squat called 'How Can I Understand The Flies?' Mick's new 'Janie Jones', 'Protex Blue', 'Mark Me Absent' and 'She's Sitting At My Party'. They round off with a first taste of the traditional Clash home dash with '48 Hours', 'I'm So Bored With The USA' and a new one that had been spawned on Mick's balcony – 'London's Burning'.

I could only read about the gig the following week in the music press. And then kick myself for missing out, despite the fact that The Clash had been roundly panned by Charles Shaar Murray in *NME*. He wrote, 'They are the kind of garage band who should be speedily returned to their garage, preferably with the motor running, which would undoubtedly be more of a loss to their friends and family than rock 'n' roll.' Later, Charles would become one of the group's most ardent champions but, at the time his criticisms hit hard – 'We were pretty done over', recalled Joe.

The sound must have been bad at the Screen On The Green, because even Giovanni Dadomo – who already knew they were hot – described it as 'poleaxing the band's nuclear potential' and reducing Joe to 'an unintelligible mumble.'

Then came the Notting Hill Carnival. By the summer of 1976, London's black youth were feeling the pressure. Racism was a major issue, especially from within the ranks of the police. The extreme right National Front was targeting disaffected white youth for support and making its sickening presence felt during local elections. The black community was becoming tired of discrimination and oppression.

The stifling heat of the August Bank Holiday provided a windless backdrop as this dam of accumulated frustration burst forth, late on during the last day of the Carnival. There was burning, looting and rioting, all of which was initially provoked by the overbearing police presence.

Joe, Paul and Bernie had gone along and found themselves caught up in the action around their Westway/Ladbroke Grove stomping ground. The main flash-point was only a few yards away from the Elgin, Joe's 101'ers stronghold. 'We were there at the very first throw of the very first brick,' grinned Joe 'Paul, Bernie and I were walking along when this conga line of policemen came through the crowd. Someone threw a brick at them and all hell broke loose, and I mean hell! The crowd parted and we were pushed onto this wire netting and nearly fell down this hole where they were doing these excavations under the motorway. A police motorcyclist came straight down Ladbroke Grove and one of our posse [Paul] threw a traffic cone at him. He only just managed to keep going.

'I decided to set a car alight, and it was ludicrous, us standing around it with the wind blowing out the flame on this Swan Vesta . . . It's one thing to say, "Let's burn the cars", but you try setting a car alight. This big, fat woman was screaming, "Oh Lord, they're going to set the car alight!" It was just a comedy, some of it. It was just a hell of a day.

'This was one time when people said, "We've had enough and we're gonna say so now." That's what gave rise to the song, "White Riot", because we participated in the riot. I was aware all the time that it was a black people's riot . . . They had more of an axe to grind and they had to guts to do something physical about it.'

Later that night, Joe and Paul were victims of an attempted mugging, but their pockets were already empty. That experience told them that they could sympathise with, and even join in with, the black man's struggle but ultimately, 'it wasn't really our story.' These experiences laid the template for the image, attitude and lyrical preoccupations of the early Clash.

Subsequently, legions of Clash detractors dismissed the group's delight in such conflicts as an aspect of 'the Clash myth'. But some form of confrontation has always gone with rock 'n' roll. There is a Clash myth, but ultimately it rests on some of the best music ever hurled off a stage, by a bunch of characters who recognised no barriers in their quest for honesty and impact.

Being inspired to write a song called 'White Riot' in response to the Carnival incident can never be considered one of the band's blunders. They were simply calling for white people to show a similar passion for change and action as the black youths at Notting Hill. Not necessarily by throwing bricks at coppers, but simply getting off their arses and not being content with their drab lot in life.

The riot furnished the early Clash with inspiration and imagery – photos of the incident were later transplanted to record sleeves and backdrops. It also woke them up further to the power of that weekend's soundtrack – roots reggae. The Carnival had throbbed to anthems like Culture's 'Two Sevens Clash', Prince Far-I's 'Under Heavy Manners' and Junior Murvin's Lee Perry-produced 'Police And Thieves', which had already been around for a while.

Since 1974 – after reading of Keith Richards' immersion in the genre – I'd been getting weekly pre-release doses from Daddy Kool's record store off Oxford Street. In the days before punk, and continuing during the subsequent explosion, reggae was the music of choice by nature of its lyrical reality and fearless sonic boundary pushing. Roots music was Rastafarian punk rock.

The combination of Paul's existing reggae fixation, the tireless promotion of the music by DJ and film-maker Don Letts – whose lone figure against a wall of cops at the Carnival would provide The Clash with one of their most enduring associated images – and now the close-to-home reality of the Notting Hill riot, gave The Clash, and especially Joe, a grounding in urban reality that they'd never lose.

A gig on 5 September at one of the Roundhouse's Sunday sessions proved to be Keith Levene's last. The Clash were third on the bill supporting pub-rockers the

The classic image of Don Letts during the Notting Hill riot of August 1976. The inscription is by Don.

Kursaal Flyers and rock 'n' roll revivalists Crazy Cavan & The Rhythm Rockers. Playing inhumanly early to just-arrived hippies, The Clash were greeted with a luke-warm response and a smattering of heckling.

Various reasons have been given for Keith's departure, with the group saying it was because he simply didn't turn up to rehearsals. Keith was subsequently quoted as saying he wasn't into all the politics. In *Uncut*'s 2003 feature he even reckons he refused point blank to play 'White Riot'. Musical differences were also cited, with supporting evidence provided by Keith's re-emergence as Public Image Ltd's guitarist in 1978. PIL's miasmic, dub-inspired music provided both John Lydon and Levene with an environment free of the political baggage that accompanied both the Pistols and The Clash. However, Pete Frame's *Zigzag* family tree simply blamed bad reviews.

Other sources insisted that the effects of hard drugs caused Keith to quit, but I only became aware that he had a smack problem much later, when I was knocking about with PIL. Before that it had been speed all the way although, when I did it with him that year, we banged it up (And I felt psychotically dreadful afterwards). As Keith told *Uncut*, 'I'd been a bit moody, *well* moody, at rehearsals, to the point that I knew they were talking about me.' 'He was doing a lot of speed,' said Joe. 'His weekend would go on 'til Tuesday and he wouldn't show for rehearsals, so he kind of walked out by himself. I thought Keith was brilliant, but I realised Keith had other eggs to fry, so we just got on with it.'

Whatever his reasons, without Keith, The Clash played their next gig in what would become their classic four-piece format: the frontline of Joe, Mick and Paul, with Terry Chimes occupying the drum stool. The show was the opening night of the 100 Club Punk Festival on 20 September and was the point at which The Clash buzz really started.

The festival was held over two days, with The Clash appearing on the first night on the same bill as headliners the Sex Pistols. Immediately afterwards, it became noticeable that The Clash were getting their own crowd. Whereas the Pistols were anti-everything, The Clash were more accessible, positive and you could imitate their look with an Oxfam shop shirt and a pot of emulsion, rather than by buying a pair of bondage strides that were well out of the reach of most kids.

The 100 Club Punk Festival is another of those occasions that's been blown up into a history-changing event – attended by the world and his dog, of course. Granted, it was tailor made for mythical status – being the first show of unity and solidarity for punks after Screen On The Green.

Before The Clash's set, Siouxsie and the Banshees played their first and only gig with a line-up that featured future Pistol Sid Vicious on drums, guitarist Marco Pirroni (later of The Models and Adam and the Ants), and eternal Banshees bassist Steve Severin backing Siouxsie's vocal exertions. The newly minted combo let rip with twenty minutes of audacious racket – called 'The Lords Prayer' because of the lyrical content – that later became the stuff of legend. A bunch of disaffected ex-soul boys from a Mortlake estate called Subway Sect also made their debut.

The Clash went down fine, but they were still feeling their way. It was during their set that another legendary Clash incident occurred, which Joe was fond of retelling; 'The Clash were in the middle of this ludicrous Stalinist vibe where we decided it was uncool to talk to the audience,' he recalled in *Q*'s Punk special. 'Inevitably we broke a string, so suddenly there's no music. Luckily, I always used to have a transistor radio with me . . . We didn't have spare guitars, so I just switched on the radio and held it up to the mic. At the mixing desk, [sound man] Dave Goodman was hip enough to put a delay on it and it happened to be a discussion about the bombs in Northern Ireland. People think it was a set-up, after that the band started speaking to the audience.'

The DIY fanzine *Sniffin' Glue* put out a special based around the festival which made you wish that you'd been there. 'The Clash are really good,' wrote Mark Perry. 'They seem to be getting better every time I see 'em. Their set was more loose and expressive than before. They've dropped a number and they are obviously the most powerful band on the scene at the moment . . . They're gonna start headlining in clubs so they should soon build up a loyal following, they fucking deserve it.'

By now, I knew it was high time that I checked The Clash out. Just the name gave me tingles and I hadn't even heard them yet. Then it was announced, as luck would have it – The Clash were coming to my hometown!

CHAPTER FIVE

LIKE TROUSERS, LIKE BRAIN

I'd rather play to an audience and them not enjoy it, if we were doing what we thought was honest. – Joe Strummer

Some gigs can change your life. Usually, you realise that later. The best ones are when you know it's happening right there and then. Bang! Your world is never the same again.

9 October 1976 was one of those nights. At the time I was living in a place called Leighton Buzzard – your average market town with amoeba-like estates, crap pubs and leery beer monsters kicking off after closing time. But it also had a fairly vibrant gig scene. A guy I'd been to school with, Chris France, put on live music in a pub backroom and had already showcased a virginal Jam, pub-rockers Eddie and the Hot Rods and the legendary local maniac, John Otway. Bigger events took place at the local Tiddenfoot Leisure Centre, which was one of those council hangars better suited to bingo and comedians.

But that October evening, Chris had booked a locally popular R&B pub band called the Rockets . . . with The Clash as support.

In the run up to the gig, my anticipation was stoked by a couple of factors. Firstly, the October issue of *Sniffin' Glue* carried the first major Clash interview. Until then, Mark Perry's photocopied missives from deepest Deptford had centred on the impact of the Ramones and London outfits like Eddie and the Hot Rods and the Damned. Davis Road squat resident Steve Walsh went to interview Joe, Mick and Paul at Rehearsals. The band sought no favours from the press – they were urgent and aggressive, talking as if The Clash were indeed the only group that mattered.

Joe went first, laying into the contemporary music scene; 'People are prepared to accept rubbish, anything that's going. I mean, every single LP anybody ever plays me in any flat I go to and they say, 'this is good' . . . it's rubbish and they have got nothin' else to play. The thing is – they've got to think it's good, otherwise they go insane. The only good one is that Ramones one.'

When asked about the band's DIY approach to fashion, Joe hit a rich vein, 'What we've got is what other people put in the rubbish bin. Like Mick's shirt was gonna be put in the bin until he paid ten pence for it. I mean, you ain't gonna go down to *Sex* with your ten quid stuffed in your back pocket and buy some stupid . . . I dunno, I've never been down there.'

Mick took up the theme, 'I think it's a bit easy to go down there and look great. I mean, their stuff's pretty good. Looks good to me, but I think the way we do it is

Peroxide punk Joe cradles his new black Fender Telecaster. He would nurse the guitar through more than 25 years of touring and recording.

much more accessible to kids. . . it encourages 'em to do something for themselves. It's to do with personal freedom . . . I don't think it's just the trousers though. I mean, the trousers reflect the brain.'

'Like trousers, like brain!', added Joe.

The Clash's Year Zero punk fundamentalism was in direct contrast to the good-time bands that had injected some energy into the pub-rock scene. Joe now viewed the sort of endless knees-up he had escaped from by quitting the 101'ers as an irrelevant dead-end. Joining the Clash had turned him around to the extent that providing a suitable soundtrack for a night's getting pissed was an unthinkably bourgeois proposition.

'Look, the situation is far too serious for enjoyment, man. Maybe when we're fifty-five we can play tubas in the sun. That's all right then to enjoy yourselves, but now . . . I'd rather play to an audience and them not enjoy it, if we're doing what we thought was honest. Rather than us go up and sing, "Get outta Denver, baby", and do what we didn't think was honest.'

The week before the Leighton Buzzard gig, I got a string of phone calls from Bernie Rhodes. This came about because I'd told Chris France, who booked the show directly with Bernie (and paid him about £20), that I wanted to write a piece for *New York Rocker*, the US publication dedicated to punk rock. Bernie also knew I'd eventually be doing a *Zigzag* piece.

Having never encountered Bernie before, I had no idea about his background or personality. All I knew was that he was the band's manager. Bernie gave me the whole street-credible spiel, all the while emphasising that this was the only band worth following and how they were going to turn the world upside down. At first, I thought it was the usual hype that you could expect from managers, but there was something more here. Bernie really knew how to stir up interest. And he was dead right. I was really never the same again.

When we arrived, the hall was about half full of local hippies, rock fans and lager meatheads, who draped themselves over the comfy chairs. There couldn't have been more than ten punters of a punky disposition in the whole joint. The first place we hit was the bar – and immediately encountered The Clash. There were no dressing rooms to speak of, so they were just hanging about waiting until the time came to go on.

For some reason, I found myself perched next to Mick – he knew he'd seen me before, and a chunk of the evening dissolved in shared rock reminiscences.

In contrast to Mick's readiness to wax lyrical about the Stones or Mott The Hoople, Joe was friendly, but remained pretty quiet. The developing punk scene must have been something of a culture shock for him. Six months before he'd been playing pub-rock standards with the 101'ers. Now he was at the centre of a whole new movement. Baggy suits had been replaced by Oxfam jackets, studs and boiler suits splattered in paint. And he was already being called a spokesman for a generation.

Then it was time. The Clash came on, exploded into 'White Riot' and it was like a bomb had gone off. Coruscating razor-chords and breakneck double-time rhythms topped with the amphetamined passion howling out of the incandescent front man, who was literally *vibrating*. The Clash's diversity and depth could evolve later. In 1976 they simply provided a declaration of all-out war on all the bullshit you'd accumulated over your whole life.

I had to review the gig for *New York Rocker*, which was like a hip collision between the US's *Punk* magazine and *NME*. It was the first press the group had got in the States. I led off with, 'The Clash taking the stage was like an injection of electricity into the smoky air. They charged headlong into a dynamite opener with shattering energy, strutting and lurching with manic, stuttering violence. Like clockwork robots out of control.

'Before they'd played a note the group hit you straight between the eyes with the visuals. Oxfam shirts splattered with paint and daubed with slogans like "STEN GUNS IN KNIGHTSBRIDGE."

'Despite sound problems they were astounding, almost overpowering in their attack and conviction,' I continued. 'In The Clash's 35 minute set I counted about six potential rock 'n' roll killer classics. Every song they do is their own, none over three minutes long, each razor sharp and rocking at lethal speed.

'The Clash are the most devastating of the new wave British bands . . . bent on reforming rock 'n' roll to topple the bored and ancient heroes and replace them with high-energy rock 'n' roll played by people with their fingers on the pulse of what's REALLY going on. The Clash are riding the movement, happy to be part of something fresh and new, but with the ease of geezers who know they'll be going from strength to strength when the bandwagon-jumpers have long since fallen into the dust and clambered onto another trend.

'The Clash are vital and different. Every gig they do – and so far there have been about half a dozen – is better than the last. They're great now. In three months they'll be staggering.'

That night still looms as one of the greatest experiences of my life. So many people lucky enough to have seen The Clash say that they had their lives changed that first time. Me too. Later that month I also saw the Sex Pistols up the road at Dunstable Civic Hall. Although impressive, the Pistols impact was diminished by the fact that there were about 80 people in a venue that could accommodate a couple of thousand. And the sound was appalling. Even in this half-full leisure centre I could stand a few feet from the stage and get knocked backwards by energy sparking off the stage.

After the Clash's show, me and my mates hit the bar to gibber disbelievingly about what we'd just seen. The band were already there. Here I ranted endlessly about what I thought about The Clash. After all, this was the best group I'd seen in years. I knew Mick felt the same way. Slowly the rest of the group got involved in the conversation too. Joe shook my hand and gave that characteristic head-leaning backward nod. He must've been drained after that performance.

Then Bernie Rhodes appeared. Discovering I was the journalist he'd been ranting to on the phone, he kind of took over. At the time he was still a used car salesman. He certainly had the gab – not to mention a motor with the number plate CLA5H. He proudly told me that the band's roadie Sebastian was actually one of

'What we wear is dangerous gear' – Fashion guerrillas Mick, Paul and Joe sport the situationist style.

the mega-rich Conran family, but worked for The Clash for peanuts because of his passion for their cause.

Having made arrangements to meet up with the band the following week, I left to go back to my nice house in Leighton Buzzard, but now everything suddenly seemed dull and boring. To quote Joe, it felt like a cog in the universe had shifted that night.

Three days later I met The Clash (minus Terry Chimes) at Rehearsals to do their second press interview. There were the pink drapes, Paul's car dump mural and three angry young men eager to expound the same radical agenda that I'd just read about in *Sniffin' Glue*. We adjourned to the Carnarvon Castle pub over the road. I had some money and got 'em in.

Mick, Joe, Paul and myself sat around the table. Suddenly, Joe disappeared underneath it. Had he dropped something? Surely not pissed already? I then became aware of something pulling on my trouser leg? It was Joe. He got back in his seat with an evil, incriminating grin on his face. 'What do you call those, then?' he demanded. He was obviously referring to my new jeans, which I'd purchased to replace the customary flares I'd sported for the previous few years. I thought they were straight legged but they still weren't narrow enough for Joe's liking.

Even a slight flare was now taboo in punk rock – which I did find a bit odd because I thought the whole idea was about doing and wearing what you wanted. But he had a point. Flares meant the old regime. Hippies and all that. Looking back at old photos – they did look fairly stupid.

'Like trousers, like brain.' Joe recalled his catchphrase with a laugh on *Westway To The World*. 'That was the difference between the flared look that was a hangover from the sixties and the new look, which was fast and trim and going places. You could tell people a mile off what they were into.'

Although I wasn't going to hear the last of this trouserial business, I'd been more worried about the fact that I was twenty-two years old, having read all the 'old fart' comments and guessing that these boys were around the twenty mark. I didn't find out until much later that at twenty-four, Joe was actually nearly two years older than me, while Mick was just over a year younger.

Irrespective of any prior influences, the three penniless urban warriors sitting in front of me were wiping the slate clean in and starting all over again. 'No Elvis, Beatles or the Rolling Stones.' All in the name of maximum impact. Mick would be jamming with Keith Richards ten years later, while Joe would be held up alongside all three when he died. But in October 1976, The Clash were on a mission.

'We're one up the arse for the rich, established groups,' declared Mick. 'There's so many useless bands around it's not even worth naming any . . . There's a lot of oppression around today. We're making people aware of it and opposing it . . . We're still rock 'n' roll though.' They talked about London. 'We love the place,' declared Joe. 'Blocks of flats, concrete . . .' 'Yeah,' agreed Paul. 'If we get any gigs where we have to stay away we'll just have to take photos of London with us.' 'I hate the country,' chimed in Mick. 'The minute I see cows I get sick! I ain't never lived below eighteen floors.' Joe added that 'London's Burning' was, 'a celebration of the Westway under a yellow light.'

They said that the only other current music they really liked at that time was reggae and the Ramones – 'They must be really intelligent to write lyrics like that,' observed Joe. Just as reggae voiced the discontent of black youths, The Clash saw punk doing the same for white kids growing up in council estate ghettos with nothing to do and no future. Okay, nigh-on 30 years have passed and the situation has got much worse. But before The Clash *nobody* was writing songs about the harsh reality and desperation of inner city life. While bemoaning the sad state of radio – one of his favourite gripes – Joe likened The Clash to a public broadcast system bringing the truth. He always harboured a desire to start his own station.

The distinct personalities of The Clash's frontline had become apparent over our two meetings: There was Joe, the ex-pub-rocker, who seemed older than the others and had obviously enjoyed a reasonable education. His passion and expression seemed drawn from deeper sources than just being pissed off with pub-rock. He was channelling the same type of wired energy that came from Jerry Lee Lewis and appreciated the importance of lyrics, especially the way they'd been used in the old American protest songs. He had a way with words and was quick witted. Plus, behind the gruff exterior was the genuinely nice bloke who would open up as time went on.

Mick was more forthcoming, obviously sensitive and in love with the rock 'n' roll world. You sensed he would adapt to life as a rock star with enthusiasm, if only to live out the fantasy he'd read about every week in *NME*. A year later, Mick's rock-star affectations would start to bring him into conflict with Joe. But, like the Stones, this friction is what propelled The Clash to greatness.

This friction was perfectly offset and complimented by the strong, streetwise and often silent Paul.

Although a damning rock stereotype, The Clash already had the essential ingredients for a classic *group* that none of their contemporaries could match – A frighteningly new and dangerous version of the old rock formula, which had come along almost by accident. I emerged from that meeting uplifted and elated. I could have said that I had just met the future of rock 'n' roll, if that phrase hadn't just been abused on behalf of Bruce Springsteen. I went home and got out one of my white shirts. Fished out a tub of paint and splashed it all over with a glaring red CLASH. Trouble is, I used gloss. It wouldn't dry, stank like hell and stood up on its own afterwards. I still wore it with pride though.

The next few weeks proved highly eventful, as The Clash became part of my life. I missed the following Saturday's gig at London University, where they supported Shakin' Stevens and the Sunsets, of all people. The punk-ted battles of the following year were brewing, as it sank into the backward brains of the more violent rockabillies that here were some people who looked different and might be worth duffing up. A standoff was narrowly averted at the gig when the group and friends armed themselves with chairs in the dressing room afterwards.

I witnessed my second Clash gig on 23 October, at the Institute of Contemporary Arts in The Mall leading up to Buckingham Palace. Home turf and top of the bill. The evening was aptly billed as A Night of Pure Energy.

London was buzzing as punk poetess Patti Smith was in town from New York for shows at Hammersmith Odeon and a press conference. I went to the lot, including the conference in a London hotel where she hurled sandwiches at a somewhat confrontational Allan Jones. Patti was the first female punk icon to arrive from the States, with her fiery combination of opiated poetry and rock 'n' roll attitude. The Clash had checked out her gig at London's Roundhouse a few months earlier and were fans. The parallels between the two camps became apparent when she announced at the press conference, 'Call me Field Marshall of Rock 'n' Roll! I'm fucking declaring war, a war where everybody's fighting the same war. My guitar is my machine gun!'

The shows were great, with Don Letts and Tapper Zukie coming on to skank about on stage near the end. On the afternoon of the ICA concert I interviewed Patti's genial guitarist Lenny Kaye. He'd heard of The Clash and, after I'd gushed my enthusiasm, said his band would try and come along that evening.

The ICA was heaving that night. I wore my new shirt and, unfortunately, those semi-flares. First on were Subway Sect, who Bernie had taken under his wing. A lot of people really liked them for their stance – four disaffected teenagers dressed down in old Oxfam gear and playing monochromic, dissonant reflections upon a grey life. One of their songs was called 'We Oppose All Rock 'n' Roll'. Sid Vicious thought they were great.

The Clash were even better than at Leighton Buzzard. Along with Rotten, Joe Strummer was now the most compulsive singer in rock 'n' roll – not just punk. He could barely contain his anger and emotion as he spat, slavered and shouted lyrics that were more like rhetorical slogans. Often Joe would end a song lying on his back, pouring sweat, face clenched as he wrenched the last drop of blazing passion from his raw throat.

Then there was Mick's force-ten guitar blizzard. His classic pop harmonising with Joe was interspersed with sorties around the stage doing scissor-jumps.

Paul Simonon was the lean, mean bass machine.

Three diverse individuals bent on tearing the system down, shredding your pre-conceptions and pinning you against the wall. They were taking that primeval rock 'n' roll piledrive hump and dropkicking it off the Westway like a scatter-bomb.

This time The Clash got the response they deserved. They were playing to their own crowd – like Mick's best mate Tony James, who'd just joined Chelsea with Billy Idol, Sid Vicious and the rest of the punk elite. There were a lot of record company people there, plus journalists and those that had simply turned up to see what all the fuss was about.

The gig made the music press for a couple of reasons. First of all, a young Clash fan called Shane MacGowan had turned up to pogo with 'Mad' Jane Crockford, who would later play bass with female band the Modettes. The pair were standing right in front of me and, at some point, got over excited in their play-fighting. Jane gave future Pogue Shane an over-affectionate nibble on the ear – and ended up causing a deep cut. Not taking the whole lobe, as was reported, but it certainly passed into punk legend after *NME* seized on it the following week. Joe saw what was going on and shouted from the stage: 'All of you who think violence is tough, why don't you go home and collect stamps? That's much tougher.' Shane would later tell *Zigzag* that Jane had bottled him – out of affection, of course.

Patti Smith had duly turned up with her entourage. Despite apparently being on another planet, she ended up leaping onstage to join in – somewhat ironically – with 'I'm So Bored With The USA'. She skipped, jumped and flung her arms around in circles while howling the chorus for all she was worth. 'I just couldn't stop myself,' she told me afterwards. Patti obviously had the hots for Paul. The feeling was mutual and she ended up leaving with him.

Having missed my last train home I ended up leaving with Mick, who said I could stay at Davis Road. The squat had now become a bit of a hangout – current inhabitants included Sid Vicious, Keith Levene, an occasional Johnny Rotten, Steve Walsh and Viv Albertine, Mick's girlfriend. But first we would have to stop off at the tower block flat, which he shared with his nan.

It was those trousers again, the same ones that Strummer had ridiculed. 'Sid won't like it if you turn up in them. You might get hurt,' said Mick with concern. 'We'll go to my nan's and I'll lend you a pair.' So we trudged off into the night to Wilmcote House, on a high from the gig, swapping stories and giggling like idiots. While I was there, Mick took me out onto the little balcony and looked down at the yellow-lit bustle of the Westway snaking through West London. 'This is where me and Joe wrote "London's Burning", he said. A lot of the first Clash album was spawned within that perfect symbol of inner city hopelessness.

I was really warming to Mick. He was open, funny, passionate and, it was becoming increasingly more obvious, extremely talented. Also considerate, as he rummaged in his chest of drawers and emerged triumphant with a pair of faded old jeans that had been taken in at the leg. 'Here's my old ones. These'll do!' I put them on and felt like Rudolph Nureyev in his ballet tights! Again we walked into the night, with me doing a good John Wayne impersonation. This time it was to Davis Road.

I was a bit wary of meeting Sid Vicious as his legend had preceded him. I'd heard all the stories about him chain-whipping Nick Kent at the 100 Club Punk Festival and the press had him marked down as the ultimate nihilistic thug. I didn't know that he was going to turn out to be a big softie, a pleasant, average bloke who just liked enjoying himself. Sitting in one of the rooms were Keith Levene, Steve Walsh, Viv and Sid, who was in the process of learning to play bass to the Ramones' 'Blitzkrieg Bop'. They were all laughing and frazzled, firing up vast quantities of punk's drug *de jour*, amphetamine sulphate. Mick was knackered and retired fairly early with Viv. Eventually it was just me and Sid, talking about the New York Dolls and the Ramones while he soldiered on with the bass.

By the time I left around eight next morning he could play along to 'Blitzkrieg Bop'. 'I can play bass now,' he proudly declared as I left. It's a shame that it would be the last time I'd see him so happy.

At this time, The Clash weren't particularly looking to clamber on the ever-accelerating bandwagon of punk rock bands signing to major labels. They were simply honing their set, their style and their strategy, while focusing on playing live with maximum disturbance.

After the ICA, Patti and Paul went together to Birmingham, where both had their next gigs. Here, The Clash found themselves supporting local band the Suburban Studs, a punk-by-numbers quartet who never enjoyed much success. *Sounds'* Jonh Ingham rated it as the Clash's best gig to date. There was none of the London pressure, a good crowd, and they were simply getting better with every show. Two nights later they played Fulham Old Town Hall, supporting pub-rockers Roogalator, and got another salivating *Sounds* review from Giovanni Dadomo.

The *NME* of 6 November carried a review of the ICA by Miles, formerly a leading figure on the mid-sixties London underground scene. He'd tuned in to punk rock as another vital, potentially epoch-making, movement. 'The Clash were really good,' he wrote. 'They are not poseurs, they are what *Sniffin' Glue* promised they'd be. It was as if they'd crystallised the dormant energy of all the hours of crushing boredom of being an unemployed school-leaver, living with your parents in a council flat, into a series of three-minute staccato blasts, delivered like a whiplash at the audience, who were galvanised into frenzied dancing.'

My next Clash gig was at London's Royal College of Art on 5 November. Appropriately the evening was called *A Night of Treason*. The Clash were supported by The Rockets (a reversal of the Leighton Buzzard bill) and Subway Sect. This was a different crowd from the ICA. Punk was starting to catch on now, while at the same time drawing plenty of aggression from anyone from teddy boys to lager thugs. The RCA was sprinkled with the Clash faithful and also some drunken students, who apparently got a bit pissed off when Sid Vicious started heckling their mates in pub-rock support band, the Tyla Gang.

When The Clash came on, it all went off. I was standing ten feet from the inci-

The truth is only known by guttersnipes – Mick, Joe and Paul peruse the press.

dent, some heckling from the students was blackening the mood of the gig. This escalated as a few bottles were thrown. Joe told them to cool it a few times. When they
carried on hurling, Joe and Paul leapt off the stage to sort out a couple of the main
protagonists. Within seconds, Sid Vicious appeared from the back of the stage and
dived into the crowd to join in. There was a bit of a skirmish, which seemed to do
the trick, then Joe and Paul returned to the stage to finish the set, now driven by
adrenaline into ferocious overdrive. Mick later said he stayed up there because 'somebody had to keep in tune'. Before the gig Joe had told me they had a new song called
'Hate and War'. 'Well, it wouldn't be 'Peace and Love' would it?' he explained.

I was sporting another of my emulsion creations, plus Mick's old strides, and
came in for some evil stares. After the show, I was standing by the stage waiting for
the band to come out when a small gaggle of herberts swaggered up. They looked
suspiciously like the mob who'd been chucking bottles. They thought I was Mick and
started mouthing threats and jibes and poking me. Suddenly, a ruckus exploded as
Sid appeared. He was making straight for the lunks and hurling abuse, while being
held back by four people. The aggressors bolted.

Afterwards, we hopped into a cab and headed back to Davis Road. It soon
became obvious that we were being followed by a Volkswagen, which parked up
nearby when we reached our destination. Ominous figures got out and I immediately recognised them as the idiots from the college. Mick also seemed to think that
they were the ones who'd been starting a lot of the trouble at the gig. 'Hold on,' said
Sid, who promptly hopped onto the front garden wall brandishing some handy

roofing slates. 'Fuck off!' Sid yelled, his lip curling and teeth bared, as he hurled the slates at our would-be-assailants. This they duly did. We laughed. Far from starting on me, it was the second time that Sid had saved me from a kicking in one night. It was also my first taste of lunk-on-punk aggression.

'Punk rock is the music of now,' declared Joe in the group's first proper music press interview – with *Melody Maker's* Caroline Coon in the 13 November issue. He'd had the hippies in his ideological crosshairs, declaring, 'The hippy movement was a failure. All hippies around now represent complete apathy. There's a million good reasons why the thing failed. I'll jeer at hippies because that's helpful. They'll realise they're stuck in a rut and maybe they'll get out of it.'

Back then, the complacent and hostile hippy was viewed as an enemy but, as the years went on, their peaceful idealism was a concept that Joe came to appreciate as he slotted in effortlessly into the spirit of traditional events like Glastonbury. 'Joe was a bit of a hippy anyway,' said Paul in 2003, adding, 'But that's fine. Live and let live.'

The gigs continued. I next caught the band on 18 November at a pub in High Wycombe called the Nag's Head, which was run by 100 Club promoter Ron Watts. Within the space of two weeks, the group had improved again. Joe had dyed his hair blonde and sported a boiler suit on the back of which he'd daubed the title of that new song – 'Hate and War'. This time the onstage attack was even more frenzied and confrontational. The rehearsals were obviously paying off as the songs uncoiled off the stage in taut, ballistic stun-bursts while Strummer was almost consumed with righteous anger.

The set was similarly lean, and included 'White Riot', 'London's Burning', '48 Hours', 'Janie Jones', 'I'm So Bored With The USA', 'Protex Blue', 'Hate and War', 'Career Opportunities', 'What's My Name', 'Deny' and '1-2 Crush on You'.

I reviewed the show in *Sounds* and tried to convey the fact that The Clash excited me in a way I'd never experienced before. I'd seldom felt this passionate in years of being inspired by music. The groups I liked were rarely more than TV images, records or dots in the distance at a stadium. This time I could have reached up and touched the group if I'd wanted to, then have a drink with them afterwards.

I wrote: 'The Clash are now firing with more compressed energy than a flamethrower at full blast. They play with almost frightening conviction and intensity, each number a rapid-fire statement delivered like a knockout blow.' I was impressed by the emergence of Joe as a totally compulsive frontman enough to compare him to 'a paint spattered Greek god'!

Admittedly, my enthusiastic outpourings might not have got the nod from more restrained and scholarly observers, but I still stand by them. At the time, I was gripped by the band's euphoric surge. Those gigs are still some of the best I've ever witnessed.

It was staggering to behold the emergence of what would soon be one of the greatest bands of all time in the space of just a couple of months. That night at High Wycombe clashed with the Miss World contest, and was half full. The little loft was awash with A&R men, who spent most of the set asking punters – including me and my mates – if they thought the band were any good. They were better than good, and improving with every show.

Walking into the cupboard-sized dressing room afterwards, Joe was spread-eagled on a table, barely able to speak because he was so spent. Or maybe he just wanted to avoid talking to the A&R men.

In my review I also took the opportunity to ask why the group hadn't been signed yet. 'The Clash seem forced to take a back seat on the new wave recording front while groups like the Damned, Pistols and Vibrators shove singles out. Why is it that the hottest group this country has got hasn't yet had the chance to get themselves on vinyl? Dunno, but going on last Thursday's set, it won't be too long before some record company wakes up.'

Polydor seemed to have emerged as the label most likely to sign The Clash and booked the band into their own studios off Oxford Street to record some demos. These would be used to convince the bosses to sign the group. Simple? Not when you consider that the group's choice of producer for the sessions was Guy Stevens – the berserk ex-Mott The Hoople producer who'd sacked Mick from Violent Luck.

The first time that the rest of the band met Guy they were accompanied by Sid Vicious. Guy had just been to see Led Zeppelin's film, *The Song Remains the Same,* and, being a fan, was appalled at the self-indulgence on display. He was so enraged he took the record and flung it across the room – hitting Joe smack in the eye. Seeking medication for Joe's injury, they found Sid rummaging in Guy's medicine cabinet.

Mick told me that Guy Stevens, way of 'method producing' could involve hurling a chair at the wall if he thought it'd get a reaction from the musician and create a more impassioned performance. Joe recalled the first meeting with Guy in *Mojo*: 'When I saw him he was wearing this dyed army jumper with pads on the shoulder, some ratty old coat, his hair all wild all over the place, mad staring eyes, gibbering like a lunatic. But not nonsense: talking fast, but talking sense.'

They recorded five songs – 'Career Opportunities', 'White Riot', '1977', 'Janie Jones', 'London's Burning' – but didn't capture the essence of the band. Joe would later complain to *NME*'s Tony Parsons that Guy had tried to make him sing more clearly and annunciate his words. 'So I did it, and it sounded like Matt Munro,' said Joe, recalling the schmaltzy sixties crooner. 'So I thought, "I'm never doing that again . . ." To me, our music is like Jamaican stuff: If they can't hear it, they're not supposed to hear it. It's not for them if they can't understand it.' Joe referred to Guy only as a 'famous producer', adding that he was 'too pissed to work.'

Guy's unconventional methods rubbed Polydor A&R hotshots Chris Parry and Vic Smith the wrong way. Their brief was to get an accurate representation of The Clash on tape. Guy responded by getting progressively more incapacitated, forcing engineer Vic Smith to finish the mixing. The results sounded flat compared to the gigs. 'Boring,' said Joe. The demos of 'Career Opportunities' and 'Janie Jones' later made it onto the *Clash on Broadway* CD set.

As Mick revealed when we spoke the following March, 'It was great recording with Guy Stevens – fantastic when we were doing it. He was really inciting us, but when it came down to the mixing it was a bit untogether.'

While the record labels were hesitating to offer the band a deal, Terry Chimes announced he was leaving. Unconvinced by the politics, and increasingly put off by the growing amount of violence around the scene, Terry agreed to fill in until a replacement could be found. As it happened, the drumming position wouldn't have a permanent incumbent until the arrival of Topper Headon the following year. In the meantime, The Clash tried out a guy called Rob Harper with Terry periodically reappearing up until March.

The Clash's first TV interview appeared in an edition of the Sunday afternoon *London Weekend Show*, hosted by Janet Street-Porter. Although mainly featuring the Pistols at one of their recent gigs, the programme did track down a wired-looking Clash frontline at Rehearsals. They talked about the usual stuff, but with a far more aggressive attitude than I'd ever encountered.

Joe looked down and curled his lip as he spat out statements like, 'You've got to have some music that's what you feel like, otherwise you go barmy, don't you?' From crusty squat-rocker to snarling, disaffected punk in only six months. But underneath Joe's golden heart was unchanged.

He was equally as full on in *NME*'s first major Clash interview, which was conducted by Miles. 'I think people ought to know that we're anti-fascist, we're anti-violence, we're anti-racist and we're pro-creative. We're against ignorance.' The conversation then focussed on violence, with Joe using the flick knife he'd been opening and closing during the interview as a prop. 'Suppose I smash your face in and slit your nostrils with this, right? Well, if you don't learn anything from it, then it's not worth it, right? But suppose some guy comes up to me and tries to and tries to put one over on me, right? And I smash his face up and he learns something from it. Well, that's, in a sense, creative violence. And this sort of paintwork is creative violence too, right?' With that he pointed to the stencil on Paul's clothes.

On 1 December, the Sex Pistols were booked as last minute replacements for Queen on ITV's *Today* show. It's one of the most infamous incidents in music history. Bill Grundy had become notorious in media circles as a drunken boor and it was evident that he'd had a few drinks that evening, as he tried to goad the band into saying something outrageous.

Both group and entourage fielded his initial forays with polite indifference, but became hostile when Grundy started leching over Siouxsie. The temperature rose as Johnny Rotten – who later confessed, 'I'd been out of my head on speed for three days' – was commanded to repeat his mumbled utterance of the word 'shit'. Steve Jones called Grundy a 'dirty sod' and a 'dirty old man'. Egged on by the porky presenter's '*What* a clever boy' Steve offered 'what a fucking rotter!'

The Press loved it. They finally had a nail on which to hang their fear and loathing of the growing punk 'threat'. The *Daily Mirror* blared the classic 'Filth And The Fury' headline from its front page and carried a report about the lorry driver who was so outraged that he kicked in his TV. Little England was up in arms over these 'foul-mouthed yobs'. Less amusingly, the shit-storm of publicity led to nervy local councils cancelling gigs throughout the country. The imminent Pistols/Clash Anarchy Tour of the UK was reduced to tatters. Even Grundy was suspended for

No fun on the bus – Mick, Johnny Rotten, Heartbreaker Billy Rath, Paul and Joe on the Anarchy Tour wagon, December 1976.

two weeks for his part in the debacle.

The Anarchy Tour had been put together by the Sex Pistols' management as a showcase for their band and punk rock in general. Originally it was planned to have the Ramones and Talking Heads on the bill too, but music biz politics intervened. The Damned came in as outsiders, with tour support from their record company, Stiff. There was also proto-punk icon Johnny Thunders, flown in from New York with his new band the Heartbreakers. Finally, The Clash were slotted in as bottom of the bill to pad it out. Considering their growing reputation it was almost insulting to see their name in such tiny print at the bottom of the tour poster. Eventually, the tour would play just a handful of shows. Even the much-anticipated Boxing Day gig at London's large Roxy Theatre in Harlesden was pulled.

There had already been a warm up gig at Coventry's Lanchester Poly on 26 November, with the Pistols and The Clash, who were trying out new drummer Rob Harper. It didn't bode well for the forthcoming tour when a committee of students had decided that 'White Riot' and the Pistols' new song, 'No Future' (soon-to-be-called 'God Save The Queen'), were fascist and tried to withhold payment.

A precursor to this kind of misinterpretation had appeared in the *NME* interview a fortnight before, when Miles mentioned that some people thought the words of 'White Riot' were racist. 'Joe lunged at the remark like a Doberman Pinscher,' he wrote. 'They're not racist! They're not racist at all! . . . The only thing we're saying about the blacks is that they've got their problems and they're prepared to deal with them. But white men, they just ain't prepared to deal with them – everything's too cosy. They've got drugs, hi-fis, cars . . .'

The first proper gig to remain from the original Anarchy schedule was on 6 December at Leeds Polytechnic. By now the tour was being pursued by Fleet Street's finest, just waiting for some dirt to fling. Paul and Steve from the Pistols were goaded by a photographer into uprooting a potted plant in the hotel foyer, which was promptly paid for. The *Mirror* subsequently reported that they'd wrecked the joint.

Later that night, Joe took the stage with his £9.17 weekly dole income stencilled on the front of his shirt. He exercised his fixation with '1984' again by announcing, 'I've been going around for two days thinking Big Brother is really here.' The crowd of curious students looked on in apathy – as they did for the rest of the night.

The opposition to punk rock didn't only apply to gigs. The Pistols were having problems with their record label EMI, who'd just released their debut single, 'Anarchy In The UK'. Tour support was withdrawn amidst protests from pressing plant workers. Pretty soon band and label would mutually separate. After days of waiting and being thrown out of hotels, the tour succeeded in playing Manchester's Electric Circus on 10 December. It went down as one of those later-legendary affairs, which sounds better than it probably was. The out-of-London masses had still to pack out punk gigs and roar their enthusiasm. However, two who did were the young Bernard Sumner and Peter Hook, who went on to form Joy Division and end up in New Order.

By all accounts – including *Sounds'* Pete Silverton – The Clash responded to the novelty of actually being able to play a gig and tore the place apart. They were angry and it all came out in one of their white-hot stun-blasts. Silverton wrote about the frenetically strumming Joe: 'I still reckon he's currently the quintessential English rhythm guitarist.' That said, Pete had to throw in a reference to Joe's 'public school past' – probably in revenge for Strummer trying to have him thrown off the bus on the way back to the hotel.

With gigs still being called off, the next show took place four days later at the Caerphilly Castle Cinema, a hastily booked replacement for the cancelled Cardiff Top Rank. It only held a hundred people and the tour was now deeply in debt.

The gig was notable for being picketed by local council officials and members of the Pentecostal Church, who warned of eternal damnation and sang Christmas carols outside. Further last minute shows were added in Manchester and Cleethorpes, with Plymouth's Woods Centre being only the third date of the original itinerary to actually take place.

The Anarchy Tour had been prevented from becoming the trailblazing nation-wide spectacle that it could have been. The furore, cancellations, disappointments and endless waiting had put pressure on everybody. EMI backing out financially halfway through had put a huge financial strain on the Pistols and the rest.

Joe later told Caroline Coon, 'When I got back to London on Christmas Eve I felt awful. I was really destroyed, because I'd got used to eating – it was Holiday Inn rubbish, but it was two meals a day and that. When I got off the coach we had no money and it was just awful. I felt twice as hungry as I'd ever felt before. I had nowhere to live and I remember walking away from the coach, deliberately not putting on my woolly jumper. I walked all the way up Tottenham Court Road and it was really cold but I wanted to get as cold and as miserable as I could.'

While he was away, Joe had been chucked out of his current pad, which was in an old ice-cream factory at Foscote Mews, Maida Vale. His possessions had been thrown into a skip and he was forced to move into Rehearsals with Paul and roadie Steve 'Roadent' Connolly.

In terms of publicity, The Clash probably came out of the tour best. But afterwards none of the participants were happy campers. There wasn't even a London show. 'That was soul-destroying', Mick told me later. 'We thought we were the greatest rock 'n' roll bands, conquering the world. Everyone was really excited, but the day before it started the Grundy thing went down and gigs started getting cancelled. The Pistols suffered quite terribly. It was really tragic, but we learnt so much from it. You knew the time had to come. There's a lot of oppression around today. We're making people aware of it and opposing it.'

'The tour turned into a cause, in a way,' added Paul. 'Us kids just wanted to play. We were stuck in hotel rooms for a couple of days waiting to play, then we'd be told the gig was cancelled and we'd wait for another three days in the hotel room.'

'It really put punk rock on the map', reasoned Joe on *Westway* '. . . Every truck driver and builder, and your grandmother and your uncle knew what punk rock was all about.'

At the end of 1976, the Roxy – a former gay bar in Covent Garden – became the punk equivalent of the Marquee. It had been taken over by Damned manager Andy Czezowski and launched in mid-December with the second ever gig by Generation X. This was the outfit launched after Tony James and singer Billy Idol had quit Chelsea. They were followed by the Heartbreakers, who provided the club with its first full house. The Roxy slowly caught on and was given a boost when Don Letts started playing reggae in the absence of any available punk records. In the wake of the Anarchy debacle the Roxy was one of the few places the punk groups could play or hang out at without hassle. Small, dark and poky, it was somewhere to go where you could see mates and get served – a big deal back then. The bands were often bog-standard Pistols-Clash impersonators, while the bar was usually packed with people like Sid, Johnny Thunders, Chelsea, Generation X and The Clash. Also, Johnny Rotten, who said, 'It's a wankhole, but fuck, Don's on!'

DJ-ing as it is today didn't really exist in 1977. Gaps between bands were usually filled by a roadie's AC/DC tape. Don used these breaks in a way that's now considered to be the norm. Back then it was startling and had a profound impact on The Clash, who got Don to spin at some of their gigs. 'I'm getting more asking me for reggae than punk,' Don told *Sniffin' Glue*'s Mark Perry. 'They come in and actually tell me to take it off. It's true. Joe and Mick from Clash, even Johnny Rotten . . . everybody! . . . I think the majority of the Roxy audience dig it. [A] Quarter of 'em really like it . . . The Clash guys, they all like it. I can talk to 'em and tell that they like the music.'

Don also managed the Acme Attractions boutique on Kings Road. He sold me a pair of fifties winkle-pickers in 1976. His enthusiasm and influence quickly became crucial to the scene, and later The Clash. After filming many classic early punk

Joe and Paul showcase the charity-shop DIY aesthetic at Ilford's Lacy Lady, November 1976.

moments and managing The Slits, he turned his hand to making videos, ending up in Mick's Big Audio Dynamite, and remaining a lifelong friend of the band members. He stoked the group's growing reggae fixation, particularly Joe's. Don consolidated his Clash connection by making his *Westway To The World* documentary.

'This was the first club for punk groups and their followers,' recalled Joe, when asked about the Roxy for *Westway . . .* 'It was a good place to hang out, and there was also a good punk-Rasta interface because the DJ at the time was Don Letts. He would play a lot of reggae records that we hadn't had the chance to come across. That gave us a lot of new information. That Rasta-punk crossover was really crucial to the whole scene.'

Subsequently, there was talk of staging the pulled London date from the Anarchy Tour at the Roxy on New Year's Day with Sex Pistols and The Clash. However, McLaren wouldn't go for it. Many said this was down to him wanting to hold on to the Pistols 'banned in London' reputation. Plus he wasn't into endorsing a new punk club that he didn't have a stake in.

So, on the first day of 1977, The Clash played instead.

I turned up about eight and encountered the band for the first time since High Wycombe. They were obviously still disappointed by the way the Anarchy Tour had panned out, but seemed determined to blow tonight's roof off to compensate. I walked into Joe and asked 'how ya doin'?' 'How do I look?' came the reply. His shirt simply had a big '1977' stencilled on it while his hair was still blonde. Joe's manner was speedy and surly. Mick was starting to look more like a rock star in his white strides and black silky shirt. His manner was speedy but friendly.

The gig was a full on Clash classic, as they roared through the set. And then did it all a second time three hours later. They'd also added a new song, 'Remote Control', which Mick had written over Christmas about the Anarchy Tour: 'Who needs remote control/From the Civic Hall?' Even though barely three months had elapsed since their glorious ICA gig, something had changed. After the manic savaging of punk rock by authority and media, and its parallel ascension as the latest 'youth rebellion' trend, the mood amongst the shock troops seemed to have darkened. Particularly amongst the Davis Road hardcore. It was like their exclusive club had been invaded by dullards and made public property. In a sense, that's what had happened, but Sid, Keith, Steve Walsh and the rest weren't the friendly nutters I'd encountered just a couple of months before. Heroin was starting to make its presence felt – having been introduced to the scene by the Heartbreakers on the Anarchy Tour.

It was also a rather strange paradox that a lot of people were slagging off the new groups who'd taken the advice of the originators and started their own bands, myself included. I guess this was a reaction to the flow of Roxy bands who hadn't taken the other bit of advice – do something new, original and true to yourself. There were so many Clash-Pistols copyists that the scene was starting to disappear up its own arse. As The Clash strove for perpetual innovation, new groups were springing up every week. But they were imitating, not originating.

This was getting Joe riled. The last time he went to the Roxy, he drunkenly protested by shouting and splattering the mirrored walls with tomato sauce. In early 1977, Joe's unpredictable, sometimes aggressive, demeanour was down to a regimen of speed and Special Brew ('Ten cans to feel normal'). Apart from affecting his moods, it started taking its toll on Joe's health.

In his biography, *Rotten: No Irish, No Blacks, No Dogs*, John Lydon describes an incident where Joe was beaten up in the toilets at the Speakeasy by a large, teddy boy. The place was traditionally a rock star's after-hours watering hole. If anything, it was the embodiment of what punk was supposed to be against. But, in the absence of anywhere more suitable, that's where we started going after the Roxy had closed. Joe, who suffered much bruising and a chipped front tooth, confirmed the incident in Tony Parsons' later *NME* interview.

Joe did everything to extremes. If he was going to embrace punk that meant whatever happened in his past life didn't exist. If he was on stage, he'd push his body beyond the limits. When the punk-teddy boy wars were raging, Joe, Mick and Sebastian would get decked out in full drape jacket regalia and frequent ted gigs and pubs. 'Slick our hair back and go to a teddy boy place in Southgate, or somewhere like that, for the whole night,' recalled Mick. 'Totally anonymous. No one knew were weren't one of them.' When Joe started drinking, he'd be the one collapsed outside the club in a puddle. That phase wouldn't last long. The Clash, who'd started the Anarchy Tour bottom of the bill, would soon be in a position to headline their own jaunt.

But first they needed to make a record.

CHAPTER SIX

STREET CORPS

*I believe there will ultimately be a clash between the oppressed and
those doing the oppressing.* – Malcolm X

With Polydor still showing plenty of interest and other labels sniffing around, January 1977 saw The Clash recording more demos. They used the National Film and Television School at Beaconsfield, outside London, an arrangement which came courtesy of student Julien Temple, who'd filmed some of the Anarchy Tour and would go on to do the same with a string of major Clash gigs. As well as the Pistols' *Rock 'n' Roll Swindle*, Temple would later direct Rolling Stones videos as well as the ultimate Sex Pistols documentary, *The Filth and the Fury* and the movie *Absolute Beginners*.

The drummer vacancy remained unfilled, following Rob Harper's departure after the Roxy gig in January. As a result, Terry Chimes stood in at several shows, as he would for the recording of the band's debut album. Joe's old mate Micky Foote, who'd started controlling the live sound, acted as producer as Bernie carried on his advisory role.

The new demos featured the same songs as the Guy Stevens sessions, plus 'I'm So Bored With The USA', but had much more of a raw, live feel. The successful translation of the band's untamed live impact to tape seemed to do the trick, and Polydor were ready to bite.

On 27 January, The Clash signed to CBS for £100,000. This came as a shock to everyone – especially the band. The common belief was that Bernie had agreed a £25,000 deal with Polydor but, on the day they were supposed to sign, he took the group to CBS's Soho Square offices.

Such machinations have to be viewed within the context of the Pistols' filthily lucrative label-hopping antics. Bernie wanted 'complete control' – as he would often tell sniggering Clash members – and acted in a fashion that aped McLaren's tactics. There had even been talk of Bernie and Malcolm joining forces to start a new label with their two charges, but Malcolm demurred. So Bernie pulled his own spectacular move by nabbing the deal with CBS – which truly dumped on Polydor A&R man Chris Parry, who went off and signed The Jam instead.

After months of struggling, Joe finally got a princely £25 a week wage allowance from Bernie. He also moved into a new squat with roadie Steve 'Roadent' Connelly, in Canonbury, North London.

On the face of it, £100,000 seemed like a lot of money, but the small print would later reveal that, if all options were exercised, it was actually a ten-album deal. A couple of years later they'd be comparing the deal to serving out a prison sentence. The group also had to pay for things like recording, a new PA to replace the knackered pink 101'ers set-up, and instruments for Mick and Paul. For his part, Joe wouldn't let go of his trusty Fender Telecaster with its 'Ignore Alien Orders' sticker. He never did.

These contractual nuances had yet to become apparent to the group and the public. There was a deluge of condemnation when the signing was announced. *Sniffin' Glue's* Mark Perry famously declared that punk died that day, and cries of 'sell out' echoed far and wide. The band didn't care. They wanted to reach a wider audience. Future DJ and TV personality Danny Baker later defended them in the same fanzine with a succinct, 'We wanna be heard, fuck being a cult.'

I sprang to The Clash's defence in *Zigzag* because I wanted The Clash to conquer the world. 'As soon as the group made their marks on the contract they knew they'd be accused of selling out. But the deal hasn't turned them into big-spending superstars. They got some new equipment, Joe got a place to live, Mick got a stereo and paid for his nan to go to America, but they're still the same group, except with a means and outlet for their music. CBS is one of the biggest record companies in the world, so it follows that more people will get to know and hear about The Clash album than if they'd signed to a small label or done a private pressing job.'

'To be honest, I'm a total idiot in business affairs, more so then, and I'm really dumb and naive now,' confessed Joe to *NME* in 1979. 'I'd freely admit I didn't know what the fuck was going on . . . I just thought, "Fucking great, we can put out a record."'

'I've been numbered wherever I go with that thing about selling out,' Mick told me a few weeks after signing. Despite some confusion and frustration at the outcry, he was excited to have the chance to record the music that was exploding live.

'I think it's important that we don't change,' he said. 'What is happening right now is that at last we've got the chance to make records. It all comes down to records . . . You've got to make records. You can do your own label and not many people will hear it. This way more people will hear our record. I don't care if they don't like it or don't buy it, as long as they hear it. We've got complete control. Everything is our own ideas.'

Joe later reflected on the stinging *Sniffin' Glue* putdown, 'I thought, "Well that's nice for you, but we were never your toy to begin with." I can see the point that we should've stayed home-made, started our own labels, the stuff people do nowadays, but it needed to break out and reach America and be global. Someone had to take that bull by the horns and shake it.' A point Joe re-iterated when heckled during the White Riot tour: 'If we hadn't signed to CBS, none of you lot would have heard of us – so stuff that down your gizzard!'

The day after signing the contract, The Clash went into the studio to record their first single. They chose to do 'White Riot' backed with '1977'. The sessions took place at CBS's own studio in Whitfield Street, off Tottenham Court Road. They had the weekend to do it and used Micky Foote as producer. This was the place where Iggy and the Stooges recorded *Raw Power* in 1973, which impressed Joe and Mick.

Simon Humphrey, in-house engineer for the single, was struck by Mick's avid eagerness to learn the ropes but detected a degree of antagonism from the band – which may have been caused by Simon's off-message hair. 'They wouldn't shake my hand because I was a hippy,' he recalled in *Uncut's* Clash special. 'Joe Strummer wasn't really interested . . . The first time I met him he was setting up to record and he put his Twin Reverb [amp] next to the drum kit. I said, "You can't it put it there," and he said, "Why not?" I said, "Because it's gonna affect the drums, it needs a bit of separation." He said, "I don't know what separation is and I don't like it.'"

Whereas Mick was like a kid in a candy shop as he strived to learn the workings of the studio, Joe worked by his own rules, like delivering the song from start to finish without doing the painstaking drop-ins usually favoured by singers and producers. 'He didn't see a vocal take as being something that you worked up to,' declared Simon. 'He just gave it 100 per cent from the word go. Which is why you, more or less, had to get it first take, 'cos that's the only one you were going to get.'

Mark Perry retracted his controversial statement in the March *Sniffin' Glue* after he heard the single for the first time: 'They're the most important group in the world at the moment. I believe in them completely. All I said about them is crap.'

Uncut's December 2003 issue, demonstrated that hindsight had further refined Mark's views: 'It sounds dramatic, but at the time The Clash meant so much to us. More than the Pistols, they were OUR band, y'know. So I wondered how you could reconcile something like "1977" with being on one of the biggest record companies in the world? I thought, "What's that all about?" But looking back more realistically, they were a very ambitious group, they just wanted to be rock 'n' roll stars like any band does. I was probably a bit too earnest to appreciate that.'

The Clash's next move was to record an album. Sessions took place over three consecutive four-day chunks, running Thursday to Sunday from 10 February. Whitfield Street's Studio Three was again the location, with Simon Humphrey engineering and Micky Foote in the producer's chair. Bernie Rhodes was sometimes there in his 'executive producer' role. Mick was assimilating production skills at an impressive rate and probably contributed more to the finished sound than anybody. 'Any guitar of note on the record is Jonesy,' confirmed Joe. Similarly, Mick's little overdub touches and backing vocals elevated the album above the level of simply reproducing their live set.

I went along to the sessions a couple of times, and recall the place being cramped and somewhat archaic. Not state-of-the-art at all. 'We were in the cheapest studio,' recalled Joe. 'I got the feeling they were going to spend the price of an egg sandwich on us.' 'We knew what we wanted to do, so we went in the studio and learnt as we went along,' added Mick. 'We just banged it out, like at the gigs,' said Joe.

The album kicks off with the white-hot intensity of 'Janie Jones', a song Mick wrote on the bus. Joe growls about a man who 'don't like his boring job' being 'in love with the Janie Jones world'. Janie was a notorious Sixties vice queen, who got banged up in 1973 and enjoyed a surge of interest as a result of the song. Later, she even got to record a single with The Clash, returning the favour for using her name on the first album.

''Remote Control' was Mick's new song about the Anarchy Tour, attacking the country's ruling bodies with a hint of Mott in his vocal. The breakneck assault of 'I'm So Bored With The USA' now featured re-written Strummer lyrics decrying American cultural and military imperialism. The rough and highly cranked version of 'White Riot' that had been demoed at Beaconsfield replaced the single version on the LP. Apart from not repeating themselves, it was simply a better representation of The Clash. The single version was a tad clipped and clean, although the touches like sirens, bells and feet stomping in the studio were fun. This was more like the live

Complete control – Clash manager Bernie Rhodes ignores the draw.

monster version.

'Hate and War' was another newer song – mid-tempo with the anti-hippy title that had been recently sprayed on the back of Joe's jumpsuit. 'It was a good punk rock blast to have a song called that,' said Joe in *Westway To The World*. 'After all those years of peace and love, it was a punk rock thump on the arm.'

'What's My Name' is one of the earliest Clash songs, and the only one to carry a Keith Levene composing credit. This is another standout Joe performance as he relays the lyrics about loss of identity and urban confusion with a sense of dark paranoia boosted by some eerie harmonies.

The anti-drugs 'Deny' not only saw Mick expanding the sound via some Shadows-like guitar picking and backing vocals, but also Joe getting into his stride with one of those never-to-be-repeated home-stretch rants that later became one of his trademarks. 'You just make things up on the spur of the moment', he said. 'Whatever's on your mind. It's just a one-off.'

Side one goes out with the song inspired by the view from Mick's balcony. That all time great intro as Joe hollers 'LAHNDAHN'S BURNING!' and the band tear in like a pack of hungry pit-bulls. From then on you wouldn't be able to mention the Westway without thinking of The Clash. It was such strong imagery – 'I can't think of a better way to spend the night/Than speeding around underneath the yellow lights.'

'Career Opportunities' was another live gem. The song rails against the way in which a person's life can be pre-planned to bored oblivion before they leave school. Nobody had spoken for the faceless thousands in this dead end boat before – one of the reasons that The Clash twanged such a hefty chord with their young followers.

Sure, it was like having your face rubbed in life's dirt, but songs like this one also stoked a feeling that you weren't alone and something could be done to bust out of it.

'Cheat' – another new song – followed, with Joe's tough opening declaration that, 'I get violent, when I'm fucked up/I get silent, when I'm drugged up.' He later said it was his least favourite track on the album.

Next it's Mick's hectic pre-Clash song about condoms, 'Protex Blue', which erupts through layers of Chuck Berry-on-speed guitars. This was the only London SS tune to make it onto the album, although '1-2 Crush On You' was recorded and would later make it as the B-side of 'Tommy Gun'.

'48 Hours' is a full tilt belter about cramming all your fun into the weekend after five days of boredom. One of the tracks that's dated purely because it sounds closest to what punk rock was *supposed* to sound like – a high-octane amphetimine rush of frustration and rage.

The Clash concludes amid the consummate final glory of 'Garageland'. The track showed a new subtlety creeping into the band's attack – a new sense of melody was strengthened by Mick's vocal harmonies, while the sound was widened by an asthmatic harmonica break. It's plaintive, moving and ultimately a roaring triumph. At the time, Mick told me it was his favourite track. 'It's where we're moving on next. The chorus is "we're a garage band and we come from garage land." That's just what we are . . . It'll always be rock 'n' roll, but we're hoping to improve the aura of the sound . . . It's also commenting on the current situation with all the groups being signed up . . . in a way, that song does pronounce that the next step is about to be taken.'

Charles Shaar Murray's damning review of their second gig inspired the song's defiant chorus, while the verses deal with the punk bands being signed to record companies. 'They think they're so clever, they think they're so right/But the truth is only known by guttersnipes,' snarls Joe. There's also a shot at The Jam, 'Someone just asked me if the group would wear suits' . . . every line's a knockout. As Joe told *Melody Maker*'s Caroline Coon, 'I was trying to say that this is where we come from and we know it and we're not going to get out of our depth. Even though we've signed with CBS, we aren't going to float off into the atmosphere like the Pink Floyd or anything.'

Once all the original tracks had been completed, the album had a running time of only 29 minutes. They needed something extra, so the band recorded a song they'd been playing to warm up in the studio – a six-minute cover of Junior Murvin's 'Police And Thieves'. The original had been produced by legendary dub nutcase Lee Perry, and addressed the violent situation in Jamaica. The song had become a bit of an anthem at the 1976 Notting Hill Carnival.

'Police And Thieves' was the big surprise on *The Clash*. Set free from punk's three-minute straitjacket, it saw the group stretching out and experimenting with the mixing desk. Joe delivered what was possibly his strongest vocal performance of the album.

With Terry Chimes supplying a solid rock beat, Mick injected a razor sharp guitar skank, which ricochets from speaker to speaker. There was a dramatic new bridge, thumping new bassline and subtle vocal harmonies. This was the first indication that within The Clash's ferocious rock 'n' roll assault, there lay a desire to branch out and move forward.

'It's a logical progression,' reckoned Mick. 'There's obviously a lot of links between us and what's happening with the Rastas. It just seemed right to do it. We had lots of our own material, but we wanted to do one song by someone else. What would we do? Not a sixties rehash. Let's do something which is '77, right? Let's try and turn people on.

'This is a rock 'n' roll track in 4/4, but it's experimental. We've incorporated dub reggae techniques. We'll probably get slagged to bits for it, but we don't care. They can't understand that what we're trying to do is redefine the scene and make it clear to people the way to move. You've got to take risks all the time. That's why we did it – as a risk.'

'My conception of it was, "Great, a reggae tune, let's do it like Hawkwind!"' Joe told *Melody Maker* in 1988. 'But Mick was more intelligent. I like it a lot because we're using punk language. We're not going, "Ninky dinky dinky poo," like the Police were to do a few years later. it was punk reggae, not white reggae. We're bringing some of our roots to it, not to mimic someone else's. I wish really we could've stayed that pure.'

In March, I managed to persuade *Zigzag* to commission a Clash feature. This would be centred around the 'Night of Action' the group were putting on at the Harlesden Coliseum in North West London, on Friday, 11 March. Normally, the large cinema showed a combination of Asian films and porn, but The Clash had secured it for a night supported by their favourite bands: Subway Sect, The Slits and the Buzzcocks from Manchester.

My review was written just two days later while still buzzing from the gig. It was the first feature about The Clash to appear in a monthly music magazine and also turned out to be an exclusive preview of the just-finished new album. This time, I did feel a sense of history being made.

First on were The Slits, making their debut and a big impression. They overcame some sound problems with pure energy, with fourteen-year-old singer Arianna stamping and screaming like a little girl throwing a tantrum at a party. I noted that the girls were propelled 'with astounding force by a drummer called Palmolive,' Joe's girlfriend, who'd met Ari at a Clash gig the previous year.

Next up was Subway Sect, who'd changed from the rambling, two-chord outfit I'd seen in November. They've been rehearsing a lot at The Clash's studio and had a stack of unusual new numbers. Then it was the reorganised Buzzcocks, with Pete Shelley replacing Howard Devoto as front man.

I wrote, 'It was The Clash's night, though, and they played a blinder – despite little obstacles like one of the hired hippy sound men accidentally pulling out a lead. It was great seeing them back onstage, in new zip-festooned outfits to boot. The crowd in front of the stage went potty, pogoing right up into the air, screaming the words, shaking themselves to death and falling into twitching heaps. They couldn't have been able to see what was going on, which is a show in itself.

'There were some great announcements from Joe. Someone yelled something about the CBS contract. "Yeah! I've been to the South of France to buy heroin," he announced. Another time "I'm Bruce Lee's son," he declared, before slamming the band into another devastating two-minute burnup. Joe had psyched himself up so much for the show that he'd been almost frothing at the mouth before he went on. Meanwhile, Paul's bass playing had improved in leaps and bounds. This turned out to be Terry Chimes' last gig with the band. To emphasise the point he had "Good-Bye" stencilled on his shirt.'

Harlesden saw The Clash unveil their new brand of stage clobber, variations upon which they would sport for the rest of their career. Machinist Alex Michon moved into the upstairs office at Rehearsals and knocked out shirts and strides festooned with zips and pockets. The new kit was paramilitary style, practical and distinctive.

Unfortunately, it was quickly contaminated that night as The Clash got their first proper taste of the fashion for spitting at bands. This unpleasant craze tended to be prevalent in those who wanted to grab a piece of the punky behaviour that they'd read about in the tabloids. Joe always despised this habit, especially when it resulted in him catching hepatitis from ingesting some flying phlegm. The Clash had caught the eye of Nick Kent, the rock journo whose writings Mick had devoured every week. Kent reviewed the gig for *NME*. 'A cool guy, this Strummer,' he decided. Being chain-whipped by Sid at the 100 Club the previous year had put Nick off punk rock for a while, but, being a man with rock 'n' roll in his blood, he warmed to The Clash and 'suddenly felt involved in this music'. Coming to punk as a non-believer, Kent's articulately expressed conversion to The Clash made for an entertaining and incisive piece of criticism.

Kent seemed most impressed by Joe, who probably came of age on stage that night. 'And Strummer dead centre, very, very authoritative. Strummer's stance sums up this band at its best, really: it's all to do with real "punk" credentials – a Billy the Kid sense of tough tempered with an innate sense of humanity which involves possessing a sense of morality totally absent in the childish nihilism flaunted by Johnny Rotten and clownish co-conspirators. *That* is what Eddie Cochran had, what Townshend had . . .' After praising 'Garageland' as 'truly subversive rock', Kent made Mick's day by concluding, 'The Clash took up exactly where Mott The Hoople left off.'

'White Riot' was released on 18 March and at last we had The Clash on vinyl, even if it didn't match the impact and intensity of the live show. The sleeve showed Joe, Mick and Paul spread-eagled against a wall – an image inspired by the cover of Joe Gibbs and the Professionals' *State Of Emergency* album.

The flip was '1977', one minute and forty seconds of raw incendiary rage, which actually seemed to represent The Clash better than the A-side. 'Have you ever heard a tune that comes in at just under one minute and forty seconds that has so much bollocks?', asked Don Letts. 'The cheek of these young whippersnappers to rail against the old, heralding in the new. Sheer bollocks, man, you gotta take your hat off.'

Mark Perry described it as 'a real rallying call ' – and it was. Total us against them. Even though I didn't necessarily go along with the Stones bit, I realised that this sounded a lot better than if Joe had put No Elton, Genesis or Cliff Richard instead. Also, that guitar riff is the evil bastard offspring of two Kinks' songs – 'All Day And All Of The Night' and 'Where Have All The Good Times Gone?'

Tom Robinson, the gay activist who'd later score some hits himself, reviewed the single for *NME*, "White Riot" isn't a poxy Single of the Week, it's the first meaningful event all year,' he raved. 'The Clash aren't just a band, and this is more than just a single . . . The Clash are the writing on the wall.'

The following year Robinson would put everything in perspective when writing about The Clash for *Melody Maker*. 'Punk didn't die the day The Clash signed to CBS, it was born the day "White Riot" reached the record shops.'

The single made Number 38 in the charts. It would've been higher if it hadn't been totally ignored by radio (aside from John Peel). A further barrier to mass exposure came from within, as the group initiated a policy of refusing to go on *Top of the Pops* because they disapproved of miming to pre-recorded backing tracks.

The state of radio in the UK became one of Joe's pet beefs. He hated the fact that London's Capital Radio used its prime position as the city's source of information and entertainment as a means of sanitising the airwaves with blandness. 'To keep you in your place all day,' as Joe wrote in the song of the same name – which The Clash started working on after the Harlesden gig. Towards the end of the month, Joe seized another opportunity to slag off the station when he was interviewed by Caroline Coon for *Melody Maker*. 'What they could have done and compared to what they have done is abhorrent. They could have made the whole capital buzz. Instead Capital Radio has turned its back on the whole youth of the city.' And he didn't stop there. The same night as the interview, Joe and Roadent sprayed the fronts of both the BBC and Capital Radio buildings with 'White Riot'.

Joe and Roadent were very tight at the time. Roadent later talked about living with Joe to Robin Crocker in *Zigzag*. 'You saw the gaff, didn't you? It was amazing. Our record collection there was really weird. I mean, we had Abba, Middle Of The Road, a lot of Cajun stuff, Tapper Zukie . . . it was, in retrospect, a fairly eclectic bunch of albums. Joe and I were completely idealistic. We planned to bomb Selfridges! It was gonna be at night because no-one would be there, but eventually we dismissed it as a futile gesture. We also thought about joining the National Front. We were hoping to infiltrate it and do some sabotage to fuck the whole thing up! Yeah, we used to talk and talk, but nothing actually materialised.' Roadent would soon complain that he wasn't getting paid by Bernie, and promptly left to become a film star in Germany.

On 21 March, Tony Parsons – *NME*'s new 'hip young gunslinger' who had been introduced to add a punky element to the paper alongside his future ex-wife Julie Burchill – interviewed Joe, Mick and Paul on the London Underground. The results were published in the 2 April issue under the headline 'Thinking Man's Yobs'. This feature probably did more to propagate the myth of The Clash than any other. The band again laid out their manifesto, with the fervently enthusiastic Parsons joining in too. I could see that Tony had caught the same bug that I'd picked up the previous October. Until Tony and Julie wrote their punk-damning book, *The Boy Looked at Johnny*, the following year with Julie, he was a staunch ally.

It was interesting to see how Joe had moved on from his feet-first immersion in the punk rock ethos the previous summer, which had been exaggerated and intensified by his escalating speed and Special Brew diet. Still just as committed, Joe was calmer and friendlier these days. In his landmark feature, Tony calls Joe, 'the mutant offspring of Bruce Lee' (a reference to Joe's comment on stage at Harlesden), going on to describe him as 'confidant, determined, arrogant and sometimes violent in the face of ignorant opposition . . . He's got a no-bullshit sense of tough that means he can talk about a thrashing he took a while back from a giant, psychotic teddy boy without the slightest pretension, self-pity or sense of martyrdom.' 'Parsons nose!' quipped the band when they picked up the paper.

The Joe Gibbs inspired sleeve to The Clash's debut single, 'White Riot'.

Reflecting on his beating in the Speakeasy's khazi, Joe observed, 'I was too pissed to deal with it and he got me in the toilets for a while. I had a knife with me and I shoulda stuck it in him, right? But when it came to it I remember vaguely thinking that it wasn't really worth it, 'cos although he was battering me about the floor, I was too drunk for it to hurt that much and if I stuck my knife in him I'd probably have to do a few years . . .'

Joe also talked about how he would cope with financial success. 'I ain't gonna fuck myself up like I seen all those other guys fuck themselves up. Keeping all their money for themselves and getting into their head and thinking they're the greatest. I've planned what I'm gonna do with my money if it happens. Secret plans . . .' The main reason those plans – which included starting a radio station – didn't happen was that within a few years, The Clash would be in debt to CBS to the tune of many thousands of pounds.

To go with the feature, *NME* ran an offer in conjunction with CBS where the first 10,000 to buy the upcoming Clash album would get a sticker that could be redeemed for a free E.P. For this, The Clash went back to Studio Three and recorded Joe's new song, 'Capital Radio', which was derived from the early 'Deadly Serious'. Staccato, hard hitting and slamming the station for being, 'in tune with nothing', it certainly made its point. At the time, Joe was reading *The Rise and Fall of the Third Reich*. The song's opening lyric goes, 'Listen to the tunes on the Dr Goebbels show.'

They also laid down an instrumental track called 'Listen', which The Clash had played at their first ever gig, and was added to the EP along with Tony Parsons' Circle Line interview. The record has since become a major Clash collectable.

Around the same time, Joe was again interviewed for *Melody Maker* by Caroline Coon. This time, far from trumpeting that he could change the world, he admitted that, 'Everyone goes "Punk! Hurrah!" But none of us is going to change anything. But . . . having said that, then I *still* want to try to change things . . . the only thing I'm interested in is my personal freedom. I just want the right to choose. Obviously, it ain't no use me having the right to choose unless everybody else has too. Everyone's got to have it, right?'

Following an examination of the violence inherent to The Clash's music,

Caroline asked Joe if he enjoyed violence; 'Well,' replied Joe, 'there's nothing better, if you're having an argument which won't resolve itself any other way, than smashing somebody's face in. I enjoy violence with honour. If someone treads on me for no reason and I get back at him and knock him over, then I enjoy that . . . But I don't enjoy punching people for no reason.'

Much has been made by the various stances taken by The Clash, and their apparent contradictions. Regardless of any amount of after-the-event theorising, it's safe to assume that whatever Joe's reasons were for making such uncharacteristic statements, he meant it at that moment. By the nineties he couldn't have been a more peace-loving bloke. But in 1977, times were hard. Joe's whole life had been hard. Apart from the blighted urban wasteland he was struggling to survive in, the movement he found himself at the very centre of had attracted the sort of violent opposition that made being gentle an impractical liability. Violent music sometimes incited violent reactions. The Clash would spend years battling ignorant crowds, hostile councils and opportunist cut-throats – as well as writers waiting for any opportunity to shoot the band down and undermine anything positive that they'd managed to achieve.

As ever, actions spoke louder than words, and on 8 April *The Clash* was released.

Nobody was more surprised than CBS when the album made Number Twelve in the chart. The label had obviously viewed The Clash as their token novelty punk group and shoved them into a tiny studio on weekend 'down-time' bookings. Now they had to realise that rising from right under their coke-encrusted noses was something a lot bigger than they'd anticipated. The sleeve featured a Kate Simon photo of Paul, Joe and Mick skulking in the yard outside Rehearsals. Terry Chimes was now officially out of the group and was waspishly credited on the back as 'Tory Crimes'. The back cover carried a photo of the police charging at the previous year's Notting Hill Carnival, which had been shot by roadie Sebastian's roommate Rocco Macauley. This image became the band's backdrop throughout the *White Riot* tour. The band had insisted that the album's title was starkly eponymous.

Reviews were mixed – either gushing with praise (Tony Parsons, Mark Perry, Myself), or predictably bad from staid fellows like *Melody Maker*'s Mike Oldfield (no relation to the *Tubular Bells* prog-bore). The latter droned on about 'the tuneless repetition of chords at a breakneck pace'. You could look at it that way – if you'd totally missed the point. Then again, in signing off Oldfield observed, 'Thank God, I'm "too old" to have to enjoy it.' So maybe he hadn't.

In *NME* Tony Parsons gave the album probably its most important review and he hit all the right targets when he described *The Clash* as 'One in the face for the prejudiced, the ignorant and the complacent. Jones and Strummer write with graphic perception about contemporary Great Britain urban reality as though it's suffocating them . . . Their songs don't lie. They crystallise growing up and getting out like no band have ever before. The Clash have made an album that consists of some of the most exciting rock 'n' roll in contemporary music.'

Mark Perry also went overboard in *Sniffin' Glue* except, instead of simply dissecting the songs, he opted to describe the drudgery of life for a vast number of kids like himself: council flat, boring job, same routine every day, just wishing away the week for the two days at the end of it. Then after reproducing the lyrics to 'London's Burning', he concludes – in capitals, 'The Clash album is like a mirror. It reflects all the shit. It shows us the truth. To me, it is the most important album ever released. It's as if I'm looking at my life in a film. A story of London. Playing in and out of the flats. A school that didn't even know what an O Level was. A job that sat me behind a desk and nicked my brain. All that shit is no longer in the dark. *The Clash* tells the truth!'

Credited as 'Tory Crimes' on the reverse, departing drummer Terry Chimes was not featured on the cover of The Clash's eponymous debut album.

Sounds' Pete Silverton was more succinct, 'If you don't like *The Clash*, you don't like rock 'n' roll. It really is as simple as that.'

The first time I actually plopped the record on my turntable, I was almost dizzy with euphoria. I'd already heard it with the band, but having the thing in your hand, to play over and over again and rave about to your mates, was something else. I'd already sung *The Clash's* praises in *Zigzag*, so I vented my joy in the *New York Rocker* instead, calling it 'the most stunning debut album ever', which was 'gonna change attitudes and perceptions of rock 'n' roll'.

The album seemed to hit plenty of other people like this. I encountered similar sentiments from hordes of kids who were just blown away. The record's status seems to have grown as time goes on, with lengthy features in magazines and regular mentions in various 'Greatest Album' charts. That isn't to say that now some of it doesn't sound slightly dated. That's not the point. It was the statement. *The Clash* was of its time, in the way that the Stones' *Let It Bleed*, or Primal Scream's *Screamadelica* were. There had been nothing else like it before. It spoke for angry, late seventies Great Britain, as a gale-force of released anger, energy and, underneath it all, perfect pop dynamics within the three-minute song barrier.

Respected US rock critic Robert Christgau gave it a maximum A grading in his *Rock Albums of the 70's* guide, calling it 'the greatest rock and roll album ever manufactured anywhere.'

The album capped my first six months with The Clash. Not a bad start. But nothing could have prepared me for the next five years.

CHAPTER SEVEN

A LITTLE JOLT OF ELECTRICAL SHOCKERS

I vote for the weirdo. I vote for the loonies. I vote for the people off the left wall.
I vote for the individuals. – Joe Strummer

Obviously, there had to be a tour to promote *The Clash*, but the group still hadn't found that elusive drummer. After Harlesden, Terry Chimes departed to form a band called Jem. This didn't last long, and after a short stint as Jerry Nolan's replacement in the Heartbreakers, Terry hooked up with Keith Levene in Cowboys International. He'd subsequently rejoin The Clash in 1983 after a spell with Generation X.

More *Melody Maker* classifieds and more than two hundred auditions followed. Finally the perfect man for the job blew in from Dover during the first week in April in the shape of Nicky Headon.

'Topper', as he became known, (he reminded Paul of Mickey the Monkey from the comic of the same name) was a gift from the gods for The Clash. He could bite on their musical fusions and bulldoze through them with staggering agility and power. His interest in the martial arts gave him the necessary stamina and muscle. Plus, he was a bit of a nutter, which helped.

Nicky was born in Bromley, Kent, on 30 May 1955, but grew up in Dover. His parents were both head teachers. At the age of fourteen he badly broke his leg playing football. 'I was in plaster for six months, one of those old fibreglass ones,' he recalled. 'I was really depressed and in bed for six months. That's why I got a drum kit.' In addition to the Beatles and blues bands, Nicky loved the powerhouse jazz giants like Billy Cobham, Elvin Jones and Buddy Rich. He also shared a mutual favourite with Joe in Captain Beefheart. 'I just wanted to be the best drummer in the world.'

The young drummer played jazz on the local pub, soul circuit with scene sloggers the GI's, stints with progressive rock outfits and had most recently been in a heavy rock band with American guitarist Pat Travers. He had auditioned successfully for the ill-fated London SS, which had come to nothing. Nicky didn't see Mick for over a year until the two bumped into each other at a Kinks gig at London's Rainbow. 'Mick asked me along to an audition but I didn't turn up. But then I saw them on the front of *NME* and thought, "I'll have some of that," because I'd just been sacked from the band I was in. I just went along and thrashed hell out of the drums. It's the best thing that could've happened.' He got the job. Now the classic Clash lineup was complete.

In *Westway To The World* Joe gives Topper credit for enabling The Clash to broaden their musical horizons, 'The rules of rock 'n' roll say you're only as good as your drummer. We became an interesting musical unit after he joined, because soul, funk and reggae didn't faze him. Finding someone who not only had the chops but the strength and stamina to do it was a breakthrough. If we hadn't found Topper, I don't think we'd have got anywhere.'

Recalling Topper's assimilation into the band, Mick explains, 'What we used to do was give haircuts to people, although I never got touched. If we invited up a drummer to an audition and his hair was a bit long, we not only auditioned him but we gave him a haircut as well. We did a lot of them, and that went right through the time of The Clash. There were all these haircuts going on, but they never touched mine! I don't think we needed to do that with Topper. We wanted Topper to join before he actually joined – like quite a long time before, but he didn't join until we started to become well-known.'

Topper's first gig with The Clash was a warm-up for the upcoming White Riot tour at the Palais des Glaces, Paris, on 27 April. This was attended by Charles Shaar Murray, who took back all that he'd said in his Screen on the Green review less than a year before – 'It was like they poured Toots, Chuck Berry and The Who into a huge cauldron and lit a fire under it until all the pieces melted into one . . . it was great.'

The White Riot tour achieved everything the Anarchy excursion six months earlier was supposed to. Now The Clash topped the bill, supported by the Buzzcocks, Subway Sect and The Slits. Plus, The Jam – who were considered to be a bit of a weird choice. They weren't mates with the band and had a retro-sixties image and sound. If anything, The Jam were a tad too palatable to fit comfortably with the rest of the White Riot bill. This was a bums-on-seats decision.

The Slits, who now had Don Letts and Leo Williams looking after them, were on the bill primarily because they were great – as disruptive but musically striking as the Sex Pistols had been, while exploring territory far-removed from the saccharine 'girl-band' stereotype. They were also close to The Clash in a personal sense – Joe had been involved with Palmolive and Mick was going out with the band's new guitarist Viv Albertine, who'd replaced Kate Korus shortly before the tour. The Slits and The Clash never talked about their respective partners in interviews, but then nobody asked. There was rarely anything about inter-punk relationships in the music press gossip columns at this time. Even if they were in the same room. I'd rarely seen Joe and Palmolive actually together as a 'couple'.

With an enlarged crew that consisted of Micky Foote, Roadent, Sebastian, Mick's old school mate Robin Crocker and Barry Auguste (who'd been hijacked from Subway Sect to look after Topper's drums and nicknamed 'The Baker' by Paul on account of his resemblance to the Pillsbury Doughboy), The Clash were ready to spread the message.

Starting on 1 May, the 27-date tour was to cover much of mainland Britain, beginning in Guildford and finishing four weeks later in Dunstable, with the expected highlight being a showcase gig at the Rainbow, in Finsbury Park on 9 May.

I caught several dates, with Dunstable's California Ballroom and St Albans City Hall standing out. These were two shows where, apart from noticing an increased size and wildness in the crowds, the improvement in all the bands on the bill was noticeable.

For the first time, The Clash utilised a backdrop – the Notting Hill riot scene from the back of the album. Topper was a revelation; his style was spot-on – thunderous, sensitive and razor-sharp. This spurred Joe, Mick and Paul on to greater effort and the energy levels of The Clash's performances hit a new high.

With the last bit of the jigsaw in place, The Clash were complete and unstoppable.

Joe had taken to hands-on communication with the audience. By St Albans he'd become pissed off by the amount of security planted in front of the stage – to the extent where he insisted that bouncers be removed from that area. Halfway through the set he suddenly dived offstage. It could have been nasty – if the crowd hadn't caught him

Ari Up and Palmolive of proto riot grrrls The Slits, who provided support on the White Riot tour.

and tossed him back up again. 'He proved his point though,' Mick later told *NME*'s Chris Salewicz. 'They caught him. They didn't trample on him . . . Of course, if they hadn't he could have broken his neck. Joe has a very forceful way of proving a point.'

Night after night, Joe would be on his knees, face to face with the punters, often offering the mic for them to sing along. When things got heavy, like at St Albans, he'd be in amongst them, either sorting out trouble or just revelling in the madness at his feet. It was never like this playing the pubs.

At the St Albans gig, the police raided the tour bus and turned up nearly 50 unreturned room keys and some pillows from the hotel in Newcastle. 'They were going to charge everyone in the band and crew individually with nicking a pillow and a key,' recalls Topper. 'But we had a conflab and decided that Joe would take responsibility for the pillows and me the keys.' Topper and Joe would have to attend court in Newcastle at a later date.

When the White Riot tour descended on the Rainbow, the levels of crowd mayhem had reached the point where the band had to issue assurances that any damage to the venue would be paid for. On the night, The Clash were on top form and their audience responded in a manner not unlike the frenzied, seat-slashing teddy boys of the fifties. Over 200 seats were ripped out and dumped in front of the stage to create pogoing space.

Never mind the 100 Club. To me the biggest punk breakthrough was making it

Wreckage at The Clash's Rainbow gig, May 1977.

as far as a venue I'd been frequenting since the turn of the decade, usually to see names like Bowie, Lou Reed and the Faces. I went to the gig with *Sniffin' Glue*'s Mark Perry and Danny Baker and we agreed that the sense of occasion was overwhelming. As did the band. Afterwards, we celebrated so hard I can't remember much of what happened. But Joe always cited that concert as his favourite Clash moment of all. 'That was the night that punk really broke out of the clubs,' he recalled. 'The Rainbow at the time was a big venue. It was like "supergroups go there!" We played there with The Jam, Subway Sect and The Slits and the audience came and filled it. Trashed the place as well, but it really felt like, through a combination of luck and effort, we were in the right place doing the right thing at the right time. And that kind of night happens once or twice in a lifetime.'

The group certainly looked like they were born for this kind of gig, as they commanded the biggest stage I'd seen them on so far. During the encores they spotted a kid being pushed around by bouncers. Mick hauled him up onstage and he sang along with 'London's Burning' and 'White Riot', before Joe gave him the t-shirt he was wearing. *Sounds*' Jon Savage wrote, 'They can communicate just as directly and devastatingly with 3,000 people, as opposed to 300. An amazing feat.' He reckoned, 'Strummer is emerging as one of the great front men', and that The Clash 'could just have that once-in-a-generation thing.'

Writing for *Trouser Press*, Pete Silverton said, 'Onstage, Strummer is obviously a natural star, forcing his body and Telecaster to ever greater heights of pain/pleasure, grabbing the mike and screaming like he really does care.' He concluded that The Clash, 'has got to be one of the most special things to have ever happened.'

NME editor Neil Spencer reviewed the gig and was not impressed by the nihilistic destruction and negative aspects of punk, although he praised their 'expertly honed professionalism'. He singled out Joe, observing, 'He takes the part of street psychotic further than anyone before him. Just as the lettering on his clothes and the backdrop spell out images of violence and alarm, so Strummer's vocabulary is plundered from the madhouse, the jail, and the detention camp. . . For pure adrenaline-rush excitement, The Clash are probably the best band in the country right now. And they depressed the hell out of me.'

Like many commentators of the time, Spencer, although recognising that The Clash were mirroring the times, didn't like the way that they set out to wipe the slate clean – dismissing the work of such artists as Bob Dylan and the hippy movement in the process. Punk had kicked its way in as loudly as possible and had yet to find a properly reasoned voice. When The Clash played an event like this they attracted a mad, rabid crowd and played mad, rabid music. The intricacies had yet to be addressed – and would be – although sometimes it seemed like their crowd were stuck in 1977 while the band moved on. This would prove to be an enduring frustration for a group committed to innovation. But at the Rainbow, The Clash were simply announcing to the world that they were here, and you better believe it.

The *Sun* opted for a predictably shrill 'Punk Wreck' headline. The impact of the damage on the band was certainly no joke – bills incurred by punks acting how they'd read they were supposed to in the papers, plus cancellations and rescheduling, ensured that the tour lost nearly £30,000.

After the Rainbow gig, The Jam left the tour claiming that they'd been denied a soundcheck. There was already ill feeling after The Jam had refused to contribute to any tour running costs outside of their own expenses.

Unlike the harmonious camaraderie of the hippy movement, the aggressive punk scene was notable for intense rivalry between the main groups. Even though the two bands hung out together, John Lydon would constantly take potshots at The Clash. The Damned had been ostracised since the early days for their Benny Hill take on punk, and The Jam were seen as suburban mods who'd leapt aboard the bandwagon. Frontman Paul Weller even gave me some stick when I turned up at an early Jam gig wearing a union jack badge with 'Clash' scrawled on it. From now on, if the two groups found themselves on the same bill at a festival there'd be an icy kind of tolerance between them.

During the tour, CBS – buoyed by *The Clash*'s healthy sales – took it upon themselves to cash in with a quickfire second single. They chose 'Remote Control'. Although it was a good enough tune, the group preferred 'Janie Jones'. The single came in a cobbled-together art department sleeve that simply re-worked the first album cover. The B-side was a live version of 'London's Burning' – supposedly recorded at Dunstable's California Ballroom but actually taken from a Don Letts video shoot. The release, which didn't chart, seriously undermined the credibility of the band's claims to have control over their creative output.

The Clash were incensed, with Mick going as far as asking Portobello Road record stall holder Kosmo Vinyl to hand over the one copy he had in stock. He also responded by writing a new number that was an unashamed jab at CBS. Called 'Complete Control', the song went against the usual Strummer-Jones working method. Joe left it lyrically untouched from Mick's original, instead injecting it with a dynamically dramatic delivery and inspired vocal adlibs. It was also the first studio track that Topper played on.

'Complete Control' is Clash perfection. Mick's guitar blasts in, followed by Topper's kick, then Joe's vocal. And they're off into this locomotive surge of howling defiance. After Joe's shout of 'You're my guitar hero!', Mick's Chuck Berry-on-speed solo drops to a haunting refrain, before the impassioned closing coda climaxes with Joe ranting – 'This is Joe Public speaking . . . This is punk rockers!' – over Mick's 'See you in control' chant. The group may have been railing against their record company but, in the process, presented them with one of the greatest records of all time.

Crackpot reggae legend Lee 'Scratch' Perry had heard The Clash's version of 'Police And Thieves' and loved it. He was promptly hired to produce 'Complete Control' at Sarm East Studios in London and sprinkle some magic dub dust. However, working with a man who was alleged to have burnt down his own studio due to 'vampires' was never likely to be easy. Joe told *Melody Maker*'s Simon Kinnersley that the liaison 'didn't really work out', although he later admitted that working with Scratch had been 'a dream come true'.

After Scratch had gone, Mick went in and remixed it with cranked up guitars. The band also recorded a version of Toots and The Maytals' 'Pressure Drop', which was shelved – for the time being.

Both Scratch and Bob Marley were impressed with the white youth rebellion that was going down. The Clash became the only white band to have their photo on the wall of Perry's Black Ark studio and Marley was inspired to write 'Punky Reggae Party', which was released on the B-side of 'Jammin''.

Throughout June and July, the Clash wrote some amazing new songs that demonstrated an expansion of their sonic palette. These included a new group anthem derived from old song 'I Know What You Do', called 'Clash City Rockers', 'City Of the Dead' and Mick's 'The Prisoner' – which was inspired by Patrick McGoohan's legendary sixties TV series of the same name. Mick also insisted they revive Joe's 101'ers tune 'Jail Guitar Doors'.

Joe was particularly excited about '(White Man) In Hammersmith Palais', a new reggae ballad written following a night out at the venue with Don Letts. On the bill were Jamaican legends like Dillinger, Jah Stitch and Leroy Smart, but they were presented in a glitzy fashion that was the antithesis of roots. Joe told *NME* that while at the gig, he saw black youths ripping off white girls' handbags and tried to intervene.

Joe's lyrics describe his night out at the Palais and the paradoxes it presented. Reggae heroes wearing flash clothes while the youth try to rob the crowd. This led him to ponder the fact that poverty-spawned punk had no shame in whisking up and parading their own trophies of achievement. Hence the pop at The Jam, the new groups in 'Burton suits' that, 'aren't concerned with what there is to be learned'.

From the middle of that year I was in the thick of it at *Zigzag*. I'd started writing for the monthly in 1975. When Pete Frame started it six years earlier, it was a lovingly crafted forum for underground music, rock 'n' roll outlaws and the unsung heroes of quality music. As the punk movement emerged, Pete gave me more space until I was writing regular features on the main movers. In mid-1977, the gracious Frame handed me the editor's chair and, while striving to retain the mag's integrity and in-depth coverage of a variety of music, *Zigzag* ended up becoming the largest widely available outlet for the new movement. I'd written about The Clash from the start and used my new position to cover every move the group made, to the point where the magazine almost became an unofficial Clash newsletter. Although there were the occasional jibes of sycophancy, we didn't care and neither did the punters, especial-ly when some of the reports were exclusives from the inside.

One night in July I was at the Vortex, the Soho club that had replaced the Roxy as the top London punk hangout. Most of the time the club was a soul boy haunt called 'Crackers', but on Monday nights it presented a selection of groups, ranging from good, to bad, to downright ugly. It attracted all the young punks, like The Clash, Pistols, Sid, Generation X, Banshees, Slits and even famous thrill-seekers such as Keith Moon. One night John Peel's producer John Walters, who wrote a monthly column in *Zigzag*, persuaded his reticent DJ friend to venture down there.

On this particular night, Mick introduced me to Robin Crocker, who I'd already encountered on the White Riot tour. Mick explained how they'd gone to school and got into music and trouble together, before Robin was sentenced to two years in prison for armed robbery. He was a good writer and, now he was out, wanted to know if I could use him on *Zigzag*. 'Sure,' I replied. Robin promptly sent in a world exclusive preview of 'Complete Control', courtesy of Clash Central. 'I first heard it at Wilmcote House,' recalls Robin. 'Mick had just written it. It blew me away and it still blows me away now.'

Robin's presence enhanced *Zigzag*'s position as a source of information from within the band. He told me, 'People involved with The Clash played a major part in breaking The Clash. They had total credibility from a fanzine base.'

Over twenty years later, Robin was with Joe in a crowded dressing room at Brixton Academy, where the Mescaleros were playing. 'Joe leaned over and put his arm round my shoulder and said, "You see this, everyone?", and went on to tell the room about *Zigzag* and how it had been behind The Clash from the start. Then we looked at each other and burst out laughing – there wasn't one person in the room that we recognised!'

In addition to being a shit-hot writer, Robin was the quintessential articulate hooligan, a great laugh, and has been credited as the glue that often held The Clash together by diffusing tension with a well-placed comment, wildebeest impression or precisely-targeted ham sandwich. Although originally Mick's mate, he got on with everybody and was intensely loyal – a quality which the band never failed to appreciate. It was worth putting up with the sticky situations he some-times ended up in.

Soon we were best mates and ended up in several scrapes together. He'd have bright ideas like, 'Let's go and see Joe!' – at 1 am. Robin was soon firmly ensconced in The Clash's circle as one of their few proper mates, and still is. One of the best things about writing this book is I've hitched up with the old goat again after being out of touch for many years. He's still skint all the time, still hanging out with Mick and remains unrelentingly hilarious company.

After the tour, Joe had a couple of brushes with the law to deal with. On 2 June, he was arrested for spraying 'The Clash' on a wall near Dingwalls, in Camden. He was fined £5 on 10 June – the same day he and Topper were due to appear in a Newcastle court for nicking hotel pillows. The pair were arrested again and taken to Newcastle, where they spent the weekend before being fined a further £60 and £40 respectively.

Topper recently said that the weekend in jail was his favourite Strummer memory. 'Joe was out on bail for nicking the hotel pillows but then he got done for the graffiti. Bernie said to me, "Hand yourself in," and face it with him. So we went to Camden Town police station and they nicked me and Joe, then sent us up to Newcastle. Joe was touched that I'd handed myself in to be with him. We were banged up for three days and we just chatted. We got really close. That stands out in the time I spent with him.'

A fortnight later, Joe took the opportunity to enhance his standing as a 'Man of the People' when The Clash, who had seen their proposed one-day punk festival at Birmingham's Digbeth Rag Market cancelled by the police, turned up anyway. The group drove up to speak to disappointed fans. While the others stayed in the car, Joe walked amongst the throng and chatted. Upset by the rest of the group's lack of interest in meeting their audience Joe confessed, 'I feel like a stranger in my own band.'

After Joe's walkabout had alarmed the lurking police, The Clash party moved on to the pub, but not before they'd managed to announce a last-minute spot at the local Barbarella's club. Borrowing dodgy equipment from the group already playing – a heavy metal outfit called Warhead – and beset by equipment failures, The Clash eventually played a 45-minute, largely instrumental, set.

The band saw out the summer by playing some European festivals. First the Mont de Marsan event in Paris on 5 August, with The Damned and The Jam, then the Bilzen Jazz Festival in Liege, Belgium on 11 August.

The first feature that Robin Crocker wrote for *Zigzag* reported on Bilzen, an event that considerably shook up the Clash touring party and showed how violently punk was being interpreted, and reacted to, on the continent. The Clash headed the bill, alongside The Damned and Elvis Costello. Writing under the *nom de plume* of 'Robin Banks', he reported that they were forced to face 'the wrath of several thousand stalwart hippies, jazz fans and assorted lunatics . . . refugees from the summer of 1967,' who were listening to 'a group of local jazz musicians who sounded like a cross between Acker Bilk and the Soft Machine.'

The group were outraged by a ten-foot barbed wire fence fifteen feet from the stage, which had been designed to protect the VIP area from the overcrowded outer arena – 'where they all look angry.' 'This ain't Bilzen, this is Belsen,' announced The Damned's Captain Sensible.

Robin's report read more like a dispatch from the front. 'Backstage the angry band make a decision about the fence. "It's definitely got to go," decided Joe.

The Damned get canned by most of the crowd. 'The general feeling is that these people aren't going to like anything they get tonight,' continues Robin. The Clash go on and, immediately, Joe's guitar plays up so he has to borrow a replacement. They start 'London's Burning' and the cans start flying, 'and it becomes perfectly obvious that a part of the crowd have no wish to see the band at all!' Paul gets a brick in the shoulder – 'I could hear the smack of it as it hit him . . . Next alternative object to hit the stage is a steel bolt, all of five inches long. It bounces twice with thuds that can be heard above the music. Then comes a rock. It hits the stage and splinters ricochet everywhere. One rock leads to another and suddenly it's getting completely out of control.

'Between numbers Strummer is trying real hard to get through, but it seems like hardly anyone out there can speak the lingo. "Break that bloody fence down! I want that fence down," he tells them time and time again. Gradually they seem to understand. The fence is slowly being dismantled and the security men are having a real job keeping the people back from where they belong – right in front of the stage.

'Suddenly Strummer leaps into the inner arena. He streaks straight to the fence and with his own bare hands he is pulling and tugging at the bastard as hard as he can. For a second nobody knows what to do. Then all hell breaks loose. Security men try to grab at Strummer. Other people leap from the stage and try and grab the security men. Somehow Joe is pushed back on to the stage, and he carries on as if nothing has happened. It really is an unbelievable scene . . .'

This goes on for the rest of the set. Afterwards, Joe lay motionless on the floor while, after throwing up, Mick came in carrying a massive rock that had just missed his face. 'That thought suddenly brings home the stark and horrifying realisation that tonight, with the Westway just a distant fancy, The Clash could quite easily have played their final set,' concluded Robin.

The issue of *Zigzag* in which Robin's despatches appeared also featured the band on the cover for the first time. In the same issue, I printed an impassioned piece by Tony Parsons, who was writing for us under the name Dean Porsche. But he used his real name to warn about a genuine threat which made the life of a young punk seem irrelevant. Never mind the local council bannings, ted-punk wars and police oppression. There was a vastly more sinister spectre hanging over the UK, as the National Front was showing signs of becoming a major political party. It seemed absurd that there'd been so much outcry over the Bill Grundy incident when networks were legally obliged to transmit party political broadcasts on behalf of thinly veiled Nazis.

In May, the NF had polled 119,000 votes in London local council elections. Whereas local councils were quick to ban The Clash from playing gigs, they readily granted permission for the National Front to march through the London borough of Lewisham on 23 August. The idea that a rock concert was viewed as unacceptable, while neo-Nazis were at liberty to parade at will, appeared to be a gross hypocrisy. Maybe it was down to the fact that the NF had polled 44% locally.

*Toxic Twins Kris Needs and Robin Banks –
Banksy's dispatches from the Bilzen front lines
appeared in the September 1977 issue of
Zigzag.*

Generally speaking, anyone capable of logical thought despised the NF. Organisations like Rock Against Racism and the Anti-Nazi League were increasingly active in striving to combat the kind of blind ignorance that leads to racism. But the whole period of The Clash's rise had this shadow looming over it until it dispelled like a bad fart as the public wised up. This was an occasion when the white man shouldn't have minded throwing a brick, but The Clash couldn't make the Lewisham march because they were in the studio. 5,000 protesters did – only to be brutally marshalled by nearly as many police.

The Clash's absence incurred Tony Parsons' wrath in his 1978 book, *The Boy Looked At Johnny*. After the effusive praise that Parsons had submitted to *NME* the previous year, he decided that The Clash weren't the future of rock 'n' roll after all. Joe was now a 'diminutive diplomat's son' whose 'hammy histrionic anger dabbled in casual destruction as a stage-prop'. Once he was in The Clash, 'All that remained was for Joe Strummer to be taught to walk by a genuine working class boy – Clash camp-follower Robin Banks.' In 1977, Tone – now a successful writer – wrote that The Clash had, 'made an album that consists of some of the most exciting rock 'n' roll in contemporary music.' Less than a year later it's the product of 'single-dimension art scholars . . . cranking out the same old chestnuts.' We were admittedly puzzled but blamed the speed. The man who apparently taught Joe to walk was less than amused to see Parsons wheeling out the tributes when Joe died.

The Clash would demonstrate their solidarity when they headlined the massive Anti-Nazi League gig in Hackney the following year. 'The National Front are against us . . . They know about us,' said Joe. He made sure he knew about them too – by reading *Mein Kampf* and *The Rise and Fall of the Third Reich.* 'And with a lot of attention,' he later told *Melody Maker*'s Simon Kinnersley. 'The whole movement started off with only a handful of people in one room. That's where the whole Hitler movement originated from, eight or nine people. And that's happening now in this country with the National Front. So when people wonder when and why I don't go around singing wimpy songs about the moon in June, it's because there's that sort of thing going on. It's pretty obvious to me which is more important.'

Equally important was the way in which The Clash's growing popularity ensured that the very youth that were targeted by right-wing propagandists at concerts, football matches and outside schools were receiving a positive message of racial unity from a credible source. The band articulated the anti-racist sentiments of an entire section of British youth that saw capitalist greed, rather than race, as the cause of the nation's ills.

But The Clash never pretended that they could change things at a government level. Lyrically, the band's prime concern was the politics of the individual. They would never stop trying to make people think and change their lives positively. And if something enraged them like the record company releasing a single without their consent, they would write about that too.

Complete with a pink sleeve featuring one of the amps that dated from the 101'ers, 'Complete Control' was released on 23 September but, without the radio and TV exposure afforded to 'safer' bands like The Jam, only made Number 28 in the UK chart. The flip was 'City Of The Dead', a passionate tirade against London punk and it's dead-end bandwagoning, which contained a sideswipe at 'New York Johnny' (Thunders) and the heroin epidemic. It showed The Clash starting to widen their sound with the addition of sax and organ.

Reviewing the single for *Melody Maker*, Ian Birch declared, 'Good though the Pistols singles are, this knife-edged masterwork makes mincemeat of them. Reggae and punk are forever talked of in the same breath . . . now the relationship has been consummated.'

In late September the band hit the continent for a fortnight of gigs that took in France, Germany, Holland, Switzerland, Austria and Scandinavia. Their Munich gig was filmed by a German crew. Eventually the footage would turn up as an extra on *The Essential Clash* DVD. The stage is stark and chaos free as the band tear through a selection where director Wolfgang Bund favours fixing the camera on one group member for long sections. Compared to Leighton Buzzard less than a year earlier, the progress and improvement is astounding.

Next came the Get Out Of Control tour, where Joe's personal powder keg was primed for blastoff every night. Scheduled to start on 20 October, in Belfast, the 24-date tour would finish with three nights at the Rainbow. Support on the tour was provided by French all-girl band The Lous and New York's Richard Hell & the Voidoids. Hell had been in the original Television before joining Johnny Thunders' Heartbreakers and was a central figure in defining the ripped and torn punk look.

Don Letts came along as tour DJ to warm up for the group.

The tour got off to the worst possible start. They got to Belfast – then at the height of the Troubles – and found the gig at Ulster Hall pulled two hours before it was due to begin when the hall's insurers withdrew their cover. The Clash had never played the city before. With the intense levels of sectarian bloodshed engulfing Belfast, The Clash's appearance was bound to be a volatile occasion. But now the gig was off, which sparked a different kind of outcry.

Angry punks gathered outside the much-bombed Europa Hotel, where The Clash were staying. The police, unsure of quite how to react, arrived in force at the same time that the band came out of the hotel to explain why the gig had been cancelled. *Melody Maker*'s Ian Birch observed, 'Back in the hotel the atmosphere was one of terminal depression intercut with pure anger. Three fans who were on the verge of forming their own band had collared Joe, whose external belligerence belies an incredibly sympathetic and understanding nature. He spent several hours clarifying the debacle and offering advice about getting a group together.'

That afternoon, the band had gone walkabout in the war zone and, egged along by the attendant music press, posed for photos in front of the army blockades and checkpoints. 'I felt like a dick,' confessed Mick. This photo-shoot sparked a backlash, as the band was accused of using someone else's suffering to enhance their credibility. The group knew it wasn't the best move they'd ever made, although they'd only gone to play the gig and then tried to talk to disappointed fans. But the incident epitomised the type of criticism that would follow any kind of political misjudgement.

There were no complaints the following December when The Clash finally got to play Belfast, turning in a frustration-releasing ripsnorter at Queens University Students Union. 'Police And Thieves' became 'Police And Priests' and the encore was 'Belfast's Burning'. The set ended in the usual chaos with a stage invasion and Joe passing the mic to a fan to finish 'White Riot'. The gig passed without trouble, which seemed to disappoint the local police, who'd turned up dressed for combat and seemed completely bemused by the whole scene.

After six days on the road, Roadent quit, ostensibly over money, but also because he didn't get on with Bernie and Mick. He later told Robin that he left because, 'Bernie was a real cunt. He didn't pay me proper, and I was forking out for the gear from that! Also, I felt that some members of the band needed a personal valet instead of a roadie.' And he wasn't referring to his squat-mate Joe either. In 2004, Robin told me that Roadent left because he simply, 'wanted to work with Lydon – because he gave him more beer.'

As a result, another essential member was added to the entourage – Johnny Green, who'd been helping out by voluntarily humping gear since the start of the tour. Or, as the redoubtable Greeny puts it, 'Roadent fucked off and I took his job.' Johnny undertook the unenviable task of road manager, Joe's spotlight operator and, after a while, the nearest thing they had to a personal manager. It was his job to make sure everything happened. That could range from sorting out a dodgy lead to putting up with physical abuse from irate European promoters. Or trying to get the group out of bed in the morning.

Johnny's real name was Broad, but it got changed to Green after he assumed a name he'd noticed on a hotel register in order to get a free room for the night. Also, his glasses would become so splattered with gob during Clash sets that they sometimes assumed a greenish tinge. Always larger than life, Johnny was an ever-willing participant in the band's on-the-road antics, enthusiastically contributing to their animal impersonations and fond of a good prank. Johnny was to spend three years with the band and later wrote about it brilliantly in his book, *A Riot of Our Own*. Johnny quickly became part of the Clash inner sanctum and his gnu impression never failed to impress.

'I loved it!' he booms. 'I'd always felt like an outsider and it was good to be with people who felt the same way. We had a perverse kind of unity. It was the "us and them" thing. I like chaos. I still do. I thrive on all that being in the eye of the hurricane.

'There was always an air of tension from the first day I came along. Mick was an awful timekeeper. There was that sort of tension. I was always amazed it didn't explode more.'

One perk of my new position at *Zigzag* was getting sent on the road by record companies to do stories on bands. In this particular case I was despatched to join The Clash on tour – all expenses paid. Heaven! My brief was to cover two dates in Derby and Cardiff to see what was going on outside of London as Punk spread across the country. My partner-in-crime was Danny Baker. He was a right laugh and got on with The Clash, so I thought he'd be fun to take along on his first press junket. Robin Banks was also along for the ride, as was – much to my delight – legendary American gonzo writer Lester Bangs, who was covering the tour for *NME*. It was the only time that I ever met my own literary hero.

Several factors still stand out from those dates. First, the utter gob-drenched, can-throwing carnage which now seemed to grip the crowds, who were especially hostile towards support bands. It was a far cry from the previous year, when The Clash would take the stage to a small sprinkling of the curious and converted, many of whom were stunned into polite applause.

Throughout the tour, Joe was in a bad way. He was notorious for the horrendous state of his teeth and it was inevitable that his dental minefield would one day detonate – which it did in the form of a painful abscess that resulted in glandular fever. Even though he was in severe pain, Joe insisted that no gigs were cancelled. His announced, 'I am not going to be known as "No Show" Strummer.'

The gobbing became more of a repulsive epidemic with each gig. Having been in that situation myself, it is a horrible feeling to stand under the green blizzard, especially when you're trying to sing. There's nothing like seeing the next incoming globule arc through the lights straight towards your face. Splat! Another direct hit. Without a doubt, it was the most negative, stupid and disgusting craze ever. No wonder Joe took to starting gigs with a plea to desist from spitting. Not that it did much good. He'd still end most sets drenched in phlegm and beer.

At the cavernous Derby Kings Hall, I was standing with Mick as The Lous played under a constant deluge. Eventually he was moved to go into the crowd himself and sort out one meathead glass-thrower. I felt like I was delivering a message from the combat zone when I wrote, 'The hurler is embarrassed and surprised that a member of the group he's paid to see tonight is acting bodyguard for the third-on-the-bill act. I've met few people who CARE as much as Mick Jones, apart from the rest of The Clash. Stranded fans are allowed to sleep on the group's hotel room floors. The group will talk to non-sheep fans with warmth and interest.

'Joe Strummer will take the stage for a punishing hour-long set a few hours after a doctor has told him he must rest for three weeks to get rid of the glandular fever which has kept him in pain for days. He apparently got that from a face-full of spit so it must be a bit of a pissoff that when the group takes the stage the first crowd response is an eyeful of gob.

'As they took the stage the Clash roared in with "London's Burning", followed by the orgasmic chord-rush of "Complete Control" . . . The set was shortened cos of bozos bunging – "The Prisoner" was left out but you should've heard the other new ones. "Clash City Rockers" will be the next single and should destroy the charts. "(White Man) In Hammersmith Palais" is . . . for a start unlike anything else The Clash have done before. Slower than usual, with a melody I love. At last a white group's assimilated reggae music into its own style without resorting to the "this is our obligatory reggae song" blatancy of most that try. It works with Paul's bass and Topper's drums pumping the rhythm with gaps while Mick's guitar soars out on a deep ring. This number throws the "we wanna pogo" brigade.

'The rest of the set is made up of album tracks, which the group can toss out with their eyes closed now and naturally seem less into than the newies. As usual the corkers are pulled out towards the end – "Janie Jones", "White Riot" – two-minute speed of light blurs. The Clash storming the outer limits of intensity is still one of the most exciting experiences in rock 'n' roll. It all comes to a head with "Garageland", perhaps my favourite Clash song ever. As usual Strummer has discarded his guitar by now.

'In the terrace chant finishing blast, Mick and Paul are on the drum rostrum either side of the machine-gun drumming Topper, guitars blazing. Joe's bent double at the front, tearing what's left of his throat apart.

'Then it's back to The Clash motel, where we sprawl around the foyer drinking and throwing salad sandwiches. Sometimes in our mouths, mostly at each other. The sombre desk clerk has a bald head. Paul lobs a bit of cake to see if he can land one dead on centre-pate. The unfortunate bloke carries on writing fiercely in his book as if nothing is happening – least of all bits of cake raining all around him!

'A full-scale sandwich battle breaks out. Joe holds up an *NME*-shield for protection. I get a cucumber in Paul's drink but then find several in my lap. Someone produces some Green Slime, which becomes the Toy of the Tour. It's wet, bendable, green and slimy. It's great fun and looks like mould when you put it on cheese. Paul flicks little pellets around for the next few hours and secretly drops

'The National Front are against us ... they know about us' – Paul and Mick picket NF Headquarters.

some in my beer. Later he proudly boasts: 'I got Bernie right in the mouth and he went "Errhh!"'

'By now Lester Bangs has been warmly accepted into The Clash camp. Although coming in for his share of the usual piss taking – Paul's decided to call him "Mo-Lester" and thinks he sounds like Kermit the Frog. But the man has a wit, wisdom and arsenal of tales that win the band over – he ends up staying on for nearly a week, leaving the *NME* screaming for his article. Paul, helped along by some strong weed, invented a new game on the bus that has stuck with The Clash until the present day. You could call it unlikely combinations, and soon we were all at it. This, supposedly the most politically-motivated group in the UK, sitting next to one of America's most prominent rock writers – "A budgie with human arms . . . hee hee! . . . A fish with a penis . . . ho ho! . . . Bernie with a giraffe's body and the legs of a vole . . . hoo hoo! . . . A cat in a leather miniskirt with the studs inside . . . That's the best one! Aha ha!" Two hours of this in the bar and we're more than ready for the gig.'

'Mercifully the crowd seemed a little more enlightened than the previous night

– The Lous go down well and escape with only a slight coating of phlegm. I really like them. Likewise, Richard Hell's lot go down much better with a more "studenty" audience. He looks pleased.

'Then The Clash. Tonight they play a blinder. Songs flash by in a maelstrom of energy and attitude – "Police And Thieves", "What's My Name", "City Of The Dead", "The Prisoner". Joe's mustering every bit of fevered energy he can while Mick leaps and struts and Paul simmers with suppressed aggression (No doubt thinking of a goat with the legs of a wildebeest).

'The mood is brighter in the dressing room afterwards, a bloke from a magazine with the original title of *Punk Rock* is talking to Joe and someone who calls himself "a social worker" keeps asking Paul what he'll do when the Clash break up. "A horse with the eyes of a gnat . . . hee hee!" was Paul's considered response.

'Another hotel bar, another sandwich fight. Paul goes mad and hurls a plateful at Bernie, places a well-aimed ham sandwich in my face and then covers my legs in milk.

'Now it's 3am. I'm sitting opposite Lester Bangs. For the last hour I've been trying to keep a straight face as Paul heaps everything from matches and paper cups to tomatoes on Lester's head, blows smoke behind his hair so it looks like he's on fire and finally builds a bonfire under his chair and sets it on fire Joan of Arc style – singeing the carpet and nearly catching Lester's now-legendary strides. Lester laughs through it all, continuing to send us into further fits with anecdotes about Lou Reed and everything else he chooses to hold forth about.'

The next morning Pennie Smith took the band outside the hotel to do the photo session with Lester that appeared in *NME* and later in her book, *The Clash: Before & After*. It was Pennie who coined the famous quote; 'Being on the road with The Clash is like a commando raid performed by the Bash Street Kids.'

The craziness sparked by those couple of days infected The Clash and spread throughout the crew until it got to the point where I'd get phone calls at two in the morning from Johnny Green, Banksy or even the band, just to tell me to imagine a parrot on stilts, or similar. Letting forth 'The Cry of the Wildebeest' was also popular. This entailed holding back the head and going 'Aarooo!!!' as loud and for as long as you could. You can hear it in the middle of 'Should I Stay Or Should I Go'.

During a soundcheck at the Manchester Apollo gig on 29 October, the impatient throng outside smashed its way through the plate glass doors and surged into the hall. Hundreds got in for nothing, causing at least £500 worth of damage. Several punters were badly cut, but the 2,000 in the hall were more concerned with going bananas during support bands Subway Sect and Siouxsie and the Banshees. Robin described the scenes when the band took the stage as being akin to Beatlemania. The gig was being filmed for the *So It Goes* TV programme – which caught Joe going mental, curled up in a ball of sweat on the stage. During 'What's My Name' he embarked on some improvisation, adding the lines, 'Here we are on TV/What does it mean to me?/What does it mean to you? . . . [glares at camera] Fuck all!'

By mid-tour, Lester, Tony Parsons, Danny Baker and several others were calling '(White Man) In Hammersmith Palais' the best thing The Clash had ever done. The band knew that they had to start thinking about a second album. They'd wanted Chris Thomas – who'd done *Never Mind The Bollocks* – to produce, but he was busy.

Dan Loggins was head of CBS A&R. The moustachioed brother of country-rock star Kenny Loggins always had a keen eye on the US market. Five years earlier, I'd encountered him trying to steer Mott the Hoople in that direction and now he'd turned his attention to his label's latest bunch of young punks. He gave Bernie a short list of potential producers and the only one that stood out was Sandy Pearlman, the mastermind behind overblown rockers Blue Oyster Cult. Mick was familiar with BOC, while the rest of the band hadn't heard his work. Joe only knew that he was your quintessential AOR rock producer and sided with Johnny Green and Robin Banks when they started predicting a nightmare battle if he worked on the second Clash album.

Flown over on Concorde by CBS, Pearlman got his first taste of live Clash mayhem at the Manchester gig. Knowing he was there, Joe vented his feelings: 'We'd like to dedicate this next song to Ted Nugent . . . Aerosmith . . . Journey . . . and, most of all, to Blue Oyster Cult!' – before launching into 'I'm So Bored With the USA'. But the gig was enough to convince Pearlman to take on The Clash.

Lester Bangs didn't disappoint with the epic three-part account he turned in for the *NME*. Along with Pennie Smith's photos, it can be regarded as the finest piece of Clash journalism on record. The features are peppered with the gonzoid observational style that elevated any subject he tackled. No formal interviews, just looking and listening and then conveying the whole scenario from gig to bar to unconsciousness.

Certainly, Lester was bowled over by the galvanising experience of catching the band at their live peak, but he saw them as something much greater than a shit-hot rock band. Lester couldn't believe the way the group took trouble to talk to the fans, never mind letting them sleep in their hotel rooms – 'That, for me, is the essence of The Clash's greatness, over and beyond their music,' he wrote. 'because here at last is a band which not only preaches something good but practices it as well . . . There is a mood around The Clash, call it "vibes" or whatever you want, that is positive in a way I've never sensed around almost any band, and I've been around most of them.'

This from the man who'd tussled with Lou Reed, hung with the Stones and transformed the conventional idea of rock writing into the bargain. I recall Lester sitting in the hotel bar with me and Baker expounding on The Clash while nibbling for titbits that might help his piece. In the same bar after the show he had the zeal of the newly converted in his eyes. Even so, he still didn't feel that The Clash had fulfilled their potential during the show. When he told Joe that he had been apprehensive about mentioning this, Joe had simply said, 'Why not?' When Lester talked of Joe being the group's leader, Joe vehemently declared, 'We ain't got no fuckin' leader.'

Lester offered a spot-on description of Joe on stage at the Bristol gig. 'Strummer

. . . is an angry live wire, whipping around the middle of the front stage, divesting himself of guitar to fall on one knee in no Elvis parody but pure outside-of-self frenzy, snarling through his shattered dental bombsite with face screwed up in all the rage you'd ever need to convince you of The Clash's authenticity . . . one of those performances for which all the serviceable critical terms like "electrifying" are so pathetically inadequate.'

Lester was not only impressed by Joe's resilience in getting through the shows, but also by the man himself. 'Strummer himself . . . conveys an immediate physical and personal impact of ground-level directness and honesty, a no-bullshit concern with cutting straight to the heart of the matter in a way that is not brusque or impatient, but concise and distinctly non-frivolous . . . He is almost certainly the group's soul, and I wish I could say I had gotten to know him better.'

Even Joe's closest friends say that now. 'I don't think anybody ever really got to know Joe,' said Robin recently. We were sad when Lester died in 1982 of a cough mixture overdose. I wish I'd got to know him better too.

Joe's illness alerted the frontman to the value of his health, so he gave up speed. 'I decided very quickly that the up wasn't worth the down,' he revealed.

In December, Joe found himself the victim of a vicious altercation with bouncers at the old Marquee Club in London's Wardour Street. He'd gone to see the Buzzcocks, accompanied by Robin Banks, who rang me the following day to tell me that they'd both been ripped off and beaten up. Robin asked if he could write about this incident, and the growing epidemic of bouncer thuggery, for *Zigzag*. Earlier that month Henry Bowles – one of Sebastian Conran's housemates – had been set upon by bouncers at a Subway Sect gig in Kings Cross after someone else had thrown a firework. The bouncers dragged him outside and put his head through a window. After three weeks in a coma, he died.

We'd already published an account of that incident. Now Robin wanted to report on the fact that Henry had died – The Clash would later dedicate *London Calling* to him – as well as this latest attack on Joe. According to Robin, he was standing at the Marquee bar with Joe, who bought a round of drinks but got no change from the barman, who then feigned ignorance. When Joe raised his voice, three large bouncers appeared and grabbed hold of him. 'They had hate and aggression stamped all over their faces and the collective expression could only be interpreted as, "Look, look, we've got Strummer, he's a star and we don't fucking well like that, we're going to give him the beating he deserves," wrote Robin. The bouncers then dragged Joe towards the toilet with the obvious intention of administering a secluded kicking. Robin steamed in – 'so a quick tug of war ensues, me pulling Joe back with one arm, and try trying to prise him free with the other, while Joe continued to put up the best fight he could. Within seconds another thug appears, and Joe and I are punched and kicked down the corridor to the back door, where we are literally flung outside, and the door's slammed in our faces.'

Robin described Joe as 'bruised and shaken' after the assault. It could have been a lot worse – he could have ended up like Henry if Robin hadn't jumped in. While the battered pair stood recovering in the alley outside, several other punters were thrown out too, accompanied by punches. Their crime was protesting at the way that Joe and Robin had been treated.

This incident summed up the violent anti-punk climate that was prevalent in the UK during 1977. Punk was everywhere, inescapable and horrendously alien to normal society. Inevitably, there was no shortage of meatheads ready to thrash some conformity into anyone who looked a bit different. John Lydon was razored by a teddy boy gang in Finsbury Park, Paul Cook needed fifteen stitches for a head wound after being hit with an iron bar, pitched battles raged between teds and punks and every day brought reports of new violence.

Robin also wrote that, despite punk's revolutionary ideology, 'nothing has really changed. The incident revolved around Joe Strummer, a figurehead of the "Punk" movement, and although it had its genesis in something quite trivial, the end result indicates that we have a long, long way to go before we can look around with a clear conscience and say, "Something has been achieved". . . I can tell you that Joe doesn't view life with that attitude, and it is highly ironic that he became the victim of an event which, coupled with others of a similar nature, throws real doubt not on what people like Joe Strummer are trying to get across, but on what has actually managed to get through so far.'

CHAPTER EIGHT

ROOTS ROCK REBEL

The thing is, we never came to destroy. – Joe Strummer

In a rare free moment during the hectic tour activity of 1977, Joe moved into a spare room at Sebastian Conran's large London house in Albany Street, near Regents Park. By the following summer, Sebastian would cease working for The Clash. It was mainly down to disagreements with Bernie and a lack of available funds, but his millionaire background being blown up in the papers as if it was some previously hidden revelation was a contributing factor.

The press furore ensured that Joe got further stick – just for finding a place to stay. 'I just get speechless with rage about the press,' Joe told *Melody Maker*'s Simon Kinnersley. 'I have to control myself from going round and sorting some of them out . . . People believe everything that's written, like that big, white mansion. Well, I've got one room, and all it's got to offer is a blocked sink. I don't even have a TV set or a stereo, and there's no carpet, just bare boards. All I have there is a cassette player. But I never get a chance to answer back. I phone some of these journalists that write these stories to say, "Come round and have a look," but they won't even speak.'

'It was a real pisshole, like a squat,' says Robin Banks, who was staying there when Joe moved in. I went round a few times to see Joe and can vouch that he wasn't living in any kind of palatial splendour. He indeed had one room – the old servants' quarters right at the top – which he'd customised with graffiti and posters. He admitted that, when he couldn't be bothered to make the downstairs trip to the toilet, he'd simply utilise the nearest available milk bottle and leave it outside the door.

One night, we went round after the pub and followed the customary practice of sabotaging Sebastian's younger (and now very successful) brother Jasper, who lived there too. He wasn't amused to be woken up by a designer torpedo lamp lobbed into his bed. Joe, Robin and me then spent most of the night talking in the kitchen, because there was more space there than in Joe's room. The 'white mansion' jibes stung him right in the Punk Cred nether-regions.

Joe didn't seem too happy at this time anyway, he'd split up with Palmolive and went on to have a brief fling with Jeanette Lee – Don Letts' former partner, who would later join PiL. He seemed pretty down about his personal circumstances but tried to concentrate on writing new lyrics.

Joe seemed to respond to unhappiness in an extreme manner: by cultivating an interest in the mechanics and imagery of international terrorism. He would regularly wear t-shirts bearing slogans like 'H-Block' and 'Brigade Rosse', after Italy's Red Brigade terrorists. This fascination would result in new songs like 'Tommy Gun' and 'Guns On The Roof'. It all seemed to be part of some compulsion to plunge feet-first into a vat of international taboos.

In November 1978, *Melody Maker*'s Allan Jones pulled Joe up over a comment he'd made in an interview with fellow journalist Chris Brazier. Joe had accorded terrorists credit for 'laying their lives on the line for the rest of the human race. They're doing it for everybody, trying to smash the system that has broken everybody.' Joe told Allen that he believed he'd been misunderstood when he'd dropped terrorism into the topic tank. Now he had to try and explain his reasons.

'Right now, there's loads of people out in their country mansions getting ready to go grouse shooting. And at the same time, there's millions of old-age pensioners who have to wrap themselves in bits of cardboard to keep warm because they've got no heating . . . And I don't think it's fair. And those people in West Germany and Italy, they decided that the only way they can fight it is to go out there and start shooting people they consider to be arseholes . . . At once I'm impressed with what they're doing, and at the same time I'm totally frightened by it.'

Joe's interviews seemed to act like an escape valve that came in handy when the band was off the road. He would get heated and pour it out. Joe always seemed to be the most intense member of The Clash when it came to causes and politics. Initially, Mick had always plainly stated that he wanted to see change, but most of that concerned the social politics of the nation's youth – the way they were treated by the establishment and police.

When we met in September 2004, Mick mentioned the issue of politics, 'Yeah, but nowadays, it's such a dirty word synonymous with corruption and stuff. It's like a bad thing to be, but we were never that side of politics. It was always more about how it affected us. Overtures were made by left wing people and parties. We didn't really want to know.'

Mick saw punk rock as an escape from dull jobs, and when it brought him success, effortlessly slipped into a lifestyle that, for a while, was veering towards how personal heroes like Keith Richards and Ronnie Wood had lived for years. He was a rock 'n' roll kid who got the chance to live the dream and had to get that out of his system. Joe had to find his feet, which in the early days meant diving in with both. As he later admitted to *Uncut*'s Gavin Martin, 'There wasn't any thinking, or any intellectual process to it. We just did it.'

The difficult second album is one of the music business's most time-honoured clichés. For The Clash, it became painfully appropriate as the making of what would eventually emerge as *Give 'Em Enough Rope*, which was started at the end of 1977, would occupy much of the following year. A complete contrast to the way in which the live set had been thrashed out in no time at all for *The Clash*. CBS's requirement for new product took the band by surprise. 'Our response was, "What do you mean a second album?"' said Joe. 'We weren't ready to make a second album. It took so much out of us to make the first one.'

The Clash wanted to progress musically while capturing and properly representing their live power. The singles released between the two albums showed that the group were expanding their sound at an impressive rate. 'Complete Control',

'Clash City Rockers' and 'White Man In Hammersmith Palais' are a remarkable trilogy, which show the band exploring new musical directions. A lot of it was to do
with Mick acquiring more studio experience and becoming able to realise the musical soundscapes rolling around his brain. This gave Joe a bigger field to roam in
when feverishly working on his all-important lyrics. Unshackled from the two-
minute punk onslaught, he could stretch out and caress the soul from these subtler
new masterworks – or 'mini operas', as Joe liked to call them.

Sandy Pearlman was duly brought in to work on the new record. It was alleged
that CBS, who still wouldn't release the first album in the States, were pressing for
a cleaned-up, more radio-friendly production, unlike the rawness of *The Clash*. As
Pearlman was a big cheese in the flares and fondue world of American Adult
Orientated Rock, he could make records that the big US radio stations wanted to
play. On the other hand, he'd just produced grossout merchants The Dictators, a
bunch of snotty American punks, and made their album *Go Girl Crazy* sound pow-
ered-up. It wasn't such an odd choice because he was good at making guitars sound
big and vocals ring clear. The Clash were a guitar band with lyrics that were cus-
tomarily tricky to decipher.

Although Pearlman wasn't The Clash's choice, they could have had the final say
by simply refusing to work with him. I remember Joe telling me on the phone,
'We've got this American guy producing.' When I spoke to Mick he sounded cau-
tious but, probably buoyed by his own progress in the studio, didn't think Pearlman
could water down the essence of The Clash.

The band knew that hiring Pearlman was a move guaranteed to draw yet more
catcalls from the self-appointed punk purists. Back in 1978, the idea of hiring a big
name American producer was tantamount to treason for fans whose idea of The
Clash started and stopped at 'White Riot'. There were so many people waiting to
shoot the band down if they put a foot outside of the Punk Rulebook. They'd been
accused of selling out by signing to CBS, Joe's public school background had been
thoroughly raked over, and now they were recording with Sandy Pearlman.

'There's this big myth about a list of ten producers, and we had to have one of
them,' said Joe in *New York Rocker* in 1979. 'All this could be true, but the only guy
I considered was Pearlman, because he was the only guy that we'd met. But the reason that we got anybody in at all was because we needed someone to be a third corner in an argument . . . It always boils down to, I'm always going, "Turn the vocals
up," and Mick's going "turn the guitars up," you know. And it's irresponsible, kind
of like we're kids.

'The idea with Pearlman was to have someone who was a bit older . . . We obviously got him first and foremost because of his technical expertise, because we wanted to try and get a sound.'

With the production issue decided, the pressure was on Joe and Mick to write
some new songs. The debut album had been a doddle because there was already a
live set to record. All they had to do was hammer it out and polish it up. Now they
had to start from scratch.

Joe and Mick had joked to Bernie that they should go to Jamaica to write songs. Apart from being suggested earlier by Lee Perry, this was a mutual fantasy derived from the group's long-running reggae fixation. The duo were surprised when their suggestion was taken up and they were duly sent off on a ten-day song-writing jaunt to Jamaica in December. This severely vexed Paul, the member of The Clash who'd been into reggae music the longest. His omission from the trip was entirely down to the fact that Joe and Mick wrote the songs, but it didn't stop him getting the hump. To placate Paul, girlfriend Caroline Coon took him on holiday to Moscow, which he enjoyed immensely. When he came back he gave us all Communist Party badges and recounted tales of the locals' fascination with his Levi's.

On arrival in Jamaica, Joe and Mick immersed themselves in Kingston culture by going out to cop some ganja near the docks. 'We came out of the Pegasus Hotel all togged up in our punk threads,' Joe told *NME*'s Sean O'Hagan. 'I tell you, we was like two punk tourists on a package tour. Completely naive. We knew Lee Perry, sort of, but we couldn't find him, so we were on our own . . . The only reason they didn't kill us was that they thought we were merchant seamen off the ships.'

This was in the days before super-strength weed began rattling the brains of UK inhalers. In Britain, the draw simply did its job. You could tell the difference when you came up against real deal Jamaican tackle. Around this time I interviewed Dennis Brown, Culture and other roots figures, who were all passing it about. I was floored. Joe and Mick plotted up in their hotel room with their stash and wrote songs, rather than venture back out into Kingston. Robin Banks says he's still got the postcard they sent. 'They just got stoned and had to stay in the hotel room!'

Although the trip to Jamaica had been disappointing, at least Joe and Mick managed to write some new material. The Clash duly spent most of January in Rehearsals working up the tunes that would become the next album. During that month the Sex Pistols split up, leaving The Clash as the most notable survivors from the Class of '76. They decided to road test their new material at three low-key gigs, which started at Birmingham Barbarella's on the 24th.

The second of the trio of gigs was at Dunstable's Queensway Hall. Like the others, it had been kept out of the press but sold out on a week's word-of-mouth and some local advertising. As a result, my review of that gig in February's *Zigzag* turned out to be an exclusive first mention of the new tunes they'd soon be working into the second album. It was also another battlefield report, as a night of chaos culminated in a full-scale stage invasion.

'Alright, so Dunstable isn't the greatest place in Earth but I still wasn't prepared for the scenes which took place later. In short, it was the wildest, most . . . frightening/exciting gig I've ever been to. Certainly the most senselessly violent. A bloody damnation of national paper punk behaviour pattern brain-feeding.'

I went on to describe how the two opening bands – The Lous and Birmingham's dire Model Mania – got pelted with beer cans amidst chants of 'We want The Clash'. At one point Joe came out during Model Mania's set to try and calm the audience and ended up jumping off the stage to shake hands all round. The Lous fared less well, and got canned off despite Topper coming out and laying into the culprits with a mic-stand.

'The situation continued to worsen. Police came in as ambulance crews treated fans with blood streaming down their faces. Fights continued to break out around the hall while cans flew over our heads in all directions. All the front monitors were trashed. Backstage The Clash steeled themselves to go on. Joe donned his 'Strum Guard' and contemplated gaffa-taping himself all over as a body suit. But somehow, rather than fear for their lives, the danger seemed to hot-wire the group. They knew it could be one of those special nights.

'And it was. They ran onto that stage and ram-raided headlong into "Complete Control". The place indeed went mad. Joe changed the next song to "Dunstable's Burning", before "Jail Guitar Doors", "Clash City Rockers", "Protex Blue" and the second ever airing of "Tommy Gun".

'By now cans are falling at regular intervals. The group don't pay much attention, or comment much on it, just hammer into the next song with even more force. Strummer is practically frothing at the mouth, face screwed up with passion. "Police And Thieves", "Capital Radio", and into "Last Gang In Town". The Clash's new stuff is incredible. What an album this is going to be.

'The fireworks really start in "Janie Jones". The crowd continue to be carried out, Topper crashes through his snare-skin, Joe drops his guitar, Mick is running all over the place, a wicked grin on his face, and Paul urgently rips at the strings of his bass . . . into "Garageland", the finishing salvo. Back on, Joe starts singing "Career Opportunities" softly, the crowd joins in, it builds, then the group crash in as one under Joe and the audience.

'It is a magic gig for The Clash . . . It's gotta be "White Riot" – they've been shouting for it all evening. Those pummelling opening chords and the dam breaks. All of a sudden about 100 fans are on stage, singing the words themselves while Mick and Paul climb on the drum rostrum, guitars raised above their heads, and thrash out an instrumental version while the crowd really does start a riot of its own on the stage at Dunstable Queensway Hall. Joe lurches around behind the kit, a look of wild delight on his face. It IS a magic rock 'n' roll moment, and for a moment the injuries and senselessness of the violence that's gone down is forgotten.

'Afterwards we're all shell-shocked and shaken. Blood fills a can-gouge on Mick Jones' face, the hall is like a battlefield, no arrests made but punk rock probably banned.'

This set the tone for that year, with the crowd mania a few notches up on the previous tour. In 1978 The Clash were leading a charge but also facing a monster. The power that Joe had over the crowd was frightening. In Dunstable he could have told them to go and burn down the town and they probably would have. Joe knew it. He never told them to riot, he hated the spitting and missile throwing, but also got cathartically fired up when the whole live beast went careering into spectacular, lunatic overload like all great rock 'n' roll is supposed to do.

The whole band was also aware that the mania they sparked could also trigger psychotic reactions in bouncers too. 'Rock and roll is played on enemy ground,' Joe told *Sounds'* Sylvie Simmons. 'We never promised you when you were a baby that it was going to be roses all the way. But we stopped more than you can imagine. You can go on about getting the shit kicked out of you and you can go on about that guy getting murdered by bouncers in London, you can go on as much as you like and I'll just sit here and listen and I'll be thinking of the times I've stopped the blood when I've had the chance to.'

Sandy Pearlman was back to hear the songs he'd be working on. Before the following night's show at Lanchester Poly, Pearlman tried to get into the dressing room, which was being guarded by Robin Banks, who promptly smacked him in the face. There was blood everywhere, which a panicking Bernie mopped up with a handkerchief while the group stepped over his supine form to get on stage.

It's been said that Robin hit Pearlman because he didn't know who he was. Not true. 'I knew exactly who he was and I'm glad I hit him!' he laughs today. 'I took the first opportunity I got because he was a fucking MOR producer brought in for the American market. In The Clash there was one faction who wanted him and one who didn't, which was me, Johnny Green, Paul . . . and Joe. I knew that this would be the most boring album ever to record. An ordeal of immense purgatory. I knew all that was going to happen, so I whacked him in the face . . . Anyway, he looked like a dork.'

For his part, Pearlman seemed to view the incident as part of his 'initiation' into Clash-world.

Work was due to start on the new album in February. However, the sessions were postponed when Joe contracted hepatitis. He was believed to have caught the disease by inadvertently swallowing some of the gob aimed at the group on stage. I thought he looked a bit yellow.

Joe's illness necessitated a short stay at St Stephens Hospital, Fulham Road. It was confirmed that he had hepatitis B, which meant nine months with no booze. Luckily there was a near-total recovery rate and while Joe recovered, Mick, Paul and Topper continued to run over new stuff at Rehearsals.

Shortly after he came out of hospital, Joe moved out of the 'white mansion' into a squat in Daventry Street, Marylebone, with Kate Korus of the Raincoats and former 101'er-mate Boogie, who was now roadying for the Sex Pistols. 'It was Tony Parsons and the music press that drove Joe back to squatting,' recalled Robin. 'But there was no difference anyway. It just wasn't fair.'

This would be the third time that Joe moved home in the space of a year. Finding a permanent place to live had been his biggest problem since moving to London six years earlier. 'My idea of ecstasy is to have a room, a typewriter, an electric guitar and a TV,' declared Joe. 'What else do you want?'

By March, Joe was back in action and The Clash went to work on demos and future B-sides at Marquee Studios, Soho. They finished work on '(White Man) In Hammersmith Palais', Mick's song 'The Prisoner' and a skanking new version of Toots and the Maytals' 'Pressure Drop', which hadn't worked with Lee Perry, but would later come out on the flip of 'English Civil War'. Joe was still debilitated from his illness, so Mick was pretty much calling the creative shots – hence a high-octane stab at his old '1-2 Crush On You'.

They also laid down a version of Booker T and the MGs' 'Time Is Tight', which had long been a soundcheck favourite and later popped up on the *Black Market Clash* compilation. The track was originally released during the glory years of Stax Records in 1969 and appeared on the soundtrack of a movie called *Uptight.* Tackling such a classic was another milestone for The Clash, as it showed that they had moved away from the nihilism of '1977' and weren't afraid to acknowledge great music from the past.

'Clash City Rockers' was the second release of the trilogy of singles that bridged the gap between *The Clash* and *Give 'Em Enough Rope.* Group policy dictated that these singles would not appear on the LPs.

'Clash City Rockers' – despite barely denting the Top Forty, the single represented another step forward for The Clash's developing sound.

The new single had been recorded before Joe and Mick went to Jamaica in December and was released on 4 March (reaching Number 35 in the UK chart). There was a row with Mickey Foote over the mixing – apparently he'd speeded up the master. It was enough to end his involvement with The Clash, although he remained with Bernie.

'Clash City Rockers' rode Mick's sharpest guitar sound yet; somewhat reminiscent of 'I Can't Explain' by The Who but packing far more punch. A wired comment on the London scene and the city itself, the song was notable for its more complicated arrangement, as well as its clipped and cleanly dynamic sound. Joe's vocal was outstanding – brilliantly surreal words mixed way up front and spat out with the intensity he'd been mustering live as the band performed the song on the Control tour.

The production also marked a major progression for The Clash. It sounded like they were mastering the studio, beginning to expand the sonic palette while Joe's words were surpassing the simple sloganeering of some of the earlier stuff with sharp lines like, 'You owe me a move say the Bells of St Groove' and 'No one but you and I say the Bells of Prince Far-I.' I loved the fact that Joe could namecheck someone like Prince Far-I, the underground reggae genius who sounded like a Jamaican Louis Armstrong impersonator from 50,000 fathoms.

Joe had a unique approach to interviews and stage announcements. He often came out with great one-liners and his songwriting improved as he made greater use of his linguistic talents. It was here that his original influences, from Kerouac to Dylan – writers who loved to tinker with language – started to make their presences felt. Not directly, but in the way that Joe was perfecting ways to make his aural barbs and observations more effective.

As ever, the sessions were undercut by a climate of conflict. 'I seem to remember that, when we did "Clash City Rockers", [Mick] and me had had a row,' recalled Paul. 'I was in one corner of the studio and Mick was in the other. He had to tell Joe what the chords were so he could come over and tell me. The guy who was recording it didn't know what was going on 'cos of this weird communication breakdown.'

The single would be backed with 'Jail Guitar Doors' – a rebel classic with origins dating back to Joe's 101'ers days.

As April Fool's Day dawned, I was awakened by the phone. 'That'll be Robin,' I thought – expecting him to helpfully inform me that Bernie had the legs of an ostrich. But this time it was, 'We've been nicked – me, Topper and Paul.' Of course, I immediately thought it was an early seasonal wind up, but it turned out to be true.

The previous day, Paul, Topper, Robin, and mates Steve and Gary Barnacle, had been on the roof of Rehearsals while waiting for Mick. They were trying out a new air rifle and shot a couple of pigeons. Little did they know that the pigeons were of the racing variety and belonged to a workman from the nearby warehouse complex, who reacted by pursuing Topper with a monkey wrench. To make matters worse, British Rail Transport Police had their office over the road and thought that the boys were shooting at trains. This was a time when terrorism was in the news, and the cops was already aware that those well-known revolutionaries The Clash were rehearsing across the way.

A squad of armed CID officers and a police helicopter swooped in to arrest them. Bail was set at £1,500 per person – which Mick stumped up as Bernie stayed away – and they were required to sign in every day at Kentish Town police station. Their plight was not helped when Robin (who had previous form) gave his name as 'Robin Banks' and started doing a loud moth impersonation against the light in the cell.

'It was nothing really,' says Topper. 'Just four kids shooting at pigeons and someone pressed the red alert button. That's all. It was totally insane. When they realised it was just four kids with air guns they went nuts on us.'

Bernie's lack of support during the affair stoked further rumblings in the camp, with Paul daubing Rehearsals with a mural called 'Bernie Is Odd'. Here you could see a naked and penile-deformed Bernie being shat on by a gang of pigeons. A few candles were added to create a kind of Bernie altar, before which band and crew would gather to genuflect and chant 'Praise him' in high voices.

By April, Pearlman had reappeared and backing tracks were laid down at Basing Street studios off Portobello Road. There had been an attempt to work at Camden's Utopia Studios but, on the first night, they were forced to leave after Sandy's engineer, Corky, introduced some top class American weed to the proceedings. Paul upturned an old plant pot and Topper brought in his motorbike to race up and down a newly created dirt track. I remember Joe looking on a bit despairingly while mayhem ruled. They wouldn't be asked back.

It soon became apparent that this album was not going to be dashed off over three weekends. Sandy Pearlman's method involved doing a song over and over until it was right. This didn't sit well with the group, especially Joe – the first take man – and Paul, who both felt that the life was being squeezed out of the tunes. Paul's response was further pranks and piss taking in similar vein to the constant stream of wind-ups he inflicted upon Bernie. Joe gritted his teeth and stuck the endless takes out. Meanwhile, Topper – who an impressed Sandy called 'the human drum machine' – got his parts recorded first time. Mick immersed himself in the music and the studio, watching every move the producer made, while religiously poring over the tapes to plot his future creative moves. He was learning fast enough to entertain ideas of producing subsequent albums.

The production process defined the roles in The Clash to an even greater extent, as Mick became the studio force, leaving Joe free to represent, write lyrics for and reincarnate The Clash as World War Three every night on stage. The group, especially Mick, subverted CBS's strategy of using a radio-friendly producer who'd crack America by using Pearlman as a means of gaining studio experience.

April also saw the start of a movie project featuring the band. The project was being undertaken by producer Jack Hazan and director David Mingay, who were known for making *A Bigger Splash* – a quasi-documentary about artist David Hockney. They would film the group right through the making of their second album and its accompanying tours. Rather than being a straightforward documentary, the film was to have a narrative based around the story of a fictional Clash roadie played by Ray Gange, an acquaintance of Joe's. Unfortunately, the film, which would end up being called *Rude Boy*, did not see the light of day until after *London Calling* had come out, by which time the band had moved on and it looked a little dated. But the following year would certainly provide plenty of excitement for Hazan and Mingay to capture.

The first gig to be filmed was on 30 April, when The Clash played the Carnival Against The Nazis rally in Victoria Park, Hackney. This was organised by the Anti Nazi League and Rock Against Racism. It was their first gig of the year and a large one. An estimated 50,000 people marched to the park from Trafalgar Square and were treated to sets by X-Ray Spex, The Clash, reggae outfit Steel Pulse and the Tom Robinson Band.

As we made our way from Trafalgar Square, through the East End to Victoria Park, me and the Aylesbury Clash squad were inwardly bursting to see the band. It sounds funny now, but around three months without a Clash gig seemed a long time then. As we got there, X-Ray Spex were parping enthusiastically away and we were quite surprised when The Clash came on at 2.30pm.

It quickly became apparent that they were victims of the kind of muddy sound that often afflicts support bands. Joe had on his 'H-Block' t-shirt and the band was in incendiary mood, blasting through old favourites and some of the new songs – which already sounded dynamite live. To Joe's annoyance, Jimmy Pursey of Sham 69 leapt up to grab a piece of 'White Riot' and they were off. Pursey's appearance had been pre-arranged as a kind of two-fingered gesture at the racist boneheads who tended to follow Sham 69 at the time. Regardless of this show of solidarity by The Clash, the self-styled 'Cockney Cowboy' made every attempt to steal the show, drowning out Joe's vocal despite the fact that he seemingly had little idea of the lyrics, or where they went. Mercifully, the plug was pulled before Pursey got into his stride.

The gig also marked Barry Myers' DJ debut with The Clash – a relationship that would last for three years, before being rekindled in 2002 when he spun on Joe's last tour of the UK. At the time Barry played at Dingwalls in Camden Town and had a regular gig at the Roundhouse. Being in close proximity to Rehearsals, The Clash were often at both.

Barry cites the July 1976 Dingwalls double-header featuring the Ramones and Flamin' Groovies as 'very much a night that changed my life.' But I was surprised when he added that it was partly because I gave him his first review in *Zigzag*. 'You're the first person who reviewed what I did. That formed the basis of it because it was the first time that somebody acknowledged my presence. That didn't happen to club DJs back then.'

Barry says that The Clash thought hard about 'creating a whole show'. Previously they'd enjoyed the services of Don Letts, or tapes that he'd made for the band. This was quite groundbreaking for the time, as pre-show entertainment usually consisted of little more than the roadies' Led Zeppelin tape. In the late eighties, the status of the DJ would become elevated through acid house, and bands like Primal Scream started employing them for tours as a matter of course. The Clash were there ten years earlier.

'I was a fan before,' says Barry. 'I ended up MC-ing at Victoria Park because, apart from being in favour of what Rock Against Racism is about, I just wanted to be like close up in front to see The Clash. So I approached Rock Against Racism, who said they'd already got Johnny Rotten. But then I got a telegram from them saying, "We need you." That was my first time with The Clash.'

The album sessions continued through May, although toward the end of the month Pearlman was bemused to discover that the band had taken off to play a one-off gig in Paris. Organised by the Trotskyite *Ligue Communiste Revolutionnaire,* the gig was organised to mark the tenth anniversary of the Paris riots. It was a bit of a farce, with awful sound, fighting in the crowd, teargas and bottles being thrown. Another mini-riot, in fact, with Joe not even participating in the 'White Riot' encore as he'd thrown down his guitar in disgust. Henceforth, the new album's working title became 'Rent-A-Riot'.

To keep the pot boiling, I carried an album progress report by Robin Banks in *Zigzag.* He'd made up with Pearlman but was still one of the main pranksters. He talked of the punishing sixteen-hour sessions (which sometimes involved over twenty takes of a single track) and hinted at the rockier musical direction. 'The end result is not only going to come as a major surprise to many of the band's detractors, but to some of their major fans as well,' wrote Robin. 'The band have always been one step ahead of their contemporaries, and the songs on this LP take them far beyond the confines of a movement that they themselves were so instrumental in founding.'

With the backing tracks complete, it was down to the arduous task of overdubbing vocals and adding the walls of guitar that Mick liked to build brick by brick. Mixing would be more than crucial on this one. Robin was at most of the sessions and would excitedly phone up at all hours from the studio. He was most impressed with the improvement in Joe's voice. 'From the vocal takes that I've been present at I can say that at last it seems Joe has made a full recovery from his recent bout of throat trouble. His voice now seems to have recaptured the raucous strength it had in his 101'ers days,' he wrote.

I went along a few times and Robin's story summed up a typical session. 'At night the studio takes on an eerie, dreamlike quality, and the tiredness and strain of getting everything as right as possible is evident in all the faces present. Johnny Green, aided and abetted by Paul and Topper, relieves the pressure by having a spontaneous competition to see who can rearrange the lounge furniture in the most unexpected style. Johnny, a tall, gangling stork-like figure, comes out just about on top. Such activities as furniture piling are all part of everyday life with The Clash . . . Meanwhile, Joe Strummer reclines on a sofa, keeping one eye on Scotland's dismal World Cup showing, while with the other expertly skinning up.'

Making *Give 'Em Enough Rope* was every bit the tortuously boring ordeal Robin had foreseen when he whacked Pearlman. When I went along it seemed there were a lot of people pissing about to pass the time while one or two pored over the mixing desk and tweaked endlessly. Or as Robin puts it, 'the sound of The Clash being neutered.'

Since the pigeon-shooting incident, the future of the group looked shaky, as Paul and Topper faced possible prison sentences. On the night before the final court appearance on 16 June I went to the Speakeasy with Mick, Robin and Tony James, who was then living with Mick. Afterwards, we went back to Mick and Tony's and – suitably refreshed – stayed up all night. As the night melted into morning Mick was getting more edgy, pacing about and finger licking the mirrors in the hope that there might be a left over coke-crumb. He seemed very agitated and definitely highly pissed off about the court case. Mick's mood was surly and unsmiling, which – it has to be said – was often the norm during early 1978.

There's a scene in *Rude Boy* when a cab pulls up to meet Topper and Paul outside the court that day. Some people get out and walk to the court: Tony James, Robin Banks, Mick Jones and yours truly. And I am seen paying for it! I've lost count of the number of people who've come up and said 'I saw you in *Rude Boy!*'

At first, the Camden Five were suspected of terrorism, but no such charges were brought. While the case dragged on through several postponements, the police had still failed to make necessary ballistic tests. In the end the Five elected not to go to Crown Court, so as to get it over and done with. They were each fined £30, ordered to pay the pigeon-fancier £700 compensation and £30 towards legal costs between them. Afterwards we rode a huge sigh of relief to the nearest pub.

By late June, with the new record still far from finished, The Clash took off on the Out On Parole tour. However, the band had recorded the basic tracks that would appear on the LP, as well as out-takes like 'One Emotion', 'Groovy Times', Joe's terrorist item 'RAF 1810' and 'Scrawl on the Bathroom Wall'.

The tour opened on 28 June at the well-respected Friars club in my hometown of Aylesbury. The venue had become famous for putting on early shows by Mott

The Aylesbury Friars 28 June gig kicked off the
Out On Parole tour and saw
The Clash hit top form.

The Hoople, Roxy Music, Lou Reed, Free, Black Sabbath, Genesis and David Bowie. After relocating to a nice thousand-capacity hall in 1975, Friars had become firmly established as a top gig. Less than an hour's drive out of London, it was popular with bigger bands about to embark on major tours.

Nothing beat having The Clash play on your doorstep, and festivities commenced in the afternoon when the band arrived for the soundcheck that included a blinding version of Johnny Burnette's rockabilly classic 'Train Kept A-Rollin' and Booker T's 'Time Is Tight'. The show was a proverbial stormer with The Clash achieving their best live sound to date. I remember falling over when 'Police And Thieves' – one of the few songs to survive from the first album – segued into the Ramones' 'Blitzkreig Bop'.

Fully recovered from hepatitis, Joe was now a man totally on top of his game. His adrenalised punk attack of early gigs had been replaced by rock 'n' roll showmanship, with moves that referenced everyone from Elvis and James Brown to the sheer presence of big screen figures like Clint Eastwood or Jack Nicholson. Mick had changed too; his onstage persona seemed to be heading towards that of the archetypal guitar hero. His hair was a cross between Keef and a heavy metal poodle cut, while his clothes and poses veered toward the archetypal 'Rock Star'.

By now, I was getting worried about Mick. He wasn't the same bloke I'd met less than two years before, even acting cocaine-aloof to his old mates. Within the band, this caused tension and even fights, as Mick seemed to be turning into exactly the kind of pampered rock star The Clash had set out to pull down. 'If you snort coke, you're in on your own,' Joe told *NME*'s Chris Salewicz in July. 'Yes, but so did I,' Topper confessed later. 'We were all nightmares in our own way. We had the music in common, but we all had different personalities.'

As if in retaliation, Joe seemed to resolutely go the other way and dig his heels further into the punk ethos. He always sported Alex Michon's custom made paramilitary gear, tended to stay away from the club ligging circuit and imbued his onstage persona with even more manic energy. He might have given up speed after contracting hepatitis, but footage from the tour shows him discarding his guitar, rolling on the ground, diving amongst the pogoing throng, while wringing every last drop of passion from his tortured throat. He seemed more at one with the crowd than any of his fellow group members.

New York's notorious audio terrorists Suicide, were signed up to support at Mick's suggestion. Since the early seventies, Alan Vega and Marty Rev had been pioneering a terrifying onslaught of primitive synthesised mayhem topped with psychotically confrontational vocals. It was a bold move for The Clash to throw them to the lions in the support slot. Even bolder for Suicide, who were heckled, gobbed on and pelted with bottles.

I remember them coming off at the Music Machine and Vega's purple suit being drenched. This willingness to stand firm and not compromise won much admiration from fellow human spittoon, Joe Strummer. 'Vega is one of the bravest men I've ever seen on stage,' he announced. 'No-one in England had ever seen anything like Suicide. The skinheads just weren't gonna stand for it. I seen a man jump up and smash him in the face. While he was singing I seen a bottle miss his head and he bent down to pick it up and threw it at his own head. He was brilliant. He'd face them off.'

When I saw Alan Vega in New York a few years later, he spoke of the tour as, 'an experience, but a lot of fun. We did take a lot of incoming on that trip but I have good memories of it all. That Strummer guy was wild.'

Also supporting was a Coventry outfit called the Automatics, who were on the bill at Joe's insistence. Bernie soon became their manager and, after they changed their name to the Specials, they became a massive force spearheading the ska-punk Two-Tone crossover. Their multi-racial approach, eclecticism and lyrics about the state of Britain drew parallels with The Clash. Unlike The Clash, Bernie kept them under wraps for a year as they honed their sound. 'Bernie Rhodes knows, don't argue,' advises the opening line of The Specials' debut single, 'Gangsters'.

Bernie had long fancied building his own management stable. Apart from the Specials, he took on The Lous, jazz-punkers the Black Arabs and a new outfit called Dexy's Midnight Runners. One night around this time, I was sitting on the last train home when Micky Foote got on with this rather serious fellow called Kevin Rowland. It was the first time I'd seen Micky since he left The Clash, although he was still working for Bernie. Both had no doubt that this new band was going to be huge. As indeed they were (for a while).

The Out On Parole tour was definitely one of the wilder Clash jaunts, and it was invigorating to see how the group was catching on in a way they probably never dreamed of. The four nights at London's Music Machine between 24 and 27 July rank among the best gigs I've ever seen by anybody. 'If you're a messenger of change it's a really nice feeling, and we were watching it grow,' recalls Johnny Green. The group was delighted when former adversary Charles Shaar Murray praised them in *NME*, saying '*This* is the heyday of The Clash.'

Johnny also summed up the excitement of the period. 'It was relentless and full of action and incident. It's hard to remember those times sometimes. How wild and how violent and how trouble-strewn. It wasn't smooth and nor did anybody try and make it smooth. In fact, we loved it like that.'

'Scratchy' Myers DJ-ed at two of the nights, and cemented his relationship with the band as a result. He recalls, 'Johnny Green came up while I was playing and said, "Joe Strummer wants you to know that he likes what you're playing and so do I." That was the start of it. It was great being in their company and also great to see a band that many times and not get bored. What a fucking brilliant drummer Topper was! No matter what was going on, or even nights when they weren't quite on top of it, Topper was amazing, in any situation. I had to drive the band a few times, which got a bit scary when Topper and Paul put their hands over my eyes!

'I just remember a lot of moments with Joe away from the stage. It was always tough, but Joe was very personal. That was his job. He always found time for the fans.'

The tour coincided with the height of the gobbing monsoon season, with every night a wet riot of stage invasions. When fights broke out in the crowd, or the bouncers got too heavy-handed, Joe would stop the music and intervene. 'Because we weren't playing along to backing tapes, we could stop,' he grinned. 'When you see somebody getting kicked by 30 other geezers you gotta stop. It was an unwritten law that we'd stop and sort the ruck out and then we'd kick it right in again.'

But at the Glasgow show – where Joe's t-shirt sported the legend 'Get Tae Fuck' – the bouncers had a field day laying into the punters and disregarded the group's pleas for them to ease off. Joe even leapt into the throng to try and diffuse the situation but retreated in the face of similar abuse.

Afterwards, Joe smashed a lemonade bottle in frustration and got grabbed by the police. Paul tried to intervene and got nicked too. Both were roughed up in custody but decided to plead guilty to avoid disrupting the tour. Joe was fined £25 for breach of the peace, while Paul was found guilty of being drunk and disorderly and fined £45. 'That's what we get for calling it the Out On Parole tour,' noted Joe.

Another feature of these gigs was that ex-Pistol Steve Jones was regularly turning up for the time-honoured rock tradition of jamming in the encores. But such manifestations went deeper than any rock star bonhomie. Steve admitted that he was in line as a possible replacement for the 'difficult' Mick. This had come from Bernie, via the suggestions of his old mate Malcolm McLaren, who said The Clash were letting the punk side down.

The three other Clash members had even practiced with Steve while waiting for the perennially late Mick to turn up for rehearsals. After a few more dates the situation came to a showdown between the band and Mick, who was reassured to the extent that he even let Steve and drummer Paul Cook play with them at the Music Machine gigs.

It was Mick who'd first hitched up with Bernie, and started The Clash. But, as The Clash got bigger, Mick started rebelling against Bernie's patriarchal approach to management. The rest of the band didn't enjoy Mick's behaviour, but they approved even less of Bernie's totalitarian tactic of simply throwing Mick out.

Ultimately, Bernie's machinations were to backfire – Mick lived for The Clash and, thinking he might lose them, decided to tackle his drug problem. This had a unifying effect on the group, who closed ranks to the exclusion of their manager. The last twelve months had seen a steady erosion in the relationship between the band and Bernie, and within a few months he would no longer be their manager.

On 24 June, The Clash released '(White Man) In Hammersmith Palais', another classic single that had originally been recorded a year earlier. Out of the whole formidable Clash canon, the song remains the ultimate embodiment of everything that was so great about the group, as well as being a daring creative move to make in the punk-ridden summer of 1978.

I first heard the song when it was just a backing track, and considered it a fine progression on 'Police And Thieves'. It was the first time The Clash had felt confident enough to ride a proper reggae beat. I was expecting Joe to crown it with reggaefied rage. Not so, he turned out his most sublime vocal performance yet, caressing what must rank among his best set of lyrics. The way Joe's vocal grows out of the ethereal beauty of the music, intertwining with Mick's gentle guitar fills, before blasting into the contrast of the glorious chorus, resulted in a wide screen sonic masterpiece. Later, when they played me the end result, I nearly burst into tears, it was so unutterably great. They had tried recording it again with Pearlman, but couldn't top that first version, which became the single.

'(White Man) In Hammersmith Palais' was backed with 'The Prisoner'. The single made Number 32 in the UK chart, and also came third behind 'Complete Control' and 'White Riot' when I ran a favourite Clash song poll in *Zigzag*. A quarter century later, the song was voted Number One in *Uncut*'s Clash poll.

'We weren't supposed to come out with something like that at the time,' recalled Joe. 'We were a big, fat riff group. We were like rock solid beats, and when we came out with "(White Man) In Hammersmith Palais", it was really unexpected. These are the best moments of any career.'

'I knew the moment we came up with the music it was gonna be a big number,' said Mick. 'Then taking it home after we'd finished it and listening to it the next day thinking, "Wow!" . . . I remember some years ago I was up in Liverpool at this party after The Farm did a gig. Suddenly all these guys started singing ['(White Man) In Hammersmith Palais']. They knew all the words. I was so moved. It was entrenched in them, y'know? That song really means something.'

Joe's lyrics commented on the state of punk. Even by mid-1977 there were few genuinely good bands about. The Clash might have been slagged for their full-tilt collision course with rebel imagery and the way they relished spreading their message around the world while easing into a rock 'n' roll lifestyle, but their music was spot-on. Most of the bands that had sprung up in their wake were crap opportunists. For every Stiff Little Fingers, who were inspired by The Clash to rise out of their troubled Belfast environment, there was a flimsy bunch of cavorters trying to stick their desperate, chart-obsessed arse in your face. Think of the Boomtown Rats or the Police, and never mind the legions of studs 'n' leather pogo merchants like 999.

My favourite part of '(White Man) In Hammersmith Palais' comes at the song's conclusion, where the band has morphed into a skanked-up guitar orchestra while Joe delivers his punch line – 'I'm the all-night drug prowling wolf, who looks so sick in the sun/I'm the white man in the Palais, only looking for fun, Put away your gun.'

'For this one you move your arse sideways instead of up and down,' explained Joe, introducing the song live.

'Maybe the greatest song ever written by white men,' reckons former Creation Records boss Alan McGee.

Meanwhile, the results of *Zigzag*'s first annual poll were published in the July issue. The Clash were voted 'Best Group' and 'Best Live Act', while 'Complete Control' got 'Best Single', with 'Clash City Rockers' at Number five. The album – although over a year old – came fifth in the 'Best LP Of The Last Twelve Months'

1978 press promo for the '(White Man) In Hammersmith Palais' single and the Out On Parole tour.

category, and Joe was voted fifth 'Best Singer' and managed number eight in the 'Best Person' category.

The Clash – although habitually hardened to music paper attacks – now had to get used to receiving plaudits. Charles Shaar Murray gave the Music Machine gig a glowing review and bigged Joe up when interviewed for *Zigzag* by Danny Baker. 'I think there definitely is a blue wave. Okay, so what has Muddy Waters to do with Joe Strummer? It's people with little money and less opportunity crammed into broom closets of areas and brushed under the carpet of society. It's those people expressing in music what they're going through. Remove the specifics and talk in those terms and there's no difference between Muddy and The Clash.'

In August, Sandy suggested that Joe and Mick get away from the distractions of London and spend three weeks in San Francisco's Automat to finish overdubs on the album that was now called 'All The Peacemakers' (after a line from 'Police And Thieves'). It was the pair's first visit to America and definitely planted a seed for the future. Mick had always been fascinated by the country and its romantic rock 'n' roll aura, which had spawned such icons as Iggy Pop and the New York Dolls. Joe was simply happy to be in the place where rock 'n' roll was born. Also, San Francisco was one of the first places in the US to embrace punk rock and Joe and Mick were treated like gods.

They took to America like ducks to water, with Joe coming back happy that Sandy 'isn't gonna turn us into Fleetwood Mac', which had been his worst fear all along. Joe managed to burst a blood vessel while singing 'Guns On The Roof' – hence the exclamation, 'There's blood in my mouth.'

Like Reherasals, the Automat also boasted a jukebox. However, this one worked regularly and was loaded with classics like Otis Redding's '[Sittin' On] The Dock Of The Bay' and 'Time Is Tight'.

Joe and Mick were particularly impressed with one particular selection – 'I Fought The Law' by The Bobby Fuller Four. One of the first things The Clash did when they all got back together was to work up their own version in rehearsal. The track seemed tailor-made for the band and many thought Joe and Mick had indeed written it. But the story of 'I Fought The Law' carries chilling undertones. It was written by Sonny Curtis of Buddy Holly's Crickets in 1958, but became a hit for

The Bobby Fuller Four seven years later. On the verge of becoming a star, the 23-year-old Fuller complained when he got ripped off by his mob-related manager and was found doused in petrol with broken fingers in the boot of his car. Although the inquest proved he'd suffocated by swallowing petrol, the verdict was suicide. Almost everyone who knew him thought that he was murdered.

After three weeks, totally knackered and missing the others, Joe and Mick took a week off. Joe headed off on a Jack Kerouac-style road trip; cross-country – via Memphis – in a '56 Chevy pickup truck with a couple of mates who included Graham Parker's keyboard player Bob Andrews, who Joe knew from his pub-rock days. He had always dreamed of doing this kind of journey. Johnny Green talked about it in the October 1999 issue of *Mojo*: 'Joe had done the drive across to New Orleans, straight roads for miles, car radio. He was gushing about it all, in this really unsophisticated way. It was lovely.' Meanwhile, Mick went to LA with Sandy to see Blue Oyster Cult.

The pair met up again in New York City, where final overdubs and mixing took place at the Record Plant. They'd spend five days mixing each track – saxophone was added to 'Drug Stabbing Time' by Stan Bronstein of Elephant's Memory, who'd also recorded with John Lennon. Some additional piano came courtesy of Blue Oyster Cult's Allen Lanier.

Mick also found time to play in the backing band at a 'welcome' gig for Sid Vicious, who'd just made his doomed move to New York with girlfriend Nancy Spungen. With the rest of the band consisting of various Heartbreakers and New York Dolls members, Joe and Mick were taken aback by the level of smack consumption going down. Unfortunately, Sid seemed to be well on the road to junkie central.

During the recording, *Melody Maker's* Stanley Mieses reported on the chilly atmosphere that had developed in the Record Plant between The Clash and Pearlman: 'it was obvious that everyone's patience had long since worn threadbare.' Describing Joe as being 'derisive' to the producer, he quoted him as saying, 'Sure, there's a big gap between Sandy and ourselves. But that's the way it should be, otherwise it comes out sounding like a load of fish. You want someone there who doesn't hear what you hear all the time. I will admit, though, that our notion of a tune stretches a bit further than his.'

In late September, Paul and Topper were flown to New York to hear the final mixes of *Give 'Em Enough Rope*. While in New York, the whole group got the bug and started kitting themselves out like a street gang with the kind of classic clothing that could be picked up cheaply at street markets. Johnny Thunders recommended a great shop called Hudson's for the heavy-duty motorcycle boots that would become one of Joe's trademarks. Joe was starting to grow his hair into a quiff – an easy enough transformation, as it happened. Mick also cut his, for the first time in nearly two years. The rejuvenated Mick told me that spending that time away from London with Joe took him away from the capital's temptations and had rekindled his motivation.

Finally the album was ready for release. As the old expression goes, 'Give 'em enough rope and they'll hang themselves.' They already knew that this one was going to put the airgun among the pigeons.

CHAPTER NINE

HANG 'EM HIGH

I was starting to turn into Keef. Then I realised, I'm in the fucking Clash! – Mick Jones

The Clash officially sacked Bernie Rhodes on 21 October 1978. With Mick back on the ball again, the band had no reason to replace him with Steve Jones and resented the way Bernie had tried to instigate this. CBS in the US were not happy with Bernie and told the press they were 'anxious for a management change.'

Aside from disliking Bernie's machinations, the band was less than delighted with his management of their finances. They were more than broke – the collective debt to CBS was around £250,000. Although their wages were minuscule and the first album only cost four grand to make, they'd had to buy a new PA and instruments. To make matters worse, the group's insistence that ticket prices be kept to a minimum, along with the usual bills for damages to halls and hotels, ensured that Clash tours always lost money.

Bernie also tended to keep the band short of cash; when I'd visit Rehearsals Johnny Green would often be wondering how they were going to practice because they had no money to replace the guitar strings which Joe would break as a matter of course. There was no float and, if we went over to the pub, I'd end up paying.

While the group were making *Give 'Em Enough Rope*, Johnny found his responsibilities increasing as Bernie became increasingly disenchanted with the lengthy recording process. 'As that relationship faded, the less they had to do with him and the more I did,' he recalls. 'I was an acting as an intermediary. He was very critical of the rock 'n' roll lifestyle. He didn't like what what he perceived to be precious behaviour.'

Making the second album had cost in the region of £150,000. Much of this was down to Pearlman's production fee and the costs of flying Joe and Mick to Jamaica and San Francisco, and the whole band to New York for the final mix.

Before his dismissal, Bernie had wanted The Clash to whack out a quick, cheap LP, but the band wanted to improve the quality of their sound – without turning into Foreigner. Rhodes was also set against recording in America, as he felt it was following an already well-trodden rock route.

'The reason we had to part company is that Bernie – although he's like some kinda genius, a great ideas man – he can't, you know, do sums,' Joe told Allan Jones. 'That and the fact that he hadn't really been friends with the group for the last couple of years.'

The relationship between The Clash and Rhodes reached breaking point over a gig at Harlesden Roxy, which had originally been set up by Bernie for 9 September. Joe and Mick were in the US working on the album and they would've been forced to return early in order to play the show. They saw the timing of the gig as an attempt by their manager to re-assert his authority, especially as Bernie didn't approve of them recording in the States. Joe and Mick stayed put. Bernie retaliated by announcing that the gig was to be postponed because the group were 'on strike' about not getting any radio play. Less than amused by their manager's antics, the duo refused to budge and didn't honour the rescheduled date on 23 September.

At the same time, all four members of The Clash convened in New York to hear the completed album. They discussed Bernie and agreed that he had to go. Bernie flew out on 26 September for what *NME* described as 'a showdown', which resulted in his dismissal three weeks later.

The Roxy show was rebooked again. This time a date was set for 14 October but was cancelled at the last minute because the venue had changed its seating arrangements, thus lowering the capacity beneath that of the number of tickets sold. The band went down to the Roxy and personally told the disappointed punters what had happened. The gigs finally took place over two nights on 25 and 26 October, by which time Bernie was gone.

Bernie immediately instigated legal proceedings against the band to recover money that he claimed they owed him. He asked the High Court to freeze the band's earnings. The group counter-claimed, saying that Bernie's accounting amounted to a breach of managerial duties. Their affairs were taken over by a squad of lawyers and accountants, with Paul's girlfriend Caroline Coon taking over as manager on a trial basis. They wanted someone they knew, and Caroline had been with the band from the start. Also, she had some grounding in legal affairs from her work with the Release organisation, which assisted drug offenders in the sixties. Caroline's invaluable help during the pigeon-shooting proceedings – when Bernie was markedly absent – counted greatly in her favour.

Rhodes felt that his boys were straying away from his original ideals, whereas the band was simply growing up. I always thought that Bernie came over as a kind of wannabe Malcolm McLaren, especially when he was phoning to fire me up before my first Clash gig. Keith Richards described McLaren as 'a half-assed Andrew Oldham' – the Stones' visionary first manager, who brilliantly steered them to notoriety via the press. But, once the Stones were established as one of the biggest bands in the world, they struck out on their own, for better or worse. Bernie was reminiscent of Oldham in the way he loved to create scams, make money and control people.

But then The Clash became a monster and Bernie found it increasingly difficult to maintain control as rock 'n' roll, rather than situationist polemics, became the motivating force behind the band. Rhodes had designs on attaining the kind of notoriety that his erstwhile partner Malcolm McLaren was enjoying. However, Joe's rock romanticism and Mick's rock star ambitions were far too strong for Bernie to reign in.

Over time, the group gradually lost respect for their manager – as demonstrated by Paul's 'Bernie Is Odd' mural, and his penchant for building salad arrangements on his manager's shoulders while on tour. An inveterate piss-taker, Paul couldn't manage to take band politics seriously and often viewed Bernie as a figure of fun. Mick, who'd known Rhodes the longest, simply favoured full-on confrontation. Joe was the only member still in favour of Bernie. But at this time, The Clash were Mick's band. He'd taken the helm while Joe was sick and had steered their musical direction into areas far removed from the original Rhodes ethos of disaffected shouting. Despite this, Bernie stuck doggedly to the ideas that he had initially used to politicise and inspire the band. Indeed, were it not for Bernie Rhodes there might not have been a Clash – certainly, this was an opinion that Joe held for the rest of his life.

Despite the fact that he would've taken the manager's twenty per cent of gross earnings, Bernie also ended up with a £25,000 payoff. If the group wanted to get money, they had to go through Bernie's accountant, Peter Quinnell – or 'Quister the Twister', as the band liked to call him. Caroline found a new agent in the genial Ian Flukes of Derek Block's agency. Now The Clash would have tour managers and a professional road crew, in addition to Johnny and the Baker, who'd both elected to leave Bernie in favour of The Clash. This meant they'd have to move out of Rehearsals.

In October, The Clash warmed up with dates in Paris and Amsterdam before hitting London. The rescheduled Harlesden concerts became the first UK gigs to promote the new album. I went to both nights and sensed a different spirit in the band from the previous July. It seemed to be a combination of relief that the album was done, Bernie was gone and certain internal problems appeared to have been sorted out. They played a blinder both nights; with the new stuff sounding great pared down and pumped up in the live setting.

Give 'Em Enough Rope was unveiled to the media with a piss-up at a porno cinema in Dean Street, Soho. I'm ashamed to admit that Robin, Topper and me scuttled around to Cheapo Cheapo Records afterwards and flogged a box of albums to finance a group pub outing. 'That was so funny!' laughs Mick. 'The record was in Cheapo Cheapo on the Thursday and it wasn't released until the Monday!'

The event was organised by the group's new PR – Tony Brainsby, who I'd previously encountered with Mott. You got a nifty press package containing the album, a poster, photo, plus Joe's group history. The poster was 'The Clash Atlas Of . . . Give 'Em Enough Rope', a map of the world accompanied by photos of the world's trouble spots, including Cambodia, Northern Ireland, Nicaragua, Brazil, the Basque region of Spain, South Africa and Afghanistan. The US was represented by the neutron bomb, while Britain was depicted with a riot and the National Front's John Tyndall. This was going to be given away with the album until somebody noticed that Pennie Smith's large Clash photo overleaf was printed backwards and the plan was dropped.

The album's sleeve – designed by New Yorker Gene Grief – was derived from a Chinese government postcard called 'The End Of The Trail'. It shows a cowboy corpse being picked by vultures as the Red Army rides in.

Give 'Em Enough Rope was released on 10 November and sprinted to number

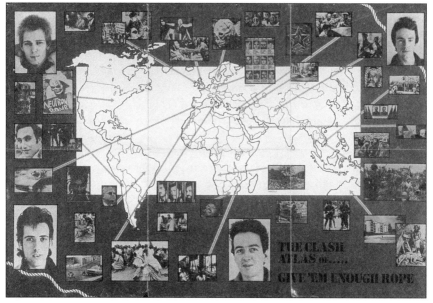

'The Clash Atlas Of ... Give 'Em Enough Rope' mapped out the volatile political landscape of the late 1970s.

two in the charts. It kicked off with the opening volley of 'Safe European Home', one of the songs that Joe and Mick wrote in Jamaica. The immediate effect is like a grenade going off, with Topper barrelling snare shots over the mighty surge of the guitar wave. The underlying feel is akin to supercharged reggae, propelled by Topper and then constructed by Mick in the fashion he was fast perfecting, where layers of guitars worked in perfect counterpart to build an awesome wall of sound. You could hear Joe's words like never before, which were joined throughout by another emerging Mick trait – intricately subtle counter vocals. Sandy Pearlman's production demonstrates the skill at handling guitar-based dynamics he'd developed from working with Blue Oyster Cult. Pearlman's expertise couples with Mick's sonic vision to produce a classic guitar sound far removed from AOR stodge.

Next up is 'English Civil War' – based on the American Civil War battle hymn 'When Johnny Comes Marching Home', with new words from Joe that railed against the rise of oppressive authoritarianism. Next is Joe's 'Tommy Gun', a blistering attack with armour-piercing snares and a storming melody, which played a significant part in the track becoming The Clash's first Top Twenty UK hit. Again, it's Mick's guitars that elevate the song, adding counter-riffs and underlying melodic touches. This was one of the songs that Joe would later play live at his solo gigs, often accompanied by the crowd on air drums.

'Julie's Been Working For The Drug Squad' was the album's first indication that The Clash were heading for different musical pastures. Joe had been getting into the delta sound of New Orleans – skin-tight Southern funk outfits like the Meters, and 'second line' Cajun rhythms, which originally emanated from swamp dive juke joints. Here, sweaty polyrhythms would mesh as a soundtrack for the wildest of all night partying. These influences were overlooked at the time because, in the midst of the bombast of the rest of the album, it was dismissed as a lightweight jazzy filler. But, with a different polish, this track wouldn't have seemed out of place on *Sandinista!* or any of Joe's later explorations into world music.

Give 'Em Enough Rope *saw The Clash in creative transition and received a mixed reception from fans and the press.*

Lyrically, the track recounted 'Operation Julie', a 1977 Drugs Squad 'sting' that involved the infiltration of a major LSD smuggling ring. This resulted in more than 1.5kg of acid being seized, with sentences totalling 130 years being dished out to those involved. The bust also caused the price of trips to more than double in the UK. 'Last Gang In Town' laid the band open to the now-familiar accusations of self-mythologising. However, as Joe told *Melody Maker*'s Chris Brazier, '"Last Gang" wasn't anything to do with us at all. I never for one minute imagined that we were the last gang in town, but the fact it was one of our song titles became a handy headline for newspaper editors . . . Every day I was hearing about new gangs . . . I just wanted to take the piss, you know? So we invented this mythical gang.'

'Guns On The Roof' was inspired by the pigeon-shooting incident in title alone. Joe is looking way beyond the roof of Rehearsals as he rails about global arms dealing and terrorist activity. 'A system built by the sweat of the money/Creates assassins to kill off the few.' The riff is wholeheartedly hoisted from The Who's 'I Can't Explain'.

Then comes 'Drug-Stabbing Time', another song that was inspired by Joe and Mick's Jamaican adventure. It's full throttle Clash, a raging blitzkrieg of guitar overdrive and breakneck groove assault. Little touches like the cowbell and roaring sax solo bring the track home.

'Stay Free' is often cited as one of the album's classic tracks. Mick is essentially singing about Robin Banks and some other schoolmates, talking about school days and how his mate ended up in jail. It's poignant and heart crunching with a brilliant sense of melody. As with 'Guns On The Roof', Mick strip-mines his influences in an inspired manner, this time lifting the acoustic guitar straight from the Stones' 'Sweet Black Angel'.

Robin was living at Sebastian's when 'Mick came around with his acoustic guitar in a case and said, "I've written a song about you." He sat me down and played "Stay Free". What did I think? "Fuckin' hell!" It was amazing. Very nice of him!' Howard Fraser, a mate of Robin and Mick's, described it as 'The greatest heterosexual love song ever written.'

'Cheapskates' is another light-and-shade rocker that sees Joe berating the band's detractors while examining the group and himself. Talking to *New York Rocker* the following year, Joe agreed that 'Cheapskates' and 'Safe European Home' were reflections on the group's rise. 'Oh sure. Those are kind of fumbling attempts to come to grips with it, or come to terms with what's happened to us. "Cheapskates" is . . . sort of a descendant of "Garageland" . . . You know, you start getting really paranoid. You start off, and you're just chancing it . . . Then you hit, you hit good and big, and you start saying "well, this is well and good.' Then they start, all those people . . . "You ain't like you used to be, you're stuck up . . . I can't talk to you, you're a star." . . . Then in the papers, you read, "The Clash are finished, a dying myth" . . . All these shitheads, but it still gets to you . . . And so you get all paranoid, and you start writing these songs like "Cheapskates", which is kind of a paranoid song.'

Finally, 'All The Young Punks (New Boots And Contracts)' rounds the album off on an anthemic note. Again, there is a melancholy undertow as Joe bemoans the current state of punk rock: 'Everybody wants to bum a ride/On the rock 'n' roller-coaster.' Like 'Garageland', Joe is commenting on how the original punk scene hadn't quite panned out like he'd hoped.

At the time he meant all this with a passion, but by the end of the following year Joe was confessing to *Melody Maker*'s Chris Bohn that songs like 'Guns On The Roof', 'All The Young Punks' and 'Last Gang' were a conscious move to deflate taking all this supposed Clash myth business too seriously.

The idea that the band were promoting their own myth was seized upon by detractors who felt that The Clash placed themselves on some cinematically heroic pedestal as gun-toting punk outlaws – untouchable men with a mission attaining godlike status through their use of self referential lyrical imagery.

There was no 'myth' from where I was standing. Just a cathartic overhaul of the senses and sensibilities every night on stage, and countless beautiful moments on record. The Clash *stood out* with their hearts proudly on their sleeves. In the process of growth, they laid themselves wide open to detractors. Such criticism was unfair, as nothing that the band did or said was fake. Ill-advised, maybe, but never fake.

CBS released *Give 'Em Enough Rope* to a hail of derision from punk fundamentalists and many reviewers. The most frequent criticism was that Sandy Pearlman had buffed up the sound to stadium proportions. However, much of the album's heretical complexity came from Mick, who overdubbed layer upon layer of guitars and then merged them into one bone-crushing whole. Although the production was far more polished than on *The Clash*, tracks like 'Safe European Home' and 'Tommy Gun' can hardly be described as AOR. Joe's voice was clear and upfront and the

Paul/Topper rhythm section meshed to produce thumping sonic booms. Punk's tinny requirements were now a thing of the past.

In the *NME* Nick Kent was swayed by *Give 'Em Enough Rope*'s enhanced sound but criticised Joe's lyrics and 'totally facile concept of shock politics'. *Sounds*' Dave McCullough gave it a five star thumbs-up, but *Melody Maker*'s Jon Savage, after pointing out the 'follow that' situation The Clash had placed them in after 'doing all their growing up in public', reckoned, 'The sharp, direct attack of the first album . . . has been replaced by a confused lashing out and a muddy attempt to come to terms with the violence of the outside world, which The Clash plainly see as hostile through and through . . . They sound as though they're writing about what they think is expected of them, rather than what they want to write about, or need to. So do they squander their greatness.'

'The first time you're slagged it really gets you here,' Joe told Allan Jones. 'But after that you get sort of immune. You get a leather heart, know what I mean?'

Robin Banks's *Zigzag* review diverted from the 'build 'em up to shoot 'em down' approach and highlighted the album's good points. I didn't care if we were sometimes seen as a fan club organ. The way I saw it, somebody had to present The Clash with honesty and the support they deserved. Groups like this came along once in a lifetime.

'A triumphant war of battles won. This album is a paean to victory that demands instant recognition and then leaves one gasping for breath, exhausted but exhilarated. It certainly must be placed among only a handful of rock albums that merit the term "classic" . . . The sound here is immensely powerful, has depth and scope, and yet is full of subtleties, delicate nuances and changes in pace.' By the end of the page review, Robin declared the album to be almost the equal of the group's landmark debut: 'The Clash have carved out for themselves a place in rock history, they have come through, against the odds, and delivered an album that is, in my eyes, the best since their first one.'

The album was too different, ambitious and widescreen in a time when punk desperately needed a life raft. The Clash weren't gonna be the ones to retread old glories and encourage more imitations. They had to move on and, if *Give 'Em Enough Rope* is flawed, it had to happen so they could move on to the great things around the corner. It's as if Joe had to go through this phase of self-doubt and terrorist chic in order to arrive at the works of genius on the next album. Mick sat for hours watching Pearlman at the mixing desk, in order to get a handle on cutting out the middleman next time.

'Mick learnt all the technicalities,' Robin later observed. 'The A to Z of how to do this. It was a conscious thing and it was brilliant. That meant he could go on to produce *London Calling*. The songs transcend the production but it still neutered them to some extent. That's not what The Clash were about, but I'm so glad that experience happened. It's probably the main reason for the dynamism of *London Calling*. They bounced back. It wouldn't have happened without Sandy Pearlman.'

There's a reflective, almost despondent streak running through the record, espe-

Jones at the controls – 'Mick learnt all the technicalities'.

cially when listened to now. Almost a swansong for the punk movement. When you think that the next album would be the panoramic *London Calling*, this is even more apparent. It was like the end of chapter one – now it was time to move on. 'Yeah, definitely,' agreed Joe in an interview with *New York Rocker*. 'That's definitely true. But I ain't gonna say what we got up our sleeve. We got an idea, but I don't want to say what it is, in case some two-bit group down the block whips it out on a coloured vinyl EP.'

Give 'Em Enough Rope did shock at first but, once you accepted that it was a linear progression and refinement from *The Clash* – not to mention a stepping stone for what was to come – it became apparent that here was an album of significant worth.

Rolling Stone's Greil Marcus praised Pearlman's production but conceded that it sometimes sounds 'overworked, and so does the vision'. Marcus also observed that The Clash sound as 'wearied' by the failure of their early ideals as 'a bunch of tenured Marxists. But these familiar contradictions follow upon the invigorating gutter truths of the first album for a reason – they're truths as well, truths that couldn't be stated more forcefully with any other music.'

Released on 24 November, 'Tommy Gun' was the first single taken from the new LP. Danny Baker had come out in sympathy with Tony Parsons, by declaring in *NME* that, 'this is a sad report on the state of things.' The single would still become the group's first Top Twenty hit when it reached Number 19 in the UK chart. Don Letts shot a promotional video at the Roxy soundcheck. The band wouldn't let it be shown on *Top of the Pops* but the clip appeared on anarchic Saturday morning kids' TV show *Tiswas*, accompanied by a studio visit from The Clash.

Next came the Sort It Out tour – so named because of the ongoing financial chaos caused by Bernie's sacking. The Slits were supporting again. Still managed by Don Letts and Leo Williams, they had replaced Palmolive with a guy called Budgie from Liverpool, a veritable Topper-style powerhouse who would go on to forge an enduring partnership with Siouxsie Sioux. Barry Myers, was on the decks. The Clash's new backdrop emblazoned flags of all nations in a typically Joe-inspired global theme.

I managed to get to a fair share of the gigs – and lived to tell the tale. Even the highly eventful night of 22 November in Bournemouth, where Johnny Green and I ended up stuck halfway down a cliff face overhanging the beach at 5.30 in the morning.

As usual, I covered the show for *Zigzag:* 'Tonight in Bournemouth Village Bowl, a huge place which looks like an underground car park, The Clash turn in just the set to lay to rest any doubts that they've "lost it", "got slick" or "turned rock stars".

'They played with all the spontaneous combustion and attack they would muster in The Old Days at places like High Wycombe Nag's Head, careering through the songs despite technical hitches onto an accelerating escalator of white hot intensity, eventually dissolving into . . . well, tonight, Joe finished with a solo just-me-and-my-guitar rendition of "London's Burning", while being swamped by singalongaClashers. The reason was, Mick's lead went in "Complete Control" [first encore] and the replacement was a dud! By the end of the Mick-less song all I could see from my two square inches was the black-clad guitarist's arms flailing yards of cable in the air like an octopus. The number finished, he ran off – presumably to get a replacement – and the bouncer wouldn't let him back on! He thought he was a stage invader and tried to strangle him. Exit Paul and Topper in confusion. But Joe starts up "London's Burning" and Paul reappears to play along. Topper can't do this because he left his podium through the drum kit and it fell over.

'With the stage a mass of singing kids and roadies fighting to save the gear, the set screeches to a chaotic, premature end.

'But I leap forward. Before the flood The Clash delivered an hour of electricity that made me feel great. Most of *Rope* kicking off with "Safe European Home" [even "Julie's Been Working For The Drug Squad"], an explosive treatment of "I Fought The Law", plus singles, B-sides and a select few survivors from the first album.

'It was the best sound I've heard them get – clear, balanced, but demonically powerful. With that advantage plus the howling thousands and the group's high-speed calorie burn-up, they couldn't go far wrong.

'Afterwards, Mick, who earlier spent a silent ten minutes with the music papers, announces, 'I'm going to be a drunken idiot tonight!' Later, Mick and I indulge in a lengthy heart-to-heart, which I can't remember a lot of (bet he can't either!). He is pissed off by those writers. If it got to Joe, he didn't really show it – his anger came out in stage rage. Mick has been an avid *NME* reader since his early teens and gets hurt easily. Mick describes himself as over-emotional, he's aware of his faults. I'd say he was a rare, caring commodity these days. Seems like his "black cloud" [of cocaine] has lifted, at last, but we both agree that it's a weird coincidence that him, me and several of our mates, all felt pretty pissed off and suffered from headaches for the past month. "Perhaps they've put something in the air."

'After the meal we hop back to the hotel and assemble in the lounge for a nightcap (where I inadvertently find myself with a huge drinks bill). "Where's Topper?" is the question. The answer comes when an excited tour geezer rushes in clutching an armful of clothes. "Topper and Dee [his girlfriend] went swimming and we nicked their clothes! They're on their way back now with only Dee's boots between them!" Sure enough, within minutes, the great drummer and his young lady nonchalantly stroll in through the foyer past the desk absolutely naked. Drunken businessmen gawp as the unclothed pair step into the lift.

'Denied further drinks and beset by the aforementioned businessmen, the group retire. Of course, drinks can still be obtained, so Johnny Green and me do.

'About an hour or so and several scotches later, the cliff incident takes place. It started as a stroll along the promenade but within minutes the crazed Greeny is over the fence and sprinting downwards like a mountain goat. "COME ON!", he orders, and before I know it I'm on the descent. Johnny's six foot-plus build gave him a distinct advantage and there are several heart-clasping moments. It was only when I got down the bottom, that I realised what I'd just done . . . without being given any rope.'

Even though it's over 25 years ago as I write this, that gig remains firmly entrenched in my memory as one of The Clash's best. Joe had overcome the hepatitis that crippled him on the White Riot tour and was once again firing on all cylinders, even if he'd suffered more dental damage when a fan bashed him in the mouth with a mic. Mick was beating the coke problem that had unsettled him over the previous eighteen months. In my *Zigzag* feature, I'd skirted over the heart-to-heart I had with Mick because I didn't want to give other writers fuel for their putdowns, but Mick had talked of his problem and how he felt he was overcoming it. He'd become close to Joe again and felt that the band was too special to blow out because of rock star drugs. He was back to the old Mick I'd met two years earlier.

The Clash had faced a year of problems; Joe's illness, Mick's drug use, Bernie's manipulations and ultimate dismissal, as well as constant scrutiny from the press. Despite these distractions, the band had succeeded in making an album that clearly demonstrated their creative development. Such difficulties played a part in creating a group dynamic which combusted internally to forge the sort of blazing magic that doesn't come out of a can. With Topper fully settled in and Paul a lot happier now that Joe and Mick were getting along, The Clash were back as a full fighting unit.

'We were very aware of each other,' Mick told *GQ* in 2003. 'We spent so much time with each other. There was that kind of telepathic thing. We knew things without even saying them; we looked at each other and just knew what the others were thinking. We were a three-pronged attack. We formed in a line, and the line was so strong that we never really thought about it.'

Pennie Smith gave me two photographs to use with my *Zigzag* piece, and they seemed to capture the essence of the band. There's one of Paul and Joe. The bass player is standing solid with legs apart, glancing at Topper. Meanwhile, Joe is looking at his guitar with murderous intent, veins sticking out on his hand because he's grasping the neck so hard. His lip is curled up in a cross between Elvis and Johnny Rotten. He was incendiary that night, as if doing the new songs was an injection of molten energy, which transcended the regulation punk attack. Now a new demon gripped Joe's body and brain in the shape of pure, five star rock 'n' roll petrol. A burning surge of adrenalised possession. And he looked so happy when he stood playing alone during that full-on stage invasion in Bournemouth. Those kids weren't trying to destroy anything. In a weird way it was like a teacher standing in the middle of an unruly class, conducting a mass singalong. A magical Rock 'n' Roll Moment.

The other photo has Mick, all in black, recently shorn and standing on the drum riser with intent blasting out of his eager eyes. Earlier in the year, he looked like a refugee from one of the bands he set out to bring down in 1976 – albeit a punked-up version. Pennie's photo spoke volumes about the change in Mick Jones. Now he was not only shorn of hair, but also the rock 'n' roll excess that threatened to derail The Clash.

Back at the tour, two gigs at Glasgow's Strathclyde University got cancelled by the band when Joe found out that only students could buy tickets. He tried it out for himself by queuing up with the punters and being refused a ticket when he couldn't produce a Students Union card.

On 19 December, The Clash played a Sid Vicious Defence Fund Night at the Music Machine. Following his arrest for the murder of girlfriend Nancy Spungen, Sid's mum had asked the group if they could raise the money to pay for him to come home. Supporting were The Slits, the Innocents and an old friend of Mick's – singer-songwriter Phil Rambow, who Mick sat in with on guitar while Glen Matlock played bass.

It was The Clash's first London gig since the release of *Give 'Em Enough Rope*, so the joint was packed. As *NME*'s Claude Bessy wrote, 'This was their band, the sound of their hearts, and may all the effete critics go to hell . . . we've left the relatively safe ground of musical values and have entered the realm of cult phenomena.' Just before the second encore a bomb threat was announced and we all had to spill out onto the street. End of gig. Not much was said about Sid's cause. There was a sense that it already seemed lost.

I was delighted when the tour rolled into town for the Friars Aylesbury Christmas party on 22 December – another instant sellout. The good spirit I'd encountered at Bournemouth a month earlier was still going strong. In keeping with a festive club tradition, some people wore fancy dress animal costumes – these were right up the group's street. Joe and a couple of the crew amazed the locals by popping next door into our local pub – the legendary Green Man from whence came the jukebox charts printed in *Zigzag*. The Clash had repeatedly held the number one spot. He wasn't mobbed but shook a lot of hands.

The tour finished up at London's Lyceum on 28-29 December, with a final gig there on 3 January. 'The Clash were unstoppable, moving inexorably towards their prime,' remembered Jean Encoule of punk website *Trakmarx* in 2003. It had only been just over two years since I'd first seen them and the band were now realising all their initial promise. The look, the attitude, the music – the whole epic, heart-lifting show and its brilliant new songs. It was undoubtedly that 'prime' of their career that Encoule talks about. He was there too and later added, 'This could well have been the group's finest live hour – it was definitely the best gig of our lives.'

The *Rude Boy* crew had been filming all year and finished up by capturing a classic performance of 'I Fought The Law' at this gig. Later that month, the band agreed to overdub some of the songs that had been filmed for the movie, which they then believed would have a soundtrack. Mick applied himself with customary enthusiasm, fired up to be finally in control in the studio and using what he'd learned making *Give 'Em Enough Rope*. *Rude Boy* Producer Jack Hazan said later that the overdubs cost twice as much as the film.

The group also cleverly used this time to thrash out what became the *Cost Of Living* EP. They were working in North London's Wessex Studios, with Bill Price engineering and co-producing. I first became aware of Bill when I visited Mott The Hoople at the same studio, sometimes seeing Mick there. These sessions would sow the seeds of what ultimately became *London Calling*, as the EP was planned as a test run to see how working with Price at Wessex would pan out.

First, they recorded 'I Fought The Law'. The Clash version sounds more triumphant than the Bobby Fuller's original, which is a classic rock 'n' roll tale of a man doing bad and paying the price. The song blazes away magnificently and there's even a clap-along session on the chorus. Joe infused the lyrics of lost love and life with a real passion, while Mick built upward spirals of guitar on the original's strident key-riff. One night somebody decided that a chain-gang effect would be good at the end, so everyone piled into the toilets and started whacking the pipes. Obviously somebody had to flush it, and that's on there too. If you listen very carefully there's another wildebeest about. At least the guitarist didn't just stop playing and take a leak in the middle of the band room, as happened with Mott.

They also did a new version of 'Capital Radio', in response to the demand for the *NME*'s limited edition. This was long sold out and the free single was now changing hands for upwards of £100. There were also new versions of two previously unfinished songs: the airy and acoustic-flavoured 'Groovy Times', which dated from *Rope* sessions in early 1978, and the lovely 'Gates Of The West', which even boasted a Bruce Springsteen influence amid its soul-vamp grooving. This had started life as a pre-Clash Mick number, 'Ooh, Baby, Ooh [It's Not Over]' and had originally been recorded as 'Rusted Chrome' at Basing Street in April 1978. Mick changed the lyrics when he arrived in New York with Joe that September and vocals were added to the backing track at the Record Plant.

My stop-press in the January 1979 *Zigzag* reported: 'The Clash have reworked their classic ['Capital Radio'] to devastating effect. Not gonna say much but would you believe The Clash go disco and Strummer meets Travolta! Also done for their forthcoming EP: "I Fought The Law" (Ooh, that new vocal sound), "Groovy Times" and "Gates Of The West"'.

NME's readers obviously paid little heed to its writers and voted The Clash Best Group in its annual poll. 'White Man' was voted Best Single and *Give 'Em Enough Rope* second best album.

In February, The Clash would embark on their first American tour. It would turn out to be one of the biggest turning points of their career.

CHAPTER TEN

IGNORE ALIEN ORDERS

We're just four blokes, like any other blokes . . . I just laugh at all that stuff,
because if you start walking around thinking that you're the last hope of
rock 'n' roll, I'd say you were finished. – Joe Strummer

After their storming Pearl Harbor '79 tour of America in February, The Clash's fascination with the States would be assimilated into their sound, their look and their whole attitude. Joe had always been fascinated with the US, ever since his early immersion in legends like Woody Guthrie, Chuck Berry and Captain Beefheart. Half the repertoire of his previous group was cover versions of American classics. His original stance and look was early Elvis, albeit transplanted from Memphis to a London squat.

When The Clash hit the US for their seven-date tour, they travelled economy. I did the same thing myself, five years later, when I was doing press and lights for glam-goth-rockers Specimen. Touring usually entails hours cocooned in the bus. It's bad enough on the drive from London to Middlesbrough, but the immensity of the USA takes the mundanity of being stuck on the road to a new level of misery. See the road signs for places you've only heard of in songs: New York City, Detroit, Chicago, Kansas, San Francisco, while American radio broadcasts its own brand of message for a country that's vast beyond British comprehension.

If there's such a thing as a 'mundane' buzz, it's being huddled in a bus at three in the morning and glancing out of the window as America unfolds before you. Then in comes New York City and the Manhattan skyline becomes apparent as dawn breaks. To be suddenly confronted by the twinkling, towering concrete flesh of a city that I'd so often encountered in films and books is the sort of rush that makes life great. And Joe caught it from the start. 'That childish thrill is essential when you come over here. "My God! We're going to New York!" I hope I never lose that.'

Going to America was the obvious next big step for The Clash. When they took off for Pearl Harbor '79 – a name designed to announce that The Clash were on their way with bombs of a musical kind – it was a move which might alienate diehard fans but could potentially catapult the group onto the world arena.

Give 'Em Enough Rope was the first Clash record to be released in America, through CBS's sister label Epic. It got good reviews – including one from Lester Bangs in the respected *Village Voice* and *Rolling Stone*'s Greil Marcus, who wrote, 'The Clash are now so good they will be changing the face of rock 'n' roll simply by addressing themselves to the form.' The album only made Number 128 on the *Billboard* chart. There wasn't even a US single released to coincide with the tour.

The Clash were keen to embrace America, but Epic were less enthusiastic as they already had most of their roster on the road. Caroline Coon paid her own fare to New York and set up the eight shows in medium sized venues, which held between one and three thousand. All but one sold out. Meeting Epic, who were obviously happy to see Bernie out of the picture, Caroline managed to squeeze $30,000 worth of tour support out of the label.

The Clash hired rock 'n' roll legend Bo Diddley as support act. Bo – real name Ellis McDaniel – scored his first hit in 1955 with 'Bo Diddley'. The big man with the square guitar was part of the explosive Chess Records set-up in Chicago, which also included Chuck Berry and Muddy Waters. To stand out, Bo customised his own guitars and amps to create a juddering, primeval stomp boogie, which magnetised the young Keith Richards and Mick Jagger. The 'Bo Diddley Beat' underpinned their first big hit, 'Not Fade Away', which Joe says was the first tune that made his toes curl. The Stones then covered many of Bo's songs and toured the UK with him in 1963. In return, they booked him on their US tours after they'd become successful, along with other blues artists they felt deserved more exposure in their native country.

Like the Stones, apart from being fans, The Clash's main reason for booking Bo Diddley was to remind mainstream America where this wild, primal music came from in the first place. They would continue this policy on subsequent tours, with such seminal figures as Lee Dorsey and Sam and Dave, while Epic consistently tried to foist their own bands onto the bill.

'We made a point of doing that,' says Mick. 'We brought them in and sort of helped to introduce them to other people who weren't aware of that.' 'I can't look at him without my mouth falling open,' said Joe, who had been into Bo's music from his early teens. Bo got on famously with The Clash, who hung on every word from the 50-year-old legend. Paul nicknamed him 'Uncle Skiddly Daddly'. Bo gladly told his tales while drinking a whiskey concoction called rock and rye and gave up his bunk on the bus to his guitar.

I guess Mick had been working towards this moment ever since that fight in the classroom with Robin Banks. He says he never mentioned it to Bo. 'Maybe I should have . . .'

During the tour, The Clash continually went against the grain. They started every show with 'I'm So Bored With The USA', and didn't take kindly to fake music-biz etiquette and patronisingly stupid journalists. They were heralded as the exemplars of punk, who would deliver where the Pistols had failed, but they were more concerned with rubbing America's nose in its own musical ignorance than sparking shock-horror outrage. If they did have anything they wanted to destroy it was America's preoccupation with radio-friendly jock groups – 'Every second we're on the radio that's a second less Boston or Foreigner,' said Joe.

Whereas Malcolm McLaren's Stateside touring strategy had involved the Pistols eschewing high profile venues in favour of a string of shows at relatively obscure redneck bars, The Clash took the direct approach – they had come to storm the barricades of FM radio blandness, by any means necessary.

On 30 January, The Clash – plus Barry Myers, Messrs Green, Baker and sound and lighting crew – flew to Vancouver, Canada, for the first show at the Agora Ballroom the following night. 'No blizzards, no snow, no Mounties – just the customs,' wrote Joe in *Armagideon Times,* the fanzine they started later to communicate directly with their fans – getting Banksy and me to act as editors. 'They go [through] everythin', confiscating studded belts, armbands, knives, cos they can't find any drugs. "If we'd known it was going to be like this, we'd have brought some drugs for you," we tell 'em. But they don't smile, they just kick us out, knifeless and beltless.'

The gig itself was a wild night of mayhem as bottles were hurled during the repeated demands for encores. Joe's usual Strum-guard didn't stop him receiving a huge gash to his arm and his perennial dental problems returned in the form of an abscess. Topper got three good head wounds. Johnny Green entered into the frontier spirit by adopting the voice of redneck cartoon rooster Foghorn Leghorn for much of the tour – especially when the band hit Texas and he bought a Stetson.

After playing Toronto, The Clash made their way to San Francisco, having hired country star Waylon Jennings' tour bus. They arrived on 3 February and were greeted by the news that Sid Vicious had overdosed on smack while out on bail for Nancy's murder.

The Clash were playing Berkeley Community Centre for Bill Graham, the infamous promoter who'd made his name staging the mid-sixties hippy concerts at the Fillmore Auditorium before taking on the Rolling Stones tours. The afternoon of the gig they visited a local record shop called Leopold's, which was run by Vietnam veteran Mo Armstrong who was once a member of late sixties UK hippy club stalwarts Daddy Long Legs.

That night's gig was pretty sedate. Mo told The Clash that the formidable Graham had a monopoly on the Bay Area concert scene and how other promoters had formed a collective to make a stand against him by keeping ticket prices low. The following night, these promoters were holding a fund-raising benefit at a new venue. The Clash volunteered to play and went down a storm.

More bad news followed, as a mortified Mick learnt that the Pembridge Villas flat he shared with Tony James had been robbed and all his music equipment stolen. The band then travelled on to Los Angeles for a show at the Santa Monica Civic Auditorium.

In his review of the show, Don Snowden of *LA Weekly* called The Clash 'the best rock 'n' roll band in the world'. 'I've never seen a performer so completely wrapped up in his performance as Strummer – slashing away at his battered Telecaster, mouth agape, left leg pumping like a piston and eyes often wide open with the look of a man who's seen his worst nightmare come to life ten feet in front of his face.' Sylvie Simmons, the veteran writer reporting for *Sounds*, wrote, 'The Clash were electrifying. Like a bloody great headline, commanding attention and belief.'

'If you can't understand the words – don't worry. You're not alone,' Joe told the audience.

After the gig, The Clash snubbed American music biz etiquette when they refused to pose for a cheesy-grin team photo with a small herd of Epic executives. 'I was disgusted that they were there,' Joe later told *Melody Maker's* Allan Jones.

'They've done nothing for us. And there they were, prancing about backstage with their slim handshakes and big smiles. I just ignored them . . . I don't have any time for it. All that record company bullshit.'

Epic hadn't put much into the tour anyway, but relations were souring by the minute. Even the Stones were party to this kind of schmoozing, and Elvis Costello and the Boomtown Rats were happily towing the party line. Joe saw it as arse licking.

In Cleveland, the band played a benefit for Larry McIntyre, a Vietnam veteran who'd lost both his legs during the conflict. Larry had recently been banned from his local swimming pool and was taking the matter to court. Barry Myers recalls Joe walking on stage and announcing, 'We're here for the geezer with no legs!'

After driving ten hours from Cleveland to Washington in the worst snowstorm Bo Diddley had ever encountered, the Clash tour party decided to visit the White House at 4am. Allan Jones was along for the ride and recalled it in *Uncut* in 2003. He recounted Joe's reaction to arriving at the nexus of American imperialism. 'Just think, if we had a mortar or a bazooka or some machine guns, we could blow it all away. Just lob a few grenades over the garden wall and wipe them all out. It's got to be worth thinking about.' At that point, Mick started to feel uncomfortable and the party drove off. The sound at the Washington gig was so awful that Mick smashed his guitar in frustration.

On 17 February, The Clash made their New York debut at the Palladium theatre on 14th Street. My New York friends still speak of that as one of the best gigs they've ever seen. The crowd included such notables as Robert De Niro, Bruce Springsteen, ex-New York Doll David Johanssen, Nico and Andy Warhol, who took the band to ultra-hip disco Studio 54 afterwards.

The next day, Joe still made it to Gaylords Restaurant to undertake a string of interviews. One of these resulted in him appearing on the front cover of *New York Rocker* under the banner announcement 'Clash Mania! Strummer Speaks Out'. The headline inside simply said 'Not So Bored With The USA'.

Writer Tom Carson observed that, 'though obviously tired, Strummer was unfailingly courteous throughout the conversation. An intense talker, he often slapped his hand softly on the table to emphasise a point: more rarely his gaunt face would crease in a Robert De Niro/Johnny Boy grin. Friendly as he was, talking to Joe was a little bit like listening

The Wild One – Joe as featured on the cover of New York Rocker, *January 1979.*

to The Clash's music – a little bit unsettling.' He asked why Joe had decided to come to America, mentioning that he'd already told *Rolling Stone* that he saw it as a new lease of life. 'Well, that's kind of part of it, and also – five times around England kind of drives you out of your mind, you've got to go somewhere else . . . if we don't accomplish anything, it's probably going to be our fault, rather than anybody else's. What I've seen so far, the atmosphere here – lots of people travelled to one of the shows from Kansas, and it was just like talking to some guys from Birmingham, or Manchester. There's the same kind of fever, the same kind of dedication.'

Tom then asked Joe about the fanaticism and pressure surrounding The Clash, with them being lauded as 'saviours of rock 'n' roll'. 'I hate that. I hated that when it first was said . . . I just shut my mind out when I hear that stuff, or I laugh at it. I don't take it seriously.'

Joe also submitted a tour report – typed in capitals – for *NME* and concluded, 'To break, crack, storm or blitz America you have to work as hard as Elvis Costello, shake hands and smile like the Boomtown Rats and sound like Dire Straits. Of the three, we could make the first bit but not the rest so we are going to go back and play the US again but we must also play Britain, Japan, Europe, Australia and it's fair shares all round. Hey! I hear they're really rocking in Russia.'

By the end of February, The Clash were back in the UK, and returned to Wessex, having agreed to provide two new studio songs for the proposed *Rude Boy* sound-track. They laid down early versions of Danny Ray's 'Revolution Rock' and a new song called 'Rudie Can't Fail' – both ska-influenced outings with the latter's title taken from a line in Desmond Dekker's '007'.

The fired-up group were preoccupied with thoughts of their next album. America had planted seeds of inspiration, while Britain didn't seem so attractive as Margaret Thatcher goose-stepped her way to power. Joe was in love with the roman-tic notion of the States, just like he'd seen in the movies back when he was at board-ing school. Musically, he felt like he'd found the Holy Grail. American music had always been his lifeblood and now he'd visited the source. I know how they felt. Joe and Mick's endless enthusing on the country's music, mystique and magic played a large part in my own immersion in the place myself a few years later. For some peo-ple it takes just that first sighting of the New York skyline as you drive in from the airport. You're never the same again, as the country's rich cultural heritage unfolds and an over-the-top bombardment of images and myths commences. Having expe-rienced this, The Clash were permanently altered.

'I got so much inspiration from America, I can't describe it,' Joe bubbled as I tried to prise snippets of info from him after the band had returned to the UK. The band's enthusiasm for the roots of rock 'n' roll made you scour the record shops for records by obscure country singers.

'That happened with Mott The Hoople as well,' recalls Mick. 'They came back from America all full of it. They came back with guitars, records you couldn't get here and stuff . . . When we went to America we made sure we plugged into the heart of the city when we visited places, like Motown's Hitsville in Detroit.'

After that first American trip, The Clash noticeably changed their look. Less zips and bondage gear – although those outfits were practical for stages soaked in gob and sweat. Offstage, they were starting to look more like a cross between a New York street gang and the cast of *The Godfather*. They particularly favoured dark suits, long coats and trilby hats. They'd all got these ultra-cool black jackets, which were hand-sewn by Vietnamese peasant women for the US soldiers, all covered in slogans and dragons. 'We don't walk around with green hair and bondage trousers any more,' declared Joe. 'We just like to look, sort of, flash these days.'

Joe had recently started going out with a friend of Topper's girlfriend, Dee – seventeen year-old Gabrielle (Gaby) Salter. He'd soon move into the flat she shared with her mum on the World's End Estate, Chelsea – now he lived by the river.

During early 1979, I conducted a one-off poll in *Zigzag* to find out the readers' favourite Clash tunes. I was pleased to get about 700 replies and swiftly realised how everyone had their own personal reasons for their favourite songs, plus how much they meant to people. 'Complete Control' won by a mile, followed by 'White Riot', '[White Man] In Hammersmith Palais', 'Stay Free', 'Safe European Home', 'Police And Thieves', 'Capital Radio', 'Clash City Rockers', 'London's Burning' and 'Janie Jones'. The poll appeared in the April issue, which celebrated the mag's tenth birthday. Inside, a plain white box said, 'Happy Birthday *Zigzag* – The Clash'.

Around the same time, I was in a punk band called the Vice Creems (Unfortunately I was singing). Mick said he would produce us when he came back from the States. The ambitious new *Zigzag* record label had hired Olympic Studios – where the Stones did 'Sympathy For The Devil' – for 20 March. But the week before the session the band split up, leaving just me and guitarist Colin Keinch. I told Mick of my plight and he just said, 'Let's go ahead. I'll get you a band.' Colin and I duly made our way to Olympic, and walked straight into Johnny Green, who was setting up some very familiar pink amplifiers. Then Mick arrived, along with Topper Headon and Tony James. 'I said I'd get you a band,' grinned Mick, as he plugged in his black Les Paul. 'Blimey, we've got half The Clash in our group,' I thought. 'That's what generous people they are, just doing something for a mate. They didn't think any more of it,' Johnny told me.

Within an hour, the assembled company were working up 'Danger Love' – the song me and Colin had written. Colin taught Mick the arrangement, which they then vamped up into a flame-breathing, mid-period Clash-style monster. 'So this must be how The Clash work,' I thought. Setting up, jamming, shaping half-songs into roof-raising anthems. With the basic track recorded, Mick dubbed layer upon layer of guitar, colliding and counteracting. You don't hear it at the time as the riffs and counter-riffs keep coming, but Mick has the end result in his head. When he gets on the mixing desk it all makes sense.

After that day, I could hear any Clash track and tell how it was put together. From watching Mick at work and observing the manner in which the band's sound developed over the first four albums, I understood what Joe had said about the way he worked with Mick. Joe was the words and the voice, while Mick was the sound and the big picture.

The great lost Clash single? Kris Needs' Vice Creems 1979 'Danger Love' featured guitar and drums from Mick and Topper.

The flip to the Vice Creems single was a cover of Fabian's fifties rock 'n' roll classic 'Like A Tiger'. Here we let rip on some Ramones-style punk 'n' roll. Tony's Generation X bandmate Billy Idol turned up and ended doing handclaps, while Robin Banks joined us in some rousing wildebeest howls in the middle of 'Tiger'. The Clash would later employ this haunting effect on 'London Calling' and 'Should I Stay Or Should I Go'.

One afternoon in August 2004, I was gobsmacked when Robin told me that 'Danger Love' had inspired Joe when writing 'London Calling'. Come again? 'It was on that Vice Creems single, "Danger Love",' he cackled at my disbelief. 'That's where Joe got the idea for the wildebeest noise.'

Because they were contracted to CBS and Chrysalis, Mick and the chaps had to adopt false names. Mick became Michael Blair, after George Orwell (real name Eric Blair), author of *1984*, Topper was Nicholas Khan, while Tony became Anthony Ross. For his trouble, Mick was given two ounces of prime Jamaican weed, and to this day, 'Danger Love' remains the great lost semi-Clash single and currently changes hands for around £25.

Meanwhile, The Clash wanted to release 'I Fought The Law' as their next single, with 'Gates Of The West' on the flip. Instead, CBS (who were looking to squeeze another single off *Rope*) put out 'English Civil War' on 3 March, with the group's version of 'Pressure Drop' on the flip. This made Number 25.

Once again, Danny Baker reviewed the single for *NME*, describing it as, 'A wise enough if miscued and rock 'n' rolly warning about all things uniformed and sinister that this chap can flow to easier than any tupenny ha'penny "Oliver's Army". But then it was a CBS choice, we hear . . . Despite myself, The Clash are still the only rock group I would cross the road for.'

On 5 May, *NME* ran an Election Special where readers voted for Joe as the preferred choice of alternative Prime Minister. A fortnight later, on the day that Margaret Thatcher was swept to power on a tidal wave of lowest common denominator voting, The Clash released the *Cost of Living* EP.

Featuring the four new tracks that had been recorded at Wessex , it kicks off with a detonating turbo-charge through 'I Fought The Law', before the acoustic-flavoured waft of 'Groovy Times'. The Booker T soul chug is a perfect vehicle for Mick's yearning 'Gates Of The West'. With lyrics such as 'Eastside Jimmy and Southside Sue both said they needed something new,' and a bewitching chorus, the song represents The Clash's most overtly US-influenced track to date. Finally comes the reworking of 'Capital Radio', with Joe halting proceedings halfway through its solid new treatment. 'Wait, we ain't never gonna get on the radio,' he declares, and they launch into a cod disco coda. The disc closes with a brief reprise of 'I Fought The Law', with Joe toasting over the top.

The sleeve is a washing powder box pastiche featuring fun photos like the band on the Wessex studio table football game, which has been altered to resemble a barbecue. The band can be seen wearing propeller hats, while pointing and laughing at an out-of-shot Sandy Pearlman.

Although the band were less than happy that the record retailed for £1.49 – they had wanted it to sell for a pound – it climbed to Number 22 in the UK and marked the final instalment of The Clash's non-album seven-inch run. The EP reached the ears of *NME* rookie Ian Penman, a cantankerous new boy despised for his pretentious manner, and thus regularly subjected to Banks's ridicule. Of course he slagged it, with references to 'Pub City Rockers' and the music sounding 'tired'.

Now that they'd split with Bernie, The Clash had to find somewhere else to write and rehearse the growing corpus of songs that they were building up. In March, Johnny Green and Baker turned up Vanilla Studios in Causton Road, Pimlico, which was basic but practical. It was up the stairs behind a garage. Certainly off the beaten track, which ensured that the only visitors would be invited ones.

'It was perfect for us because we were sort of a bit with our backs to the wall,' Mick told *Clash* magazine in 2004. 'We needed some place private, I think, just to work. You wouldn't know there was a band there unless you were specifically invited. Otherwise you'd never have known.'

The band started working up new material through May and June. After the obsessive effort that had gone into making *Give 'Em Enough Rope*, the group had become close again as they shared their American adventure. So they plotted up at Vanilla and got down to the business at hand with renewed vigour and unity. A garage band, in the true sense of the word.

Robin would phone regularly with enthusiastic progress reports, telling me about the daily football matches played over the road in a concrete playground. Mick invited me along to check it out and, being stupid, I wandered around for half an hour before I found the place. Here I encountered the re-born Clash. Hammering away at new ideas, getting on famously and riding the crest of a creative wave.

We did have a game of football. I've always been crap and floundered around like a beached seal, but Johnny recalls that 'Paul was quite hard and enthusiastic . . . Topper was skilled and nimble; Joe would be well-meaning and try hard but wasn't very good, and Jonesy was really flash, but we all laughed at his style, because he wasn't as good as he thought he was. As soon as they were back inside they'd roll a joint. Rather than sedating them it had the opposite effect – it would fire them up. Very unusual for white boys.'

Mick has credited the daily kick-about for the eventual stunning album: 'I just think we really found ourselves at that time and it was a lot to do with the football, because it made us play together as one.'

Everyone seemed to be pouring their newfound musical influences into one big melting pot. Joe was reliving his early Woody Guthrie and rock 'n' roll fixations and had started writing on piano. Mick strummed gentle country songs. Topper battered out the dance grooves he'd picked up. As ever, Paul was into his reggae, but – realising you could make money from songwriting royalties – made sure he wrote a song, 'The Guns Of Brixton', which evolved from a bassline he'd been hammering at rehearsals.

Joe took the 'London Calling' title from the BBC World Service reports that he had first tuned in to whilst visiting his father in Malawi in 1960. Inspired by the view of the West End provided by Joe's daily trips to Wessex studios on the number 19 bus, the song was originally about tourism. However, Mick suggested he rewrite it against the apocalyptic fear generated by the 1979 Three Mile Island incident – where a nuclear reactor in Pennsylvania went into partial meltdown.

Mick also had an instrumental with the pithy working title 'For Fuck's Sake', which became 'Working And Waiting' and, finally, 'Clampdown'. Joe and his piano came up with 'Death Or Glory' and a song called 'Four Horsemen'. The new songs came pouring out as The Clash wrote together as a band – for the first and last time.

Topper's jazz leanings begat 'Jimmy Jazz', which Joe turned into a Lenny Bruce-style free-associative ramble when the band performed it live. In the mid-nineties I realised where the title came from after I happened upon an old clothing shop of the same name off 125th Street in Harlem. I bought a pair of strides with the shop's name on the back.

'*London Calling* was the last album that we actually wrote, rehearsed and recorded,' Topper told me in September 2004. 'That was the time I was happiest with the band and I feel that we were at our peak, musically. There was very much a band feel of four guys working together. It was an amazing thing, the four of us then.

'I do think that I allowed them to play other styles of music, like funk and jazz. I like to think that The Clash wouldn't have got as big if I hadn't been in them and, obviously, it could've been even bigger if I hadn't fucked up.'

The most common false assumption made about *London Calling* was that it was designed to 'crack America'. Not so. When they poured out the new songs, The Clash were *inspired by* America. It had opened the door for their already-inbuilt influences. They now felt that, with punk becoming a clichéd dead-end, they didn't want to – indeed, couldn't – simply recycle the first album to order. Before their time in The

Englishmen abroad – Mick and Joe take a tea break during their US tour, whilst Dead Kennedy Jello Biafra mocks.

Clash, Joe had listened to soul and rock 'n' roll, Mick cut his teeth on the New York Dolls and Topper had played with a soul band. Even the ska that Paul grew up with sprang out of American R&B. The album was simply a *gestalt* of these influences.

'It was there already,' says Mick. 'All we did was write a few numbers and do our thing.'

At the end of June the group were ready to demo the new songs and thus began the story of the fabled *Vanilla Tapes*. Johnny and The Baker called up their mate Bill Pridden, soundman for The Who, for advice. They knew him from hiring gear from The Who's hire company. He suggested they use a TEAC four-track recorder linked to a portastudio, which were new products on the market. Bill helped them set up and taught The Baker how to use the new kit. They taped several rehearsals and laid down a bunch of new songs in their most basic versions.

When *London Calling* was reissued to celebrate its 25th anniversary in September 2004, it came with a bonus CD called *The Vanilla Tapes*. For years it was believed that Johnny Green had lost the cassette on the London Underground while pissed. With the knowledge that the group taped everything, Clash-spotters slavered over the possibility there was an album's worth of material gone missing. The legend grew and the tapes became known as The Great Lost Clash Album.

'What a load of bollocks that all is – I did lose 'em!' foghorned Johnny Green at how such a small incident has been blown up into one of rock's great mysteries. Johnny revealed that Guy Stevens was already a candidate to produce the next album and wanted to hear the new songs. 'But he didn't have a tape recorder. I thought that was great. The previous producer had flown over on Concorde and was an expert in gourmet cuisine. So we get this new producer and he don't even have a tape recorder!'

Having blagged the money off Quister the Twister, Johnny went to Tottenham Court Road and got the cheapest mono radio-cassette player available. Then he went to Vanilla where The Baker copied a cassette of the band rehearsing from the portastudio.

'Then I had to deliver it to Guy, but first we went to the pub on the corner and had a few beers. Then I caught the train. I nodded out and woke up at Seven Sisters. It wasn't until later that I realised I'd forgotten the bag. I went back to Baker Street, where the lost property office is, but it never turned up.'

'So I went back and told the band,' recalls Johnny. 'They just said, "You're a silly cunt." Then The Baker ran him off a duplicate. And that's the story of the tape. Nobody thought a lot of it. The tracks were just sketches in the studio. At one point Joe wanted to release *The Vanilla Tapes* as the record because he was so pissed off with CBS.'

But, in 2004, BBC2's *Newsnight* would deem 'The Great Lost Clash Album' to be of enough significance to merit a report and interviewed Mick, Paul and Don Letts.

I asked Mick about it the following week. 'For years they told me, "Oh no, Mick, the tapes were erased. He left them too close to the train magnet near the engine of the train." And I bought that. For years. But it's only recently come out that he fell asleep on the train and left it on the platform. By the time he realised and rushed back they'd gone.

'Then I found them when I was moving in March [2004]. I knew exactly what was on it when I found it in a box of cassettes.'

The 21 tracks on the CD are a fascinating glimpse of The Clash at work, laying the foundations for what would become *London Calling*. There are bare-bones versions of fifteen of the songs that made the album, including 'London Calling' with an alternate lyric, delivered in a lower key by Joe. Some are still just backing tracks under different names. There are bona fide previously-unheard gems in 'Where You Gonna Go (Soweto)', 'Lonesome Me' and 'Heart And Mind', robust rockers which would have sat comfortably on the album alongside tracks like 'Death Or Glory'.

There are a couple of surprises on the disc – a bluesy instrumental called 'Walking The Slidewalk', and a vibrant new version of 'Remote Control'. My gratitude goes out to the band for the inclusion of their cover version of Bob Dylan's 'The Man In Me', then a popular single by reggae band Matumbi. I'd been hearing it at soundchecks around that time and always thought that they should record it.

Mick always described the creation of *London Calling* as 'a natural, organic process'. This is where the seeds started sprouting.

CHAPTER ELEVEN

HEART AND MIND

You couldn't have known that punk would have such an effect. We were supposed to be a punk band and yet we were doing whatever we wanted to do. I never would've thought that twenty-five years later they'd bring London Calling *out in a reissue, like it's* Sergeant Pepper *or something.* – Mick Jones

There was supposed to be another US tour in June 1979, but lack of record company support and the manner in which Bernie had tied up the group's funds meant it was a no-goer. Caroline Coon had even got as far as booking dates – New York's Palladium had already sold out – but it became painfully clear that the tour would have to wait.

On 16 May, the band contacted Caroline, who was in New York trying to placate the promoters over the Palladium cancellation. She was told that she was no longer The Clash's manager. While she flew on to Los Angeles to work on the punk movie *DOA*, The Clash opted to manage themselves.

Around this time, Paul cut Caroline loose too. Robin Banks was very close to his fellow pigeon-shooter at the time and observed that they decided to sack Caroline because 'She wasn't any good.' He adds, 'Typical Paul. He always had an eye for the main chance.'

Once again, The Clash cleaned up in the annual *Zigzag* readers' poll. Best Group, Best Live Act, Best Album (*Give 'Em Enough Rope*), Best Songwriters, and Best Singer for Joe. Also fifth Best Single '(White Man) In Hammersmith Palais'), with the *Cost Of Living* EP four places below. Joe was voted second Favourite Person, with Paul eighth Sexiest – beating me by one place!

We held a party in June at The Venue in Victoria to present the awards and also celebrate *Zigzag's* tenth birthday. Entertainment was provided by Levi and the Rockats, Jayne County, John Otway, Doll By Doll and reggae band Merger. The event, which quickly descended into a drunken, rip-roaring knees-up, was attended by The Clash, PIL, Siouxsie and the Banshees, Gen X and probably every punk in London.

Although they didn't perform, it turned out to be The Clash's most high profile UK public appearance of the year. The whole band turned out and spent most of the party talking with fans. I tried to present the awards (a selection of joke items and cuddly animals), but any sense of ceremony quickly disintegrated as only the Banshees came on stage to pick up their giraffe. Mick said he was 'too shy', while Joe was simply so pissed he couldn't find the stage. I'd seen him earlier, grinning and staggering around. By the time he found the stage, all the prizes had gone, including the pair of hairy gorilla feet I'd got him.

That month, Joe was interviewed by *NME's* Charles Shaar Murray and spoke of his desire to open a musician-owned venue in London, which he would call

Kris Needs presides over the chaos, capering and a cuddly giraffe at the 1979 Zigzag awards show.

Buckingham Palais. He also said he was trying to get in touch with London Weekend Television about starting a decent rock 'n' roll show, admitting that the group's anti-*Top of the Pops* stance was, 'tough shit for us now, because all we get is 22 or 23 in the chart, but in the long run it's gonna be for the best.'

As with his projected radio station, Joe's TV show and dancehall failed to progress beyond the pipe-dream stage. However, the group's debt to CBS was real enough. 'I shouldn't say this, but I'm a man whose knees are dusty from begging on record company floors,' opined Joe. 'I got no pride – but I wanna survive and I want The Clash to survive. The only thing that we got is The Clash . . . We got all these things cooking and we're trying to bring 'em to the boil. We've had our fill of bull-shit, and now we're back to the drawing board. We're really fucked, but I don't think we're fucked enough to quit. We're way beyond that.'

At the time of this interview, the songs that would ultimately make up *London Calling* were starting to catch fire at Vanilla. As the sessions gathered momentum, it was evidently becoming clear to Joe that they were creating a monster.

As Robin Banks, who was there most days, explained, 'It wasn't so much what went on at Wessex later, it was what was happening at Vanilla that was interesting. It was just a very creative time. There was a real feeling of camaraderie and a lot of football. There was a real sense of freedom because they'd got rid of Bernie, so there was no money, they were skint and they could hardly afford to book the studio. But it was the most productive period for The Clash. That's when they were most relaxed. There was no friction, only creative friction. The friction before was partly because Mick was slipping into his rock star persona, but he was at the tail end of that now. Their backs were against the wall but it was an amazing time.'

'That was a great place,' remembers Johnny Green. 'Nobody came in because it was so hard to find. Nobody used to come there. I used to pay extra to keep an extra set of keys to that door. No one was allowed up when they were playing.

'But they loved it when people like you and Robin came down for the football. They really were so pleased to see you, but they'd often say, "Go and have a drink and we'll be with you in an hour." That takes quite a lot of determination. They were so hard at it.'

One day Johnny caught Annie Lennox, who was rehearsing in the downstairs room with her band the Tourists, listening behind the door while The Clash were playing. First he told her to fuck off. When she wouldn't move he assisted her down the steps. 'She looked a bit crestfallen, but those rehearsals were tight as arseholes. We just didn't want things to degenerate into a party. We just had cups of tea on an old tea tray.'

On 6 July, The Clash played the second of two 'secret' gigs at Notre Dame Hall, off London's Leicester Square, to determine how the new songs would be received. It was a good night, and while material like 'Jimmy Jazz' was never going to impress the leather 'n' studs punks, the band went down well. Luckily, my trusty cassette recorder switched itself on during their set! My tape contained early versions of 'Hateful', 'Rudi Can't Fail', 'I'm Not Down', 'Jimmy Jazz', 'Revolution Rock', 'Death Or Glory' – an indication that much of the material that would appear on *London Calling* was already fully formed.

Backstage afterwards, the group obviously felt they'd taken a giant step in debuting so much new material. They were expecting to incur criticism, but their attitude was, 'Just wait for the album.'

That evening, we had limbered up in the Admiral Duncan in Soho's Old Compton Street. As usual I was with Robin. Somehow we ended up talking to two new faces that would quickly become part of the Clash entourage – Jock Scott and Kosmo Vinyl.

Jock was instantly likeable and it was no surprise that he ended up remaining good mates with the Clash crew until the present day. Whereas Jock charmed with his dry Scottish wit and Bacchanalian abandon, Kosmo had his sights set higher. He desperately wanted to get in there and hang with the band, become accepted and thus pave the way for his employers, Blackhill Enterprises, to step in as management.

Kosmo worked for Ian Dury and Stiff Records as both PR and tour MC. They were associated with Andrew King and Peter Jenner, who ran Blackhill Enterprises. They'd started off by promoting the Hyde Park free concerts in 1967, which featured the likes of Pink Floyd and the cream of the London underground – the first gigs the young Mick went to. They ended up managing the Floyd and Marc Bolan.

To those who had been involved with The Clash from the early days, Kosmo was initially perceived as an opportunist interloper – while Kosmo was attaching himself to The Clash, Ian Dury's career was starting to go off the boil. 'Why did the band accept him?' Johnny Green mused. 'They were always very wary of outsiders but they took to him with gusto, although at first he was regarded as someone who didn't understand where the band was coming from. Maybe because he introduced some lightness and frippery at a time when it was quite hard going and getting anything done was hard work. The Clash were beleaguered and he breezed in with freshness and life and colour. What he didn't know was that he was out of his depth.'

From where I was standing, it seemed evident that Kosmo strove to be a text-book embodiment of The Clash's rebellious romanticism. A working class kid who tried to look like Elvis with the requisite quiff, suits and knowledge of music. He could be best mate and confidante to every man at any time, with enough lightning patter to sway the sternest scribe.

'I felt he was a usurper,' asserted Robin. 'After a while we were treated like sec-ond-class citizens, illegal immigrants. He made me so sick at the time. Mick said to me one time that he was "a professional cockney". He played that element, but he was great in some ways. He was into clothes, which me and Mick were too. But he ended up causing a whole lot of negativity.'

'He was the ruin of the band,' insisted Johnny. 'At first he was the acceptably hip face of Blackhill. He opened the door for them to step in. He had very little to do with *London Calling* because he came in at the back end. I call that the "silly hats time." That was Kosmo's greatest legacy with The Clash. But I think it had the effect of hijacking them from the real issues. I think he was just mainstream. The Clash thought out every aspect. They were a radical rock 'n' roll band. Kosmo understood a certain amount of style but underestimated the content.

'He was like Henry Chickenhawk on Foghorn Leghorn. As Foggy said, "A loud-mouthed schnook"!'

By the time The Clash set off to tour the US in September, Kosmo was cement-ed in place as The Clash's PR guru, and Blackhill were managing on, what was ini-tially, a trial basis.

On 14 July, The Clash returned to the Rainbow, which was now minus seats, for a benefit in aid of the Southall Defence Fund. This had been set up by Rock Against Racism after protesters had been arrested during an anti-fascist demonstration in Southall, where London reggae outfit Misty In Roots were beaten up by the Special Patrol Group. RAR set up two concerts to help with court costs, with The Who lend-ing their sound equipment. Pete Townsend, Misty and the Pop Group played the first night, with The Clash, Aswad and The Members appearing at the second gig.

'Both shows were attended by capacity crowds and a good time was had by all with no trouble,' wrote Mick in *Armagideon Times*. In his review of the gig, *NME*'s Paul Morley described The Clash as 'a sort of blank screen upon which the entire history of rock 'n' roll achieves a comprehensive focus: corny, splendid and, er, rebellious.'

Meanwhile, the group continued working at Vanilla, with Guy Stevens, who'd finally heard the demos, lined up as producer. As much as this came as something of a shock, it also made perfect sense. This was the madman who had knocked Mick back when he was in Violent Luck, and made Joe feel uncomfortable during the Polydor demos. However, Guy's manic enthusiasm was a welcome contrast to Sandy Pearlman's ascetic production methods – certainly, Joe and Paul hadn't liked the painstaking way in which Pearlman worked.

Mick didn't care – he'd taken sufficient notes to have the confidence to go in and do the job himself. As Robin Banks puts it, '*Give 'Em Enough Rope* was the sacrificial lamb that allowed them to make *London Calling*.' Mick just needed a good technician who he got on with – which he'd found in Bill Price – a shit-hot studio like Wessex and a manic creative catalyst to make things bubble and detonate. Hello Guy.

Recording was due to start at Wessex in August – but first, Guy had to be found. After a quick search of his usual haunts, Joe discovered him in a West End pub.

Still keen to crack the US market, CBS wanted to engage another big-name American producer. Their A&R department was horrified by the idea of letting a maverick like Stevens produce the record. The label's dismay only served to strengthen The Clash's resolve to hire him. More importantly, freed from Pearlman's AOR-wash, the Vanilla sessions had seen The Clash white-hot, and Guy would be in tune with that. Also, he'd worked with Bill Price before on the Violent Luck sessions, which helped. The only problem was, Guy was drinking even more than usual.

'Guy is that private thing called an X-factor,' said Joe. 'He comes in and grabs me by the throat and says, "I deal with emotions," and that's it. He doesn't deal with knobs or whatever else producers deal with. He's very off the wall, and he understands the spontaneity of the moment – priceless. If you can get that moment when you play a song just so in front of a tape machine, you got a million dollars. He understands that.'

'Guy Stevens brought a lot of R&B into this country,' Mick told me in 2004. 'Before Mott he was doing the Sue label and responsible for bringing in a lot of R&B. Then he did Mott. I think it's all connected . . . turning people on and then the bands he was working with at the time. It all connects.'

Guy also had an extensive knowledge of rock 'n' roll and soul music, which would come in handy with the group's new direction. In the States, Joe had got on particularly well with Bo Diddley, a true original with yards of yarns about the golden age of R&B.

Punk restrictions were now lifted, Joe's 'Chuck Berry Is Dead' t-shirt was in the dumper as he pursued his interest in rockabilly. But, being Joe, he didn't just go out and buy a few records.

'No way could it be ordinary with Joe around,' recalls Johnny Green. 'He really got into rockabilly. He'd think nothing of jumping in a car and going to Bedford to see Ray Campi and his Rockabilly Rebels. His passion was unlimited and it communicated itself to you. He wasn't a dilettante about it.'

The sessions took place over six weeks in August and early September, with a short break for the quick financial injection of the Russrock festival in Finland, which provided a very necessary £7,500 toward studio expenses.

On the first day of recording, Guy set out his stall by arriving equipped with a shopping bag containing two bottles of tequila. The Clash kicked off with a bang, recording twelve tracks during the first three days alone. These were mainly cover versions at Guy's suggestion, such as Bob Dylan's 'Billy The Kid', a couple of Bo Diddley tunes and Vince Taylor's 'Brand New Cadillac', which was the only one to make it to the album.

Guy was in his element, behaving with all the mania that had got him shunned by the music biz establishment. Here, it was encouraged, at first, and paid for. He could throw as many chairs as he liked, swing a ladder at Mick during a solo, or pour beer into the studio TV before upending it – as he did the night the band recorded 'Clampdown'.

I started making regular visits to the studio. One night I was sharing a cab with Joe, Johnny and Robin. As we rounded the bend to Wessex, we spotted a familiar wild-haired figure, running frantically with a look of sheer panic on his face. It was Guy. We wound down the window and asked what he was up to. 'Got to make the off-licence before it shuts!' he panted, and sprinted on. He appeared at the studio, triumphant, ten minutes later, glugged down a large bottle of cheap cider, and promptly zonked out.

Once, Guy turned up with a bloke who sat there for eighteen hours while the producer supplied him with drinks. The man turned out to be a cab driver! His taxi was outside with the meter running. Bill's engineer and tape op, Jerry Green, was left with the £60 bill.

Often he would insist on travelling to the studio in a cab, which would be required to pass the nearby Arsenal football ground so he could salute the hallowed turf. He'd then crank proceedings up for the day by blasting out the commentary from Arsenal's recent dramatic Cup Final victory over Manchester United, waving a scarf and bellowing.

When CBS chief Maurice Oberstein visited the studio, Guy – full of booze and hoping to make an impression – laid down in front of his Rolls Royce and refused to budge until Oberstein admitted that the new material was 'brilliant'.

When Guy spoke to you, he was in your face with force ten passion and phlegm flying. I was his friend for life when he discovered I'd run Mott's fan club and was treated to many a story about Ian Hunter, who Guy often insisted on phoning for advice. Guy's tendency to spit as he spoke led to Joe fashioning his own cardboard face-protector. 'The spittle guard!', remembers Mick. 'Guy would be talking and spitting and Joe'd put a bit of cardboard up with his eyes poking over the top.'

Joe wasn't without his own little studio eccentricities. He still played unplugged guitar and stamped his foot so loudly during vocal takes that the others, not wishing to spoil the take, slipped a square of carpet foam under his foot. He always wore the towel and gaffer tape Strum-guard on his forearm, but the force of his strumming also took its toll on his battered fingers. Keith Richards has a similar condition, to the extent that his fingers have developed clubbed tips, which he calls his 'hammerheads'.

The *London Calling* 25th anniversary reissue comes with a DVD by Don Letts about the making of the album. There's some brilliant footage of Guy in full chair-demolishing action.

'Now you can actually see it!' enthuses Mick. 'There's a film of it now. There's extras of us in the studio. Johnny, Baker and Paul shot it. There's one bit . . . the only bit I remember of the whole filming is, do you remember *The Golden Shot*? [A crossbow-centric sixties game show]. Get the target, then going up a bit, left a bit, left a bit, up a bit – fire!'

It got to the point where Guy would engage Bill Price in grappling matches to win control of a fader. If Guy was perfect for extracting wired-up performances of already-written songs, he was less patient with the painstaking technicalities of mixing the results. The arguments with Bill would go past the shouting and pointing stage and often end up with the two grown men rolling around on the floor.

After a while, Guy's antics and the damage he caused, began to get in the way of the creative process. Sure, his behaviour had kick-started much of the studio action but sometimes I would turn up and Guy would be asleep. It seems that, once the basic songs had been stuck down, Guy's job was done and he faded into the background, or simply passed out. The overdubbing and mixing process fell to Mick and Bill, with the rest of the band in attendance to make suggestions or add necessary parts.

During the *London Calling* sessions, Epic finally relented and released *The Clash* in the US. The label had originally insisted that the album was 'too raw', but import sales of over 100,000 and the way in which The Clash were taking off in the US persuaded them to rethink. The American version leaves off 'Deny', '48 Hours, 'Cheat' and 'Protex Blue', in favour of 'Complete Control', 'Clash City Rockers' and 'White Man In Hammersmith Palais'. There was also a free seven-inch containing 'Groovy Times' and 'Gates Of The West'. They also released 'I Fought The Law' as a single but, with no promotion, it bombed.

Talking to *Uncut* more than twenty years later, Joe observed, 'It was a relief to see it go out 'cos they didn't want to release it in the first place. It makes a good collection. If you've never heard of the group before, it's kind of a good bunch of tunes really . . . We felt that we had our say on the tunes and we got sick of arguing with them.'

The Clash were gathering popular momentum in the States, which was enough to prod Epic into setting up a second US tour in early September. Still hard at work on *London Calling*, the group literally finished the last song and got on the plane. This left the mixing to Bill, with Guy 'overseeing' – sometimes from a position standing on the mixing desk with his hands around Bill's throat.

This tour was dubbed The Clash Take The Fifth – after the Fifth Amendment of the American constitution, which grants citizens the right to remain silent in the face of incrimination. The band liked the anti-establishment sound of the phrase, which they had grown up hearing in gangster movies. It was also in honour of the group gaining a fifth musician in the form of keyboard-player Mickey Gallagher, one of Ian Dury's Blockheads.

Mickey had been recommended by Kosmo, initially to add keyboards to *London Calling*, and subsequently became part of the band's live set up. 'I got sent a copy of

'You grow up and you calm down' – *The Clash in serious mode ahead of their US tour.*

Give 'Em Enough Rope, had a listen, and thought; "My God – what do they want me to do?"' This time around, The Clash took a bigger entourage to America – this included Joe, Paul and Topper's girlfriends, Johnny, Baker, DJ Barry Myers and the Blackhill crew of King, Jenner and Vinyl. They also took their four-man sound and lighting crew. Ray Lowry came along to draw tour images, which would appear in *NME*. Pennie Smith was there in her capacity as Clash photographer. As well as taking snaps for *NME* it was hoped that she would snap an image that would serve as a sleeve for the new album.

The tour was a near sell-out success, but did not run totally smoothly. This was mainly down to the large entourage and the constant struggle to get enough money to keep the whole show on the road. One night in Chicago, *Sounds* journalist Pete Silverton had to book the entire party into a hotel for three nights on his credit card.

Live, The Clash were still opening up with the two-fingered barrage of 'I'm So Bored With The USA', although later in the tour they started kicking off the set with the nightclub vamp of 'Jimmy Jazz' – which must have been very confusing for the young Stateside punks. The Clash insisted on serving the notoriously unadventurous US crowds with a welter of new material. It was a slightly awkward situation because the group didn't like to see their latest songs get a lukewarm response, but weren't so keen on providing an appropriate soundtrack for the frequent eruptions of 1977-style mayhem.

This, along with the constant cash hassles, led to a lot of on-the-road pressure. Joe blew up at *Creem*'s soon-to-be-editor Dave Di Martino before a gig because he was smoking throughout the interview. Five years later I became *Creem*'s UK correspondent and got to know the genial Dave quite well. Aware of my involvement with The Clash, he told me how Joe had become progressively more aggressive during the interview and then just upped and left.

On another night at St Paul, Minnesota, with the sound going awry, Joe's guitar cut out. He threw it aside and carried on singing. When the crowd applauded he berated them with, 'It's no good. It's a pile of shit. You gotta say, "Fuck off, you limeys." Give it some stick, you cunts.' The next day, the *Minneapolis Star* reported Joe's forthright honesty as 'punk rock offensiveness.'

During the late seventies, *NME* devoted many pages to covering Clash tours and interviewing Joe. For the band's second US jaunt, eager cub reporter Paul Morley – now a TV pundit – was sent along to cover the tour. He succeeded in catching Joe at the right moments between gigs and persuaded him to open up, on subjects like the black support acts, who this time included Sam and Dave, Bo Diddley and Screamin' Jay Hawkins – who performed his hit, 'I Put A Spell On You', from inside a coffin.

'Never mind The Clash, what about where the music came from? For every satin-suited, platform-soled, macho-strutting guitarist sniffing coke, there's like 50 or 60 black men starving in the same town who invented the music with their own sweat, and this guy is ripping it off and posing away. It's shit!'

Paul asked Joe if he'd lost anything during his time with The Clash. 'I've certainly lost my youth. I'm 27 . . . You have to say goodbye to some stuff, torturing your body with all kinds of stuff. You can't do that, once you're past 25 it leaves a mark, scarred face and all that.

'Actually, it's a great relief for me to be 27 in a way, 'cos I think the worst time of my life was when I was 24, 'cos I used to lie about my age. . . and then I thought, "Fucking hell, I feel great!" . . . 'cos I'm older than this lot, I've got a little bit extra to add.'

The show at New York's Palladium was the biggie. 'Strummer seemed possessed, bent on making the crowd understand something, trying to break through every way he could – screaming, whistling, going into the front rows, scaling the amps – and finally, on the encore, he found his moment. Simonon and Headon began an echoed dub vamp, with only a blue spotlight shining up from behind and below the drum platform,' reported *NME* stringer Van Gosse. 'Strummer waited and then came out, grinning, from backstage, holding aloft a torch . . . He made his way over to the mic, gaunt and fevered like some Hamlet among the graves, and quietly began to sing one of the new ones . . . "A lot of people gonna get it" . . .'

This 'new one' was 'Armagideon Time', a cover version of reggae heavyweight Willie Williams' recent hit. The song was based on 'Real Rock', an instrumental originally recorded by Sound Dimension at Jamaica's legendary Studio One in 1968. It also featured elements of Horace Andy's 'Jah Give'. Williams' vocal cut boosted the popularity of the rhythm to the extent that it has now been 'versioned' over 250 times by different artists. The Clash had started jamming the rhythm at soundchecks, and as they built upon Williams' words of apocalyptic dread, quickly realised that they stumbled on another classic. The cut would later appear on the B-side of the 'London Calling' single.

The Palladium gig would climax with Paul smashing his bass onto the stage in frustration – inadvertently providing Pennie Smith with one of the classic rock 'n' roll images of all time. 'The frustrating thing was the sound wasn't particularly good and the audience weren't allowed to stand up and dance,' Paul told *Uncut*. 'When you're annoyed you tend to smash things. Well I do . . . things that you love or whatever. So I did regret it because, after breaking the bass, I had to play the spare one, which was a lot lighter and didn't have the guts of that one.'

That night, Pennie had broken her usual habit of standing on Mick's side of the stage and relocated to Paul's. Talking to *Clash* magazine, she recalled how, 'he looked really, really pissed off and continued to look worse and worse and worse. Then I saw his bass in a really peculiar angle . . . And that was it. I just clicked.'

Afterwards on the tour bus, the group were looking through Pennie's photos for a possible *London Calling* cover. When the shot of Paul came up, Joe said, 'That's great! That's gonna be it!' Pennie was against it because it was out of focus, so the pair started to argue. Pennie says that the argument continued all the way back to the hotel. 'And he stuck his bottom lip out, so I said, "Sod it, it's your album. You do it then" – and I was completely wrong!'

'When I think of The Clash, I think of Paul Simonon slamming the bass,' Joe told Charles Shaar Murray in 1999. 'When all's said and done about the songs and the lyrics, I always think of Paul Simonon smashing that thing around, and that says it all: I'd like to think The Clash were revolutionaries but we loved a bit of posing as well.'

Pennie ultimately published many of the pictures from the tour in her *The Clash: Before And After* photo book. This captures the essence of The Clash and the group's own captions perfectly illustrate their sense of humour. For her classic cover shot Joe wrote, 'Paul don't like RotoSound,' referring to the make of bass string. Mick describes what was going on at the same time stage right, where he rescued a female stage invader from a bouncer, 'and whisked her to safety – leaving the stage as the kit exploded into the orchestra pit. This all happened within the space of three minutes. The whole thing felt like a scene from a movie.'

Back home, *NME* was publishing Ray Lowry's illustrated dispatches from the front. In one he wrote, 'The Clash are looking more than ever like the bastard offspring of Eddie Cochran out of Gene Vincent and a Harley Davidson. Dumbfounding to see the most intelligent, positive rock and roll on earth at the present time, being presented nightly by a band who look like the wild ones who haunted the troubled skies of the fifties. America is being reminded of how rock and roll looks, as well as how it's never sounded before.'

The report also carried Ray's own adaptation of the cover of Elvis Presley's first album – substituting The King's name with 'The Clash'. This design would ultimately form the basis of the *London Calling* sleeve, with the distinctive green and pink lettering framing Paul's moment of bass-smashing cartharsis. 'The sleeve has dogged me ever since, with most informed observers understanding that it was intended as a genuine homage to the original, unknown, inspired genius who created Elvis Presley's first rock 'n' roll record and that it was not a calculated rip-off,' explained Ray when he was interviewed for Storm Thorgeson and Aubrey Powell's

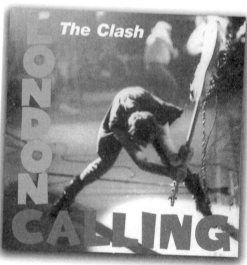

Pennie Smith's classic shot of Paul's moment of rock 'n' roll catharsis provided the perfect image for Ray Lowry's Elvis-inspired sleeve design for London Calling *.*

book, *100 Best Album Covers*. Throughout the tour, Ray was drawing the band every night, and many of his creations appeared in Johnny Green's *A Riot of Their Own*.

The Clash made it into *US Revolutionary Worker* magazine, who said, 'What I saw in this band was a concentration of all the pain and outrage this system has lodged in my gut.' More mainstream media attention came from US TV show *20/20*, who asked Joe what punks had in common. 'Short hair,' was the tart reply.

During the US tour The Clash, particularly Joe and Johnny Green, sparked up a strong friendship with Texas dynamo Joe Ely, who supported on some of the dates. Johnny was a big country buff and turned The Clash onto the music, including Ely's material.

Thanks to The Clash, I picked up his eponymous 1978 debut, and the following year's *Honky Tonk Masquerade*. We all checked out his May 1979 gig at London's Venue. Maybe it was the fact that Ely was injecting good old country music with a young man's swagger and punk-like soul, but this wayward, troublesome American troubadour was right up Joe's street.

'Joe Strummer came up to me after the gig and asked where he could get a shirt like mine,' Ely explained during an interview I did for *Zigzag*. 'They were the first words he said to me.' The two parties renewed acquaintances at the Monterey Festival and the relationship was cemented through a series of support slots.

'Yeah, Joe Ely came from me!' Johnny told me. 'I was already really into him and the others got into him too. We first met him at the Monterey Festival, and Joe and Joe started really getting on. You know all that Spanish stuff The Clash did, like "Spanish Bombs", *Sandinista!*, "Should I Stay or Should I Go", Joe Ely did all the translation work, and sang on some of 'em.'

Joe saw country music as an oasis of genuine feeling amid the desert of American AOR FM. 'I come over here and I switch on the radio and all I hear is the Eagles and Steely Dan . . . so I turn it to a country and western station.' At gigs where both bands shared the same bill Ely would join The Clash for encores of his own 'Fingernails' and their 'White Riot'.

The camaraderie of the two outfits was a strong pointer to the wider musical horizons that were already attracting The Clash. Few other bands would have considered presenting a bunch of Texan honky-tonkers whacking out swing, lovelorn country ballads and deep-fried rock 'n' roll to hard-core American spikeheads who had come along for a White Riot. Ely was a likeminded soul intent on smashing barriers – in return, he fixed it for The Clash to support him at a tiny redneck club in Lubbock, Texas – birthplace of himself, Buddy Holly and Stones sax-man Bobby Keys.

Strummer and the boys could not fail to have been smitten by Ely's stories, like the time Elvis played Lubbock and signed a girl's panties, annoying her boyfriend so much he stuck a rag in the gas tank of Presley's pink Cadillac and torched it. After The Clash played there, the pissed-up party moved on to Buddy Holly's grave and held a small celebration in honour of their rock 'n' roll forebear. As the reverential festivities wound down, the band laid plectrums on his grave.

A worrying taste of things to come occurred later that night when Topper overdosed on smack and had to be walked back to consciousness. His girlfriend Dee was heavily into heroin already. 'I started taking it around then because she was on it,' says Topper. 'But it didn't get to be a problem until the following year.'

Despite Topper's near-OD, nights like this provided welcome light relief from the drudgery of travelling, the financial and technical problems and everything that comes as unwanted baggage on lengthy tours. Mick seemed to suffer the most. The other three had their girlfriends with them, but he was alone, aside from an old mate from art college called Rory Johnson, who came along for part of the tour as a kind of personal roadie.

'The Clash is everything to me,' he'd confessed to Paul Morley. 'I'm under the impression that I have given everything else up for it. I'm under the impression that I have lost everything: home, personal life, everything. So my dilemma is, in a way, that I resent The Clash.'

Mick was referring to moving out of his flat back to his nan's after losing many of his possessions in a burglary, and also splitting with Viv. His unhappiness would come pouring out in a Motown-influenced song he'd write on his return called 'Train In Vain'.

By the end of the tour, Johnny Green was increasingly seeking solace in the traditional road diet of booze and drugs. On 13 October in San Francsico, The Clash encountered Bill Graham, the powerful promoter who they'd irked by playing a benefit for a rival organisation on the previous tour. Backstage at the Kezer Pavilion, Graham took some verbal shots at the band, so Johnny laid into him, before being wrestled away by bouncers.

By the penultimate gig in Seattle on 15 October, Johnny was in no fit state to work the stage. Barry Myers offered to stand in. 'I said to Joe, "I don't mind stand-

Two Joes Clash – Strummer meets Ely backstage at the Monterey Tribal Stomp festival, September 1979.

ing in for Johnny but I'm really feeling fucked. Please don't throw your guitar at me." You know how he'd just sling the Tele through the air and Johnny would catch it? So what did he do? He chucked it right at me. I was all fingers and thumbs but I did manage to grab it . . . Joe was a bugger like that.'

The US jaunt finally wound up on 16 October in Vancouver with another restrained crowd and a showdown with the US crew over payment. But, despite the hardships and frayed nerves, the tour had severely boosted The Clash's profile in the US, as well as providing band and crew with some top memories.

Back from America, finishing touches were put onto the album at Wessex. From time to time, I'd pop in to see how things were progressing. Apart from Joe and Mick, the rest of the group had basically done their bits. Joe was a happy man as what had started life as a stream of manic activity became honed into what he felt would be a landmark record. I would often hear him booming out of the speakers unaccompanied. He sounded so relaxed compared to the previous two albums: shouting, whispering, singing and howling some of his best lyrics to date.

The Strummer-Jones songwriting partnership hit a glorious creative zenith, as the pair wrote in the same room, trading ideas, while the whole band were obviously firing on all cylinders. Later, Topper looked back on these sessions as the point when he found his feet in the band. 'On *London Calling* I was a member of the band. I *felt* like a member of the band. When I joined I had to play the first album, which I wasn't on. By *London Calling* I was an integral part of the band. That's when it peaked.'

155

The secret of this successful *gestalt* was the unity that existed from the start of the Vanilla rehearsals and continued through to Wessex. Even the US tour hadn't taken away the momentum. This might have been totally opposite to the building block process used by Sandy Pearlman, but as Topper explained, 'It wasn't a decision to go against anything we'd done before. We just progressed and took it on because we were able to. It's what happened when we started playing together as a proper band. It was the four of us playing together, really loving what we were doing.'

One afternoon in November, I rang Mick to see how the album was going. He said they might have it finished that night, and invited me over. I duly made my way up to London for teatime. It would be over twelve hours before I finally escaped.

There was a full squad in attendance – the band, a pissed-up Guy, Bill, Johnny, Robin, Baker, Kosmo and others. Bill and Mick were undertaking the delicate task of sequencing the tracks and determining the final mixes and running order. At the last moment Mick had laid down his new 'Train In Vain'. Originally it was intended to use the song on a giveaway flexi-disc for *NME*, but that night it was decided that they would keep it for the album.

I'd gone along expecting a mixing session, but walked in and Mick was in the vocal booth singing passionately over a contagious funky guitar groove: 'Stand by me, or not at all.' He'd only written 'Train In Vain' the day before, then recorded the backing track with the band in the evening and was now putting on the vocals. Later on, he mixed it with Bill. The track was so last minute it was too late to list it on the album sleeve, but it was sneaked onto the end of side four with the title scratched in the run-out groove. Good job too – it went on to become the group's first Top Forty hit in America.

We were all back the following night for the sequencing and final playback. While final touches were put on the mix and running order, we killed time before the big moment. I remembered that the last time I'd been present at something like this was in 1973 when Mott The Hoople were doing the same thing to their *Mott* album at AIR Studios – with Bill at the controls on that occasion, too.

Waiting around during mixes involved those time-honoured Clash studio pursuits of drinking, getting stoned, playing endless games of 'Space Invaders' and making animal noises. It was a dementedly celebratory evening, definitely one of the happiest nights I ever spent in the company of Joe, who said words to the effect that, with this album, he'd finally realised his lifelong rock 'n' roll dream.

Joe's high spirits became particularly evident when he led the others in wrapping me from head to foot in gaffer-tape, so I ended up looking like a black, shiny version of the Mummy. I was dumped helplessly on top of the pool table while Joe topped things off by positioning the cue ball in the centre of my trouser-seat ('Try and fart that one off, Needsy'). Finally, Topper's motorcycle helmet was placed on my head. Normally, I'd have expected this kind of tomfoolery from Paul, Robin and Johnny – the masters of the stitch-up. Why Joe would want to subject me to such indignities remains a mystery. It was probably the Guy Stevens influence, but he was asleep in the corner by now.

'That was an interesting way to hear the album,' sniggered Mick 25 years on. In retrospect it was, but also bloody uncomfortable. It was worth it though. Then, as the sun was coming up, it was time to hear *London Calling* for the first time all the way through. I didn't realise at the time that I was witnessing a piece of rock 'n' roll history – albeit in a highly unusual, not to mention very uncomfortable, position.

When I eventually got home, I was buzzed up and hand wrote a stop-press report for the Christmas *Zigzag*, which I was in the process of finishing. Obviously the feature – like 'Train In Vain' it was too last minute to list on the cover – came completely off the top of my head, as I'd hardly been in any position to take notes.

I wrote; 'Two hours ago The Clash finished their new album. There I was, trussed from head to foot in gaffer tape, sprawled on the pool table where I'd been dumped minutes before. A billiard ball was sellotaped in a very delicate place. Meanwhile, Mick Jones, Joe Strummer and Paul Simonon were all grinning and gloating. The word came that the tracks were sequenced and ready for their first continuous airing.

'It was five in the morning and we'd all been there for over twelve hours. All the 10p's had run out for Space Invaders, so food fights, water fights, toilet utensils in the tea and much pool passed the time until this – the crowning boredom-beater . . .

'The weeks of work were now that vinyl hour. So they carried me downstairs to Wessex Studio One, put a crash helmet on my head and rolled the tapes. Know what? By the time "Rudie Can't Fail" powered out of its ska-faced shell one side later I'd burst my bonds Hulk-style and the old legs could pump free. Free to join the other beat-soaked bodies smiling with pride.

'Background: *London Calling* took half the time to make twice the vinyl of *Give 'Em Enough Rope*. In the producer's chair, but more often on the floor, was Guy Stevens . . . He acted as a kind of manic catalyst to fire up the latent new energy surging through The Clash last summer. The mood in the making was up from the outset.

'*London Calling* is the most danceable Clash album yet. It shows them branching out into a wide variety of styles. If you hold them to their past you're strapping on a straitjacket – but you probably will. This album features a gamut of styles streamlined into a new Clash direction, which has been budding more and more since they exploded into the world. Vital, exciting elements from what's great – Clashified and concentrated into an optimistic, positive record. More instruments – keyboards, sax, brass on many tracks. Greater reggae assimilation, more dynamics and a severe injection of classic wild rock 'n' roll shivers, particularly on a great version of Vince Taylor and the Playboys' "Brand New Cadillac"'.

Since I wrote those words, the stature of *London Calling* has grown to that of one of the greatest albums ever made. This reached a peak in 2004 when the LP was reissued to coincide with its 25th anniversary.

Before the reissue, I'd done a Strummer and resolutely stuck to my battered original vinyl copy. The CD marks the first time I've heard *London Calling* in its entirety from beginning to end, like I did that night in the studio. Before then I'd only caught fragments; endless fiddling with backing tracks, manic Guy-detonated runthroughs, unaccompanied vocals and unmixed sonic walls. These had brought home the true extent of Mick's visions, as his subtly woven sonic layers interlocked.

I'd caught some finished mixes too, but it's only on hearing the nineteen tracks in a continuous sitting that the genius running rampant in the songs and sequencing hits home. For instance, with four sides of vinyl you had to stop and flip, therefore missing moments like the gorgeous segue between 'Rudi Can't Fail' and 'Spanish Bombs'.

In the interviews that have accompanied the reissue, the surviving members of The Clash have all remarked how the record hasn't dated. To my ears – now out of the crash helmet – many tracks sound *better* with age. Like the unearthly title track.

'London calling to the faraway towns/Now that war is declared, and battle come down.' One of the most memorable opening lines and one of The Clash's finest songs, with chilling lyrics belted out in one of Joe's most impassioned performances to date. 'I read about ten news reports in one day calling down all variety of plagues on us,' he told *Melody Maker* in 1988.

Tom Vague's notes, which accompany the reissue, say that the song is in the tradition of William Blake's late eighteenth century poem, 'London', where he writes of wandering 'through each dirty street, near where the dirty Thames does flow.'

'London Calling' is the most evocative piece to carry the Clash name. It can be held up as a late seventies answer to the Kinks' immortal 'Waterloo Sunset'. Joe wanted it mixed to sound like the foggy river, and it does. The liquid imagery enhances the feeling of impending apocalypse, which is also bolstered with Mick's effects and touches.

Halfway through, Joe lets fly with the cry of the wildebeest, which Robin and Johnny say was inspired by my 'Arooo!' at the end of the Vice Creems single. It wouldn't be the last time that this favourite Clash noise popped up in a song. 'That all came from you and Crocker,' says Johnny. 'Paul and Topper were always doing it. That Vice Creems record started it.'

After this monumental opening comes The Clash's raw version of Vince Taylor's 'Brand New Cadillac', which I described as, 'Stinging and soaked in sinister Gene Vincent intensity.' This is the sole survivor from the cover version warm-ups that Guy instigated at the start of the album sessions. The band didn't even know it was being recorded. It was definitely the most traditionalist thing that Joe had sung since the 101'ers but works through its sheer intensity.

The song originally appeared in 1959 and was one of the early UK rock 'n' roll outings to hit big, while Vince Taylor was one of the first British rock 'n' roll rebels. An odd twist is that when Taylor relocated to France, where he enjoyed stardom, he started believing he was Jesus Christ or an alien after one acid trip too many. Apart from inspiring David Essex's character in the film *Stardust*, David Bowie credits Taylor as a major influence on his Ziggy Stardust character.

'Jimmy Jazz' slinks straight into a Harlem nightclub, or it could be a West London blues dance in the fifties. Definitely Tom Waits territory here – with clinking glasses, lazy jazz beat and Joe scatting and howling a snatch of the Abyssinians' 'Satta Massa Gana'. The Baker whistles and the Irish Horns add to the atmosphere. The Clash had never struck out like this before, whooping and hollering the early hours away.

The previous two albums saw The Clash singing about what happened to them, people they knew and situations that cropped up in the news. On *London Calling* they broadened their scope to tell stories about mythical characters in the blues tradition.

A concrete example of this is Joe's lyrical extension of the legend of Stagger Lee. This myth has its origins in the tale of a late nineteenth century St Louis hustler who shot a man dead in an argument over a hat. Stagger Lee (also known as 'Stagolee', 'Stack O' Lee', or 'Stackalee') is one of the most enduring characters in black music, with the badman ballad 'Stagger Lee' being adapted from prison work songs through Robert Johnson's blues through to Lloyd Price's number one hit in 1959.

Under different guises, this persona has populated many blues songs, as well as jazz, folk, and even the macho rock of groups like Bad Company. In the 1960s Stagger Lee's folkloric status led to his being adopted as a symbol of the fight for black freedom. He pops up later on 'Wrong 'Em Boyo' and 'The Card Cheat', while 'Jimmy Jazz' seems to be another operator with the police on his back.

'Hateful' shifts the album back into top gear with Topper's barrelling Bo Diddley beat. Rhythm tracks like this confirmed that The Clash had a drummer who was up there with Charlie Watts when it came to controlled power. Topper gives the credit to Paul's rock-solid style for enabling him to apply such subtle manoeuvres. 'If it hadn't been for Paul I wouldn't have been able to do half the things I did on the drums.'

Mick's chorus is indicative of his own drug hell, as he belts out lyrics like, 'Oh, anything I want, He gives it to me/Anything I want, He gives it but not for free.' I can vouch for the fact that the band *were* free of hard drugs at the *London Calling* sessions. They could still write about it though. 'This year I lost some friends' can only be a reference to Sid.

'Rudie Can't Fail' closed side one and was one of the tracks that really knocked me out of my gaffer tape. The celebratory counter vocals, scorching brass figures and tumbling bassline are pure ska-in-your-face. In *Zigzag*, I wrote that it should have been a single – 'As on many tracks The Clash steam through changes with reckless abandon, sharp as a needle.' The song features a tricky array of rhythmic twists but, as ever, Topper steers the beat home effortlessly.

'Rudie' is a contemporary updating of the Stagger Lee mythos, transplanted to Kingston, Jamaica. The term 'Rude Boys' was coined in the early sixties for Kingston's bad boys, who had a thing about spaghetti western movies. They achieved their own legendary status when immortalised in songs by such groups as the Wailers. Perhaps the ultimate rude boy was Jimmy Cliff's character in *The Harder They Come*, a major Clash favourite. Perry Henzell's hard-hitting 1972 film had been modelled on Jamaica's outlaw hero Ivan Rhygin, who went on a gun-blazing rampage in 1948, cementing another bad boy legend in the process.

The Clash weren't romanticising the rude boy, although he pops up in the 'chicken skin suit' reference. Joe was more inspired by the things going on around him and trying to give some advice to ersatz rude boy Ray Gange – 'Don't you be so crude and feckless.' The 'drinking brew for breakfast' line is mainly inspired by Robin Banks.

'Spanish Bombs' goes for a lighter feel with acoustic guitars and demonstrates the increasing subtlety of Mick's intricate backings – another result of his 'natural, organic process'. He's got the counter-point vocals down to a fine art now – all gossamer inflections and subtle dynamics.

Joe got the idea for 'Spanish Bombs' in an early hours cab back home from

Wessex, where the song was created. Here he constructs a modern protest song in the way singers like Woody Guthrie and Phil Ochs drew on world events to illustrate the various injustices of the day. Tipping his hat to the anti-fascist International Brigades of the Civil War, Joe sings about the Basque bombings of tourist hotels on the Costa Brava as well as the IRA's violent activity of the time. He manages to juxtapose Spanish holidays with the country's internal conflicts and also brings in Spanish playwright Federico Garcia Lorca. Mick was right to compare the song to 'a musical history lesson'.

The line 'Spanish bombs in Andalucia/The shooting sites in the days of '39' could have been inspired by Palmolive, who hailed from the region. Joe wrote enigmatically in *Armagideon Times*, 'This song was written in seat 18B of a Brannif Airlines DC10. The Spanish is Clash Spannish and it means "I love you and goodbye! I want you – but, oh my aching heart!"' Irrespective of such subtext, there's a hitherto-unheard tenderness in Joe's delivery on what amounts to another of the album's standouts.

'The Right Profile' came about after Guy lent Joe Patricia Bosworth's *Montgomery Clift: A Biography*. Johnny recalls Guy handing the book to Joe and saying, 'If you're going to write a song about somebody, write one about Montgomery Clift.' He was one of the earliest and most intense method actors, who appeared in films including *From Here to Eternity* and *The Misfits* with Clark Gable and Marilyn Monroe. Joe was intrigued enough by Clift's doomed life-behind-the-screen to write this suitably wired tribute.

'Nembutol numbs it all/But I prefer alcohol,' he intones, referring to the addictions Clift built up after his 1957 car crash. The title comes from the fact that the left side of the actor's face was paralysed and all his close-ups had to be shot from the right. By the end, Joe sounds like he's frothing at the mouth, at one point simply howling instead of finishing the chorus.

The backing was already in place by the time of *The Vanilla Tapes*, in the form of an instrumental called 'Uptoon', which, in turn, had previously been referred to as 'Canalside Walk'. 'Deep-fried piano and whacking brass provide suitable tough guy backing,' I scribbled in response to this swaggering sleaze-grind knees-up.

Another classic arrives as 'Lost In The Supermarket' eases its way in. Although sung by Mick, the words were written by Joe, after an experience in the supermarket in the block of flats where he lived. 'It was 5am and the song occurred to me as I stumbled around, dazed by the colours and the lights,' he told *Q* in 1999. In the *Clash on Broadway* booklet, Mick says, 'Joe wrote the lyric, but I always thought he had me in mind, that he was writing about me. What he must of thought it was like for me, living off Harrow Road.'

The words reek of loneliness and disaffected childhood: 'I heard the people who lived on the ceiling, scream and fight most scarily/Hearing that noise was my first ever feeling.' Joe's words are given an extra plaintive edge via Mick's fragile delivery and the impossibly sensitive backing. A pinnacle for the Strummer-Jones partnership, with all egos cast aside for the good of the song.

The mighty 'Clampdown' follows. In my *Zigzag* review I wrote, 'Heaviest track in literal sense with metallic piledriver beat emphasising the monotony of factory work. Ultra-brittle sheet metal guitars, another chorus classic and hilarious "Move On Up" quote at end.'

One of the album's strongest songs, this was an instant live corker where Joe would shout, 'Let me take you to the engine room,' and point at the unstoppable Topper. 'Clampdown' is anthemic, air-punching Clash Heaven with shrieking feedback and a wild, live feel. It was another one where I witnessed Guy in full throttle – leaping, screaming in Joe's face, gurgling and hurling whatever came to hand. Definitely worth the damage bill.

The lyrics confronted racism, the drudgery of labour and factory-line facelessness with lines like, 'No man born with a living soul, can be working for the clampdown' and 'It's the best years of your life they want to steal.'

In *Armagideon Times,* Paul had drawn a cartoon of a bloke squashed under a sixteen-ton weight. '16 Tons' would be the tag-line for the band's next UK and American tours – inspired by Tennessee Ernie Ford's 1956 hit of the same name. 'Clampdown' carried the same drudgery-of-labour message as this early rockabilly classic. Despite the track's weighty rhetoric, The Clash's humour was again evident as Joe swiped the 'What are we gonna do now?' opening line from Spike Milligan's insane *Q* series.

For 'The Guns Of Brixton', Paul's *Armagideon Times* cartoon showed a gun firing at the relevant London Underground sign. The track prodded me to scribble, 'The singer-songwriting debut of Paul Simonon and totally creditable. Perched on black, watery guitars and steady reggae beat. Builds in intensity on a scene of urban terror – police at the door, sus and guns.'

When Paul came up with words for the rhythm that began life at Vanilla as 'Paul's Tune', Joe insisted that he sing them. Live, the pair would swap instruments to perform it.

The original 1967 version of 'Wrong Em Boyo' by the Rulers was one of the 45s on the Rehearsals jukebox. Paul cited the Rulers as his favourite band in the first *Sniffin' Glue* interview. 27 years later he included their song in the selection he provided with Mick for *Mojo's Radio Clash* CD giveaway as a taster of *Revolution Rock* – an album he compiled for Trojan of artists that influenced The Clash. The Clash's version kicks off with a few bars of Lloyd Price's 'Stagger Lee', until Joe waves his arms – 'No, no, start all over again,' and they bomb into the mutant ska-Stax stomp and its steaming chorus. The mood is impossibly buoyant, thanks to Topper's springy groove and Mick's intricate backing vocal patterns.

'Death Or Glory' is the track that bears the closest similarity to The Clash's earlier output, and is another where Guy ran riot to plant an energy bomb beneath the band. 'This is considering the beat of time, which must come to everyone. Youth – juice – misuse – the truth means one day your account will be opened . . . Some people die young – Because that way you never see the debt sheet,' wrote Joe and Topper in *Armagideon Times*. It's a song about growing up and getting old. You start life as the young rebel and end up 'making payments on a sofa or a girl'. The song contains one of Joe's finest pieces of iconoclasm: 'But I believe in this – and it's been tested by research/That he who fucks nuns will later join the church.'

Another outbreak of moths and wildebeests pops up halfway through. It's a bit hazy but I seem to remember it was Joe, Robin, Johnny, me and a highly excitable Guy Stevens baarooo-ing at the top of our lungs. Obviously Guy approved of our bellowing and continued with gusto long after we'd stopped. Forget Joe's spittle-guard, we needed umbrellas!

'Koka Kola' starts like the 1970's comedy series *Are You Being Served?*, with a cash till and Joe's 'Elevator – going up!' before briskly setting out the group's punk-speed take on corporate America. At the time, the band had been reading C. P. Snow's novel, *The Corridors Of Power* – all big business, Whitehall politics and yuppie cocaine abuse. Joe's lyrics demonstrate this influence – 'Sure a packet is expensive, Mac/But you can use a Kredits Kard!' The song's Vanilla title was 'Koka Kola, Advertising And Cocaine'.

'The Card Cheat' gave me the biggest jolt from my position on the pool table. Mouth hanging open, I later wrote, 'Shocked and slayed me. The Clash meet Phil Spector! A miles-high wall of booming sound, pokey fanfare in middle and saxes like an ocean liner in orgasm. Pumps BIG and ambitious. Nearly called "King Of Hell".'

Joe and Mick's *Armagideon Times* description went, 'For those in peril on the sea. The waves were a gigantic 25 foot the night this tune was cut.' So is the sound, achieved by Mick recording everything twice when the track was conceived at Wessex. The Clash lay on the bottomless overdubs to create an epic home for lyrics revolving around a Western card game where the Grim Reaper deals the winning hand.

'Lover's Rock' ranks as one of the most lightweight songs the Clash ever record-ed, but then lover's rock was the most commercial form of reggae at the time. A Clash love song was quite rare and this skirts the romantic issue by dealing with sex and birth control, or as Joe liked to call it, 'The Chinese way of fucking.'

In *Zigzag,* I described 'Four Horsemen' as a 'Gutter-in-the-face hard rocker with Joe's Jerry Lee joanna and ouch hooks.' Although boasting lyrics such as 'Four horse-men and it's gonna be us,' Mick insisted that the song was 'Not to be taken as biog-raphical.' The group were poking fun at themselves and the mythology that had grown around them. By invoking the Four Horsemen of the Apocalypse, the band subverted this mythology by extending it to an intentionally ridiculous degree.

Without a pause, 'I'm Not Down' comes in as a statement of defiance from Mick, who is possibly referring to the break up of his relationship with Viv Albertine, being burgled, and his personal problems of the previous year. At the time, I misquoted the words – you try scribbling with your hands gaffer-taped to your sides! The strident descending riff – another mutation of the Kinks' 'Waterloo Sunset' – and smooth chord changes perfectly compliment the nature of the words, which are about taking the knocks and still standing afterwards. I know several people who've used this song to gee themselves up when feeling a bit low and it certainly beats the shit out of Elton's 'I'm Still Standing'.

'Revolution Rock' was a cover of the Danny Ray reggae standard, which the group had been playing at soundchecks during the previous year. The Clash's cut is lengthy, dubonic and tailor-made for live audience participation.

London Calling concludes with the late arrival of, 'Train In Vain'. In November 1979 I said, 'Sleeve says "Revolution Rock" is the last track, but on the Saturday Mick came in with a new song. They learnt it, laid it down and, by Monday night,

"Train In Vain" was finished . . . Glad they got it on 'cos it's great. Irresistible punchy groove with harmonica and heartfelt vocal from Mick.'

It might have been a last-minute addition but 'Train In Vain' is one of the strongest songs on the LP. Funky and loaded with enough attitude to appease the hardcore Clash lover, but melodic and groovy enough to subsequently dent US radio.

And with that the first complete playback of *London Calling* was over. Stunned is the only way I can sum up my initial reaction, but only when it was over did Joe remove the gaffer tape and crash helmet.

'So what'cha think?' said Joe, still cackling but now also glowing with pride as this had been the first time The Clash themselves had heard their new masterpiece from top to bottom.

'Load of bollocks,' I teased, then ran away and wrote my review.

Only now do I appreciate the magnitude of that night and the period of unique creativity that made *London Calling* a reality. I had no idea that I was witnessing a bit of history that would merit twenty-page magazine features, news stories and rave reviews a quarter of a century later. To The Clash, the album was a make or break effort, delivered under financial duress. But it ended up catching fire, created a whole legend of its own and hoisted the band to the top of the post-punk pile. As *Uncut's* Gavin Martin said, 'As remarkable now as it was 25 years ago.'

London Calling was ready to roll and, exposed to more considered inspection, still lived up to its initial impact. However, it would be some years before the album was recognised as The Clash's creative peak. Upon release, *London Calling* came in for much criticism from fans and press alike. Now the LP is regularly cited in 'Greatest Album Of All Time' listings, as with the January 2003 edition of *Q*, whose readers voted it the fourteenth Greatest Album Ever.

NME's Charles Shaar Murray gave the album its best review: '*London Calling* is the first of The Clash's albums that is truly equal in stature to their legend, yet for the most part it disposes of the more indigestible portions of that legend,' he wrote. 'Parts of it sound totally unlike anything they have ever recorded before, yet it is the most quintessentially Clash-like Clash record this far . . . *London Calling* makes up for all the bad rock 'n' roll played over the last decade.' In reference to Joe's expanding vocal range, Murray added that the album was, 'virtually Strummer's debut as a singer'.

Elsewhere, James Truman of *Melody Maker* reckoned 'The Clash have discovered America and, by the same process, themselves.' *Sounds* astutely gave the album to the relentlessly right-wing Garry Bushell, who shocked nobody by giving it two stars and whining that, 'Unable to go forward, they've clutched at straws, ending up ret-rogressing via Strummer's R&B past and Jones's Keith Richards fixation to the out-law imagery of the Stones and tired old rock clichés.'

Mick, who used to be such an avid *NME* reader and was most affected by the paper's earlier sniping, learned to shrug off the press as time went on. In 2004 he observed, 'One week's review is next week's chip paper. Overall, if you make an impression, it's never down to the reviews. It's down to the group.'

The album seemed to polarise Clash fans. Obviously the diehard 'real punks' hated

'London Calling' was The Clash's final single of the 1970s and saw them continue to move away from the sonic template of 1977 punk.

it as much as they had hated *Give 'Em Enough Rope*. Lovers of thought-provokingly rousing, emotional music were won over.

By 1979, many of the young punks from three years past had struck out in their own directions. John Lydon was out on his own with Public Image Limited, having left the floundering Sex Pistols in favour of exploring the furthest boundaries of what rock and punk were supposed to be about. The Jam delivered watered-down social conscience in a suit. There was rivalry, but Weller didn't have Joe's animal rage, charisma or knife-sharp lyrical surrealism. The Damned had splintered and were getting back together without Brian James. The Buzzcocks had refined their sound to a perfect pop celebration distinguished by Pete Shelley's teen angst visions. There were worthwhile stirrings underground, like The Slits and the Pop Group. Everything else around seemed to be either cod-punk, cod-metal, cod-pop or just rotten old cod.

The Clash now had post-punk rock 'n' roll reality sewn up. Levelled off from the amphetamine stampede of the first album, the band could now live and breathe, exhaling all the music that meant something to them in the process. Joe bridged the gap between punk figurehead and true rock 'n' roll star, without giving an inch or losing his edge.

'London Calling' b/w 'Armagideon Time' was released as a single on 7 December – the group's first release on the increasingly popular twelve-inch format. Despite The Clash maintaining their ban on playing or allowing their videos to be shown on *Top of the Pops*, the single reached Number Eleven in the UK chart. In his *Melody Maker* review, Ian Birch wrote, 'An irresistibly rolling gait, finely underplayed performances and sweet harmonies on the title words. The lyrics are still apocalyptic clarion calls, but now Joe sings them with a natural assurance and clarity that makes them much more forceful.'

It seems like every aspect of *London Calling* attained perfection through chaos. From its humble beginnings behind a garage, through the madness of Guy Stevens, to the magic moment of Paul's frustration-born bass demolition on the classic cover. Don Letts' video is so right as the group, now out of zippers and into the realms of street gang sharpness, blasted out by the rainy Thames.

Don Letts filmed the video on Battersea Pier, which had been erected for the

1951 Festival of London. Apart from PiL's debut single, it was his first major shoot, although he'd filmed a lot of performance footage.

'I was sort of learning as I went along, much in the spirit of punk rock,' he told *Uncut* in September 2004. While the group was set up on the pier, Don filmed from a boat. But he hadn't reckoned on the tide going out and had to wait for the right water level. The tides also ensured that the boat kept drifting off and the pier went up and down too. The combination of waiting for both conditions and the band to fall into position meant that night had fallen by the time they started filming. Then the heavens opened.

'Blinding stroke of luck!' says Don. 'Without the rain, I have to say, I don't know how good that video would have been . . . It was a textbook punk situation, turning your problems into assets.'

'That was an epic,' recalls Johnny Green, who had to oversee setting up the gear and getting the band to the same place at the same time. After getting to the location with The Baker in the morning to set up, he recalls that 'it was one thing after another and people were late. "Is Mick here? Is Topper here?" This went on for ten hours before they were ready. Then it started raining. But it turned out for the best. I said, "They can't play without a bottle of brandy," so I was in this little hut and drank nearly all of it.'

Once the shoot was over, Johnny famously turfed the hired equipment into the river. 'Only the hire stuff, not the band's,' he stresses. 'The monitor wedges floated off and we all cheered. We saluted them! If I'd have worked for U2 I'd have been sacked. The Clash thought it was hilarious.'

The album itself was released on 14 December. 'Only superstars and lunatics release albums before Christmas,' deadpanned Joe. It still climbed the album chart to Number Nine – but not before another battle with CBS. Having tasted defeat over CBS's pricing of the *Cost Of Living* EP, the band was keen to even the score.

With *London Calling*, The Clash put forward the idea of including a free single, as had been the case with the US release of *The Clash*. CBS agreed to that, and even the group's secondary request to make it a twelve-inch. By the time they found out the 'free single' boasted eight new tracks it was too late, and The Clash still managed to sneak on 'Train in Vain'. The band had managed to push through what amounted to a 65-minute double-album retailing at the current single album price of £5. 'I'd say it was our first real victory over CBS,' grinned Joe.

Struggling to repay their advance, the support they needed to keep their ever-expanding show on the road with low admission prices ensured that they owed CBS even more money. The Clash wanted the whole cake – a big, expensive show but with cheap tickets. As Tennessee Ernie Ford had sung in 1956, 'I load 16 tons and what do I get?/Another day older and deeper in debt.'

It did seem like The Clash were getting deeper in debt with every move they made, and that situation would get worse with the next album.

Debt or glory? The Clash would go for both.

CHAPTER TWELVE

ROCKERS GALORE

They teach you there's a boundary line to music.
But man, there's no boundary line to art. – Charlie Parker

To round off 1979, The Clash played a couple of secret Christmas gigs at London's Acklam Hall, below the Westway. The poster showed Mick sporting a red nose. The first show took place at five o'clock on Christmas Day to a sparse crowd, while the second was on Boxing Day. By then, word had got around and the place was rammed. Like an unwanted Christmas present, Jimmy Pursey turned up for the 'White Riot' encore, thus ensuring that his bonehead following was also much in evidence.

Vice Creems guitarist Colin Keinch phoned me up on Christmas Day evening. After the usual festive pleasantries I asked what he'd been up to, expecting the usual turkey 'n' TV reply. 'We've been to see the Clash,' he gloated. The lucky fucker went to both concerts and described them as 'very laid-back', and 'fuckin' brilliant!'

The gigs provided an opportunity for the band to test-drive a lot of the *London Calling* material, and they also unveiled a new number, the 'Bank Robbing Song'. Additionally, the two concerts acted as warm-ups for a joint Kampuchean benefit gig with Ian Dury and the Blockheads at Hammersmith Odeon on 27 December, where The Clash had been billed as 'mystery guests'.

The official *16 Tons* tour warm-up took place on 5 January at Friars, Aylesbury. By now, the place was a Clash stronghold, with 'London Calling' holding the Number One spot over Christmas on the jukebox chart in the Green Man pub next door – as had all their other singles. The chart had become so well known locally as a taste-barometer that I'd now started printing it every month in *Zigzag*, which must have made it look even more like a Clash fanzine.

The support was going to be Ian Dury and the Blockheads, plus . . . the Vice Creems!

Kosmo phoned me up a few days before the gig and asked what I was doing on Saturday. 'Nothing', I replied. He told me about the last-minute Clash gig. 'Wa-hey!' But then he told me that I'd be playing it too with the Vice Creems. I took a big gulp. This followed the group's policy of booking local bands to open up when they were on tour. There was just one problem – we still hadn't got a band together since recording 'Danger Love' with Mick. This didn't seem to bother Kosmo. 'You're playing, so better get one,' he replied.

In retrospect, this incident exemplifies the rapid rise of Kosmo Vinyl. Six months earlier he was tapping me up to get in with the band. Now, The Clash have spoken and Kosmo is their messenger. I had my orders.

I phoned Mick, who said, 'Yeah, seriously, do it. I already got you one band . . .'

Once Colin and me got over our initial panic, we roped in a bass player and drummer that we'd been jamming with, had two practice sessions in someone's garden shed, and managed to come up with about six songs. It could have been a total farce – and probably was! But the experience was once-in-a-lifetime stuff. It was just so weird to have Joe Strummer giving me a pep talk and handy hints on stagecraft.

I saw the considerate side of Joe that night – even if his arrival somewhat unnerved the rest of our band. They were sitting in the dressing room, running through a couple of cover versions on the guitars to get warmed up. Just as they were striking up 'Career Opportunities', Joe walked in. 'You're not fucking doing that,' he declared. You could feel the band's collective stools hit their pants. But, once assured it was only a bit of fun, he relaxed and told us to just go on there and 'whack it, boys.'

The gig went fine. I ended up singing Art Garfunkel's 'Bright Eyes' with a pair of Bay City Rollers knickers on my head while hopping about like a rabbit. Maybe this behaviour had something to do with the backstage presence of Mikey Dread, who would be supporting and mixing on the tour. He had his own personal rider – the most potent weed around, so the atmosphere was even sillier than usual. The Clash crew might have been offering encouragement, but they couldn't hold back from taking the piss. However, this was more than made up for when promoter David Stopps paid us with £30 and the band gave us a large bag of Jamaica's finest.

This was the sort of night you pinch yourself about later. Apart from us supporting The Clash and being the first group to play the 16 Tons tour, the next killer punch came when we caught the Blockheads performing at the peak of their powers. Finally, the knockout blow was The Clash playing the full *London Calling* set live for the first time. After tour DJ Barry Myers had spun Tennessee Ernie's '16 Tons', the band – augmented by Mickey Gallagher on keyboards – bowled on and hammered straight into 'Clash City Rockers' and an energised 'Brand New Cadillac'. They proceeded to tear through a lengthy set that covered about two-thirds of the new album, a smattering of its predecessor, the recent singles and only 'Police And Thieves' and 'Janie Jones' from the first.

The tour proper kicked off in Canterbury on 6 January, winding up with two nights at London's Electric Ballroom in Camden Town on 15-16 February. Support was originally due to be provided by reggae luminaries Toots and the Maytals, but that fell through. In came Michael Campbell, a Jamaican DJ and toaster, who was better known as Mikey Dread. He would have a huge influence on The Clash throughout their 1980 gigs and the recording of their fourth album.

Mikey emerged in 1976, when he started *Dread At The Controls* – his berserk radio show for Jamaica Broadcasting Corporation. Tapes filtered through to London – all mad exclamations, crazed jingles and sound effects like police sirens going off between severe roots music and prime dub plates. Producers like Lee Perry and King Tubby gave him exclusive mixes, which brought him to the attention of a larger audience. Mikey began making his own records under Tubby's wing, which came out on his own Dread At The Controls label. At one point, there would be a new release practically every week, all capturing the mood of his show. By the time Mikey's show stopped in 1979, he was legendary in the UK – especially with the dub-conscious Clash.

Mikey had recently released his seminal *African Anthem* album – a vinyl representation of his radio show. Some of the gigs saw a proper mix of dreads and punks in the crowd and Mikey's set would be well received. Then there'd be the inevitable occasions where the bonehead contingent couldn't handle it and hurled the predictable abuse. As Mikey recalled, 'There were a lot of times I been to places where skinheads and punks wanted to kick my butt, as a black man, and [The Clash] would warn me, 'Tomorrow don't go out alone, have one of us follow you." They start to wear their Doctor Marten boots, and they buy me a pair as well so they know we're on the warpath. Anybody come, we just mess them up.'

An evening's entertainment on the 16 Tons jaunt commenced with Mikey's solo spot, where a backing tape would crank out the dubs and he would chant and rap over the top. Highlight of the set was 'Rockers Delight', where he would be joined by a posse from the touring party – which seemed to expand as the gigs went by. As Mikey toasted over the contagious beat, these figures would emerge from the wings, skanking and swaying around the stage behind Mikey. The cast, which was variously billed as 'The Mystery Skankers', or 'The Magnificent Seven', included Joe, Johnny, Robin, Jock, Kosmo, Mick and a skinhead called Don who the group had bailed out of jail in Dundee. They'd take the stage sporting trilby hats, long coats, shades and red bandanas wrapped around their faces. Usually, nobody had a clue who those masked men were.

After the Stafford Leisure Centre gig I got roped in too, as Joe was going down with flu. So I borrowed his hat, coat and red bandana and skanked about with the others for the next few nights. I've still got the bandana hanging on my wall.

In early February The Clash took two days off from gigging to book into Manchester's Pluto Studios with Mikey Dread and record 'The Bank Robbing Song', which was now called 'Bankrobber'. This was planned to be the first in a series of what Joe liked to call 'The Clash Singles Bonanza', where the group would slam out a new 45 every month to keep the pot boiling.

Joe's original track followed his ska influences, which had also underpinned such recent outings as 'Wrong 'Em Boyo' and 'Rudie Can't Fail'. But Mikey felt the song, which featured a poignant vocal melody, should be planted against a slow, heavy dub backdrop. Some studio experimentation led to two versions being produced for the twelve-inch release – 'Robber Dub' and Mikey's 'Rockers Galore . . . UK Tour'.

I managed to catch around a dozen dates, which included an extended stint when I took the train up to Stafford Bingley Hall with the intention of seeing one gig, but didn't get home for another week. My partners-in-crime were Messrs Banks and Jock Scott.

Bingley Hall, where Barry Myers and me had seen Bob Marley a year earlier, was a bit too big for that essential Clash atmosphere. I remember it more for what went on backstage. By now, Joe had developed quite a quiff, while Paul going for the James Dean look. The touring party continually took the piss out of my hair as I had a Keef-style that was not unlike Mick's before he'd had his cut. I was under pressure to either cut if off or slick it back, particularly from Joe, who seemed to take a particular interest in my appearance. 'Needsy, you look like Rod Stewart!' he decided. Sitting in the dressing room, Joe led a barrage of 'go on!'-style taunts as I was hectored into reluctant submission.

Finally, I had no choice. Joe, Kosmo and Jock sat me in front of the mirror and smeared my barnet with Black & White hair gunk. I was then given a mean quiff, which made me look like one of Gene Vincent's backing group. And still they laughed. Joe, my self-appointed style guru, was cracking up every time he clapped eyes on me. What with my trilby, leather jacket, red neckerchief and new quiff, I was now firmly in Clash uniform circa 1980. They even gave me one of their red and black shirts, which I was most upset to have stolen by an ex-girlfriend years later.

In the larger venues I could appreciate that the show had got bigger than ever, with the flag backdrop, banks of lights and a longer set. Compared to the raw, amphetamine-driven assault of the early gigs, the group had now assimilated plenty of stagecraft into their live antics. Paul was still the moody, straddle-legged bassman, but imbued with a James Dean-style cool. He took centre-stage for his 'Guns Of Brixton', swapping guitars with Joe so that he could concentrate on his vocals. Joe attacked the bass like he did his battered Telecaster. Mick strutted, galloped and leapt like a mountain goat, while Topper had honed his raw attack and had no qualms about letting his funk apprenticeship shine through.

Probably the biggest change was in Joe. This tour saw the full-emergence of what would constitute the Strummer live legend. His live announcements – still surreal as ever – were now delivered in the style of a US soul revue: 'All aboard the soul train,' before 'Train In Vain'.

He was still as galvanised and committed as ever, but his stance now encompassed and exaggerated Elvis's twitching limbs, the intensity of Gene Vincent and the simmering aggression of Jerry Lee Lewis. Likewise, Joe's guttural extortions and stop-start signalling echoed James Brown, while the trance-like states he'd work himself into during songs recalled the eyes-closed spiritual charisma of Bob Marley. But whoever had rubbed off on Joe's stage persona over the years, he was now the most riveting frontman in the UK. He hadn't traded in any of his commitment for hollow rock star poses, just learned how to channel his passion with a drama that bounced off his amazing natural charisma. The fact he was riding the coolest live onslaught in the country helped.

The extended sets meant that, on the whole, the band didn't cane it so much offstage. Joe had to treat his throat like a delicate object because his vocal style stretched it so much. As well as contracting a sore throat and flu for a few days, toothache remained a perennial problem. But, irrespective of his physical state, stick Joe on a stage and it was like he was plugged into the mains.

Because of his experience with hepatitis, Joe was even more impatient with the gobbers on this jaunt. At the Birmingham Top Rank gig, the rain of gob was so heavy that the band stopped the show and brought a giant fan onto the stage. Joe launched into an anti-gobbing rant and they played a couple of songs from behind the fan. He got so annoyed with the crowd at Coventry Tiffanys that – after announcing, 'I've taken a thousand gobs and I'm not going to take no more' – Joe leapt into the throng and clobbered a gobber with his Telecaster.

The tour gave The Clash their biggest prime time TV spot to date, when they appeared on BBC's teatime news show *Nationwide*. Joe was filmed drinking his honey and lemon and strolling from the tour bus with a Martin Luther King speech ringing out from his ghetto blaster. He's also seen with roadie Terry McQuade letting fans in through the dressing room door. At the Brighton gig Pete Townshend went on for the encore. Back then, a Townshend cameo meant you were really up there with the big boys.

The Clash and entourage travelled the country in two customised mini-buses. One was fairly state-of-the-art, with blacked-out windows, padded aircraft-style seats and a hefty sound system. The other one was more Spartan, and was intended to transport those still hell-bent on continuing the revelry.

While group members who wanted to catch up on their rest travelled in the luxury vehicle, Johnny Green would be driving a variety of reprobates in the loony-bus – although it wasn't uncommon to find the odd band member coming along to check out the debauchery.

Throughout the week I spent up North, I tended to end up in the rabble-van with Johnny, Robin, Jock, and usually Topper. Undaunted by his recent brush with Babylon, Topper brought along an air pistol – which he'd fire out of the window at will. 'It's a miracle that we didn't kill anyone,' he says.

One memorable journey saw Robin attempting to throw one of the seats out of the window on the motorway. On another he set the curtains on fire, which flapped flaming out of the window, giving the bus the appearance of a mobile Viking funeral. By the end of my stint, that poor vehicle looked like a travelling wreck, covered in Clash graffiti.

The combination of the group's considerate on-the-road attitude and the auto-destruct mechanisms being activated by some of the party did occasionally prove volatile enough to backfire. There were those occasions when the band would help punters who couldn't get into the gigs to gain admittance – either by putting them on the guest list or, sometimes, getting them in through backstage doors or dressing room windows. That was group policy though. But it was the hotels that often bore the brunt of our antics. Sometimes it was like a street gang had holed up within the ranks of the Clash entourage. This could lead to sticky situations with the management.

As we were using the centrally located Leeds Dragonara Hotel as a base for four or five days, word got around that The Clash were in residence. Apart from the huge numbers gathering in the hotel bar afterwards, the accompanying misbehaviour escalated. Sandwich hurling was now Paul's major offstage hobby so, as had been the case on previous tours, food fights were rife.

The night after a particularly storming gig at Leeds University, Joe took the cult of the sandwich to a new level. As usual, we'd set about lobbing cheese sandwiches at each other. Joe, maybe sensitive to the annoyance this could understandably cause the other guests and hotel staff, tried to calm the mayhem by suggesting that the sandwich was too good a thing to waste. 'You should appreciate that sandwich,' he declared. Of course, this got mutated – first into love, then worship. Before long Joe was acting as a kind of high priest, presiding over a weird ritual which deified the humble sandwich.

Onlookers were treated to the bizarre sight of assorted Clashers, road crew and various others dancing in a circle around a tray of refreshments chanting, 'Sandwich! Sandwich! All hail the sandwich!' Grown men were dropping to their knees, arms raised in supplication, weeping and moaning like a gospel service with Joe the Reverend Sandwich leading the ceremony, until the knife went in and the sandwich was righteously speared. Surrounding fans and hotel guests looked on in bemusement.

Such rowdiness eventually resulted in the bar being closed and activity adjourning to the guestrooms. Me and Robin had a room, in which we were also harbouring Jock and Don. As we had managed to lose our room key during the course of the evening, Robin gained entry to by kicking in the door. At five o'clock in the morning. Unfortunately, it wasn't our room. The naked businessman, who we had woken up, was not amused and dialled the desk. He was immediately relocated. We had to hide in a cupboard before sneaking back out into the now doorless room, and passing out. I came to lying on the displaced door with a maid towering over me.

The following morning, The Clash party was nearly thrown out of the hotel. This was avoided when it was arranged that Robin, Jock, Don and me would find alternative lodgings. We were banned from the hotel and left to make our own arrangements. But what goes around comes around, and we ended up crashing around some fans' places. I did feel a bit guilty though. The band and their crew laughed about the incident, but the booking agency and band management were not amused as this simply added to the tour bill.

In retrospect, I can see how silly and irresponsible it was, but this was a bunch of mates in their twenties with free booze at their disposal having the time of their lives. Also, it has to be taken into account that this sort of behaviour has always accompanied rock 'n' roll on the road, often to far greater extremes. The Clash weren't besieged by hordes of female groupies, but there were more than enough young punks willing to hang out and party.

By this tour, The Clash had split into two factions as far as post-show shenanigans went. Topper and sometimes Paul were main instigators, while Joe and Mick were more laid back and, while amused by the stupidity, couldn't help but worry about the financial hole the band were sinking into. 'No wonder we're in debt,' said Mick, ruefully. After the Night Of The Sandwich, the post-show carnage was cooled down. Maybe it had cleared the air, but I noticed more sitting about talking bollocks than furniture re-arranging after that.

'That's why I got shit,' says Topper. 'I was always hanging out with Robin, Johnny and you and when anything got trashed it was like, "Topper was there so it's a band expense." If I'd been in my room like Mick and Joe it would have saved a lot of money!'

Joe had also started to change personality-wise. Before, especially when he was ill, he had tended to keep himself to himself, sometimes verging on the unapproachable. He could be quite gruff, but that was usually to mates. I never saw him less than accommodating and friendly to the fans, unless there was a really good reason. On this tour he'd be talking to them before and after soundchecks and always after the gigs. Not just signing photos either. He'd make the kids feel like he was genuinely interested in them and what they did. If they were stuck to get home they

Jones – Strummer – Simonon; the classic Clash front line.

could crash in his hotel room, and he was always handing out beers from the dressing room. Sometimes the band would simply open the back doors and let ticketless punters in. Privately however, he just seemed more chilled out and amenable. He stayed in his room a lot, saving himself for the night's performance.

When I visited Joe's room, he'd be sitting there with a spliff and his ghetto blaster, playing reggae and reading his war novels. For some reason, the gaffer taping episode and my stunning new hairstyle seemed to have made him more open and friendly. One time he admitted that he had a 'built-in safety net' concerning journalists but also said that he didn't regard me as one anyway – which was good. I never made notes (but wish I had now!).

Joe loved to talk about music, often getting passionate about some record he'd just discovered. His general vibe was that, now The Clash had broken out of punk's restrictions, he could explore and participate in the wonderful spectrum of music without a straitjacket. Joe only got frustrated when he wasn't permitted to graduate from the Class of '76 and, as time went on, I noticed how he never stopped trying to find new sounds to get excited about. 'I never go back, I move forward,' he said.

It wasn't all sandwich rituals and stoned guffaws. After the Sheffield gig on 27 January, Joe and Mick had a disagreement in the dressing room, which ended up with Joe smacking Mick in the mouth. Hard. The popular story is that it was because Mick refused to play 'White Riot' as an encore, as normal, and then threw his drink in Joe's face.

'It wasn't really about that,' says Mick now. 'I said some unconscionable things to Joe about the encores. Not about the choice of track, but about the stage in general. He thought I slooshed him with a drink, which I didn't, and we had . . . a bit of a scuffle, bit of a fight, and then went back on.

'Sometimes I'd think we'd just got the crowd to quieten down, but it'd be, "Well, we got one more number yet – 'White Riot'," and the place would erupt again. It was like, "What are you doing?", you know. I don't know if we wanted to push it that far. Sometimes, there were so many hairy situations.'

The Clash did go back on and play 'White Riot', although Mick, who now had a 'Rockers Delight' style bandana covering his bashed face, made his point by walking off halfway through. They didn't play 'White Riot' again until the last night of the tour. The fight might not have been specifically about that, but Mick still didn't like playing it any more.

'"White Riot" had become a running sore at that point,' says Johnny Green. 'It was a fair argument. They were progressing so fast. The records show it. Mick did have a point there.'

This incident may have been caused by a build-up of tension on Joe's part as his relationship with Mick was up and down. Mick wasn't very happy on the road at this time, and spent a lot of time alone in his room. 'Mick lived a separate existence to the rest of the band,' says Johnny. 'There's that photo in Pennie's book where he's wearing his hat and coat eating upstairs in a deserted room. That was indicative of the situation.

'People always saw Joe as this tough, hard man but I would say there were many instances when he bottled it within the band's dynamics. He was a very accommodating man, a diplomat, a listener. Mick never bottled it. He was tough as old boots. He was always uncompromising and always stood by his particular principles. He stood his ground. That sometimes meant he was on his own.'

Joe made sure he had Gaby with him all the time. 'Never underestimate the power of a woman,' declared Johnny. 'Naturally you're going to be isolated if you take your girlfriend on tour. Mick never had a woman with him on tour, except one time in 1978. The first and last time.

'That point has never been brought up. If you've got a girl on the road with you it does take away some of your energy from the band. You're going to spend more time in your room. They want attention, and they can't get that at the gig. Joe was a very attentive man with women. But then he was very attentive to everybody. When you spoke to him you were the centre of his attention. He still found time to talk to the fans every night. It was just the band that were starting to drift apart.'

By the time the group hit London on 15 February, for two nights at London's Electric Ballroom, they were wired and tired. But even The Clash at half-cock still battered the opposition. Plus there was the added attraction of Mikey Dread and his all-star dancers. Also, for these gigs, Joe Ely and his band were on the bill.

Although Ely's firebrand country initially befuddled some of the crowd, a large chunk got into it as he came on like a Texan Strummer. Later, he joined The Clash for a barnstorming rendition of his own 'Fingernails' and 'London's Burning', which also featured Mikey in a unique cross-pollination of cultures.

These were the last gigs of the tour, and garnered a slagging from *NME*'s Gavin Martin: 'They need a rest. The tour has fatigued them and sapped them of willpower and cohesion.' This could have had something to do with Topper sailing through the usual booze and spliff intake into murkier drug waters. As the star of The Clash rose, so did Topper's penchant for personal self-destruction. This frustrated the others, who realised that their mate was looking at a very slippery slope. The 'Human Drum Machine' could still turn on the heat, though. Topper says that it was only towards the end of his time in The Clash that his timekeeping started to waver.

Topper was also turning into a walking disaster area, first cracking his pelvis horsing about, then injuring his hand enough to require stitches and cause the cancellation of the last three dates. The press story said that he'd torn some ligaments. Later, Joe told a journalist that Topper had actually been stabbed in the hand with a pair of scissors during an altercation at a drug-crazed party in his flat. Ask Topper about it today and he hasn't got a clue how it happened.

'I've got no idea! Joe said that, but I can't remember anything about it. I just thought I'd been fucking about. I was out of my head. You know when you make an excuse and then start to believe it yourself. I really don't know what happened. It's over 25 years ago. By then I was using, I was drinking excessively and making up stories. I made up so many excuses. When you lie, you end up wondering what are lies and what's the truth. A lot of it's myth because of the way the band were. I won't deny that I behaved like a wanker. I was just completely out of my head.'

Topper tried to explain it to *Record Mirror*'s Lesley O'Toole in 1985. 'Joe was the spokesman, Paul was the good-looking moody one and Mick was the sensitive songwriter. The only role left over was the wild one, and I found myself creating an image I had to live up to. I always had to be the first at a party and the last to leave.'

At first, Topper was doing 'loads of coke and drinking, but then I started getting into smack too. I used to go on tour and do a bit of Charlie, then we'd come off tour for a month, so I'd get bored and go and sniff smack. One day we got two months off and I started getting a habit. I started smuggling it, in my underpants, up my arse, everywhere.'

There were always druggy goings-on at Topper's flat. I stayed there one night after some event I can't recall. All three of us ended up collapsing bollocksed into bed, but I had no idea that things were going to get as bad as they did. Topper told me that he ran into his old girlfriend, Dee, at a halfway house in 1995 – toothless, addicted and on the game. Now she's dead. From my own angle, the 16 Tons tour was the final nail in the coffin of my already punk-strained first marriage. Looking back now, there was pressure on people both in and around The Clash. At the time we were having too much fun to notice.

A week after the Electric Ballroom, there was a very special night when Joe, Mick and Mickey Gallagher joined Joe Ely and his band onstage at London's Hope & Anchor. Earlier, I'd got a phone call from Kosmo telling me to get along to the pub-rock basement that night. Joe Ely was recording a live album, and his backing group was going to include members of The Clash, who had some time off from touring because of the cancelled dates. It was another of those once-in-a-lifetime gigs as Ely, who was introduced by Jock Scott, pumped out his set with his backing group, before being joined by Joe, Mick and Mickey Gallagher. With the spotlight off them, Joe and Mick went full tilt. The results were captured on the resulting live album, *Live Shots*, which boasts another appearance from The Clash Wildebeest Male Voice Choir.

After a belting 'Fingernails', there was a big surprise when Strummer kicked off 'Jimmy Jazz'. It was a longer version than on the album and sounded spectacular with the addition of accordion and pedal steel from Ely's crew. Here Joe got to stretch like he never did at Clash gigs, scat singing and ad-libbing. By now the little basement was awash with delight. Joe S then launched into Gene Vincent's 'Be-Bop-A-Lula', harking back to his 101'ers days. 'Here's one from my home town,' announced Joe E, as they tore into Buddy Holly's 'Peggy Sue'.

Joe Ely was a wild card who liked a drink. The following Saturday he played London's Venue. With The Clash back on tour, I went along to represent the troops. The Clash influence on Ely – particularly Strummer's as a front man – was much in evidence. There'd always been a strong classic rock 'n' roll element in his country sound, but now it was tinged with a punk-style attack and intensity.

After the gig, the pair of us got stridently pissed. Having liberated a bottle of brandy from the bar, we climbed up onto the Venue roof. Here we stared at the stars, spouting on about music and The Clash. Joe talked about Texas and I recalled the days before he met the band. Ely saw a spiritual bond that existed between the two groups, which transcended any genre boundaries.

Unfortunately, the bouncers caught us and we were unceremoniously thrown out onto the street. Pissed up and outraged, Ely was hell-bent on mayhem. First he put his cowboy boot through the front door's plate glass window and followed that with the nearest dustbin. He was threatening at the top of his voice to do the same to every shop in the street, so I ended up steering him away from the inevitable police confrontation and back to the Sherlock Holmes Hotel in Baker Street. Later, Joe gave the Venue bouncers – who 'can't take a joke' – a mention on the sleeve of his live album.

Given The Clash's association with Joe Ely and their fascination with America in general, it was inevitable that the US would once again beckon. 'Train In Vain' was issued as a single on 12 February and it became their first Stateside hit, climbing to Number 23 in the *Billboard* chart. 'What happened was "Train In Vain" went on the radio,' Mick told *Uncut*. 'They thought, "Wow, this is like totally crossed over," and that really helped us.'

With The Clash now clucking for another fix of America, a return visit was lined up. On 2 March, with Topper sufficiently recovered from his injuries, they embarked on their third American tour. It was to be a short one, just over a week, with the same name of 16 Tons. In came Ray Jordan, a bona-fide minder – big, black, no messing, but with a heart-of-gold cool as his essential ingredient. He would remain with the band through to the post-Mick Clash and stay in touch after that. Mickey Gallagher played organ again. Supporting this time were Mikey Dread, all-girl punk band the B-Girls and Lee Dorsey, the New Orleans R&B legend whose big hits had been 'Working In A Coal Mine' and 'Yes We Can Can'.

The Clash were punting *London Calling*, which had come out in January to mixed reviews. Tom Carson praised the album's eclecticism and humour in *Rolling Stone*. He set the tone with his opening gambit, where he stated, 'It's not simply that they're the greatest rock & roll band in the world . . .' On the other hand, *Creem*'s Billy Altman was so bowled over by the opening title track that he felt 'the rest of the album's lyrics just seem to be a weak addendum to a case already stated as well as it can be.' New York's *Village Voice* called it 'the greatest double album since *Exile On Main Street*'.

The album went on to sell over 600,000 copies, peaking at Number 27 on the US chart. Further evidence of the band's impact on the States came in the form of an invitation to appear in an advertisement for Dr Pepper's fizzy pop. Although the band were pleased with the penetration of the American popular psyche, they were hardly about to suckle on mammon's carbonated teat, and duly turned the offer down.

At the opening gig at San Francisco's Warfield Theatre, Mick met a fan named Freddie, who was about to join the Marines. He dedicated 'Stay Free' to him and found him a job as a roadie for the tour. They also saw Mo Armstrong, who gave them bandanas and posters he'd bought from the Nicaraguan Solidarity Campaign. Mo also gave Joe some literature about the victory of the Sandinista freedom fighters – *Fronte Sandinista Liberacion National* – over Nicaragua's military dictator General Somoza.

The show at New York's Palladium on 7 March was attended by a small posse of notables, including Debbie Harry, Bianca Jagger, Robert De Niro and Martin Scorsese.

Afterwards, an impressed Scorsese approached the band to contribute music, and maybe even appear, in a pet project he'd been working on called *The Gangs Of New York*. The projected movie centred on life in New York's gangs during the mid-nineteenth century, and tied in directly with the group's street-gang fascinations. However, the project drifted into the background and Scorsese wouldn't see it become reality for over twenty years.

After New York, The Clash played New Jersey, Boston's Orpheum and wound up at Detroit's Motor City Roller Rink on the 10 March. The gig was a benefit for soul legend Jackie Wilson – best known for 'Reet Petite' – who'd been in a coma since collapsing onstage after a heart attack in 1975. Redneck rocker Ted Nugent turned up and asked to jam. The Clash replied by imposing one of their hairdressing ultimatums. Johnny approached Ted with a pair of scissors and told him he could join The Clash on stage if he cut off his flowing locks. Ted refused but Blackhill were forced to write a letter of apology the next day, while Joe and Mick went for a tour of Hitsville USA, the home of Motown.

After the tour, Johnny surprised everyone and quit. The country-loving Foghorn Leghorn made flesh felt that The Clash was becoming routine and that much of his role had been usurped by Kosmo. When he told Mick the news, he was surprised and quite touched by the guitarist's concern. Joe just shrugged and got on with business.

During his time with The Clash, Johnny had been intensely loyal, a massive fan

MICHAEL WHITE presents

THE CLASH

RUDE BOY

Produced and Directed by
**JACK HAZAN
DAVID MINGAY**

Great live footage – shame about the plot. The 'unsympathetic' Ray Gange features on a promo poster for Rude Boy.

of the band and thrived on the mayhem surrounding them. Coupled with his upfront efficiency, there really were many times when he was the only bloke who could look after the band. He'd regularly turn down much more lucrative offers from other outfits, including the Pretenders.

'I got offered loads more money, but never considered it because The Clash were so fucking good. When they were making records I knew it was fucking good. I had complete belief in it. Above everything else, I was always a fan. It was never just a job.

'I had to be fan-minded and quit when I thought it was getting too safe. When they got sucked into the mainstream there was so much going on for them, but they couldn't keep their eye on the detail. It was getting a little bit predictable. I just wanted to be a bit more maverick. Not just a fun excursion occasionally. I wanted it to be full time.'

Johnny married his girlfriend Lindy at this time. There is a lovely photo of the event in Pennie Smith's book. Having struck up an even bigger bond with Joe Ely, he moved to Texas to become his tour manager. I was gutted. He was almost part of the band – he is on the cover of *The Cost Of Living*, playing table football with a leg of pork, and robbing a bank with the Baker in the 'Bankrobber' video. To my mind, The Clash didn't start to decline the day they sacked Topper, they must have already been tottering if Johnny had opted to quit.

Johnny inadvertently had a ready-made swansong when *Rude Boy* was finally released in March. The group said they didn't approve of the film because of the way black people were depicted as thieves. Also, much of the material was around two years old and The Clash had since moved on. If they'd just tried to make a straight-forward film that captured the intensity of The Clash live, and the group's beliefs, it would have had a focus. The live footage provides all the highlights here. It captures the group at the peak of their rise, mainly on the Sort It Out tour, and also at the Christmas 1978 Lyceum gig.

'I found the film depressing, muddled and full of redundant symbolism,' wrote Robin Banks in *Zigzag*. 'That said, sporadically, it can be amusing, moving, ironic and even exhilarating – thanks to the live footage.' Robin continues to use words like 'wanky' and 'wet', adding, '*Rude Boy* was never meant to be "a Clash movie". In that it succeeds entirely . . . it presents a series of cluttered images that eventually say nothing. It poses no tangible questions and provides even fewer answers.'

NME's Neil Norman called it 'an innovative piece of cinematic art'. Although identifying some parts as 'flabby', *Sounds*' Phil Sutcliffe described it as, 'a must for Clash-watchers', praising the live footage but finding Ray Gange 'hard to bear at times . . . a lurching parody of a young Cockney Brando/Dean.'

After Joe died, *Rude Boy* came out on DVD – with the extras proving that Gange was still alive and well. He reckons that it was Joe's suggestion to star him in the film, but 'can't remember half of it'. After leaving The Clash, Gange went to the US to try to carve out a film career, then returned to the UK, where he faded into obscurity.

Johnny Green describes the film as, 'an actual reflection of our lives . . . chaos indeed – delightful, splendid chaos. We loved it. No-one was after a quiet life.' He adds that the filmmakers often 'saved the day' by bunging the hard-up group money for fags, cafes and pubs.

The general feeling in The Clash camp was that Robin should have had the part of the Ray Gange character – especially as he inspired it. Gange comes over as a free-loading slob with blinkered views. On screen, Johnny is much more of a natural, especially the doleful surrender of his bed to a horny Gange, which left him trudging the hotel corridor wrapped in a blanket.

Robin himself says now, 'It never bothered me at the time and it doesn't bother me now. It's just a shame that Ray Gange was such an unsympathetic character. That's the way he comes across. Everyone now says *Rude Boy* was about me anyway. Mick came into the dressing room in Cambridge after a Carbon/Silicon gig last week and I was sitting there. He said, "Ah, rude boy!" It was probably because I had my hat on.'

As the poster said, 'Nobody knows what the Rude Boy knows.'

CHAPTER THIRTEEN
PARADISE GARAGELAND

Who gives a shit whether a donkey fucked a rabbit and produced a kangaroo?
At least it hops and you can dance to it. – Joe Strummer

After the 16 Tons tour, The Clash decided to start work on their next album. Mikey Dread was still firmly in the camp and the idea of making the next LP a reggae/dub version excursion was given serious consideration. In March 1980, the band flew to Kingston, Jamaica, to record at the legendary Channel One Studios, which had spawned so many great records since opening in the early seventies.

This went down particularly well with Paul, who hadn't forgiven Mick and Joe for going to Kingston without him two years earlier. He took to the city like a wildebeest on heat, despite the generally heavy atmosphere around where the studio was located. Mikey, who says that Paul was, 'a great reggae bass player', took him on a guided tour of the neighbourhood.

The Clash settled in to start a cover of the New Orleans R&B standard 'Junco Partner', which Joe had done in the 101'ers. Joe remembered 'sitting at the out of tune Channel One piano trying out the chords . . . but then we had to run.'

As in run for their lives. Kingston had got worse since Mick and Joe's first visit. While The Clash were there a fourteen-year-old boy was shot dead on Hope Road, just minutes after they'd driven through. Inflation and unemployment had boosted the poverty level and therefore the amount of gun-related crime.

The last British guests at the studio had been the Rolling Stones. Keith Richards owns a house on the island and was familiar with rude boy etiquette, which involves handing out fistfuls of cash to keep the locals happy. With another white rock band in town, the studio was soon swamped with visitors, ranging from the simply curious to those who were aggressively looking to get paid.

The sessions started to resemble a rammed blues party. Mikey was there as a protective buffer, but soon the demands for money became overwhelming and the atmosphere increasingly oppresive. This resulted in The Clash's sudden retreat. They then holed up in Montego Bay, while waiting for money to be wired through so that they could fly out of the country.

Paul was committed to a movie role and flew to Vancouver, Canada to start filming *Ladies and Gentlemen, The Fabulous Stains*. Directed by top LA record producer Lou Adler, it centred on an American girl band called the Fabulous Stains. Paul was playing a member of a UK group, which also included Steve Jones and Paul Cook, plus future *Sexy Beast* Ray Winstone. It never saw a UK release.

While Paul was filming, the rest of The Clash, plus Mikey, opted to continue the recording process in New York. They holed up in the Iroquois Hotel on 44th

Joe and Paul get rude and reckless on the 16 Tons tour, 1980.

Street, near Times Square. The Clash liked the fact that James Dean used to stay there. It was one of those tolerant establishments already geared towards what was emerging as the highly lucrative rock 'n' roll business. Late bar, late everything and untidiness accepted.

Joe, Mick and Topper used the Iroquois as a base while they commenced serious work on the next album. They managed to book a few days at the Power Station studio on West 53rd Street. Ian Hunter had recorded there and raved about its acoustically receptive wooden domed ceiling.

The studio was also the home of the Chic hit factory. In fact, Nile Rodgers and Bernard Edwards were using the place at the time to record Diana Ross's *Diana* album. Nile, a great bloke who'd become familiar with the New York punk explosion through his work with Blondie, became an unexpected new mate. The syncopated disco precision of Chic seeped through the studio walls to give The Clash another new musical influence.

Initially, The Clash – with Mick playing bass – planned to warm up with some cover versions, as they'd done with *London Calling*. These included 'Louie Louie', Prince Buster's 'Madness' and the Equals' rousing 'Police On My Back', which had been a tour bus favourite. It sounded like it was written by The Clash after they'd finished with it, an 'I Fought The Law'-style rabble-rouser with siren guitars. It was the first one in the bag.

As the studio hours ticked by and the band had to arrange their sessions around other acts that had booked earlier, it became apparent that they would have to find somewhere cheaper and more readily available. A three-week block booking was secured at Electric Lady Studios. Situated on Eighth Street, before you hit Sixth Avenue, it's the place that Jimi Hendrix had built to realise his album of the same name. It's still got the psychedelic murals on the walls.

The absence of any new songs ensured that the trio would be writing their new album in the studio – the complete opposite to *London Calling*. They didn't mind at all, seeing as their new studio home was where Hendrix had done exactly the same thing in the late sixties, their ticket to unlimited creativity.

They decided to produce themselves. Sandy Pearlman had tarted them up, while Guy Stevens had been inspirationally anarchic, but now the band felt that they needed a smoother, in-house working method to replace outside pressures and chaotic destruction – without losing any edge. By now, Mick had learned enough about the studio to assume the role of *de facto* producer.

With Paul absent, it was decided to draft in outside musicians to add extra input. Guitarist Ivan Julian was one of the first contacted. He'd become friendly with the band when he was a member of Richard Hell's Voidoids. Ivan, who was starting a new band called The Outsets, turned up when they were playing with a new funk inspired anti-draft outing titled 'The Call Up' – which shows how the Chic influence rubbed off in its chiming bells and chunky riffing. He ended up adding some spectral guitar lines.

Next, they got Blackhill to call up Blockheads Mickey Gallagher and bassist Norman Watt-Roy. They arrived on Easter Monday, 7 April, and started off with a new track, which Mick said needed to be funky because Joe was planning to do a rap. They struck up the riff, looped it up and, two hours later, 'The Magnificent Seven' was on the way.

'At the start it was called "The Magnificent Seven Rap-O-Clappers",' recalls Mick. 'But it was also like a slice of life too. Something which we felt, which we got as well, kind of what was happening at the time when we talked about it, like with records like "The Message" later on.'

On the six-minute original, the band rock like a funky locomotive with Joe riding the rhythm with his rap-slanted vocals. It would turn out to be one of The Clash's epoch-making tracks, marking their first stab at assimilating the new hip-hop style currently busting out in New York.

Hip-hop was a musical form that the Clash took to and adapted in the same way as they did with reggae. The way its attitude and production techniques were assimilated into their sound was further evidence of how adept the group were at soaking in and spewing out their own take on music they'd encountered on their travels.

Rapping derived from original African forms of voicing a message over a drum, which was taken up in American ghettos in the sixties by agitating outfits like New York's Last Poets and LA's Watts Prophets. This developed into hip-hop – the modern blues.

It was a similar way of expressing anger, frustration and personal politics as punk rock except, instead of using guitars, black kids took to the streets with ghetto blasters pounding out grooves derived from cut-ups of classic rock and funk, while topping them with their own party chants and comments. The DIY ethos came to upset the mainstream via its irreverence, invention and, eventually, commercial potential.

The hip-hop explosion started to bubble in the mid-to-late seventies in Harlem and the South Bronx. Clubs like Disco Fever saw DJs such as Afrika Bamabaataa, Kool Herc and Grandmaster Flash cutting and scratching breakbeats while MCs like Melle Mel and 'Lovebug' Starski led the party. The first major rap record was 1980's 'Rapper's Delight' by the Sugarhill Gang. This was the tune that inspired Joe to write the words of 'The Magnificent Seven', which he delivers in a similar style.

As with his take on reggae toasting, Joe had a unique approach to the process of rapping. 'Vacuum cleaner sucks up budgie' and 'Italian mobster shoots a lobster' are two examples of his surreal ad-libs. But Joe also used the medium to convey a message about the drudgery of work with lines like, 'Clocks go slow in a place of work/Minutes drag and the hours jerk.' It's interesting to note that rap wouldn't really start making social comments until Grandmaster Flash dropped the graphic urban imagery of 'The Message' a couple of years later. This would help pave the way later in the decade for Public Enemy, who subsequently cited The Clash as a major influence.

During their time in New York, Joe and Mick soaked up the vibrant sounds that were reverberating from uptown. They acquired large 'ghetto blasters', on which they could tune in to hip local radio stations like KISS FM and WBLS, where spellbinding DJs like Red Alert and Chuck Chillout cut and scratched live on air. It was fresh, original, and a truly urban underground movement.

Before it got sanitised for today's mass market and tarnished by escalating violence, rap's original premise fitted squarely with Joe's principles. Records like Bambaataa's 'Planet Rock' were calls for unity via the block party, while the harsh reports of KRS-One boasted similar powers of journalistic observation. With The Clash, Joe's main concern was sculpting his confrontational, witty and thought-provoking lyrics. Technically, Joe had always been a rapper anyway; as he often delivered his vocals in spoken, or rather shouted, form. The new genre was paradise garageland for Joe, who now had a licence to rant about anything that came into his head over the funked-up grooves. Rap made his top-of-the-head vocal style legal tender instead of the outpourings of a nutter. So Joe assimilated rapping into his arsenal of punk anger, classic rock 'n' roll, Jamaican patois and country lament.

While Joe saw the oral parallels, Mick was most struck by the studio techniques and the possibilities offered by the electronic beatbox. His instant obsession with New York's rap scene eventually became a major factor in Mick's gradual estrangement from Joe and the band. 'I was in the group going, "Come on, let's dance," and they were saying, "No, let's riot,"' he later told Paolo Hewitt. 'Ever since I hit that New York club for the first time, I thought, "God, beatbox", that was it for me. I knew I was still a guitar player and I stuck that on top of it.'

Despite the groundbreaking way that Mick applied his new influences to The Clash, he never consciously thought that the band were making music that would be subsequently viewed as ground-breaking. 'We never thought that, at any time,' he told me. 'We were just sort of knocking out some numbers. It's like that's all we wanted to do. We just wanted to do our thing. We didn't necessarily wanna be part of this big, happening thing that was so cool. We just did what we wanted to do. I guess it's because we had that kind of attitude. We were so open to other things, and we attracted it so well. We were open to meet other artists in other fields.'

'I think The Clash's involvement in the start of that whole thing was by luck really, if anything,' explained Mick. 'We were in the right place at the right time. If you travel with a group like that you find out all about all the things that are happening much quicker. It's like a fast track to what's culturally happening in whatever place you go to. We were fortuitous in the fact that we *had* to be there. We met all these graffiti artists and stuff. They did a banner for us at Bond's. There were quite a few of them. It was a new thing, but clubs always interested us. We attracted all the sort of different, creative people to what we did. They came and checked us out.'

'He's always so modest!' laughed Robin when I told him that Mick puts it all down to luck. 'He's always so modest – unless he gets pissed! He's been ahead of his time all the time I've known him. On *Sandinista!* Mick was streets ahead, being into hip-hop and stuff like that when nobody was really aware of it.'

A lot of hot air was expelled about the 'Americanisation' of The Clash with *London Calling*, to which Mick always replied that he'd grown up with American rock 'n' roll culture so he didn't need any converting or further influencing. 'We were just progressing.' 'The Magnificent Seven', and the other strains of music from around the globe that were surfacing in on their new material, represented another benchmark in The Clash's development.

Largely thanks to The Clash's ceaseless absorption of new music, and Mick's gen-

'What have you been doing?' – The effects of his habit are evident in Topper's face.

erous habit of making me tapes from New York radio shows, I leapt in head first to find out more. The end result was that I later moved to New York for five years.

'Yeah, what started as a punk group turned into a multi national,' observed Mick. 'It took on international, different concepts of what people were doing and tried to make it part of it, but still retaining our own thing. We did it our own way. We didn't do it by slavishly following fashions. You said yourself it helped some people find a way in to these things. You wouldn't have known that – even when hip-hop was in its genesis, its birth – it would become one of the major forces of music later on.'

To even think of taking on funk and hip-hop, you have to have the beats. Hip-hop producers use drum machines. The Clash had 'The Human Drum Machine'. Topper had already proved his amazing flexibility on *London Calling*, but the new tracks called in the funk he'd picked up when playing with soul groups a few years before. It has to be said that The Clash could never have delved so deep into these waters without Topper's effortless pulse providing the firm foundations.

'I like to think so,' says Topper. 'But the hip-hop was Mick more than anyone. What I thought I did was – if Joe wanted to play rock 'n' roll, I could play it. If Mick wanted to play hip-hop, I could play it. If Paul wanted to play reggae, I could play it. Without sounding arrogant, I was also powerful on stage. Again, without sounding arrogant, I think because I was in the band we were able to explore these different avenues of music.'

The clipped funk of 'Lightning Strikes (Not Once But Twice)', features another of Joe's excursions into rap. The track opens with a scene-setting snatch of New York radio and is an unashamed celebration of the great city – its sights, sounds and diverse cultures. Joe's rhymes are barbed and funny, delivered with a genuine enthusiasm and sense of wonder. It's like now Joe's been over the Brooklyn Bridge he can't wait to tell you about it. The groove is as tight as a gnu's foreskin.

During the Electric Lady sessions, Joe built his Spliff Bunker. Joe, Topper and lighting man Warren 'Stoner' Steadman, who'd taken over Johnny's role, built a bolthole in the middle of the studio out of flight cases – 'a place to retreat and consider, for musicians and groovers only,' said Joe in the *Clash on Broadway* booklet. After Joe realised that he'd written most of the lyrics for the new album in his bunker, he continued the practice for the rest of his life.

'You can't have a load of idiots partying in the control room, because the engineer can't hear and no decisions can be made,' explained Joe. 'I was keen to hang with people, because otherwise you're in an isolated bubble, but it has to be done carefully, because you can't have people pouring wine into the mixing desk. Behaviour like that has just not gotta happen.

'So, I invented the Spliff Bunker, which was a place where you could smoke weed, hang out and talk – in the main body of the studio as far removed geographically as possible from the control room, so that in the control room sanity could reign, and people could EQ things and get things rewound correctly. The Spliff Bunker was where you could think up your next thing while they were fiddling with your last thing.

'As soon as they'd got a rough mix down, we'd be like "fresh tape on the reel, get the mikes out because we're gonna go like this and this and this." We'd just keep doing that, day and night. And that's why it had to be a triple album, even though it would have been better as a double album, or a single album, or an EP. Who knows? The fact is that we recorded all that music at one spot at one moment.'

Joe's bunker got a mention in one of the new tracks – 'If Music Could Talk', a reggae-influenced tune which evolved out of 'Shepherds Delight', from the Manchester session with Mikey Dread.

The creative trickle turned into a tidal gush. For the next six months the band assimilated their influences at a frightening rate, striking out in diverse musical directions, prompted by a world that was suddenly full of inspiration.

As usual, Joe was writing lyrics that reflected his surroundings. Just as he had depicted the view along the Westway from Mick's flat in 'London's Burning', for 'Broadway' he used the street-life of New York to create an equally evocative backdrop onto which he projected the outsider's perspective.

In the eighties, the homeless were a regular sight around the city, as rapidly rising rents forced people out of their homes. In the *Clash on Broadway* booklet, The Baker talks about this bloke they saw every night when returning to the hotel. He'd be sleeping or standing over a heating vent up the street from the Iroquois. 'I remember one night we came back from the studio, it was about four in the morning and Joe was looking at this guy quite intently. I always thought it was about him.'

Joe assumes the character of an angry, disillusioned street bum, and demonstrates how much his songwriting and performance had matured in just a few years. With its smoky, pulsing mood perfectly capturing the atmosphere of New York winding down in the early hours, the song is an underrated Clash classic. This is largely down to the emotional power of Joe's vocal, which could be emitted from any gutter in the world. 'Broadway' could be argued to be Joe and the group's most subtly brilliant realisation of their American dream.

Other NYC-inspired tracks include 'Lightning Strikes (Not Once But Twice)' and the reggaefied 'One More Time', which recounts the violent plight of the city's disenfranchised youth. The Clash loved to walk the streets, absorbing the electric atmosphere for the next song.

There's nothing like a full-on gospel knees-up New York-style, and The Clash capture it perfectly on 'The Sound Of The Sinners'. Preacher Joe sounded so convincing that *Trouser Press*' Ira Robbins was moved to comment that the song 'may very well embody Strummer's new faith. Or maybe it's just a *triple sec* in-joke.' Joe told *NME*'s Paolo Hewitt, 'I was just thinking that a spiritual solution is as important as a social solution.'

During these sessions, Topper worked with Mick and Joe on much of the music, playing guitar and piano as well as drums. On 'Ivan Meets GI Joe', he sings Joe's lyrics about superpowers clashing in the disco over a supercharged urban funk work-out splattered with arcade game noises.

'Stop The World' came out of Joe and Topper jamming around a Booker T-style organ vamp, with Joe later adding lyrics about global disarmament.

During these sessions, Mick was walking down the street and bumped into Joe's old busking partner Tymon Dogg. Mick invited him along to the studio. After the great reunion, Tymon fiddled out his own 'Lose This Skin', with The Clash backing him up. This mad, Cajun-Celtic mutant would be released as a single in June on Tymon's own Ghost label, and also turn up on *Sandinista!* The next time Tymon worked with Joe would be twenty years later in the Mescaleros.

Mick renewed another friendship when Chrissie Hynde, who was now riding a wave of success with the Pretenders, dropped by. Five years earlier, the pair used to play songs together at Wilmcote House, including the Spencer Davis Group's aching soul ballad, 'Every Little Bit Hurts'. Mick went straight into Electric Lady and recorded it with The Clash. It got left off *Sandinista!* but would eventually surface on *The Clash on Broadway* retrospective. Which is just as well, as it shows a gorgeous, sensitive side to the band that was rarely glimpsed at the time.

The film *Apocalypse Now* had a profound effect on the whole group which would linger through to *Combat Rock*. It inspired the gentle roto-blade shimmy through the killing fields that was 'Charlie Don't Surf'. The hook comes from Robert Duvall's memorable speech, while the anti-war sentiments are made more effective by the fact that the groove and melody recall the innocent style of a classic New York soul ballad from the Drifters era.

In *Westway . . .* , Joe later described the spirit of adventure which surrounded the album 'If someone had come in and gone, "Let's play this with balalaikas," everyone would have gone, "Give me the biggest balalaika!" We were open about stuff. Mick Jones bringing in the new sound of New York and stuff, and Simmo with his reggae thing, and me with my R&B thing and Topper with his soul chops. We could just do that.'

The rough proto-rockabilly of 'Junkie Slip' was another of Joe's, partly inspired by Topper's growing heroin-related tribulations. During this period, Topper got busted a few times copping on the streets. Back then, you only had to walk across Eighth Street for twenty minutes to encounter the Alphabet City shooting galleries and corner vendors. Getting busted was an occupational hazard, which usually resulted in an overnight stay in a cell before being released with a caution. Topper's heroin immersion wouldn't reach full bloom until the group returned to London, but his New York experiences certainly paved the way.

On 24 April, with Paul back from filming, The Clash made their major American TV debut on the *Fridays* show. With Joe sporting his new skinhead haircut, they showcased each of the front line's vocal talents with 'London Calling', 'Train In Vain' and 'Guns Of Brixton', before all getting down on a mighty 'Clampdown'.

Meanwhile, Mick's personal happiness took an upward turn when he was introduced to a young singer called Ellen Foley. She'd cut her teeth singing with Meatloaf and had her first album produced by Mott's Ian Hunter.

Back in Britain, CBS boss Maurice Oberstein – usually a Clash champion – tried to scupper plans to release 'Bankrobber' as the opening instalment of The Clash's projected monthly singles series. He hated the record, saying, 'it sounded like David Bowie backwards.' This pissed off both the band and the fans who'd grown to love the song at gigs. It had already been voted Best Unreleased Song in the previous year's *Zigzag* readers' poll.

'Bankrobber' would eventually see the light of day in the UK after the group sneakily planted it on the flip of 'Train In Vain' in Holland and it did well on import.

Meanwhile, as recording continued at Electric Lady, Joe and Mick achieved the then-ultimate accolade of making the cover of *Rolling Stone* under the banner, 'Rebels With A Cause And A Hit Album'. The success of *London Calling* gave them a new respectability that neither of our two cover stars could ever have imagined.

May 1980 saw The Clash back on the road – this time in Europe, with the dates that were rescheduled on account of Topper's injury tacked on the end. Barry Myers was no longer DJ-ing. 'Blackhill were fucking me around,' he claimed. 'They wanted to clear the decks, I think.'

As the sixteen-date tour made its way across Europe, The Clash found that the rest of the world was trying to catch up with 1977, with sheeplike latecomers in their mail-order bondage gear wanting 'White Riot'. But The Clash were charting different waters now. 'It's become everything it wasn't supposed to be,' Joe complained to *NME*'s Roy Carr. Now Joe talked about the mohican-and-leather brigade in the same way as the rock 'n' roll revival bands he'd derided in 1976 – 'junior punks in their expensive designer uniforms with concrete heads and no ears.'

On 20 May, during a volatile night at Hamburg's Markthalle, Joe got so annoyed by one individual's aggressive behaviour that he clobbered him with his guitar. The police were called but let him off after a breathalyser test proved negative. 'I was emotionally shattered . . . completely disheartened to see what's happened to the seeds of what we have planted,' Joe told the press afterwards. 'If those pricks and kids like them are the fruits of our labours, then they're worse than those people they were meant to replace.'

Topper remembers that the band often travelled separately on this tour – which nearly led to disaster. Like the time, accompanied by Ray Jordan, he tried to make the trip between France and Milan, Italy. 'We were three hours into the journey but still in the Alps. We'd gone out of our way and knew we'd be late. We were three hours late. When we pulled up at the gig, I thought, "They're playing our records," but the band had already gone on stage and started without me! They were using the support's drummer. Ray bust past the policemen and I ran straight up to the stage. Joe said, "It's alright, he's our drummer." I hadn't changed or anything.

'We started playing but they were well stressed. Mick had got pissed. He was blind drunk! We got to the encore and they started playing "March Of The Mods". Then Mick bumped his head. He was pretty bashed. Joe went, "You cunts! Can't you see he's gone blind? He's blind drunk!"

'They were mad days. The four of us were pretty mad at the time. Mick was completely insane. We were four conflicting personalities. The only thing we had in common was The Clash.'

The rescheduled UK dates kicked off in Derby on 9 June, running on to Bristol and Hanley, before winding up with two nights at Hammersmith Palais on the 16 and 17. Mikey Dread was supposed to support but The Clash couldn't afford to pay for his whole band to come over, so there was a bit of a spat. He was replaced by Blackhill's resident punkabilly outfit, Whirlwind, but returned for the encores at the Palais.

NME's Chris Bohn delivered a slagging, writing, 'Ever conscious of their future position in the history books, they've fashioned their collective rock 'n' roll persona to fit it even more perfectly since their American tour.' The man's a prophet. In 2004, The Clash are a towering presence in those history books. Except it was never contrived. As Mick says, 'We just did our thing.'

By now the Clash were knackered after all the touring and recording, so they took July off. Joe found it hard not to be active, so he produced a single, 'I Need A Witness', for London R&B group, the Little Roosters. For Joe, this represented something of a return to his roots – the Roosters were popular on the same pub circuit that Joe had slogged through with the 101'ers.

On 9 August, CBS begrudgingly gave 'Bankrobber' a UK release with Mikey's 'Rockers Galore – UK Tour' on the flip. It still made Number Twelve, despite negative reviews all round. *Sounds* lambasted Joe's 'daddy was a bank robber' line, bringing up the old chestnut about his background with a Bushell-style 'I once met a real criminal' dogshit. *NME*'s Paul Morley confusingly declared, 'I just wish they'd smash out of those traditionalist restrictions.'

Morley's comments seemed particularly strange, as 'Bankrobber' further mutated the Clash's rock/reggae fusion, extending the band's use of reggae into dub territories and pushing the sonic boundaries courtesy of a swelling, twisted choir. Like 'White Man', this is a song that, when experienced in the aftermath of Joe's death, takes on a

Originally released as Black Market Clash, *the* Super Black Market Clash *CD is a superb collection of B-sides and previously unavailable rarities.*

new poignancy as his delivery hits a gorgeous balance between resigned melancholy and steadfast defiance. It's another human tale, in the Guthrie/Dylan tradition. And again, the musical bed Joe chose to lie in was well made.

In the 'Bankrobber' video, Mikey Dread can be seen grooving away while Joe records his vocal. Eyes shut and swaying, clutching his red handkerchief as he delivers one of the most touching performances of his career. As ever, The Clash refused to go on *Top of the Pops*, so had to suffer the comical ignominy of dance troupe Legs & Co dancing to it in convict style mini-skirts!

After the US success of *London Calling*, CBS put together a ten-inch album called *Black Market Clash* for American release, consisting of various rarities and B-sides. The cover was the famous photo of Don Letts facing the massed ranks of the London police at the Notting Hill riots. The album led off with the original 'Capital Radio One' from the *NME* freebie, before heading through classic B-sides 'The Prisoner' and 'Pressure Drop', the UK album version of 'Cheat', 'Complete Control''s B-side, 'City Of The Dead', and a Bill Price mix of The Clash's March 1978 version of Booker T and the MGs' 'Time Is Tight', which had evolved from a soundcheck favourite. This, along with the hard-to-get original version of 'Capital Radio', provided the tempting carrots for any indecisive bunnies.

Side Two was a highly listenable Clash-in-dub selection, kicking off with 'Bankrobber' and its 'Robber Dub' counterpart, before leading into 'Armagideon Time' and its towering version excursions, 'Justice Tonight' and 'Kick It Over'. The selection demonstrates that a whole Clash reggae-dub album, in collaboration with Mikey, could have been something of an aural feast. Paul's guest appearance on Mikey's *World War Three* album further underlined The Clash's dub-fusion vibe.

However, Blackhill saw a limited commercial potential in such excursions. Mikey says they actually tried to steer him away from the band and, halfway through the *Sandinista!* sessions, realised that he was becoming marginalised.

Talking to Mikey in 2004, he feels that he hasn't received due credit for his work on the album, both financially and personally. Many of his reggae contemporaries have talked about the cutthroat exploitation and pillaging of their music. In Jamaica, it was common practice for labels to hijack hot new studio rhythms and release their own versions of songs that could be on the streets by the next day. On the world stage, Jamaican artists griped about having their ideas appropriated by British and American acts. Although Mikey feels he was ripped off, he stresses that his main beef is with the record company and Blackhill. He says he should have got publishing royalties on the songs he co-created, or at least a gold disc.

'I feel like those guys owe me that. Back then, they were like my family. I blame the people round the group. I trusted in them to work on my behalf. It ticked me off for a long time, that little joke money, but I'm still pleased about it. It was a very creative project. We were truly collaborating. I showed them the way we make reggae music. But when my involvement finished I had nothing to show. I didn't benefit from it. That's why I stayed away.'

Asked about Joe, Mikey responds with warmth and fond memories. 'I feel he was a great lyricist. Joe was a philosopher, a messenger. He didn't go for the glitz and the glamour. He had a humble image. Every time I saw him he was reading the prophecies of Nostradamus. We smoked a lot. He was a hard smoker.'

In August, Joe and Gaby moved out of World's End into their own flat on Ladbroke Grove. The Clash recommenced work on the new album at Wessex. The band was still employing the method of chucking every new idea onto tape, while trying to polish up the tracks they'd started in the US and Jamaica.

The sessions, which went on into September, would often run from early afternoon well into the following day, with Joe and Mick particularly fired up. While Mick was steering the music from start to finished mix stage, Joe was occupied writing lyrics and surfing the endless creative wave. I went along a few times and remember getting quite confused. One day Joe would say, 'we're done, just got to finish the mixing.' The next he'd be going, 'oh, that's a new one that just happened'.

Joe's musical focus shifted from hip-hop back to reggae, particularly dub. The trip to Jamaica, hanging out with Mikey Dread and watching Kosmo start a label called Dread At The Controls, provided Joe with plenty of inspiration. Ensconced in Wessex, Joe was writing portentous dub slices like 'The Equaliser' and the historic battle reflection of 'Rebel Waltz', which was a strange dubbed-out mutation in waltz-time.

Having been away, he could reflect on his own country in songs like 'Something About England', which roped in military brass. This track – which railed against the fact that, despite wars and progress, the class system was still in effect – had an almost Olde English folky feel.

Mick sang 'Somebody Got Murdered', which Joe wrote after the car park attendant at the World's End Estate was stabbed to death for a few pounds. Originally written for, but not used in, William Friedkin's *Cruising* movie, this is another song that only really got noticed in later years. Listeners were so swamped with the sheer size of *Sandinista!* that many didn't notice that it was studded with gems, such as this one. It bristles with subtle melodies, that wistful sadness from Mick's vocal, and works via its deft dynamics pushing it to a glorious climax. Even Topper's dog, Battersea, is thrown into the mix.

Another trip to the Notting Hill Carnival on August Bank Holiday sparked Joe's interest in soca music, which originated in Trinidad – Joe wrote 'Corner Soul' and the mad calypso of 'Let's Go Crazy', and brought in steel drum players to add flavour. 'Street Parade' mixed the tones with a loose jazzy feel, enhanced by Gary Barnacle's saxophone but all held together by a behemoth of a riff from Mick.

Mick and Ellen Foley duetted on 'Hitsville UK', the lyrics of which take another pop at CBS by fêting the UK independent record scene. The song was inspired by the daddy of all indies – Detroit's Tamla Motown, a.k.a. Hitsville USA – which The Clash had visited during the 16 Tons tour.

Joe was the driving force behind a cover version of jazz organist Mose Allison's 'Look Here', which Topper relished for its light jazz groove. Joe's rockabilly influences resurfaced on 'The Leader' and 'Midnight Log', which slinked dark and rumbling as it speared multi-corporate corruption.

'The Crooked Beat' was Paul's tune – kind of 'Guns Of Brixton' revisited. 'Up In Heaven (Not Only Here)' was a rare rocker, which saw Mick mentioning 'the towers of London/Those crumbling blocks.' With the 'piss-stained lifts' reference, he could have been reminiscing about Wilmcote House.

During the last American tour, Mo Armstrong had ignited Joe's interest in the politics of Nicaragua. Subsequently, Joe became fascinated with the background to the Sandinista freedom fighters' struggle. In the early 1900s, Nicaragua had been under the oppressive rule of its National Guard, who were backed by the US. The Sandinistas were a bunch of guerrilla activists who joined together in the sixties as the collective legacy of pioneering freedom fighter Augusto Cesar Sandino. After Sandino was assassinated by the National Guard in 1932, he became a national hero and martyr figure. Five years later, the country was taken over by Anastasio Somoza Garcia, who established a US-backed dynasty of dictatorship that would endure for over 40 years. Under this regime, social conditions deteriorated and necessities such as education and medicine were ignored.

Resistance built to the point where a variety of independently formed guerrilla factions combined to create the Sandinista National Liberation Front. After a long struggle, the Somoza regime collapsed in 1979, leaving the Sandinistas to rebuild the country, despite opposition from President Reagan.

These events provided the hook and became the title of the album, while Joe also managed to work in American CIA intervention in Chile and Cuba, the Russians, British mercenaries and dodgy arms deals. Of course, this brought accusations of 'political chic', but the group had a more substantial reason. 'There was a media blanket covering the whole bloody thing, and people didn't even know there was a revolution there,' said Mick in *Rip It Up* fanzine. 'We really wanted to have a title that was useful for once. It was something that would draw people's attention to something that was going on at the time.'

Despite the never-ending spew of sonic lava, there was noticeably more tension between Joe and Mick than during the *London Calling* sessions. Bill Price reported them fighting quite often, sometimes going beyond the necessary creative grit. Robin recalls the atmosphere as being 'quite heavy'.

It's a major paradox that The Clash had such a monstrous number of tracks to hand when there had been little of the camaraderie that had underpinned the making of *London Calling*. With this one, they were up against the wall in a different way.

'They were never in the studio together,' recalls Robin. 'Mick and Joe were growing apart, which was just natural. I think Joe and Mick just progressed in different directions. That added to the problem. There were problems with Topper. Everyone was worried about Topper.

'Then there was the Kosmo influence. He made me so sick at the time. That whole experience with Blackhill was pretty negative. It didn't do anything to hold the band together. Joe certainly wasn't too enamoured with them. They needed a Bernie figure.'

The lengthy recording process left Topper to his own devices. As Robin says, everyone around The Clash was concerned by his heroin use. He even had his own bunker – but that didn't seem to be weed that he was smoking.

'I started using during *Sandinista!*,' recalls Topper, adding how the inter-band relationships were getting strained after the initial buzz of the New York sessions. In Electric Lady he'd been co-writing tracks and playing instruments like piano and marimba. In London he joined his girlfriend Dee shooting heroin. 'It got regular when we were back in London. After I'd done my drum parts I had nothing much to do except get into trouble. There was me using smack, Paul didn't give a toss, Mick and Joe were at loggerheads. It was a band in name only by now.'

That month, Ian Dury and the Blockheads dressed up as policemen to perform their single, 'I Want To Be Straight', on *Top of the Pops*. After the show, they travelled to Wessex and faked a raid. No one really laughed. Joe wasn't amused either when, in late September, he was picked up by SPG police officers near Kings Cross station under the SUS laws. They made Joe take them back to his flat, where they found several ounces of his homegrown. He was later fined £100.

In September, Mick declared that the album was going to be a triple set – previously the unthinkable domain of self-indulgent progressive rock dullards. Having made the grand announcement, the band then found that they were about a side short. The inclusion of adjoining dub versions of 'One More Time' ('One More Dub'), 'Washington Bullets' ('Silicone On Sapphire'), 'Junco Partner' ('Version Pardner') and 'Shepherds Delight' ('If Music Could Talk') might have been considered space-filling by some, but it was rooted in the reggae tradition of letting the song play through, before switching over to dub mode.

'That was an old idea that they always did on the twelve inches,' says Mick. 'They'd do the version of the song first, and then they'd do a toast. That was quite fun to put them together like that. But, again, we didn't think anything more of it.' He stresses, 'It was quite English too. The ideas and the imagination are English. The humour is English. You retain all that stuff, y'know, even though we were going all over the shop.'

This was the Mikey influence – a more authentic way of dealing with the genre than the kind of rocked-up cod-reggae associated with bands like the Police. A New York-meets-Jamaica-in-London touch was added when the group segued some of the tracks into each other via sound effects or Mikey's vocalisations. It was like

Mikey's bombastically audacious DJ style mating with the cool hip-hop cutups from NY radio stations. Occasionally, like on 'Version City', the effect predates what the Orb and other sample-devotees would get up to later in the decade.

However, I did think it was stretching the spirit of experimentation to include Mickey Gallagher's kids singing 'Guns Of Brixton' and 'Career Opportunities', or simply running 'Somewhere In England' backwards and calling it 'Mensforth Hill'

Ultimately, Mick had embarked on a never-ending sonic voyage, with Joe supplying the narrative and catching the moods. Mikey Dread was the MC/DJ, while Paul and Topper brought up the grooves with supporting cast behind. It had to be a triple album to capture what would turn out to be a uniquely freewheeling episode in the short history of The Clash. 'Warts 'n' all,' grinned Joe.

'We never wanted to be totally up in a box, I thought,' said Mick. 'We didn't care. We just tried anything we wanted . . . We always take on the music that was going on around us on board and make it our own.'

There was a promotional interview twelve-inch pressed up called *If Music Could Talk*. On this, Mick explained the album's length: 'It's pretty much designed to last for six months to a year of listening. People don't have to listen to it all at once. They can listen to it a bit at a time. However much they can take.'

If being manoeuvred into issuing a cheap double album with *London Calling* had left CBS cheesed off, they were likely to have an embolism when they heard that *Sandinista!* was to be a triple. What's more, The Clash wanted it to retail for the price of a single album, which was then a fiver. There had to be some compromise and, eventually, the deal was that the album would sell for £5.99. CBS insisted that *Sandinista!* counted as a single album in a contractual sense, and the group waived their royalties on the first 200,000 in order to preserve the low retail price.

This was mad, obstinate and even flamboyant. Was it worth it? Hell, yeah. Not every track was a stone Clash killer, but it was a magnificent statement of defiance, apocalyptic stoned vision and fearless experimentation that became more apparent with repeated listenings. They'd taken their expanded palette of influences and made them sound like The Clash, without being patronising or pretentious. CBS considered the project an act of misguided indulgence. 'Let's put it this way,' Mick told *Q* magazine. 'If it had happened in Japan, all the record company executives would have killed themselves.'

Sandinista! was the last straw for Blackhill. By the time the record was finished, group and management had parted company. There had been numerous fallouts precipitating the split. Blackhill had wanted to sack Johnny Green after the 16 Tons tour. They had a major problem with Topper's behaviour. Joe felt they were too straight, like the kind of authority figures The Clash were supposed to be kicking against. Paul took it one step further and insisted that he wouldn't go to business meetings unless he wore a rabbit suit. Although this was provided for him, his bunny boy antics hardly served to enhance the disintegrating relations between band and management.

Blackhill had always found it hard to rationalise the group's value for money ideals with The Clash's insistence on taking a full-blown rock 'n' roll show on the road. The *Sandinista!* royalty sacrifice was just too much to take. They kicked up about it and The Clash cut them loose. Both parties felt that they just couldn't maintain a working relationship any longer.

Peter Jenner is still obviously a man with a bitter taste in his mouth. 'I'm not going to be part of a book about Saint Joe,' he harrumphed. And Peter is a nice, well-respected fellow who I'd met before The Clash. He did tell me, 'The Clash put us in the dumper in 1982.' Basically, the company went bankrupt.

On the sleeve of *Sandinista!*, Jenner and King are credited as 'the Two Ogres'. Kosmo stayed with The Clash, of course. Although taken on as press officer, his duties had long since stretched to encompass personal management, including those he'd taken from Johnny.

With *Sandinista!* complete, Pennie Smith shot the cover – this time against a wall behind Kings Cross station. The album would come with issue three of *Armagideon Times,* which presented the lyrics in newspaper format.

'The Call Up', was released on 28 November, reaching Number 40 in the UK chart. The track was a broadside against the military that featured a sombre Joe with 'hup-two-three-four' backing. The music pursued the hybrid of skin-tight rock-funk with dub splashes that fired much of their later work, while the crystal counter-melodies are pure New York mutant disco. Don Letts shot the black-and-white video at former sixties pop star Chris Farlowe's North London warehouse of military regalia, with The Clash all done up in uniforms.

By now, such writers as Jon Savage were promoting a new fad, which they liked to call 'New Musik'. Essentially this meant music that didn't acknowledge any roots and used modernist groups like Kraftwerk as a jumping off point to a brave new world where men were robots, sex didn't exist and lyrics were as obscurely pretentious as possible. It was a bit like New Romanticism's bully brother in its wilful dismissal of anything played in more traditional style. This made The Clash, and their pure explorations of different musical forms, sitting targets for the portentous new manifesto carriers.

Paul Morley had a right pop at 'The Call Up', writing that the group were now 'old fashioned', 'too stuck inside a political phase', 'in the doldrums', while the song didn't 'seem right for the times'. He wasn't to know that over twenty years later it would still be played at the coolest clubs and get a rousing cheer.

With the recording of *Sandinista!* behind them, the band

'The Call Up' – The Clash's 1980 disco inspired anti-draft single found little favour with the critics of the day.

Sandinista – *to some; a vast, sprawling melting-pot of diverse influences, to others an over-extended exercise in self-indulgence.*

switched their energies to Mick's girlfriend Ellen Foley's second solo album. It was basically the same team: The Clash playing the music, recorded at Wessex with production by Mick – credited on the sleeve by Ellen as 'my boyfriend'. Mick asked Joe to write six songs with him for the project, which would be called *Spirit Of St Louis* and released the following March. Tymon Dogg also contributed three tracks and played violin.

The resulting album was far from the dub and rebel rock explorations that peppered *Sandinista!* In fact, it's probably the most unusual thing The Clash ever got involved in and marks one of the few times that the Strummer-Jones partnership operated outside the group.

Ellen didn't deal in political comment and harsh reality. Her rich voice caressed damaged love songs, happy or sad. The players cooked up an intoxicating backdrop that ranged from torch song ballads to luxurious Euro-pop, with even a hint of Greek MOR-stress Nana Miskouri creeping in at times.

Joe's words graced six tracks: 'The Shuttered Palace', 'The Death Of The Psychoanalyst Of Salvador Dali', 'MPH', 'Theatre Of Cruelty' and the melodramatic 'In The Killing Hour'. Mick sang counter-vocal on 'Torchlight', which is the only track that bears any resemblance to The Clash's sound. But the group seemed to relish escaping from the expectations and pressure of being The Clash and plunged enthusiastically into something completely different.

The band would have had to be in a good mood to offset the shitstorm of negative press that greeted *Sandinista!* It was so predictable that a Clash triple-album originated in the USA would be greeted like a wildebeest's wind emission at a wedding.

It wasn't a good start when *NME*'s Nick Kent laid in with all guns blazing, giving possibly the worst review The Clash ever had. Phrases such as, 'precious little substance', 'ridiculously self-indulgent', 'tepid' and 'cul-de-sac' pepper the broadside, which concluded that *Sandinista!* 'perplexes and ultimately depresses'. Kent rips into the mix and production, the funk grooves, and describes Joe's singing as, 'simply duff', with lyrics that are 'neatly glib.' It has to be said that Nick, who I still hold up there with Lester Bangs, had been a huge Clash fan. It obviously pained him to do this, but at least he presented an honest, reasoned case. Maybe he was just taking the wrong drugs.

Melody Maker's Patrick Humphries called it 'a floundering mutant of an album. The odd highlights are lost in a welter of reggae/dub overkill.' He did concede that

The Clash 'really do still care, and remain a radically committed band,' and that he couldn't wait for the next Clash album.

It came as a bit of a shock when Robbi Millar, of the usually anti-Clash *Sounds*, praised the record as 'an adventure of diversity and wit, of struggle and freedom, of excellence and dross,' even if she found the American influences 'a bore'. But she liked the lyrics and the emphasis on the groove – ironically a trait they picked up in the States.

As might be expected, my stop-press review for *Zigzag* bucked the negative trend: 'They say *Sandinista!* is two and a half hours of self-indulgent sprawl, enjoyable for nobody except the musicians involved . . . A recent Saturday afternoon bending the ears to the 36 new Clash tracks – with a depressing letdown half expected – proved to be a severely uplifting experience. However – the mind boggled – two and a half hours of assorted musics all with rhythm in common. And all for six quid!'

The following year, Mick became animated when I mentioned how the press sought to bury The Clash: 'They would love to . . . Maybe because I've been away on tour so much I haven't read many music papers. Hip? Hip hop hippity hop! What would they put there instead? Perhaps they can give one of Paul Weller's old suits to Martin Fry and it'll be all right. All that stuff's really nice and it works well in a small environment, like London. People can be hip putting down other people. It don't work so well in a place like America. It's a bigger deal, a different league.'

For The Clash the accusations of over-indulgence became an albatross. Such hostile press was similar to the reception accorded the Stones' *Exile On Main Street*. Dismissed as a 'sprawling mess' at first, hailed as the embodiment of early seventies wasted cool 30 years later. The point is, you can still listen to *Exile* now. And *Sandinista!* Apart from hearing how it eventually influenced later groups – especially the indie-dance movement of the late eighties – it's great for dancing to, and tells you exactly what was going down in 1980.

Stung by the vicious criticism, Joe's enthusiasm for the album began to wane, to the eventual point where he almost disowned it. But over the years he warmed up, and so did a new generation of critics. The album started getting mentioned as a major influence on a wide range of music.

In late 1999, Joe told the *Music Monitor*'s Howard Petruziello that he'd seen a feature in *GQ* magazine that said, 'Hey, what about this for a piece of good stuff.' He added, 'I started to get more and more proud. At first I was a bit worried because self-indulgence is the worst crime. Musicians can commit two crimes; they can bore people or they can be self-indulgent and it usually goes hand in hand . . . Then after a few years I thought, "to hell with it," and now I'm beginning to feel really proud that it's so mad. It's mad as hell!'

As Joe said the same year in *Westway To The World*, 'I can only say I'm proud of it, warts 'n' all, as they say. It's a magnificent thing. I wouldn't change it even if I could. That's after some soul searching. Just for the fact it was all thrown down in one go. It's outrageous . . . It's doubly outrageous! . . . It's *triply* outrageous!'

As would be Joe's next move – instigating the return of Bernie Rhodes.

CHAPTER FOURTEEN
MORTAL COMBAT

You couldn't have written it, or contrived it. – Mick Jones

In December, Joe handled most of the press interviews to promote *Sandinista!* This was an unenviable position to be in, considering the vitriol that was being squirted in the album's direction and, consequently, at the group. He'd become used to The Clash being taken to task from the offset. The first album offended non-punks, the second offended punks for its polished production, and then *London Calling* pissed off punks and the music media. *Sandinista!* seemed to irritate everybody. With Mick away in New York with Ellen, Joe faced Christmas with Gaby and a pack of ravenous press hounds for company.

Christmas 1980 turned into a time of reflection for Joe. He wanted to get his life sorted and started by getting his driftwood teeth fixed. He was also desperate for a decent place to live. Now with a long-term partner, he was fed up with squats, spare rooms and dodgy lets. The Clash were vastly in debt to CBS – around half a million pounds. Plans to tour the UK had been shelved because of the bad press, disappointing record sales and a corresponding lack of support from their label as the band still tried to keep their ticket prices down.

For Joe, there seemed to be one answer to The Clash's problems: Bernie Rhodes. Joe's main reason for wanting to split with Blackhill had nothing to do with their efficiency. Blackhill's attitude was consistent with their role – sod the mad ideas, let's make money. Joe missed Bernie's schemes, scams and visions. With the bad press still ringing in his ears, he blamed Mick for the excesses of *Sandinista!* Bernie – Mr. Complete Control – would never have countenanced an epic like that. Joe believed in The Clash with a passion, but didn't feel they could carry on losing money and acclaim on projects like *Sandinista!* The ensuing year would see Joe try to regain control of The Clash from Mick, who'd dominated the last two albums.

'Mick had a really tight line and Joe wobbled about under all that,' observed Johnny Green. 'Paul was an agent provocateur who just sided with the band. It was Mick who had everything together and pushed things through. Mick was the tough guy, who had the vision and the determination. Joe could be really tough, but there were times when he could be less than tough. Sometimes with his dealings with Mick, he would want a tighter approach. But Joe was very inconsistent. Mick is not inconsistent. He knows what he wants. Sometimes Joe was with it but he also liked his own solitary space. I think Mick was always prepared to be a really strong character. I only understood that when they split.'

If he wanted to seize the balance of power from Mick, Joe would need reinforcements. One fateful night in January, he bumped into Bernie on the street and took his phone number. He made his mind up to bring him back. When the rest of the group baulked at this outrageous suggestion, Joe threatened to quit the group. This was one of the times that Joe did get tough, as he would right through the inception and painful birth of the next album.

For a change, Joe was thinking about himself. He'd devoted his life to The Clash since that fateful overnight decision to ditch his old band, lifestyle, image and even background, for a punk rock springboard. Now The Clash had become much more than a band bashing out social comment over two minutes of high-octane guitar. They had moved musical mountains in their sonic laboratory, made a stand for the fans in ticket and album prices, and come to represent a blast of rebel-fresh air in the mainstream music business. However, this perpetual creative motion came at a price – as the UK press withdrew their favour, the band's credibility nosedived.

It was Bernie who had originally pushed Joe into assuming his gruff, 'punky', persona of the band's early days. 'The reason he had to do that was because Bernie actually cultivated him to help Mick in a big way,' says Johnny. 'All that was to help them identify what they should be. As soon as Bernie put his finger on the button they were off. They were wholeheartedly into it. They understood it.'

Since Bernie's dismissal, The Clash had pursued many paths which led away from the Rhodes ethos – double and triple albums full of lengthy explorations into traditional forms of music, extended US trips and paying homage to rock's past. Joe felt that the band could still have the world at their feet, without compromising their original vision.

Bernie still had The Clash's income tied up since his dismissal over two years earlier. All this would be dropped if he came back to the fold. Could Joe still realise his rock 'n' roll dream and get his just rewards, while still making people think and dance at the same time?

Mick, who hated Bernie, was the hardest to convince, but, faced with the prospect of Joe quitting and the band disintegrating, he relented. 'I could quite easily have walked out then,' he told *NME*'s Paolo Hewitt. 'But it's like a marriage, or the people you love: you cling on hoping it's gonna work out.'

Mick even agreed to the humiliating task of approaching Bernie, who must have loved it. At this time, the Rhodes stable of bands was looking pretty empty; Subway Sect and the Black Arabs had split while the fast-rising Specials and Dexy's Midnight Runners had moved on. Now he had his original boys back, even if he would be on a percentage of profit instead of gross – which gave him the incentive to get some money coming in.

Towards the end of the previous year, I'd started managing Basement 5, a groundbreaking punky reggae outfit. The band were mates of The Clash, who I went to see play after they'd been recommended by Youth, the ex-Killing Joke bassist who became my flatmate when I moved to London in 1982.

Basement 5 was fronted by Dennis Morris, who'd made his name with photographs of Bob Marley and the Pistols. He wrote hard-hitting words about inner city life with titles like 'No Ball Games' and 'Riot', which were set against a turbulent mutant backdrop of dub and punk. This was supplied by guitarist JR, who subscribed to the Keith Levene school of coruscating sonic attack, and dub-shot bass-master Leo Williams, Don Letts' mate who'd worked with The Slits and would later join Mick in BAD. The drummer was Richard Dudanski, Joe's old pub rock comrade. He told me he was planning a retrospective album of 101'ers material with Joe.

Richard was a good, rootsy drummer but didn't see eye to eye with the volatile Dennis and departed after a December tour with Ian Dury. The last night of the tour, at Finsbury Park's Sobell Centre, was a blast. Robin Banks, John Lydon and Topper came to say hello, with the latter getting up to play percussion on the Blockheads' encores.

On 24 January, 1981, CBS released 'Hitsville UK' with Mikey's 'Radio One' on the flip. 'Insipid junk from old time punks,' cracked *Melody Maker*'s Ian Pye, while *NME*'s Penman gurgled, 'What do they see when they look in the mirror? Third world guerrillas with quiffs?' It wasn't that bad, but probably wasn't the right choice for a single and peaked at Number 56 in the UK.

Joe had seen in the New Year playing a 101'ers reunion gig at the Tabernacle community centre off Portobello Road. Under the name the Soul Vendors, it saw Joe, organiser Richard Dudanski, Mole and other ex-members back on the same stage and hammering out the classics.

Richard's 101'ers compilation dug out live and studio material, which would emerge through a deal with Virgin. Joe, Richard, Clive Timperley, Dan Kelleher, Mole and Micky Foote became directors of Andalucia!, a label created for the project.

There was some conflict of interest with Chiswick, who released 'Sweet Revenge' and 'Rabies (From The Dogs Of Love)' as a single and kept control of most of the Jackson's and Pathway studio material. But Andalucia! could still glean versions of 'Rabies', 'Sweet Revenge', 'Five Star Rock 'n' Roll Petrol', 'Keys To Your Heart', 'Motor Boys Motor', 'Junco Partner' and others from some Pathway and BBC sessions. The rest of the album came from a tape Micky Foote had of the 18 April 1976 gig the 101'ers played at the Roundhouse supporting prog-rockers Van Der Graaf Generator.

The album would be released at the end of March as *Elgin Avenue Breakdown*, named after a jazz record by Arthur Blythe that Joe had seen in New York called *Lenox Avenue Breakdown* (referring to the main drag through Harlem). The hand-lettered, roughshod-looking sleeve recalls the homemade punk ethic – or the way Joe later approached the Mescaleros artwork. The front photo is of the Metal Man; a legendary tramp whose chosen spot was over the road from the *Zigzag* offices in Talbot Road, a few doors along from the landmark Globe restaurant. Around this time I did a photo session with him, modelling *Zigzag* t-shirts!

Allan Jones – now *Melody Maker*'s editor – turned in an unsurprisingly rave review, writing that, 'Joe's coarse vocal still carries an enthralling potency.' *NME*'s Adrian Thrills – former editor of punkzine *48 Thrills* – declared that the collection was only of use to Clash completists, although he still praised 'the unmistakable, unexpurgated dementia in Strummer's coarse vocalising.' I found it a fascinating peak at formative Strummer, although the studio material Chiswick were hanging on to would have sounded a lot better than the bootleg-quality live stuff.

Meanwhile, Mick co-produced an album for his old hero, Ian Hunter, alongside

Mick Ronson. The latter had been the bleach-haired lead guitarist in Bowie's original Spiders from Mars, before hitching up with Hunter after the last incarnation of Mott The Hoople collapsed. Mick had only gone along to New York's Power Station to help out with one of the tracks and, on a roll with his recent projects, ended up taking the reins for the resulting album. In came Topper and Tymon, while Ellen was already singing backing vocals. Mick also followed a traditional Clash pursuit and got the shaggy-maned Hunter to have a haircut – hence the album's title, *Short Back And Sides.*

At the end of March, Joe shocked everybody by competing in the London Marathon. Most people expected Joe, who was not noted for his athletic leanings, to drop out before the finish. He hadn't trained at all, but it appears that he called up the same sheer determination that got him through all those live shows when feeling like shit, and made the finishing line sporting a 'Take The Fifth' t-shirt.

A year after its inception, 'The Magnificent Seven' was finally released as a seven-inch single on 10 April. This was followed two weeks later by the mighty twelve-inch. It may have only reached Number 34 in the UK and hardly dented the US charts, but the shockwaves it sent through the club underground were far more significant and enduring.

The American twelve-inch had been released on 27 March, with CBS filling out the disc with 'The Call Up', plus a new, Mick-mixed instrumental called 'The Cool Out'. Later on in that decade, this would be considered a normal promotional tool. But, in 1981, expanded mixes on twelve-inch singles were usually only encountered on disco, hip-hop and reggae outings. By the end of the eighties, remix culture would be rife with big names earning more money than the artist to reassemble a single for the dancefloor. But The Clash kept it in house, adopting the mythical moniker of Pepe Unidos – reportedly a pseudonym for Joe, Paul and Bernie.

By the spring of 1981, tapes of mastermixes from New York radio stations were being traded and copied in London. On some of these, you'd find the dub of 'The Magnificent Seven' – 'The Magnificent Dance' – enhanced with samples taken from films and television. While The Clash were later acknowledged as the first white rock band to explore rap, at the time none of the New York DJs playing the record had any idea of who was responsible.

'It was quite inspiring, because there was a whole new thing,' remembers Mick. 'They did things like putting bits of movies on top. There was this mix on WBLS. It's actually called the "Dirty Harry Mix". You know that bit that goes, "Do you feel lucky today, punk?" Also it was characters from *Bugs Bunny.* "The wabbit kicked the bucket." That was a kind of a pointer, yeah.

'For us it was amazing because they'd picked up on this record and they didn't know what type of group we were. They picked up on the instrumental, especially, and they didn't know who we were. Everyone was playing that record, y'know? And it turned out to be us! It was really funny, because we were like punk rockers [laughs]. And we'd come all this way. That's what I was saying about how it was just lucky, really, and just right. You couldn't have written it, or contrived it. I guess we did the first proper twelve-inch dance mixes too, but it wasn't planned that way. It just happened.'

The twelve-inch came with a dancefloor-targeted dub version, which was leapt upon by New York clubs like the Paradise Garage. Here their legendary DJ, the late Larry Levan, fearlessly pushed the musical boundaries and mashed up different styles. I remember going to the Garage myself in 1983, where the 'Magnificent Dance' remix was dropped in the middle of a housey-disco set and tore the roof off.

In 1983, NYC producer Man Parrish hijacked the bassline for the massively successful electro 'Hip Hop Be Bop (Don't Stop)', which used exactly the same bassline. In 1997, when I interviewed Masters At Work 'Lil" Louie Vega and Kenny 'Dope' Gonzalez – two hugely influential dance music figures – they both cited 'The Magnificent Dance' as a crucial tune. 'I used to play that dub when I was DJ-ing at these real underground dance clubs and the crowd would go nuts,' said Louie. 'It was a really groundbreaking record. Do you think you could fix us up to work with The Clash?'

'The Magnificent Seven' and New York's club scene redefined Mick's attitude and approach to music. It also steered him further away from Joe's tastes and methods. For Mick, traditions were now deconstructed and genres blurred. Dancefloor heaven was an ultimate goal, while the tactics and newness were pure punk as the DIY ethic survived and independent labels ruled again. Meanwhile, Joe and Paul were more at home with reggae and rockabilly. It was a case of ye olde 'musical differences', as cited by many a fragmenting band in the past. Joe and Mick were bound to lock horns sooner or later.

April 1981 saw the band return to Vanilla to work the *Sandinista!* songs into their set and develop new material. In an attempt to reunite the band after their disparate activities, they reactivated the football matches. Unfortunately, Mickey Gallagher broke his arm and wouldn't record with The Clash again. Topper's mate, Gary Barnacle, was once more drafted in to provide sax.

By now, Topper's heroin addiction was tipping the £100 a day mark and his wasted state was becoming a real problem for the band. Earlier in the year he'd been busted for smack possession and given a conditional discharge by Horseferry Road magistrates. The group tried moving Steve Barnacle – Gary's brother – into his flat to try and sort him out. This didn't work as the place was already a non-stop dealers convention.

'I took anything to stop me feeling how I really feel,' says Topper. 'I used a bit of Charlie in *London Calling*. On *Sandinista!* I was smacked out, but by *Combat Rock*, it was all over. For a long time I was going, "Joe, sack me!" Imagine how they must have felt. It must have been so difficult for them. They were in one of the best bands in the world and one bloke was fucking it all up. You just end up hurting the people closest to you.'

Over in Texas, Johnny Green had left Joe Ely because his band had no ambitions beyond playing weekend honky tonks. Ely himself 'wanted it to be more rock 'n' rolly,' and so did Johnny. The duo ended up going on a sightseeing tour around landmarks like Mount Rushmore, Deadwood and the Devil's Tower from *Close Encounters*. They ended up in New York's Chelsea Hotel – most recently famous as the place where Nancy Spungen was murdered.

One day Johnny drove to the bank and cleaned out the band account, which was in his name. He signed the withdrawal slip 'Charles Penrose' – after the music hall bloke who made 'The Laughing Policeman', one of the greatest records of all time and a firm Clash favourite.

When Johnny came marching home, he was offered his old job by the band. 'I went back for one day when I got back from America. The job was always open, so I went down to Vanilla to have a look, but it all seemed diluted to me.

'Me and Joe went to the pub and had a long talk about it. I just said, "Nah, the music's crap and you don't look like a band." He had tears in his eyes. There was Kosmo and Bernie around and I could sense that there was something unsettled going on and it wasn't being sorted out. Before, all matters were always addressed by Joe, Mick and Paul. I thought it over but just kept thinking, "It's not being addressed."'

After Johnny declined to rejoin The Clash, he asked if I needed a road manager for Basement 5. I would never have dared to ask because I knew he'd been in demand when he was working for The Clash and we had little money. But Johnny was game for a laugh and, as always, relished a new challenge. The group had a new drummer, a young London kid named Michael, who came over like a black Topper with his power and agility.

We did a European tour in May, which was great fun – reminiscent of earlier Clash excursions. This ahead-of-their-time band of punky dreads caused uproar with their blistering live shows and post-gig festivities. Me and Johnny shared a room and got through the whole jaunt on copious amounts of speed and alcohol. We were banned and fined by one hotel for painting a large cat/antelope mural in the shower with emulsion and got arrested outside Brussels when Johnny insisted on driving the van down the middle of a traffic island. 'I just loved watching the bollards going "ping",' he remembers. 'I have nothing but fond memories of my time with Basement 5. That was one of my favourite ever tours.'

The tour ended up swallowing all the money I'd made from selling the marital home after my divorce and signalled my departure from management. I wasn't cut out to be a Bernie!

After the group disintegrated, Johnny started working for Fifth Column t-shirts on Portobello Road, alongside Jock Scott. He still kept in touch with The Clash but, as he told me on one of the drunken nights on tour, he could never go back to a group in such a state of disarray. We both agreed that some kind of golden age had ended.

It was different around The Clash now. I didn't see them so much, but kept in touch with Mick. He was always stoned but never less than pleasant, still determined to push the band toward further creative triumphs. But the group were far from the close-knit family I'd first encountered. That old spark just wasn't there. Kosmo had worked his way up to plotting the strategies with Bernie while presenting himself as the Voice of The Clash. However, no amount of pep talks and grand plans could bridge the gaps that were growing between the original members.

Mythic America endured as a Clash influence, although Joe and Mick were focusing upon different aspects of US culture. Mick was enthralled and inspired by the New York hip-hop scene, whereas Joe remained gripped by *Apocalypse Now* and the welter of Vietnam-related cinematic spin-offs and documentaries it inspired. He also wanted The Clash to adopt a more traditional rock 'n' roll sound.

For the next Clash album, Vietnam and its effect on America would furnish Joe with as much lyrical inspiration as London gave him for *The Clash*. Away from the jungle, the plight of the Vietnam veteran loomed large in America's cities as incapacitated and disturbed ex-soldiers found themselves jobless, homeless and often committing antisocial acts resulting from their shell-shocked derangement.

Martin Scorsese's controversial 1976 movie *Taxi Driver*, which sees Robert De Niro's Travis Bickle character mired in the seamy underbelly of New York's Times Square, particularly affected Joe – even to the point where he later adopted Bickle's fat Mohican hairstyle. Vietnam war journalist Michael Herr's book of recollections, *Dispatches*, became essential reading for the whole group.

Joe's interest in the fallout from Vietnam illustrates the way in which he ran with whatever he was interested in or reading about at that time. A combination of movies, literature and his own experiences of being in the US was inspiring him to write about the long-term effects of the Vietnam war on American society, while using it as a springboard for his more global observations. Joe saw the war as a representation of just how crazy a nation can get.

Joe was writing about everything but the continuing decay of his own country. The fact that there were Cruise missiles stacking up and the British Government were spending millions on advising the populace what to do when the country got nuked didn't seem to come into it. But that wasn't the point any more. The Clash long since had moved away from the *verité* of their earliest outpourings. Songs had become more like films with Mick writing the soundtrack and Joe the script. The Clash's life was no longer social security and tower blocks, so they didn't write about it. They spent a lot of time in the States and saw it as the ultimate symbol of what man can do to man. And, of course, that set them up for yet more criticism.

Mick and Joe's fascinations with hip-hop and Vietnam ran parallel then collided on one of the new songs they wrote at Vanilla, then recorded at Marcus Music studios in Kensington. 'This Is Radio Clash', which wouldn't be released until the end of the year, followed the willfully innovative path that made The Clash so exciting, while puzzling die-hard punks. Now they'd added a disco feel to their take on hip-hop – they were now rocking the dance floor instead of storming the barricades.

By the early eighties, the disco stereotype epitomised by the likes of the Bee Gees had given way to a startling mutation of the form in the New York underground. The beat was dirtied down with a funk injection and the cheesy topping replaced by a reckless dub sensitivity, spacing the music into uncharted territories.

Producers like Francois Kevorkian, Arthur Russell and the aforementioned Larry Levan were dancefloor punks hurling groove bombs. There was also another movement called No New York that was partly comprised of funked-up and confrontational outfits such as ESG, James Chance and the Contortions, and Defunkt – who I called the black Clash.

New York's radio stations continued to take their mastermixes to daring new

Mick and Joe discuss new material on the road, 1980.

heights in the hands of deejays like Tony Humphries and Timmy Regisford, led by the coolest announcers like KISS FM's Yvonne Mowbly. Even the ads were fun. Once again, Joe was made keenly aware of the drab, chart-orientated state of the airwaves back home.

'This Is Radio Clash' represented a projection of Joe's longtime fantasy of a free radio station, 'on pirate satellite'. He delivers his message over a riff hijacked from Queen's 'Another One Bites The Dust', which itself was adapted from Chic's 'Good Times'. The disco anthem had already provided the groove for the Sugarhill Gang's 'Rapper's Delight', which had also influenced The Clash vocally on 'The Magnificent Seven'. 'This Is Radio Clash' starts with an appropriation of the music used for the villain's entry in silent movies, over which Joe emits a suitably malefic cackle.

It was borrowing central in those fearless, pre-sampling war times. Later in the decade, the essence of the acid house explosion would be based on taking someone else's music and making something new out of it. Passing it along. The Clash's interpretations of early eighties New York hip-hop/disco innovations cannot be overestimated in their influence on later dance music trends.

Did The Clash invent acid house and remix culture? In my opinion, they certainly played their part. There were no other groups that came close to capturing that excitement at the time. The Clash pioneered the methods several years before the whole dance thing exploded.

Take 'Outside Broadcast', the epic dub version of 'This Is Radio Clash'. It stretched the track into a ghostly groove-voyage, with Gary Barnacle's eerie sax, an endlessly mutated funk riff and Joe's slowed down rap.

This track is one of the highlights to be found on Don Letts' superlative 2004 compilation, *Dread Meets The B-Boys Downtown (The Soundtrack To New York 81-82)*. Don became immersed in New York hip-hop via The Clash and got his reggae sensibility knocked sideways by landmark tunes like Afrika Bambaataa's 'Planet Rock' and 'The Adventures Of Grandmaster Flash On The Wheels Of Steel'.

On the compilation, 'Outside Broadcast' sits comfortably amidst Don's selection of proto hip-hop grooves and demonstrates that The Clash were at the forefront of another musical form that would shake the world.

The Vietnam conflict provided Joe's lyrical inspiration for two other Vanilla recordings, both of which would end up on the next album. 'Sean Flynn' was about the son of famous wild man actor Errol, who was a Vietnam war correspondent and went missing in Cambodia. They were Joe's most overtly anti-war lyrics yet. Dark of message but devoid of bombast, 'Sean Flynn' contained simple observations like, 'No one mentions the neighbouring war,' referring to the often-ignored bloodshed that took place in Cambodia itself. The accompanying music painted an ethereally bleak backdrop with marimbas and sax hovering over a muted jungle pulse.

'Car Jamming', with its tempo upped to a futuristic take on the Bo Diddley beat, is one of Joe's most complex lyrical offerings, delivered in unison with Mick. He starts in a radio-blaring gridlock before intoning, 'A shy boy from Missouri/Boots blown off in a sixties war riding aluminium crutches.' Joe works up a head of steam through a litany of brilliantly graphic images that provides an evocative summation of New York's homeless taking refuge in drugs.

The music may have carried a modern jolt but Joe's lyrics were now grounded firmly in the surrealistic protest-barbed tradition of early Bob Dylan. Of course, Joe could never write about Vietnam firsthand, but he could use his talent to convey the situation and move the listener in the manner of a film director. Later that year, he would actually write about that situation on 'Death Is A Star', which talks of seeking solace in the cinema and escaping in its portrayals of violence. 'Sean Flynn' was like a four-minute movie scene on record. Whatever muse was gripping Joe, the resultant album would boast the most intricate, inspired and downright brilliant lyrics of his life.

Sandinista!, which had its US release in January, had been greeted with similar confusion in the States as in the UK. *Creem*'s Jeff Nesin wrote, 'Generally, the further The Clash stray from their great theme, the Dying of England, the more specious and patronising their songs become.' However, *Rolling Stone*'s John Piccarella raved about this 'everywhere-you-turn guerrilla raid of vision and virtuosity' and awarded it five stars. The album would go on to sell nearly half a million copies in the US and reach Number 35 in the charts.

The Clash had initially planned a 60-date tour in late April to consolidate their position in the US. It didn't get further than the planning stage because Epic –

maybe put off by the mixed reviews both home and abroad – wouldn't finance it. The return of Bernie, who they'd suggested dismissing in 1978, might also have been a contributing factor.

Instead, the band decided to tour Europe. In the past it had been hit-and-run short jaunts. The Impossible Mission tour would run a month, playing uncharacteristically large – 8,000 and upwards – venues. Maybe they'd make some money this time. Starting on 27 April, in Barcelona, Spain, it went on to visit France, Holland, Denmark, Sweden, Germany and Italy.

The tour was a success, with sets now going on for two hours. Short, sharp stage raids had been replaced with a selection mainly drawn from the two most recent albums, encompassing live dub and jamming excursions and slower stuff like 'Charlie Don't Surf'. The full-tilt final stretch provided the required first album highlights.

Jock Scott was on the tour and tells the classic *Carry On Abroad* tale of getting to Madrid and trying to check into a hotel that hadn't been built yet. 'It was a building site.' The gig was at Real Madrid's Bernabeu stadium and, when the Clash convoy arrived, the team were practising on the pitch. Conversation was struck up and the team ended up on the guest list.

'We had a fantastic corrugated backdrop with all graffiti on it. It used to get knocked about in transit. Bernie and Kosmo said, "Jock, go up and touch up the bits that have come away." So I went up the ladder with a paint pot and brush, sploshing away. I got a huge cheer from the punters because they could see right up my kilt! Traditional Scottish underwear was discarded. I got an enormous cheer.

'I got down the ladder and it was nearly showtime. Joe's going, "Jock! Jock! Come here!" It happened that Bobby Sands, the IRA prisoner of war, had just died on a hunger strike in Ireland. Joe had composed a long speech that he was going to start the show off with. "Bobby Sands has died, starved himself to death. The British Government are out of order and we'd like to dedicate tonight's performance to the struggle of the Irish people for freedom in their own country." But he had it all written in Spanish. He was going, "Here, test me on my words!" But that's what he's like. He's on tour, he's on the ball. He's going, "Learn me my Spanish," before he went on stage. He's not backstage fucking swigging champagne and shagging Spanish birds. He's fucking on the ball, man! It's one of the qualities about the man.'

Instead of the big US tour, The Clash decided to play a week-long residency at New York's Bond's Casino, on Broadway and 46th Street, near Times Square. Mott The Hoople had done this in May 1974, when they played a much-trumpeted string of dates at the City's Uris Theatre on Broadway. It was a more economical way of doing the US than going from city to city and carried a certain amount of romance that would be followed through later with similar stints in places like Paris and Tokyo. The Bond's residency ultimately became one of the most enduring aspects of the Clash legend.

The band arrived in New York on 25 May and took over the Gramercy Park Hotel, a docile rock 'n' roll lodge just walking distance from Union Square and the East Village. Mick was with Ellen, Paul with US singer Pearl Harbor, who was DJ-ing at the gigs, and the party soon attracted an ever-growing entourage. Graffiti artist Futura 2000, old school rapper Fab 5 Freddy (as immortalised in Blondie's 'Rapture') and legendary beat poet Allen Ginsberg all paid their respects and hung out.

The group called a press conference on 27 May. An American journalist mentioned that Paul Weller had accused The Clash of selling out and asked the band what they felt constituted a 'sellout'. 'What happens is that all the tickets go on sale for a concert and people go and buy them and if as many go and buy them as there are tickets – that constitutes a sellout,' explained a helpful Mick.

The residency kicked off the following night, and punters were perplexed to see firemen swarming around the building after the show. The next day, the New York City Fire Department imposed a restraining order limiting the capacity to 1750. Bond's had already sold 3500 tickets for each of the seven nights but estimates reckoned only 1800 would get out in the event of a fire. A summit meeting between The Clash, the fire department and the managers at Bond's arrived at a solution whereby upcoming gigs by the Stranglers and Gary Glitter were cancelled, ensuring that The Clash could extend their residency for a further seven days and accommodate all the ticket-holders.

This sort of club chaos happened a lot in New York City. The Fire Department held more sway than the police in these matters and, in the corrupt NYC underbelly, the ruling could have been the result of some dirty inter-promoter tactics or even an unpaid bribe. The point was made that, less than a fortnight earlier, 4000 people had gone to Bond's and seen shock-punk group the Plasmatics blow up a car onstage.

Whatever the reason, it was all over the news, and the next night riot police were on hand to deal with irate ticket holders who'd been told to come back a week later. The City hadn't seen scenes like this since Frank Sinatra in the fifties. The whole area around Times Square came to a halt. The Clash had inadvertently stopped the traffic and made the headlines in the world's most famous city. Simultaneously, 'The Magnificent Seven' was all over the hip radio stations.

Don Letts had accompanied The Clash to New York to film the Bond's dates for a projected film, *The Clash on Broadway*. Bernie didn't pay the rent on the place where the film was stored and only a few minutes of Don's personal footage survives. The remaining clips were used on the video for 'This Is Radio Clash', and later showed up as an additional feature on Don's *Westway To The World* DVD. These few minutes of clamouring crowds, cops-on-horses, breakdancers and car jam chaos perfectly capture the traffic-stopping mayhem that The Clash brought to the core of the Big Apple. 'It has to be said, for the time they were in New York, The Clash ran New York,' recalled Don.

Further complications arose when the New York Buildings Department slapped an order on the club, closing it down completely. There were further crowd-and-cop confrontations as both the Saturday afternoon matinee and evening shows were cancelled.

Charged with handling the press, Kosmo had a field day and the near-riot was all over the TV stations and papers, even making the front page of the *New York Post*. Finally, the New York Building Commissioner stepped in and, prodded by his

Clash-fan daughters, agreed to let the shows go on if the fire restrictions were adhered to and security improved. This furore drew further publicity, making Bond's the hottest ticket in town.

The gigs provided an opportunity for The Clash to renew acquaintances with Martin Scorsese and Robert De Niro. Joe became good friends with both, enjoying several all night pool sessions with Scorsese, who wanted The Clash to make a cameo in *The King of Comedy*, a movie he was filming with De Niro. The band's appearance in the film was an archetypal blink-and-you-miss-'em scenario, as they pop up as extras on a Times Square street corner. 'We just kind of stood there, bumbling around,' Joe told *Uncut*'s Gavin Martin.

The Clash's choice of support acts for the Bond's shows was typically daring. Grandmaster Flash and the Furious Five came on with their lethal rap attack but were pelted with bottles and abuse by a crowd who consisted largely of 'bridge-and-tunnel' out-of-towners. Fellow Sugarhill label-mates the Treacherous Three fared little better. Another night, Lee Perry came on and baffled everyone with his surreal reggae excursions. Other guests included The Slits and ESG.

The Clash took the stage to Ennio Morricone's 'Sixty Seconds To What?' theme from Sergio Leone's spaghetti Western *For a Few Dollars More*, and again, played for well over two hours every night. At one show, Allen Ginsberg – a big hero of Joe's – took the stage and read a poem before the encores, with The Clash supplying backing. This collaboration would lead to further work with Ginsberg on the band's next album.

Don's footage shows The Clash at their performing peak and the Bond's residency marked the point at which the quartet finally made an impact on the American popular consciousness. 'You can't march into a city like New York and take away the night life,' explained Joe. 'We were presented with a situation that escalated beyond control. We were on the news . . . That was fantastic!' He added, 'Doing that fifteen nights in a row. It nearly killed us. But to go to New York and take New York. That is great.'

Joe had given up the lease on his Notting Hill flat before the US visit and, on his return, moved into Tymon Dogg's squat in Bloomsbury, London. By the end of the year he would be looking for a house and a mortgage.

With work on the new album set to continue, Joe's attitude, as ever, was to bang it down quick. 'The greatest records are the ones made with a couple of microphones', he later told *NME*. Joe felt that The Clash simply couldn't afford to do another value for money multi-set, especially after the drubbing given to *Sandinsta!* Certainly, Bernie would never allow any of the indulgences he felt had started with *Give 'Em Enough Rope*.

In August, The Clash started writing and recording at Ear Studios in Freston Road, West London, using the Rolling Stones Mobile to capture the results. These included Joe's 'Know Your Rights', which was built on a panting strum-guard rockabilly hump. The song was indicative of his growing rift with Mick who, having pushed his hip-hop fixation even further with the just-completed remixes of 'This Is Radio Clash', was becoming increasingly besotted with the infinite possibilities of the mixing desk. Conversely, Joe's enthusiasm for hip-hop and dub was cooling and his predilection for Americana was leading him back to the roots of rock 'n' roll. The 101'ers were no longer a dirty word.

In 1981, Joe didn't realise that The Clash were starting a bandwagon rather than joining one. By the time he filmed his *Westway To The World* interview in 1999, Joe could appreciate the groundbreaking path, along which Mick was trying to steer the band. 'Mick was always looking for the new thing. There are mixes of "Radio Clash" with typewriters going like machine guns all over them. People hear it and go, "Is this a new remix? Who remixed it?" And I say, "No, that's The Clash in 1981." We didn't realise we were doing something big by putting that stuff together.'

'I was so gone with the hip-hop thing that the others used to call me Wack Attack,' grins Mick. 'I'd walk around with a beatbox all the time and my hat on backwards. They used to take the mickey out of me. I was always like that about whatever came along, sort of get excited for a while.'

Other new Ear songs included 'Overpowered By Funk', a powerhouse express train collision between the JB's and Prince over which Joe chants a stream of abstract phrases like 'a phone box full of books'. Following his increasingly more surreal path with words, Joe shouts 'Benny Goodman' (veteran jazz player) at one point, 'dust-carts at sunrise' at another. Later Futura 2000, the New York graffiti artist who'd now hitched up with The Clash in a kind of Mikey Dread capacity, tossed in a rap.

'Ghetto Defendant' also started taking shape at Ear, coalescing as a shimmeringly haunting dub vehicle for Joe's lyrics about inner city addiction to 'Afghanistan medication'. Undoubtedly inspired by Topper's plight, its fine lyrics are elegant and thought provoking. 'Ghetto defendant, it is heroin pity/Not tear gas nor baton charge, that stops you taking the city.'

By now, Joe was able to convey his ideas and hit his lyrical targets with passion and accuracy. When you combine this with his anger at societal inequalities and the soul he'd inherited from his love of the blues, it was lethally effective. Joe meant every crafted word he wrote, and now had the skill to make his point with subtlety and emotion. The combination of that lyricism and Mick's poignant guitar line on 'Ghetto Defendent' is a classic example of how The Clash had matured into a modern soul outfit. Mick's production echoed the spaced elegance of Norman Whitfield, pioneering studio genius behind the Temptations and Undisputed Truth.

On 29 August 1981, Guy Stevens overdosed on pills prescribed to combat his alcoholism. We were all sad but not shocked by the news. On 17 September, The Clash responded by recording a sensitive tribute called 'Midnight To Stevens', which wouldn't see the light of day until *The Clash on Broadway* box set was released ten years later. It sweeps along in the manner of a classic Mott slowie, riding a doleful guitar riff – Mick throwing in a snatch of Mott's 'Violence' is a nice touch. The song is a rare thing because Joe is genuinely lamenting a lost friend. When he delivers the last line he sounds like he's welling up. In the *Clash on Broadway* booklet, Joe describes the song as, 'the lost track, everyone had forgotten about it . . . I don't remember recording "Midnight To Stevens" at all.'

The Clash were cover featured posing outside the Apocalypse Hotel in West London for the November 1981 issue of Zigzag.

Guy would subsequently be credited for providing 'Inspiration' on the sleeve of the new album. This mostly manifested itself on Mick's 'Should I Stay Or Should I Go' and its block-rocking power chords. The song concerned Mick's relationship with Ellen Foley and would later come complete with Clash Wildebeest Choir interlude and Joe Ely on backing vocals.

'Inoculated City' was one of the album's few actual Strummer-Jones collaborations, matching another set of anti-war lyrics delivered call-and-response over an up-tempo groove lathered in subtle melodies.

The group later got in trouble when Mick – getting into the sampling craze early – added a sample from the cheesy '2,000 Flushes' American toilet-cleaner commercial near the track's end. The company's lawyers swung into action and CBS/Epic were forced to remove the ad from subsequent pressings of the album.

In late September, The Clash took a break from recording to tour Europe. They kicked off with seven nights at the 2,000 capacity Theatre Mogador in Paris – all of which were attended by Robin Banks, who gave *Zigzag* the opportunity to feature another Clash front cover along with his report. The band were really getting into the idea of plotting up in a city, playing a week and causing a bigger splash than the old hit-and-run one-nighters. It also meant much less travelling.

Robin reported on The Clash's striking new stage set, which consisted of two twelve-foot checkpoint barriers, painted black and yellow, backed by a huge plain backdrop on which Futura 2000 sprayed a graffiti mural during the two-hour show. Bravely, after the air-raid sirens, they started the set with 'Broadway', Joe's haunting ballad from *Sandinista!* Having set the tone, the group continued to steer off the beaten path with 'One More Time', the new 'Radio Clash' and 'Should I Stay Or Should I Go'. Then 'Guns Of Brixton', 'White Man', 'The Magnificent Seven', 'Train In Vain', Topper's 'Ivan Meets GI Joe', 'Clash City Rockers', 'Koka Kola', 'Junco Partner', 'The Leader', 'Washington Bullets', a first airing of 'Ghetto Defendant', 'I Fought The Law' and 'Clampdown'. Joe would often introduce 'Clampdown' as 'the angry one', but that night chose a more cryptic announcement – 'We're just waiting to be melted down . . . Have you ever seen a burning puma?'

At this point in the set Futura would climb down from his ladder to rap through 'The Escapades Of Futura 2000', with The Clash backing him. Then it was 'Somebody Got Murdered', 'London Calling' and off. Every night they were called back for three encores, which took their pick from 'Janie Jones', 'Armagideon Time', 'Safe European Home', 'Police And Thieves', 'Brand New Cadillac' and 'London's Burning'. On the final night, the band were joined by Pearl Harbor for a rendition of Ray Charles' 'Hit The Road Jack', while The Beat's Ranking Roger came up for 'Armagideon Time', and a just-arrived Mikey Dread led a version of 'Bankrobber'.

'To witness The Clash in top gear is an almost orgasmic experience, exhilarating and devastating at the same time,' enthused Robin. 'They are unrivalled and unbeatable . . . No other band could reinforce or substantiate what The Clash attempt and succeed in doing. They erode the empty and putrid barriers of racial mistrust and establish a positive and creative force that is a genuine threat to the evils of the so-called establishment.'

Robin went on to describe the post-gig outings to clubs and restaurants – pointing out that all The Clash were vegetarians – and the consumption of 'vast amounts of alcoholic beverages'. Paul also had a bone inflammation in his hip and a raw shoulder from humping that heavy Fender Precision through the lengthy sets.

Robin also mentioned a row sparked by Bernie over Topper's condition, adding that the drummer 'is probably the most physically fit member of the band, doing 50 press-ups before the show.' Today, Robin agrees that this glowing account of Topper's physical health was probably the actions of a mate trying to deflect some of the rumours that had been popping up in the music papers about Topper's addiction. 'I was probably as fucked as he was!' admits Robin. 'I can't remember a lot of it,' confesses Topper.

NME had sent Paul Rambali to Paris, where he described Joe as 'nursing a cold beer, an aching throat, a sore conscience and wounded pride.' He was referring to the paper's seemingly unrelenting criticism of The Clash, of which Joe remarked, 'I don't care – my skin is thick enough by now, otherwise I wouldn't be able to get on stage . . .They have a cupboard with a ruler in it which is called the Clash standard of honesty and truth . . . and they take it out and measure us with it and then they go off on a fucking nineteen-day whisky and cocaine binge!'

Paul asked Joe about a supposed 'Clash Book of Rebel Poses'. 'You either attract people or repel them,' reasoned Joe. 'And if you repel them, then you're wasting your time and theirs. That's what I say about the Clash Book of Rebel Poses. Look, we could write the same songs, perform the same way on stage, but we could all wear C&A outfits. Either you go up there for people to look at you or you stay at fucking home!'

Rambali grappled with the way in which opinions polarized around Joe – held up as a new Messiah by some, and mercilessly lambasted by others. 'I am honestly touched by the anger and compassion in Strummer's voice . . . It's easy to see why some people at *NME* lionise him as they do (despite his protests) . . . Hard to imagine how anyone could live up to being Joe Strummer – heir apparent to rock's rebel crown.'

Pennie Smith told Rambali that the band were having more arguments since the return of Bernie, who had even ruled that they shouldn't wear hats. Joe had said that the smooth running during the Blackhill period had made the group too comfortable. One of his reasons for wanting Bernie back was to reinstall an edge. This is what he was doing, and would continue to do until The Clash imploded. But in 1981, the arguments were more like 'lovers' quarrels', according to Pennie. 'Most of the quarrels can be traced back to their laundry anyway!'

The Radio Clash tour opened in Manchester on 5 October and wound up two weeks later with seven days at London's Lyceum Ballroom. It marked the band's first UK dates for eighteen months.

It came as little surprise when *NME* panned one of the gigs. Barney Hoskyns laid into Joe's performance and the diverse musical strains in the music – 'Strummer's earnest attempts to make cultures clash are always a case of hit-or-miss. Certain Clash signatures have got pretty wearisome – the screeches, the painfully contrived angst, the "genius is pain" grimaces, perhaps the whole Clash beat – that decisively unloose funk-rock.' Barney also dismissed most of the recent two albums as 'piffle', as did many – then.

When I went to the Lyceum, there seemed to be a lack of the riotous dressing room unity that I'd encountered on those tours between 1977 and 1979. Both front and backstage were packed to sardine level. It was more like a reunion, with the band members in separate pockets with their own cliques. 'There'd be two dressing rooms on those tours,' remembers Topper. 'Joe, Mick and Paul would be in one with their friends and I'd be in the other one with all my druggy mates.'

The shows had moved on from the previous tour, especially with the graffiti presentation and length of set. It was a truly eclectic selection now with little to please the fundamentalist spiketops. The Clash were now a mature, spectacularly creative rock 'n' roll band, taking you on a sonic world tour rather than coming on like the old commando raid, even if they did start the shows with an air-raid siren.

After the constant stream of negative press, The Clash were surprised and delighted at the success of the gigs, which were all sold out. 'That's another bum steer that the *NME* gave me,' recalled Joe. 'I believed them when they said we weren't liked there. In fact the guy on the street was digging us.'

After the UK tour, the band returned to New York to recommence recording at Electric Lady studio. This was at the insistence of Mick, who delivered a similar ultimatum to that which Joe had issued over Bernie. Of course, this rankled with Joe and Bernie, who'd been all for recording the album at Ear on a TEAC. This was a vastly more expensive operation.

It didn't help later when Mick said that he'd only been joking. Or when he announced that they'd be re-recording much of the Ear material from scratch, in addition to writing more new songs. A power struggle was definitely underway. Mick, unable to prevent the return of Bernie, had retaliated by calling the shots on the music, which – up until now – had been his territory. Plus it meant he could see Ellen and further feed his New York fixation. One all.

Despite the conflicts, some great stuff was emerging. The new songs included 'Straight To Hell', which is regarded as one of Joe's all-time greats in terms of lyrics and performance. Possibly his best ever. The song began life as a Mick guitar riff over an unusual drum pattern set up by Topper, which he based on a bossanova groove. Joe provided the low percussive resonance by whacking Topper's bass drum with a lemonade bottle wrapped in a towel. The end result is an ethereal outing of total beauty. One of the few pieces of music I've encountered where time seems to stand still.

The vivid lyrics deal with the way in which society consigns its perceived outcasts to the dumper. Joe refers to unemployed steel workers, the offspring of American GIs, Vietnamese women and immigrants in general. Rather than romanticising America, the track is actually laying into the country.

As easily as The Clash paid homage to US musical styles on tunes like 'The Magnificent Seven', the new album saw them demonstrate that they could just as easily highlight the gross injustices going on in that country with their own creative assault. Joe's hook on the new song was an approximation of the old Monopoly board game's stern 'Go To Jail'. 'There ain't no need for ya/Go straight to hell boys.'

The sessions also produced the finished version of 'Death Is A Star', which featured Tymon Dogg on piano, in a brilliantly wide-screen piece of music that managed to combine a psychedelic baroque flourish with some before-its-time spaced ambience. Joe, who semi-spoke his words, later told *NME* that the song was about, 'the way we all queue up at the cinema to see someone get killed. These days the public execution is the celluloid execution. I was examining why I want to go and see these movies, because deep in my heart I want to see a man pull out a machine gun and go blam, blam, blam into somebody's body.'

Joe extended his cinematic obsessions on 'Atom Tan', where he describes a Phantom style superhero figure in a rain-battered motel with 'the guns dying at sunset'. He wrote 'Red Angel Dragnet' after reading about the murder of a Guardian Angel, New York's red-bereted subway vigilantes. Paul sang Joe's pleas for, 'Just freedom to move, to live/For women to take a walk in the park at midnight.'

Further work was carried out on the desolate dubscape of 'Ghetto Defendant'. Allan Ginsberg came in on several nights and, acting as 'the voice of God', came up with several lines that provide an eerie counterpart to Joe's inner city anguish.

Ginsberg was no stranger to the cutting edge of art and music. He'd spearheaded the new poetry in the early sixties, brought it to London and hitched up with New York's Fugs when they launched their fiery brand of agit-obscenity into the world.

In the mid-eighties, when I lived in New York on 12th Street before it hits Avenue A, Ginsberg occupied the apartment below. When he wasn't entertaining a stream of fellow writers and young male friends, we'd chat sometimes. He talked about Strummer's work being on a par with the great writers he'd come up with, although he did wish that The Clash had included some more of the several poems he'd laid down with them at Electric Lady. Even William Burroughs heaped similar praise when I hunkered in his bunker around the same time.

Originally, 'Ghetto Defendant' was a lot longer, with a full verse from Ginsberg being left off the finished product. Joe's explanation for the edit was, 'It was kind of long, so we shortened it.' The song eventually appeared in its original form on the *Clash on Broadway* compilation.

Meanwhile, Topper had been fiddling with a distinctive piano riff for some time and started working on it when he arrived at the studio early one morning. The band arrived and took a fancy to it. Mick added some guitar and Joe, impressed by the speed at which this was happening, immediately wrote the words for what would become 'Rock The Casbah'.

'I had the idea with the piano riff at Electric Lady,' recalls Topper. 'No one was there one afternoon so I thought, "I've got an idea." So I put down the drums, piano, bassline and percussion one by one. Then Joe came in and wrote the words. Not a bad afternoon's work.

'With *Sandinista!* and *Combat Rock* we just made it up as we went along. It was a four-way thing. If I'd not been an addict I'd have loved it. On *London Calling*, they told me how to play but by *Sandinista!* I was writing stuff. On *Combat Rock*, I was really contributing. If I'd have played my other instruments I could have done more. When I did "Rock The Casbah" I was stoned out of my head, but I put everything down. I could've gone on like that because I was all right when I had some gear. But then when I ran out I'd disappear again. Either I'd be trying to score, or I'd be in my room sick. I wouldn't come out – "Fuck off! I'm trying to score."'

The lyrics were partly sparked by a news story that Joe had encountered which reported that Iranians were being flogged and jailed for possessing Western rock and disco albums. Joe's opening line comes from one of Bernie's more famous comments, comparing The Clash's new stuff to the endless improvisation commonly found in Indian ragas. 'We found that whenever we played a tune on the *Combat Rock* sessions, it would be six minutes minimum,' said Joe in the *Clash on Broadway* booklet. 'After a few days of this, Bernie came down the studio, and I think he heard "Sean Flynn" and he said, "Does everything have to be as long as a raga?" From then on we called everything we did "ragas".'

The song would later become The Clash's first top ten hit in the US, but what happened next illustrates the capricious nature of Topper's addicted existence. He got busted again. Now his future with The Clash was in real doubt.

'The 1981 bust was when the band thought, "Fuck it." We were in New York, recording *Combat Rock*. I'd met this nice bird and I was concentrating on her. But then I phoned my girlfriend in London, who was an addict and she told me there was a drought. Nothing to be found. So I thought I'd pop back to London for 24 hours and take some gear over for her. I was stoned out of my head and woke up on the plane at Heathrow, but I had all this gear, so I just stuffed it down my underpants. That was it. All over.'

Topper was arrested for smuggling heroin at customs and appeared at Uxbridge Magistrates Court on 17 December. It looked like he might go down, but his defence said he had recently been voted 'one of the top five drummers in the world' and had recording commitments to fulfil. Topper admitted to being an addict but said he wanted to clean up and would do so.

While fining him £500 the judge said, 'Unless you accept treatment, you will be the best drummer in the graveyard.' Although he avoided jail, Topper recalled that the bust haunted him for the remainder of his time with The Clash. 'Now everywhere the band went we got pulled apart because we had a convicted heroin addict in the band.'

The band returned to New York in January 1982 and continued work on the album – which was supposed to have been finished the previous month. Ironically, now that work had been transplanted to Electric Lady, birthplace of *Sandinista!*, the record was ballooning lengthwise. Under the working title, 'Rat Patrol From Fort Bragg', they got up to around seventeen tracks, many of which were raga-length.

By now, Joe and Mick were usually working separate shifts to do their overdubs. Joe sent over to London for Jerry Green, who'd worked as tape operator on the previous two albums and recorded his vocals at night. Mick worked during the day with house engineer Joe Blaney. That was the only way they could avoid arguing.

Topper now describes the sessions as, 'The ones where we'd just bump into each other occasionally in the studio. We were hardly speaking. Mick and Joe rowed about everything. Mick was always late and stoned. He hated touring and just wanted to be in the studio. I was right out of my head, fucked up on heroin. That was affecting my timekeeping. All four of us were fucked up – we were a band in name only.'

There was another touring break that month when The Clash – literally downing tools and heading for the airport – visited Japan for the first time, followed by dates in New Zealand and Australia in February. From all accounts, Joe was on manic top form throughout the jaunt and the group was welcomed like visiting royalty.

'Every time we come to a town, they go, "Oh, we've been waiting five years for you"' Joe confided to *NME*'s Roz Reines. 'I'd rather come as an extra, a bonus to the local scene, not like the staple diet was in town for twenty minutes then left.'

Again, The Clash favoured playing extended stints at 3,000 capacity venues rather than making the obvious killings in bigger arenas. On 24 January, they embarked on seven nights at Tokyo's Shibuya Kohkaida, playing over two hours of 'greatest hits' and bringing on the less than tactfully named Pearl Harbor to sing her single, 'Fujiyama Mama'.

In Sydney, before they played seven dates at the Capitol Theatre, the press conference caused a bit of a stir. Consistent with the band's animal fixation, it was held in the 'mammals' section of the Museum of Applied Arts & Sciences. Joe gave one of his most memorable performances – ranting, expounding and coming on with 'a holy rollin' one-man standup, political flag-waving harangue by a man who – if he delivers one tenth as good live on stage – must be a performer to leave others flat-footed,' according to *Rolling Stone*'s Australian correspondents Bruce Elder and Ed St John. 'We're here because we're exciting,' proclaimed Joe. 'We jump about, wiggle our bums, and there's nothing wrong with that!'

After his periods of illness and the times when he left the direction of The Clash to Mick, Joe was now asserting himself in a big way, really diving into any situation with both feet. It was an approach he would maintain for the next twenty years, as he got up really early – sometimes at around six in the morning – and immersed himself in the local culture while constantly scribbling ideas, band suggestions and lyrics on scraps of paper. When The Clash hit Auckland, New Zealand, Joe acquired a ukulele and went out busking. In Perth, Australia, the effort of being constantly hyperactive became too much and he collapsed from exhaustion during the gig.

With the album still unfinished, the group attempted to finish mixing while on tour, booking studios in Australia and sometimes going in after a show to record through the night. Eventually, Mick reckoned that *Rat Patrol From Fort Bragg* was complete. At this point, it was a double album with fifteen tracks. 'It sounded terrible,' says Topper. 'It just wasn't Mick. After that we all tried to mix it on the world tour. I had a go in Australia after a gig, when my ears were ringing, so I had every fader on full.'

A CD came into my possession called *Rat Patrol From Fort Bragg – Mick Jones' Original Mix For Combat Rock*. The disc isn't in the actual running order, but it's a fascinating glimpse of what *Combat Rock* would have sounded like if it had been a double album in Mick's hands. Tracks are allowed to breathe, stretch and hit levels of transcendental beauty rarely glimpsed on rock albums. Those ragas are great!

Rat Patrol starts with 'The Beautiful People Are Ugly Too' and 'Kill Time', which have never been released. The former was inspired by a visit to Studio 54 and rides a suitably uptown disco-funk groove, with a touch of calypso. Likewise, 'Kill Time' cites The Clash's Caribbean influences with its jumping steel drums. Then comes the original 'Should I Stay Or Should I Go', before Glyn Johns forced Mick to re-record his vocals and replace the 'around your front or on your back' line with 'if you want me off your back.' It did sound a bit messier with more upfront Spanish vocals but, understandably, Mick sounds a lot more chilled. 'Rock The Casbah' lost a saxophone riff, while 'Know Your Rights' is the version before Joe re-recorded his vocals. He sounds like Captain Beefheart on 'Ice Cream For Crow'.

'Red Angel Dragnet', which features a hilarious Kosmo rap that sounds like Nick Cave impersonating Ali G, and 'Ghetto Defendant' are simply longer, although the latter places more emphasis on Ginsberg's contribution and, with the extra verse, builds a formidable atmosphere. I think that's the key to this version of the album – Mick was into building textured moods within extended versions of the songs. It's a shame such a lot of good bits ended up on the cutting room floor – like the drifting coda of 'Sean Flynn', which is nearly three minutes longer. 'Car Jamming', 'Inoculated City' and 'Atom Tan' are also taken further.

The slinky drug bust funk vamp, 'First Night Back In London', and reggae-lite 'Cool Confusion' were relegated to B-sides of the US releases of 'Should I Stay Or Should I Go'. 'Overpowered By Funk' appears in its original stripped-down hot-wired incarnation, while 'Death Is A Star' still sounds like an out-there psychedelic tone poem.

The real gripper is the instrumental 'Walk Evil Talk', also never released, which is basically a space-jazz piano instrumental, with Topper excelling on his Elvin Jones style rolls and rimshots. It's the furthest out The Clash ever went and totally uncommercial – but absolutely startling.

Finally, 'Straight To Hell' is preserved in its full magnificence with an extra verse about Alphabet City. On this evidence, I'm sure there could have been some greater compromise reached. For instance, using Bill Price again.

However, war had been declared and Bernie and Joe were determined to win.

The spark that had galvanised The Clash and enabled them to record the first album in three weekends had been replaced by business requirements, touring *ennui* and internal tensions to the point where Joe often acted as the middleman between Mick and Paul, even if they were in the same room. The pair had to abandon one session after spending two hours arguing over the bass sound on 'Know Your Rights'.

Mick was always falling out with Joe, which left Topper – the band outlaw on account of his habit – as the nearest thing that Mick had to an ally. Joe had once drawn a line on the floor between the two factions and described Mick and Topper as the 'musicians', while he and Paul were 'the entertainers.' Now the great divide had become reality.

The Clash wound up the tour with a pair of one-off shows; in Hong Kong on 25 February, followed by a gig at Thamasat University in Bangkok, Thailand. This is where Pennie Smith shot the session for the album cover. The lack of unity within the group is clearly evident on the image that was selected for the cover of *Combat Rock*. Clash photos used to boast an indefinable ring of energy, which saw the four members bouncing off each other. Here, they simply look uncomfortable in each other's presence. Mick and Paul stare away from the camera in their own worlds, Topper looks wasted and Joe sports a look of mild panic while covering most of his face with his hand.

'Somehow they seemed to dissolve in front of my eyes!' recalled Pennie, 'I knew

Thousands of miles from The Westway, The Clash dissolve during the Combat Rock *cover shoot.*

something was wrong.' Matters were not helped when Paul then went down with a debilitating bowel complaint. Despite being advised by local medics that he had a twisted colon, which required an operation, Paul opted to seek out a second opinion once he was back home. This was just as well, as his illness turned out to be nothing more than a particularly nasty bug.

When the group returned from the Far East, they were nowhere nearer finishing the new album than they'd been when they'd left. The Bond's experience and touring virgin territories to mass adulation had shown Joe that The Clash could indeed become huge – especially if they delivered a knockout blow of an album.

Joe had got Bernie back in as an ally but Mick had continued to dominate the recording – with results the others weren't satisfied with. Now it was Joe's turn to reassert his influence. He got everyone to overrule Mick and, with the approval of a panicking CBS, brought in veteran producer Glyn Johns to pump, prune and panel-beat a killer single album out of it all. Joe seized creative control, with the intention of turning the LP into an unashamedly commercial weapon in the war against Foreigner and Boston's domination of the American masses.

Glyn Johns had an impressive CV, which included The Faces, The Who, the Rolling Stones and The Beatles. He went into Wessex with Joe and the pair set about racing against time to try and meet a late April release. Having heard the *Rat Patrol* bootleg, I wish they hadn't bothered.

The remixing and editing process deprived tracks like 'Straight To Hell' and 'Ghetto Defendant' of essential verses. The new sound was often dry and punchy, whereas the original mixes were experimental and atmospheric. For the first time, Mick did not attend the mixing of a Clash album, preferring to stay away and quietly fume.

Joe and Glyn emerged with twelve tracks, which ran at about 48 minutes. These could be crammed onto a single disc with minimal loss of sound quality caused by compressing the grooves. Tracks left off were 'First Night Back In London', 'Long Time Jerk', 'Kill Time', 'The Beautiful People' and 'Cool Confusion'. The songs which made it were 'Know Your Rights', 'Car Jamming', 'Should I Stay Or Should I Go', 'Rock The Casbah', 'Red Angel Dragnet', 'Straight To Hell', 'Overpowered by Funk', 'Atom Tan', 'Sean Flynn', 'Ghetto Defendant', 'Inoculated City', 'Death Is A Star' and 'Walk Evil Talk'.

Flexing his influence still further, Joe changed the title to the more slimline *Combat Rock*, which I hated because it sounded desperate, and too paramilitary. In retrospect, it made sense – single album, snappy title, no messing. It makes even more sense when you consider the conditions it was created under.

Trimmed of flab and straight to the point, The Clash's music had now entered a different dimension to their previous work. The dub vibe remained in terms of sonic possibilities, but the sonic textures echoed electronic foraging, classical experiments and a technique that used to be known as 'sound painting'.

You would not have seen the band devoting time to heavily treating a violin during the first album sessions. Here, the aim had been to plant the message, often via spoken word, against a futuristic but sympathetic aural backdrop. It should have been that double album.

'Mick's attitude was that I ruined his music,' said Joe in a 1984 *Creem* interview. '50 per cent was great rock, but the other 50 per cent was what Phil Spector would have called "wiggy".' Ironically, Glyn Johns had seen his back-to-basics version of the Beatles' *Let It Be* album rendered into stringy slush by Phil Spector.

Joe later cited the album's agonisingly extended birth as a major factor in the group's demise. As he explained to the *San Antonio Current* in 2001, 'There was a bit of friction. When friction builds up people stop communicating – or maybe that's the cause of friction – but whatever it is, the result is that people don't tell each other what they think any more. Then you're really in bad water. And we couldn't get out of it. I think that kind of finished us off.'

CHAPTER FIFTEEN

THE RUNNING MAN

The enemy you know is better than the enemy you don't know. – Joe Strummer

With the gruelling recording sessions and extensive touring, Joe desperately needed a break. He even had 'I may take a holiday' stencilled on his guitar during the 1981 tours. This he got in April 1982 when, on the eve of a nineteen-date UK tour, he did a runner.

Although sudden, Joe's disappearance was hardly spontaneous. Worried by slow ticket sales in Scotland, Bernie had recommended that Joe visit his old mate Joe Ely in Texas for a few days, while calling in every day to confirm his whereabouts. Bernie reasoned that the dates subsequent to Joe's return would sell out, in addition to boosting sales for any gigs that would need rescheduling. What Bernie *didn't* reckon on was Joe genuinely vanishing for a few weeks, in a show of strength designed to demonstrate that Bernie couldn't control him and the group couldn't work without him.

The Know Your Rights tour was supposed to start in Aberdeen on 26 April. Joe disappeared on the 21st. Bernie then dressed up the situation for public consumption via the *NME*. 'Joe's personal conflict is: where does the socially concerned rock artist stand in the bubblegum environment of today? I feel he's probably gone away for a serious rethink . . . I think he feels some resentment about the fact that he was about to go slogging his guts out just for people to slag him off, saying he's wearing the wrong trousers. A lot of people want to destroy the group, but we won't let that happen because we're an international group. But they could destroy The Clash in this country . . . I think Joe has just gone away to examine what it is all about. We've got to find this bloke. He'll get a bollocking when he comes back but it's still better that he comes back.'

Having instigated Joe's vanishing act as a McLarenesque stunt, Bernie was thrown into panic when Joe didn't call. With their frontman's whereabouts unknown, the whole tour was rescheduled for July. The press had a field day with 'Strummer's runner', with Joe being cast as Lord Lucan in combat gear. I heard so many rumours: Joe living in Amsterdam, being found dead in a Scottish river, going to deepest Africa or working on the Marseilles docks. The group didn't have a clue, although they knew he was okay because he'd phoned his mum. They just didn't know when, or even if, he'd be back.

'I thought it would be a good joke if I never phoned Bernie at all,' said Joe on Channel 4's *Wired* in 1988. 'So he was going to be *thinking* he was acting, "Where's Joe gone?" and after a few weeks he'd be going, "Where HAS Joe gone?" I stayed with a bloke I know in Paris and I ran the Paris marathon too.'

'Well, obviously I called my mom,' Joe recalled in *The Big Takeover* in 2000. 'I said, "Look, mom, I'm going to have to disappear for a while. Don't worry about it." You know, I chilled her out. But she didn't even know where I was at . . . The funniest thing was, I got on the boat-train, and we got into a compartment . . . and the guy already inside reached into his bag and pulled out a copy of the *NME*. He started to read it and I was going, "Oh God, why did we have to get into this compartment of all the ones on the train?" But he didn't notice.'

In fact, he did. The guy was Steve Taylor, who wrote for *The Face,* and promptly told *NME* who he'd travelled to Paris on the train with.

Eventually, Kosmo managed to wheedle the address of Joe's hideout from his mum and was dispatched to bring him back on 17 May. He dressed as Viet-superman Rambo for the task. Joe's attitude was, 'It's a fair cop,' and he returned rejuvenated.

After a month in exile, Joe returned to face the inevitable barrage of 'where you been?' queries. Joe said he and Gaby had initially set off for Paris, 'without even thinking about it', and 'dicked around for a while'. He grew a beard and nobody recognised him. 'I guess it's not the place you'd look!' he reasoned later. He also gave *NME*'s Charles Shaar Murray a full explanation – 'It was something I wanted to prove to myself: that I was alive. It's very much like being a robot, being in a group. You keep coming along and keep delivering and keep being an entertainer. Rather than go barmy, I think it's better to do what I did, even for a month . . . I only intended to stay for a few days, but the more days I stayed, the harder it was to come back because of the agro I was causing that I'd have to face.'

'I went to shake The Clash up, to shake the Clash fans up, to shake the Clash haters up, and to shake myself up too,' he told *Sounds.*

Later that year, I interviewed Mick and mentioned how the press had *loved* this one. 'Yeah, I loved it an' all,' he replied, coldly. 'No, it was horrible. I guess I'm envious.'

You wish you'd done it?

'Yeah,' admitted Mick. 'But once it's been done, it's been done. You can't do it. You have to do something else. Maybe I'll top meself.'

Thankfully, he laughed after the last comment. Far from bitterness or contempt, Mick's reaction to his partner's runner seemed to be one of great mirth. He genuinely found it funny, especially America's hysterical reactions.

'They made a big thing about it in America. Once we said in an interview when they asked what's happening with Joe, I said, "he's gone off to have a sex change operation." So then you see all these pictures of girls doing aerobatics [sic], and the caption is, "Joe Strummer – the operation worked out"! Put him right in it there, but he didn't mind. You only have to get one gullible bloke to go, "Oh really, I'll alert the Media immediately!"'

While Joe was away, 'Know Your Rights' was released as a single on 1 May, with 'First Night Back In London' on the flip. It did little better than 'This Is Radio Clash', hitting Number 43. This one actually got a good *NME* review, with Paul Du Noyer writing, 'Orator Joe storms back with a bitter-edged pep-talk for the troops, and The Clash make their best single in a long time.'

The sleeve is notable for the five-pointed star, which Paul got the idea to use when he visited Moscow four years earlier. Inside the star is an open book inscribed with 'The Future Is Unwritten' on one page and a gun on the other. This actually originates from a Strummer doodle of the time, which would form part of 2004's *Joe Strummer – Past, Present and Future* exhibition.

On 14 May, *Combat Rock* was unleashed. The album broke with recent tradition and garnered enthusiastic reviews: Five stars from *Sounds*' Dave McCullough' while *Melody Maker's* Adam Sweeting picked up on the cinematic vibe – 'Like editors of old documentary film, The Clash re-process imagery through the shifting lenses of their music.'

NME raved its approval, with X Moore (a.k.a. Chris Dean of leftist skinhead band the Redskins) calling it 'easily the best Clash album since *Give 'Em Enough Rope.*' Dean, who had claimed that his ambition was to 'sing like the Supremes and walk like The Clash', declared that the LP, 'spells out the sides, nails the real war and says all that needs to be said about the farce that is the Falklands War.' Obviously the Falklands link wasn't planned, but The Clash had managed to release an album called *Combat Rock* while Britain was at war.

The conflict had started in April when Argentinian ruler General Galtieri ordered an invasion of the remote British colony in the South Atlantic. Back home, Margaret Thatcher was looking for a way to boost her party's rock-bottom popularity in the long run up to the next General Election. The Argentinian invasion was an absolute gift-horse for Thatcher, allowing her to enact her Churchillian penis envy fantasies, while sending her opinion-poll rating soaring amidst a tide of jingoistic ravings in the tabloid press.

That over a thousand young men lost their lives fighting for an island that most people in the UK couldn't find on a map was a secondary consideration for a gov-

An illustration from one of Joe's many notebooks, as displayed at the Joe Strummer: Past, Present & Future *exhibition in London during September 2004.*

ernment determined to ensure re-election at any cost. The tabloids had a jingoistic field day bellowing about 'our boys' stomping 'the Argies', who were mostly hapless conscripted youngsters. At the time I was on tour with Motorhead and the merchandisers dished out 'FUCK ARGENTINA' t-shirts to the touring party.

By 1982, my relationship with *Zigzag* had soured considerably with the arrival of repugnant new publishers who stripped me of my powers, ripped off writers, banned me and Robin from the office and turned the venerable old mag into a lightweight travesty. A golden age when the magazine had really meant something and The Clash were like family was gone.

Even though *Zigzag* had distanced itself from The Clash since my departure, at least new writer Marts didn't (quite) pan it: '*Combat Rock* shows The Clash in a harsh light. It shows them as they are: uncompromising, enthusiastic and alone . . . As for Joe, well he sounds as ill as ever. The Clash have grown up. Maybe I have too. Maybe that's the problem.'

Combat Rock became the most successful Clash album of all, narrowly missing the top of the UK chart, and went to sell over a million copies worldwide. 'I never thought we'd be Number Two in Britain,' a shocked Joe told Charles Shaar Murray. 'I really didn't. There really seems to be something against us here . . . since we started going round the world.'

Joe's runner cleared his head on what should be done with Topper, and showed him he had the power to do it. Joe and Bernie now wanted Topper and his addiction out, while Mick stood up for him. In *Westway To The World*, Paul points out that they felt uneasy singing anti-drug songs when Topper was sitting behind his drums in an opiated daze. Mick felt that Topper was still his mate and should be given a chance and offered help with his problem. But Joe forced the Topper issue after he had shown how easily he could shut down The Clash.

Joe joined the band to play the Lochem festival in Holland on 20 May. Although Topper didn't know it at the time, the gig was a last chance to see if he could still hold it together. It turned out to be his final gig with The Clash.

Topper didn't pass the test, as he now recalls. 'Joe had been saying, "Topper's got to go" for a while, but Mick and Paul were saying, "Give him a chance." So they did at this gig, but I blew it. I was nodding out in my breakfast at Heathrow. Then at the gig I was scoring coke and everything else.

'When we got back to London, they called a group meeting. I said, "Tell me about it in the morning." But they said, "No, you've got to come." I thought, "What's that about then?"'

The meeting took place at Paul's flat, with the band, Bernie and Kosmo present. 'So I went round and Joe just said, "You're sacked." First of all I burst out laughing. Then they told me again, and I burst out crying. It was horrible. Mick was crying. He was really sensitive.'

Topper left, walked around the block, then came back and promised he'd clean up if they let him stay. Unfortunately, they'd heard this one before. Then Topper made an offer he thought the band wouldn't refuse. He was wrong.

'I came back to the flat and said, "Why don't you take Terry [Chimes] on the tour and I'll go too? You can give him my wages. I'll just be there and I'll be drug free. If you suspect I'm doing drugs I'll go." But they wouldn't have it, except for Mick.'

'That's when my heart went *ping*, y'know,' Joe told *Record Mirror*'s Jim Reid in 1986. 'It just rose up in me to say, "Look, he's come back. That's enough, isn't it? What more do you want? Let's work with him. Let's help him!" Instead, I just shut my mouth, like everyone else in the room.'

'Bernie was actually behind it,' says Topper. 'He was sitting beside Joe when he said it. Bernie was such an idiot. I never got on with with him from the start. I was always kind of like the new kid on the block. It was Bernie that killed it. He played a big part in my sacking. As much as I love Paul, he took the easy option. If Joe and Bernie wanted me sacked, Paul went with them. Mick wanted me to stay.'

Robin Banks was – and still is – particularly close to Topper. 'When Topper got thrown out it was the beginning of the end for The Clash,' he says. 'Mick stood up for him and Topper's never forgotten that. Paul just sat on the fence, like he's always done. Topper always says, "I'd kill for Mick or Joe but I wouldn't cross the road for Paul," because he knows Paul wouldn't cross the road for him, and he didn't.'

'Joe didn't have a lot of choice but to get rid of me,' reckons Topper now. 'For a long time I didn't give them a lot of choice. I had lots of warnings. I know I fucked it all up. Mick didn't want me to go, but if I'd stayed I'd have just let Mick down. I did when I started playing with BAD.'

Kosmo told the press Topper had quit due to 'a difference of opinion over the political direction the band would be taking'. That fooled nobody, especially after the recent Strummer farrago.

Joe was still obfuscating the real reason for Topper's sacking when *NME* interviewed the band a few days after the event. 'It was his decision,' he told Charles Shaar Murray, ' . . . it's not easy to be in The Clash. It's not as simple as being in a comfortable, we're-just-entertainers group, and he just wanted to do that, just play music. He had to sort of strike out in another direction, because I don't think he wants to come along with us.'

Or Joe didn't want him coming along in that state, anyway. The truth is, the door was never totally shut on Topper. If he'd shaped up he probably could have walked back in as the real Clash never had a permanent drummer after him. Topper was one of the finest drummers of all time. He was uncannily perfect for The Clash, feeling, driving and accentuating every nuance of the music while, as Sandy Pearlman put it, remaining the Human Drum Machine.

But, as Topper says, 'You can play anything else and be fucked up but if you're the drummer then it just can't work because it throws everyone else out.'

'If you try and imagine a group and the drummer is falling apart, then no matter what you're putting on top, it's going to fall apart,' declared Joe. 'You need to have someone firing on all cylinders. You can't have any passengers on board because it slows the whole thing down, you lose the spirit and you grind to a shuddering halt . . . it was the chemical mixture of those four people that makes a group work and you can take one away and replace them with anyone you like or ten men, and it's never gonna work.'

In 1982, there wasn't the rehab techniques, armies of counsellors and facilities for weaning people off drugs that there are now. It was usually cold turkey or the also-addictive methadone. Only later in the decade would rehab centres like The Priory become the rock star's holiday camp. Topper was genuinely surprised when I told him that Joe had later said that he wished The Clash had tried to find some kind of help instead of sacking him.

'That's Joe. He was really nice. One of the most caring people that I ever met. I know he felt really guilty afterwards. Bernie pushed him, and to sack Mick, so it's no detriment to Joe. I didn't envy Joe's position. It was Bernie who killed it.'

However, the group didn't give up hope that Topper would one day sort himself out. When I talked to Mick a few months later he glumly observed 'I don't know what's happening with Topper.'

What did happen was that Topper – after a stint with former Motorhead guitarist 'Fast' Eddie Clarke – tried to form a band with ex-Pretenders bass player Pete Farndon, who was also a heroin addict and overdosed in April 1983. Topper then embarked on a short-lived solo career and released an album called *Waking Up*. But he couldn't stay away from the dope. He used to go to CBS and blag records to sell in the secondhand shop – he was also compelled to sell his drum kit. Johnny Green recalls how The Clash used to get sponsorship deals, 'then the kits would mysteriously disappear.' Eventually, Topper had to resort to selling his silver and gold discs.

'After I was sacked it was just, "Say you've got nervous exhaustion,"' says Topper. 'They left the door open if I cleaned up my act. Then Joe was pissed and said in an interview, "Oh, we had to get rid of Topper, he was a junkie." All of a sudden, I went up to being a heroin addict. I thought, "Fuck it, then." Within weeks I was injecting all the time. But I've got no bad feelings. The Clash was my life. The Clash was brilliant for me, but five years and it imploded.'

Topper only really beat his addiction in early 2004 – over twenty years after leaving The Clash. On *Westway . . .* , he says that if he could do it all over again, he'd probably do the same thing. 'I'm that kind of person . . . I remember when the band sacked me I promised them I'd try and stop misbehaving and taking substances. I feel a lot of guilt about that, because if I'd have kept my act together I could see the band possibly still being together today, in a way.'

'I'm an addict, I was still using then, so I looked a bit gaunt,' he says of his *Westway . . .* appearance. 'Up until six months ago, that's all I knew. Of course I regret it, but I was just being honest. If you made me 21 again and put me in The Clash I'd react the same. I love it too much. I'd do all the coke, shag all the women, do loads of smack, get drunk. That's how I am.' Today Topper realises that he can't even have a can of beer without embarking on a bender.

Later, Joe would always describe Topper's departure as 'the beginning of the end' for The Clash. 'He's the best,' he reflected sadly when talking to *Punk*'s Judy McGuire in the late nineties. 'I hated it when we sacked him. The day The Clash died was the day we sacked him.'

Topper's sacking meant that The Clash were faced with a familiar problem. Who was going to play the drums? Especially when, in just over a week's time, they were due to start a month-plus US tour at Asbury Park, New Jersey. Fortunately, no auditions were necessary. They simply called up Terry Chimes, who was available following the disintegration of Generation X the previous year and agreed to fill in on the gigs booked until the end of 1982.

Apart from reuniting the first album's line-up, the tour was notable for the fact that the band had finally sold enough of their previous albums to be considered out of debt to the record company. They might even make some money this time.

When Topper left so did his faithful roadie, Barry The Baker. During his time with the band, The Baker had become as much a part of The Clash family as the sorely-missed Johnny Green, quietly getting on with his job while still boasting that indefinable essential spirit and humour. Barry moved to New York to be a truck driver but, after a road accident, somehow ended up becoming manager of the large Strand bookshop on Broadway. Baker's departure was another example of how this family was starting to unravel.

Before the US tour, Mick had a chance to regain his dented studio pride by remixing 'Rock The Casbah' for a US twelve-inch single release, complete with a dub called 'Mustapha Dance'. This he did at New York's Power Station with another established engineer, Bob Clearmountain, who'd worked with the Stones and Ian Hunter.

Meanwhile, the first US single off *Combat Rock* was 'Should I Stay Or Should I Go', which was released on 10 June with 'Inoculated City' on the flip. Two weeks later it came out again coupled with the non-album 'Cool Confusion' – and then again on 20 July as a limited edition flipped by 'First Night Back In London'. The latter version generated some controversy by depicting Ronald Reagan on the sleeve wearing a pasted-on Clash armband.

The original version of 'Rock The Casbah' was released in the UK on 26 June with 'Long Time Jerk' on the flip. It managed to reach Number 30. Don Letts' video – filmed during the US tour – deposits the band in a massive oil field in the Texas desert. While Joe sports his new Travis Bickle-style Mohican, Mick covers his face with a camouflage netting bandana, which could be taken as symbolic, or simply as a bit of dressing up, as Mick told the press. Joe whips Mick's mask off towards the end, which was also manna for Clash conspiracy theorists.

Ironically, the song was later co-opted as a kind of anthem by the US military during the first Gulf War in 1991, and has become synonymous with war and destruction in the Middle East. 'But if you listen all the way through, Joe's lyrics are really funny!' counters Robin Banks.

With Terry Chimes in tow, The Clash embarked on a lengthy period of touring under the Casbah Club banner. Starting on 29 May and supported by ska revivalists The Beat, they toured the US for nearly a month, winding up in San Francisco on 23 June.

In Atlanta on 2 June, fourteen people were arrested, mainly for disorderly conduct, when local communists tried to distribute leaflets outside the Fox Theatre. The tour also saw The Clash sell out five nights at the Hollywood Palladium – all

Pull up to the bumper – Mick, Terry Chimes, Paul and Joe head for Shea Stadium.

the more satisfying, as The Jam had barely managed one. Joe was bowled over to hear that Bob Dylan was in the crowd for one of the nights.

From 10 July, The Clash played the UK dates rescheduled from April. The plan was to turn each venue into the Casbah Club for the night courtesy of the support acts and DJs. The opening night at the 4,300 capacity Fair Deal – now the Academy – was a belter. With a good sound and rabid crowd, it was a consummate Clash show, with the *Combat Rock* songs starting to sound great.

NME's Richard Cook wrote about the Clash's 'brilliant revitalisation': 'Every one of perhaps twenty songs was dealt out with surly, scorched-earth bravado, spilling accents of suspicion and untempered wrath; purpose in every turn.' He said how the group had reinvented their roots – 'The Clash have learned to channel sound as never before,' – and talked about 'this steeled rush, this fluorescent razor's edge.'

The Aylesbury gig saw the Friars club take over nearby Stoke Mandeville Hospital's 3,000-capacity stadium, which quickly sold out. In the afternoon, Joe toured the wards and met patients at the world's top spinal injuries centre. He visited as many beds as he could and afterwards said he had been moved and humbled by the experience, 'It kind of puts it all in perspective.'

By now, I was living in Ladbroke Grove and Johnny Green was still working at the Fifth Column t-shirt shop at the top of Portobello Road with Jock. We decided it would be a great idea to run a mini-bus to Aylesbury and embarked upon the evening with gusto.

The gig was not The Clash's best, as the inadequate power supply from the stadium generator emitted a loud hum throughout. As a result, the group were rattled. Also, gobbing still ruled in Aylesbury, which didn't improve the band's collective mood. I came away feeling deflated.

I didn't know the true extent of the inter-band ructions then, but I could sense that something wasn't right. The dressing room atmosphere was decidedly different as the familiar faces of Greeny and the Baker had been replaced by a stern new crew; men in black whose attitude seemed to say, 'We are The Clash.' There was no Topper now, and the other band members seemed to gravitate away from each other. I found the mood unsettling and depressing.

Only later would I think back and realise that this was the last time I saw The Clash. When I recalled the countless amazing gigs and the dressing room antics with my extended family, I felt like I'd lost something special. The group must have known it too, as this falling out had been bubbling under for the last two years.

The UK tour wound up in Bristol on 3 August. Six days later, The Clash were off to the US again for the ten-week long *Combat Rock* tour. New York was covered by three nights at the capacious Pier 84, which started on 31 August. On the second night, Allen Ginsberg joined the band for 'Ghetto Defendant'.

Around this time, Mohican haircuts came into vogue. The cool dudes modelled theirs on Travis Bickle in *Taxi Driver*, while the new wave of cartoon punk bands like The Exploited and GBH tended to take their fashion tips from *Mad Max 2*. Kosmo opted for the former, and Joe was so impressed he got one too. Someone pointed out that wigged-out Vietnam GI's favoured Mohicans when they thought their number was up. Joe just said he wanted to look as ugly as possible. This was punk rock! On the other hand, Mick sported cool suits, changing into the regulation combat gear for gigs.

Back in the UK, on 17 October, 'Should I Stay or Should I Go' was paired with 'Straight To Hell' as the second single to be taken from Combat Rock. 'Though it could well be the rambling, Stonesy "Should I Stay Or Should I Go" that will pick up most of the airplay, it is "Straight To Hell" that is the reaffirmation that there is still life in The Clash,' wrote *NME*'s Adrian Thrills.

That week, *Melody Maker* had John Taylor of Duran Duran reviewing the singles. After confessing that he didn't like the recent albums, he wound up by predicting that the A-side would see, 'the first Top Twenty hit they've had in . . . God, it's a long time!' He was right, as the single strode up to Number Seventeen – their first Top Twenty showing since 'Bankrobber' over two years earlier.

In a surprise move, The Clash took up an offer from The Who to support them on a series of 50,000-plus capacity stadium gigs, which started at the end of September and ran sporadically throughout the next month. To the hardened Clash-watcher this came as a shock. The band had usually eschewed dealing with their audiences in one fell swoop of a mega-gig in favour of playing extended stints at smaller venues. They had also given up support spots in 1976, unless it was a special occasion or charity event. This was a very conventional music biz move, but now The Clash just wanted to play to as many people as possible – even if they had to limit their set to 50 minutes.

Mick was totally honest about it when I interviewed him that December. 'I'm not that into the big ones, but when we went out and played with The Who it was really good for us. We [big grin] sold lots of records, y'know? And probably picked up a lot of their fans. So we shouldn't complain. We went out there and did a job really. No big deal. We're matter of fact about it. We just went out and played, trying not to be fazed by it all.'

It was like The Clash had finally hit upon the most effective way to carry out their anti-AOR campaign: play them at their own game. It had been staring them in the face all the time while they tried to do things their way. Mick reckoned this first major stab at playing to the American masses had won some of them over.

'Yeah, I think we did. People haven't got anything else to do as far as America goes. Let's say they still believe in music more. It's their way of life, which is why you get thousands and thousands of them in row after row of mega-stadiums. It was The Who's audience, but we did good there.'

Just how good can be seen in Don Letts' video for 'Should I Stay Or Should I Go', which was shot on 13 October. The band dressed loud for the occasion, with Mick sporting a red jumpsuit and beret, and Joe coming on in shades and Davey Crockett hat. Don filmed the band driving to the gig in an open-top Cadillac.

The size of the audiences on that tour may have increased a thousand-fold, but Joe was still up to his old tricks, getting the fans in the back door. Roger Goodman, who would later become one of Joe's closest mates, was on the merchandise stall, selling *Combat Rock* gear. The Clash were ferried to the Shea Stadium gigs on a bus from their Manhattan hotel. The rule was that if you missed the bus you had to make your own way to the venue.

'It didn't matter if you were in the band or in the crew,' recalls Roger. 'Me and Joe missed the bus. At that time, Joe was so laidback it was like he was in a coma, although he was still lovely. I offered to get a cab, but Joe said, "Let's go by subway." So we went on the subway and he had a big ghetto blaster on his shoulder playing reggae.

'By the time we got to the gate we had 360 people with us who he'd invited to the gig on the train journey. Me and Joe were the only ones with a backstage pass. When security asked to see our passes Joe said, "If they don't get in, I ain't playing." So they sorted out a pass for everyone there. That's how I met Joe.'

For better or worse, there were now no pretensions of being anything other than rock stars. Mick just admitted it, and Joe must have either been going along with the flow or suffering severe inner turmoil. But then, hadn't he expressed his ambition to be a star back in the early seventies? Of course he wanted to be successful. Who wouldn't get the maximum buzz out of several thousand punters all going apeshit?

For a long time, Joe had been a composite showman born out of all his heroes, who were mainly *legends*. Joe saw himself as more of a Dylan figure than a Rod Stewart. That he would ultimately be held up there with Marley and Lennon probably never crossed his mind, though he wouldn't have said no. But in the video, Joe's look is either rock star parody or a caution-to-the-wind outrageousness that comes from too much touring.

Joe later observed, 'It was fun to play "Career Opportunities" in a situation like

Shea Stadium when we'd been writing it four years earlier in Camden . . . These are the things that make the world so interesting.'

On 9 October, The Clash appeared on cult comedy show, *Saturday Night Live,* alongside former *Happy Days* star Ron Howard. The band played two tracks, 'Should I Stay Or Should I Go' and 'Straight To Hell'.

In late October, 'Rock The Casbah' was released in the US and went to number eight. The album had reached number seven and sold over a million. All this conventional rock group behaviour was indeed paying off.

It's ironic that the band scored their biggest US hit after its composer had left the band. Topper still gets royalties for composing 'Rock The Casbah' and doesn't feel any bitterness about other songs that he contributed to being overlooked.

'To be honest, I got the money. Anyone who knows about the band, the fans, know I wrote "Rock The Casbah". I considered Mick and Joe to be the songwriters. They were fucking brilliant. I wasn't going to go, "But I wrote that." That's a bit childish. The band was great because we had Mick and Joe songwriting with me and Paul contributing.'

The Clash's last gig of the year was on 27 November at the Jamaican World Music Festival at a new stadium dedicated to Bob Marley in Montego Bay. Obviously this one was special. Jamaica had loomed large throughout the group's career. This was some kind of pinnacle, and also a bit of a treat after all the graft that year. Playing alongside names like Black Uhuru and Peter Tosh, The Clash went down well, leaning their set towards the reggae end of their musical spectrum. Writing for *NME*, the respected journalist Richard Grabel noted, 'The Clash took their chance and made it mean something.'

The Clash also made their best showing in the *NME* readers' poll for a while, scoring third Best Band, second Best Album, third Best Songwriters and third Best Live Act. The Jam were still on top, but Paul Weller had already decided that they would soon cease to exist.

Towards the end of 1982, with *Zigzag* in ruins, I started writing elsewhere and ended up editing a teenybopper magazine called *Flexipop!* Their attitude was fun and irreverent, but they wanted to steer away from endless Duran Duran and Culture Club photo-spreads.

My first cover feature was an exclusive with Mick. It was the first time I'd seen him since the Stoke Mandeville gig, where he'd been a little unapproachable. After Topper's sacking and rumours of discontent within the Clash ranks, I felt slightly trepidatious. I didn't see the band all the time like I used to, mainly because they were on tour or recording abroad so much. I'd had to apply and wait for this interview, whereas two years earlier I'd just pick up the phone and have a chat. But any doubts went out the window as we convened to Mike's Cafe off Portobello Road, both in buoyant pre-Christmas moods. I'd had a list of probing queries but we kicked off with a discussion on the animal kingdom.

'Some people are crazy about pigs,' mused Mick. ''78 was a very popular year for the wildebeest. I feel that this is the Year of the Goat, overall . . . or the Year of the Amoeba!'

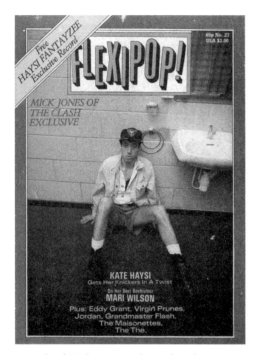

An isolated Mick was cover-featured on this 1982 issue of Flexipop! *magazine.*

Mick bemoaned the lack of excitement on the current scene. In 1982, vapid synth-pop ruled, and The Jam were the most popular group in the country. 'It's pathetic here! It's *really* pathetic. At least we've been interesting. We ain't been boring in a suit. I mean it's terrible. The state of music in this country is dreadful. It's also a see-through plastic bag and so much washing powder really . . . I just don't see it as a creative contemporary scene.'

With The Jam on the way out, I asked why the far more volatile Clash were still going strong. Mick's answer was a passionate spontaneous volley, belying any inner discord in the group.

'We respect each other and because of that we've got our own self-respect. We still believe in what we're doing and we enjoy it. Give me any other reason . . . Show me a contemporary scene here and I'll laugh it off. There really isn't anything in Britain that doesn't tend to look back totally.'

Mick seemed genuinely happy that day, for the simple reason that the group he'd started was finally a massive success, on both sides of the pond. Six years earlier we'd both staggered back to Wilmcote House after a gig without a pot to piss in.

'Yeah! it's really nice. It makes a change at the end of the year to be able to look back and not feel like you've wasted 365 days. Some of the things that have happened this year have balanced it out, you know what I mean? I think that losing Topper really had a great effect on us.'

Having known Mick when he was struggling, I asked if he and the band now actually *felt* big. I meant in terms of success, but Mick came back with, 'No, I'm my normal size. I know Joe feels funny he has to do things. He's got to get a flat now.'

Joe was trying to get his personal life together at this time. He still didn't have a proper home and was looking to obtain a mortgage. This was one of the reasons why a proposed US tour for the New Year had been shelved.

'We were going to go but . . . after a while you just look in the mirror one day and steam's coming out of your ears,' said Mick, in a rare serious moment. 'You know you've got to stop for a couple of days.'

At this point, Paul Simonon wandered up to the cafe window with his dad and peered in. Mick waved but Paul didn't see him and walked off. Or, as Mick put it,

'He saw me and ran away!' I *thought* he was joking, but, given the parlous state of relationships within the band, it was hard to be sure.

Mick also told me about a project with infamous vice-queen Janie Jones, who had just been released from prison. The band wanted to repay using her name by recording a single with her. While in hiding, Joe had written her a tune called 'House Of The Ju Ju Queen' (its original title was 'The Judge'). The song was recorded in Wessex on 28 December with a band comprised of Joe, who also produced, Mick, Paul and Blockheads Mickey Gallagher and Charley Charles on keyboards and drums, respectively. This swampy, sleazy little outing was released a year later, on Big Beat Records, under the name Janie Jones and the Lash. The B-side saw the Clash/Blockheads ensemble tackle James Brown's 'Sex Machine'.

During our conversation, Mick recounted an anecdote that took on additional significance, when viewed with hindsight: 'We went down to San Antone, pretending we were at the Alamo. We all played! Paul was Colonel Travis, Kosmo was Davey Crockett, Joe was Jim Bowie and I was the wall! Bernie was a cannonball. Joe Ely was there too – a real authentic cowboy riding round on his cow!'

As we were saying goodbye, Mick pressed a cassette into my hand and said, 'Happy Christmas.' He'd drawn a little cover with a New York skyline fronted by a dollar sign and an apple, and given it the title 'NY Hits'. The cassette was a succession of highlights Mick had taped off New York's dance radio stations on his last US visit – a top selection which included Indeep's 'Last Night A DJ Saved My Life', audacious mastermixes of Marvin Gaye's 'Sexual Healing' and Vanity 6's 'Nasty Girls', plus other prime slabs of hip-hop/electro boogie. It was indeed a happy Christmas.

After such a hectic year, The Clash took a break for the first three months of 1983. In reality, they had been on the go since 1976, the only respite being when Joe did his runner. They should have kicked back earlier – it might have saved the group.

Joe finally found himself a permanent place to live when he secured a mortgage on a house in Lancaster Road, near Portobello Road, and moved in with Gaby.

Any further activity was put on hold for a while after Paul's father and second wife Marion were involved in a car crash on 26 February. Marion later died in hospital, so Paul started spending a lot more time with his dad.

During the break, Joe pursued some extra curricular activities, including financing and helping out on a Tymon Dogg album, which was never released. More

Mick's self-drawn cover from his Christmas 1982 New York themed compilation tape.

235

surprising was when I noticed a copy of *The Sun* in early March, and there was Joe posing happily with 'TV celebrities' Lennie Bennett and Kenny Lynch. This unlikely union – not to mention, Joe's *Sun* t-shirt – was due to the fact that he'd signed up to run the London Marathon as part of the newspaper's campaign to raise money for leukaemia research.

Around this time, Joe was offered the part of a hitman in UK director Stephen Frears' upcoming film *The Hit*. Maybe feeling that he wasn't ready to star alongside acting legends John Hurt and Terence Stamp, Joe recommended that the role be offered to Tim Roth, who he'd just seen in a TV play called *Made in Britain*.

Joe was determined to keep busy and decided to make his own movie. This resulted in the legendary *Hell W10*, which he wrote and directed. The original 16mm black-and-white film had been thought lost but finally saw the light of day when it was included on *The Essential Clash* DVD. The cover notes reveal that a couple of fans found a rough copy in a car boot sale!

There is no script and any dialogue pops up on silent movie-style boards. The film is set around the Westbourne Park-Portobello Road area and comes on like an old gangster movie with a simple plot involving drugs, violence and dodgy deals. Paul plays a street kid, Mick a zoot-suited hustler and the supporting cast includes Kosmo, Ray Jordan, Pennie Smith, Tony James and the band's girlfriends. Joe himself appears as a policeman with a moustache.

As a curio and a taste of Joe's personal celluloid vision, it's fun and fascinating. The soundtrack is prime late-period Clash, featuring excerpts from the last three albums – many in instrumental form – and also some *Combat Rock* out-takes like 'The Beautiful People' and 'Cool Confusion.'

Johnny Green still kept in touch. I saw him regularly up until early 1983 – partly because we'd both developed an unfortunate penchant for the Topper lifestyle since the Basement 5 tour. I'd go round to Johnny and his partner Lindy's flat in Hampstead, where they lived with their two baby sons, practically every day.

Then, in February, tragedy struck when Lindy succumbed to meningitis, followed by the youngest boy. It has been reported elsewhere that she died from a heroin overdose, but I can vouch that she had given up while pregnant as she was still breast-feeding the baby when she died. Two people, in particular, helped Johnny through his grief – Robin Banks and Joe Strummer.

'Banksy was brilliant,' recalls Johnny. 'He saved my life. I just shut the front door and took Harry [heroin], but he would sit outside and wait for me to open the door for hours. Then we'd walk to the Heath and he'd make me have something to eat.'

'I'll never forget the time Lindy died,' adds Robin. 'Johnny was just taking gear, so that sparked off the whole thing where I went to Joe and said, "I want to take Johnny away to Greece. He needs to get away."'

'So Banksy went to Joe and he stumped up the money to go on holiday,' explains Johnny. 'We met him in a pub near Shepherds Bush roundabout and he handed over the dough. He was good as well, really asked how I was, even though I was a fucking mess. Joe was so emotionally helpful. Then Banksy went to Joe and asked him if he'd help out with the funeral. He sorted that out too. Joe helped me out hugely when Lindy died.'

And it didn't stop there. Johnny and Robin went on a bender in Greece and ended up stranded in Athens with no money. Joe came to the rescue again by sorting out return air tickets. 'He didn't need to do any of that,' says Johnny. 'He stood by us.'

When they returned home Johnny got himself together to the extent where he became a drug and alcohol counsellor. He saw the group one last time, at rehearsals. 'I found they now had a huge entourage around them. I found it all a bit Elvisy. They were surrounded by sycophants laughing at their jokes. But this wasn't the Memphis Mafia, I thought something was dumb and stupid. I noticed it looked really floppy. My memory of their rehearsals before was hard work. Back then they didn't fuck around. But now everyone was just lying around. There was a serious loss of energy.'

In March, The Clash went back to the building that housed Rehearsals in Camden Town. It had been refitted with a rehearsal room and sixteen-track studio, so finally they had an HQ where they could do the three R's – rehearse, record and, er, write. The much-discussed Clash club was going to be called the Lucky Seven (a reference to the Skatalites' 1965 hit), so the new studio was named the Lucky Eight.

Out of the blue, the band was then made an offer they couldn't refuse. Apple computer tycoon Steve Wozniak was organising a major three-day festival at Glen Helen Regional Park, San Bernadino, and offered the Clash $500,000 to headline the opening New Music Day on 28 May. The Unite Us In Song (or Unuson, or simply Us) Festival, aspired to being an updated version of Woodstock and probably went against everything The Clash had once stood for, but who would turn down that kind of dough? It would even be worth the inevitable sell-out taunts.

However, they still hadn't got a permanent drummer. Terry Chimes had only agreed to do the 1982 bookings and had gone off to become a chiropractor. In April, The Clash held auditions via a *Melody Maker* ad, which drew around 300 applicants.

Eventually, they settled on Pete Howard, from Bath group Cold Fish – who were already on CBS. As with Terry, Pete was brought in solely for the function of providing a beat for the three-pronged attack. You couldn't replace Topper and The Clash didn't try to. After a five-date warm-up around the Southwestern USA starting on 10 May, they were ready for the festival.

Despite their hefty fee, The Clash had insisted that tickets for the Us Festival be kept to a $17 maximum but, when they got to the site, discovered that the organisers were charging up to $25 plus parking. The group called a press conference, which saw the ever-voluble management duo of Bernie and Kosmo doing most of the talking. Angry at what they viewed as Woodstockian pretensions masking a blatant desire to make money, the double act lambasted the event and declared that The Clash wouldn't play unless the promoters donated $100,000 to a Southern California centre for disadvantaged children.

The promoters eventually agreed to donate $32,000 to the charity, while the band also tried to get other acts to donate part of their large fees. (Van Halen were playing the following night and getting $1,000,000.)

The Clash went on two hours late and played for 80 minutes in front of 140,000 people. 'You don't want to hear me going on about this and that and what's up my arse. Try this one for size,' snarled Joe from the stage in front of the biggest crowd The Clash had ever faced. Some of the Us Festival footage surfaced on *Westway To The World* and shows a band about to implode. The growing distance between Joe, Mick and Paul is evident; each seems completely disassociated from the others, consumed by the gravity-well of their own performances.

'Onstage, that's how it was backstage,' recalled Paul in the documentary. 'Mick all the way over there, me over here, and Joe in the middle. Me and Mick didn't talk.'

'Here we are in the capital of the decadent USA.' Joe's announcements were deliberately confrontational. Behind the band was a banner bearing the not entirely accurate legend, 'The Clash Not For Sale'. After the set the band got into a scuffle with the festival bouncers and in-house crew. It was ugly all round, and the group didn't come out of it in a good light. It's possible that the aggressive attitude the band adopted was driven by an element of guilt at succumbing to the ultimate big money gig. Combine that with their perpetually raging internal tensions and you had a ready-to-detonate powder keg.

The following year, Joe talked to *Creem* about the festival, and attempted to put a gloss on The Clash's appearance. 'We have to deal with the music industry, and that weekend, the whole industry was looking at the festival as the state of rock 'n' roll,' he told Bill Holdship. 'So we had to go in there and show them that we wouldn't be pushed under the carpet. Our second purpose was to spoil the bloody party, because I'm not going to have some millionaire restaging Woodstock for his ego gratification and tax loss in his backyard and get away with it.'

Around the same time, John Mendelssohn of *The Record* asked Joe why The Clash didn't simply donate part of their fee. 'We needed it for London,' he replied, referring to The Clash's plan to open a club. 'We don't have people in London who want to throw Woodstocks as a tax write-off. If Wozniak wants to be a sucker and give us half a million dollars, we'll take it.'

In explanation of his adversarial attitude during the show, Joe explained, 'I wanted to wind them up. There was too much self-congratulation in the air. I wanted to get a reaction, and I felt that we'd never reach them – it was too vast . . . We had to go there. Otherwise we'd have been condemning rebel rock to the basement.' Ultimately, the gig left a bad taste. The only reason that it's remembered is because it turned out to be Mick Jones' last ever gig with The Clash.

On 1 September 1983, a 'Clash Communiqué' from Bernie and Kosmo dropped the bomb – 'Joe Strummer and Paul Simonon have decided that Mick Jones should leave the group. It is felt that Jones has drifted apart from the original idea of The Clash. In future it will allow Joe and Paul to get on with the job that The Clash set out to do from the beginning.'

This appeared in the 10 September issue of *NME* and I still couldn't believe it, even though I'd heard about it the previous month on the Clash grapevine. Then I'd phoned Mick and, although obviously shocked, he kind of shrugged it off. 'I don't feel nothing,' was one phrase he used. 'Don't worry, I'll be alright. Got to keep going,' he added. I think we were more shocked than Mick, who seemed to go from initial numbness to determinedly dealing with the future.

The same news story carried a statement from Mick issued through the CBS press office. 'Mick Jones would like to state that he feels the official press statement is untrue. He would like it made clear that there was no discussion with Strummer and Simonon prior to his sacking. Jones does not feel that he has drifted apart from the original idea of The Clash and in future he will be carrying on with the same dedication as in the beginning.'

Two unidentified sources 'close to the band' added their opinions. The first said there had been 'some kind of power play' to do with Bernie and that Mick didn't have any warning. The second said, 'Joe Strummer and Paul Simonon are trying to make Mick Jones a scapegoat in their bid for new credibility. Everybody knows that Mick was the one who had arguments about *Combat Rock* because he thought it was too commercial and was a sell-out in terms of credibility. They've set him up to make it look as if he was the one who was interested in grabbing the money, and that's not true.'

Tony James said it was like throwing Keith Richards out of the Stones. Although that nearly happened in the mid-seventies when Keith was fucked up, the rest of the Stones were astute enough to realise that this would be unthinkable. Mick Jagger's ill-fated solo career bore that out. Like Mick 'n' Keef, Joe and Mick were chalk and cheese, but if they'd both been cut the same, there wouldn't have been the edge of brilliance which the two goaded out of each other in The Clash. Strops and fallouts were necessary to add the danger that made the band so exciting.

First they sack one of the best drummers in the world, then the genius behind the group's whole sound. Joe might have been an amazing lyricist but he needed the right setting for those words to spark off. It would be another fifteen years before Joe found anything even remotely approaching the kind of creative alchemy he shared with Mick.

Joe couldn't take Mick any more, and was putty in the manipulative hands of Bernie and Kosmo. 'Mick was intolerable to work with by this time,' said Joe. 'I mean no fun at all. He wouldn't show up, then when he did it was like Elizabeth Taylor in a filthy mood.'

'I didn't know personally about self-control,' admitted Mick. 'I didn't know about that stuff until later. We lost communication with each other. Even though we were in the same room we were looking at the floor . . . I was just carried away really. I wish I had a bit more control. You wish you knew then what you know now.'

'I missed a lot of The Clash because I was so self-involved,' Mick confessed to *NME*'s Paolo Hewitt in 1986. 'Like when we toured, I'd get on the coach, and I wouldn't look out of the window I was so far up my own arse.'

The cards had long been on the table but the Us Festival was the incident that forced the issue. After some of the money was held back under US tax laws, there were rows about what to do with the rest after some had gone into sprucing up the Lucky Eight. Mick brought in New York attorney Elliott Hoffman to look after his interests – a move that obviously rankled Bernie on a management level, but also personally annoyed Joe.

'I could take the moaning and the not wanting to work and the lack of enthu-siasm,' Joe told John Mendelssohn of *The Record* the following year. 'And did until I had all that up to the neck. But what *really* got me was when he started saying he'd have to check things with his lawyer first. I thought, "Since when was lawyers involved in this team?" We never had a lawyer to begin with . . . I finally said, "Go and write songs with your lawyer, and piss *off!*"

'Me and Joe had been talking about it, and we got to the point where I said, "We're grown men, I can't take any more of this,"' recalled Paul. 'We were both in agreement that we were fed up, we wanted to get on with the job, rather than wait around for Mick. We were in this rehearsal room and Joe said, "Mick, we want you to leave." Mick said, "What do you say?" and I said, "Well, yeah." I think he felt let down by that.'

'I asked the band who they wanted, me or Bernie,' Mick told Paolo Hewitt. 'The group said they wanted Bernie, and then just looked at the floor. I couldn't believe my ears. I stood there for about ten seconds, stunned. then I just picked up my gui-tar and walked out.' In a 1989 BBC2 documentary, *That Was Then This Is Now* – which explored The Clash's split – Mick claimed, 'I was set up really. Bernie came running after me with a cheque in his hand – you know, like a gold watch – which added insult to injury. But I took it anyway.'

Relating what The Baker had told him about that day, Johnny Green recounts, 'Baker went along to pick some money up. When he arrived he saw Mick sitting outside with his guitar case. He asked him what he was doing. He just said, "I've been sacked. I don't really know why, but they just sacked me." He had tears in his eyes. Barry was just sitting there with Mick in this hotel foyer. He said he felt angry and really sad. He was just . . . lost.'

Mick knew that Bernie was the motivating force behind all this. Joe had always tended to leap straight into something, regardless of the consequences – as he did when he saw the Sex Pistols, underwent Bernie's indoctrination and swiftly jetti-soned the 101'ers, who he'd been slogging away with for the previous two years, in favour of a complete makeover to join The Clash. Six years later, Bernie struck again and got him to nudge out Topper.

Now it was Mick. That Mick's aloofness and difficult behaviour were pissing Joe off is without dispute, but there was a little bespectacled devil sitting on Joe's shoul-der, convincing him that the only move would be to sack Mick. At the time it suit-ed Joe's ego too, because then he would be the one calling all the shots. In complete control – or so he thought.

It would take Joe a couple of years to identify Bernie's hand in this, as he admit-ted to *Record Mirror*'s Jim Reid in 1986. 'Sometimes I feel that I've only been a pawn in the game between Mick and Bernie. If you wanna look at the Clash story, the Titans in the struggle have been Mick and Bernie. They put it together, and then Mick said, "Let's get rid of Bernie," so we got rid of him.'

As Johnny Green has observed, Joe could be a hard man when he wanted. By 1983 his power struggle with Mick had been raging for over two years. Prodded by Bernie, he chose to make the ultimate hard man move by leading the push to sack Mick. It would take him less than a year to regret it.

Joe was more candid with *NME*'s Gavin Martin the same year, when he explained, 'What you must realise is a large percentage of people like me are idiots. I sit in a room and write ditties while others are selling stocks to Malaysia on the vodaphone. It's easy to manipulate people like me . . . Bernie sort of coerced me into thinking that Mick was what was wrong with the scene. That wasn't hard because, as Mick will admit now, he was being pretty awkward. Plus my ego – a bad thing an ego – was definitely telling me, "Go on! Get rid of the bastard!"'

The Clash fragmented because Bernie wanted to silence any opposition and thought he could keep the band going with personnel that he could control. Why else would Bernie be going around for months saying, 'Mick's not going to be in the band much longer,' to anyone who'd listen – including me, when he knew that I was a close friend of Mick's? Conversely, how can you take anyone seriously when he's sitting there outlining plans to take over the world and one of his group is methodically building a salad on his shoulder?

The previous December, Mick had taken some delight in telling me, 'Paul really does torture Bernie. They lift him off the ground and play with him like he was a toy. But I think that's rotten!'

The day they threw out Mick out was the day Bernie Rhodes became a fully-fledged member of The Clash, followed close behind by a hopeful Kosmo Vinyl. Those who were there before Kosmo appeared watched him work his way into the band's inner circle, attaining a status that allowed him the conceit of seeing himself as the fifth Clasher. Even that wasn't good enough for Bernie, who wanted to go one better than Malcolm McLaren in the Svengali stakes – from now on Clash songwriting credits would read Strummer-Rhodes. At last – complete control.

As Mick told Lisa Robinson in 1986 for *Hard Rock Video,* 'Basically, what happened was that Bernie wanted to sit where I was sitting in the group. The good seat, the comfy seat, the best seat in the house . . . [Joe] sat by and let it all happen.'

The 'source close to the band' in the *NME* news story showed uncanny foresight when they commented, 'Just wait and see how long it takes CBS to rush-release a double-live Clash album and a quick Strummer-Simonon album which isn't very good. And then watch Joe Strummer move into films.'

In 1999, speaking evocatively in *Westway To The World,* Joe confessed that sacking Mick had been a ghastly mistake. 'Whatever a group is, it was the chemical mixture of those four people that makes a group work. That's a lesson that everyone should learn. You don't mess with it. If it works do whatever you have to do to bring it forward, but don't mess with it. We learned that *bitterly.*'

'That's one thing that Joe had to live with for the rest of his life,' says Robin Banks. 'He knew he'd been involved in the most profound mistake. A huge error. He never came to terms with it. Every time I came across him after that he would always say, "That was one of the dumbest things I ever did." But it wasn't Joe, it was Bernie Rhodes. Joe found it hard to live with that, he really did. It haunted him. It really haunted him.'

CHAPTER SIXTEEN
TIME IS TIGHT

The hotter you are now the colder you're going to be. – Joe Strummer

Now reduced to a trio of Joe, Paul and Pete Howard, the new Clash set about finding a replacement for Mick. This was always going to be a tall order considering that Mick's talent had blossomed within the group and, more than any other factor, defined The Clash's unique sound. This was year zero again and, with the crowds that came to see them wanting the greatest hits, any thoughts of breaking down musical barriers would have to be put on hold. Joe and Paul had already expressed a desire to get back to their punky roots instead of following Mick's technological obsessions. Now they had no choice and were set on a path to becoming their own tribute band.

Rather than add a name guitarist to become a punk supergroup, an advert was placed in *Melody Maker*. Auditions were held at Camden's Electric Ballroom in October and, out of the 350 hopefuls who had to play along to a backing tape, two guitarists were selected because Joe said he wanted to stop playing guitar. This caused some head-scratching for those who recalled Joe being unable to record a vocal without having his Telecaster to thrash along in time with. It's more likely he realised what a huge gap he had to fill with Mick gone and such a statement would cover up the fact that it would take two men to replace him. If the new Clash were going for a more guitar-orientated sound, it would make sense to double the firepower anyway. This was virgin territory for Joe. Previously he'd only had drummers to worry about.

When the bogus Clash started gigging, Joe *was* playing guitar – although one critic remarked that this was so he could make 'a big production' out of flinging it to a roadie in time-honoured fashion.

Enter the new boys. First they chose 23-year-old Nick Sheppard from Bristol, who had been in a band called The Cortinas in 1977. I saw them play once, supporting Blondie, and they sounded like a Clash copy band. Then there was complete newcomer Vince White, from Southampton, also 23. When the new line up was announced, the *NME* revealed that 'Vince' had actually been a Physics and Astronomy student at University College, London, whose real name was Greg.

Joe's first post-split interviews let out the anger he'd been building towards Mick. With Paul becoming more of a peripheral figure, the spotlight was firmly on Joe. 'I wanted someone who knew that the guitar is for accompaniment and not for ego-tripping,' he told John Mendelssohn of *The Record*. 'The ones we chose changed their playing for each of three backing tracks they had to play along with for their final audition. And they were punks – they'd been in the punk rebellion in '76, been excited by it, swept up in it. So they don't moan.' In other words, two yes-men. The first group publicity photo looks like the Cortinas with Joe Strummer in the middle. It was notably not taken by Pennie Smith.

The new Clash had to start gigging double quick, because Mick had instructed his lawyer to freeze all band earnings that dated from before his departure so that his old work wouldn't be financing the new band. I found this extremely funny because it was the same stroke that Bernie pulled when The Clash had sacked him. Mick had also suggested that he might use The Clash as the name of the new group he was forming so the bogus quintet had to make a speedy showing to stake their claim.

Joe did all the talking in interviews and was back in gruff punk mode, denouncing America, advocating guitar lessons and forming bands, while attacking Mick at every available opportunity. From his soapbox he undermined his previous four years' work by slagging America to *Jamming!*'s Ross Fortune – 'I don't like it!' he declared, before laying into the food, signs, 'plastic buildings', music and government.

Joe's zeal extended to insisting that his new platoon be drug-free so that they could carry out their mission. 'If you take drugs, wear a kaftan,' he shouted at *NME*'s Richard Cook. 'Be honest. Wear a bell round your neck. I've smoked so much pot I'm surprised I haven't turned into a bush.' This from the man who built the Spliff Bunker, but it was obviously a thinly veiled dig at the weed-loving Mick.

This was all very *Sniffin' Glue*, circa 1976 and embarrassing for those who'd grown up with the band. Maybe Joe was disowning us too and aiming at the younger generation – hence the hip schoolteacher-cum-sergeant major routine.

It was all very confusing. Times had changed since 1976, when the enemy was rock behemoths like Led Zep and progressive noodlers such as Emerson, Lake and Palmer. In 1984, pop music meant names like Wham!, Duran Duran and Culture Club ruling bedroom walls, while rock was dominated by the likes of U2 and Queen. Students liked indie bands and worshipped at the altar of Morrissey. The last embers of the ever-narrowing punk scene had died out and few of the bands that had been part of the initial explosion were still standing. Ironically, Billy Idol, from the second raters Generation X, had risen to become one of the hottest stars in the US.

Joe slagged off *everybody*. He was offended when Bob Geldof didn't ask him to appear on the star-studded Live Aid single. He knew about it because it was being recorded just around the corner from his house, at Basing Street Studios.

Considering that punk rock was now a thing of the past, it didn't seem wise for Joe to be steering his new band straight back down that particular cul-de-sac, alienating a whole mass audience in the process. Anyway, now the real action was in the underground world of electronic dance music, with New Order and Soft Cell bringing their own interpretations of the medium to British white kids just as The Clash had. Seeing as that was the world of Mick Jones too, Joe appeared to be painting himself into a very small corner.

Bernie had arranged for the band to begin 1984 with a January tour of the US, followed by a series of dates in Britain the following month. The set for these dates would lean heavily on the punky stuff from the first two albums, because it was easier to learn, although they did have a bash at 'The Magnificent Seven'.

Never mind 1984, it was back to 1977 as the 'new' Clash, in their Kings Road

Joe distances himself from Paul and the new recruits.

retro gear of old Sex t-shirts and leathers, seemed about to join the punk cabaret circuit. All the excitement, innovation and danger that had surrounded The Clash seemed to be gone. Still, maybe Joe had some good new songs. We'd have to wait to find out, as more than a year would pass before the new line-up made it to vinyl.

In Joe's defence, he wasn't reverting back to 1976 as a career move. He'd spent a large part of the previous two years in America and, now ensconced back in the UK, was able to take in the way the country had gone downhill since The Clash first sang about it. Unemployment had mushroomed while Joe had been focused on New York City and the killing fields of Vietnam. He felt angry at himself that he'd ignored his own country and lightened his approach in the sometimes whimsical outings that appeared on *London Calling* and *Sandinista!*

Joe wrote several new songs that eschewed musical invention and variety in favour of basic punk structures. After the breathtaking lyrical masterpieces he had carved into *Combat Rock*, Joe's new titles didn't bode well. 'Glue Zombie' (anti-drug), 'Sex Mad War' (anti-pornography), 'Ammunition' (anti-war) and then 'We Are The Clash' (no you're not). 'Dictator' once again laid into US-funded Central America, but such obvious titles and themes hinted at a degree of creative bankruptcy.

The first gig that the bogus Clash played was at Santa Barbara's 2,000-capacity Arlington Centre on 19 January 1984. The January tour centred around Southern California – always a Clash stronghold. As it was a hit tune in the US, the group were duty-bound to do 'Should I Stay Or Should I Go', so they got Nick Sheppard to sing it. This met with such derision from the Mick supporters in the crowd that it was quickly dropped.

After the show, Joe and Kosmo talked to John Mendelssohn. Now Kosmo not only sorted out interviews but gave them too. With Bernie still behind the scenes, the three visible Clash representatives were Joe in the middle with Kosmo and Paul on either side. And Paul remained silent for much of the time. Joe was mustering a lot of bluster to justify his great mistake, but Paul now seemed to melt away from the spotlight. He once said that he loved it when Keith Levene got sacked because it gave him more room to do his Pete Townsend routine. Now he was one guitar in four. His impact was diminished and his band was shit. Paul would hardly play on this group's only album and he said nothing in interviews. Perhaps the thrill had gone, which is why he switched to painting.

Even when he wasn't laying into Mick, Joe remained stuck in full rant mode. 'When we said, "let's have a punk rebellion," we didn't mean for everyone to become copies of The Clash . . . We've been through everything in the book. We've been through drugs. We've been through pretension. We've been through studio bullshit. You name it – I bet we've been through it. But, I'm still walking the stage without a crutch.'

Joe was setting himself up as a veteran survivor of the punk wars, who'd beaten off the deadly threat of Mick Jones and now, surrounded by his old generals and eager new recruits, was going into battle again to do what the original Clash should have done before they were sidetracked.

To ram the point home, Joe explained his crusade to *Creem*'s Bill Holdship using a battery of military metaphors. 'In my mind I liken us to a new platoon. We're going to go and crawl out in front of the enemy lines, get fired upon and then look at each other to see how we're bearing up. Can I rely on this guy when my gun jams? We're under fire, and we're sharing that experience. And that's what's going to make our record great.'

Despite their commanding officer's bravado, Joe's concert party now had to face the most hazardous part of their mission – the UK. The lack of ideas was underlined as Out Of Control was again trotted out as the tour's title. The trek kicked off on 2 February in Dublin.

After two shows in Belfast, they played Glasgow Barrowlands on the 10, followed by three further dates around Britain, before traversing Sweden, Germany, Switzerland, Italy and France. There would be five nights at Brixton Academy – in two stints between 8-10 and 16-17 March, with more gigs in Ireland in between.

While on the road, Joe wrote 'This Is England', which many consider to be the last great Clash song, and the only decent tune that the new group came out with. Having seen the country again, Joe described the rotting council estates, brutal police and unemployment-riddled towns up North.

One of the Brixton gigs, where support was provided by The Pogues (Shane McGowan's raucous Irish knees-up ensemble) was reviewed for NME by Gavin Martin, who had a field day with this lot. 'This new Clash are no big departure, they are still entangled with all the old faults. The new young bloods in the pack haven't brought fresh drive and commitment, they've merely grown into and expanded the idea of The Clash as posed-perfect rebels.'

Melody Maker's Lynden Barber was even more condemnatory, using the word 'pathetic' and describing the current show, which sounded like, 'one giant heavy metal thrash', as 'nothing more than a reactionary surrender to the forces of nostalgia, Punks-on-45, a Greatest hits runthrough . . .'

Those two reviews set the tone for the new Clash and explained why they would never catch on. They started off playing a welter of new songs, but this wasn't like Notre Dame Hall where the old band tested out *London Calling*. This was a new band, but it called itself The Clash so it had to do Clash songs. It cannot have escaped the original two members that they were playing music written by the guy they'd just chucked out of the group.

I refused to go and see them out of loyalty to Mick. I just couldn't stand the thought of witnessing the classic catalogue of songs being mauled and abused. Robin, Johnny and Jock were braver men than I, and they all said that it was appalling. 'A travesty,' spat Robin, after his first gig. From now on he referred to them as, 'the placenta of The Clash'. Or just, 'that abortion'.

Surprisingly, *Zigzag* turned in a good review – and it wasn't by me or Robin. We were long gone, but our shoes were filled by Paul O'Reilly, a former fanzine editor and long-time Clash fan who I'd employed in 1977 under the *nom de plume* Suspect O'Typewriter. Paul was a lovely fellow, who is sadly no longer with us.

Paul wrote about Joe's stern treatment of the new boys at the soundcheck, a 'demanding boss' who made the guitarists run through 'Safe European Home' endlessly, pulling them up if it wasn't right. That was the one Joe and Mick wrote together in a Jamaican hotel room. How would anyone else capture it?

In Manchester, Paul described drummer Pete taking the piss out of the support band's kit, and Joe coming down on him, 'Like a ton of bricks. "You'd still be playing a kit like that if you hadn't been picked for The Clash!" he thundered. "Just fuckin' remember where you came from!"'

Paul had some sympathy for the new band, pointing out the impossibly hard task in front of them. As he was also manning the t-shirt stall, he heard a lot of favourable comments and concluded, 'I just defy anyone to call The

The new band's Out of Control tour was featured in April 1984's Zigzag.

Clash a dead band. This isn't dead, it's the liveliest band I've seen in years. Let the critics scoff. If The Clash have reverted to guttersnipes – all the better.'

Johnny Green also went to Brixton and popped backstage. 'Bernie saw me, and shouted, "Who let him in?" I watched the show and it was just frustrating. I was hanging out with the roadies and went onstage. They had two springboards by the amps so the guitarists could jump in the air!'

After the show, Johnny hung around in the corridor to see Joe for the first time in over a year. 'I was wearing a Burton's suit and drinking Special Brew,' recalls Johnny. 'I'd given up the gear and put on a bit of weight. I was mushrooming! So I had on this tight, cheap suit. Joe came out and said, "Crap suit, Johnny. What did you think of the gig?" I said, "It might be a crap suit, but it's not as crap as your band." And he started crying. Like, he knew it. He always regretted sacking Mick and Topper. He had so much remorse. Joe always said to me, "It's my fault that The Clash broke up."'

On the other hand, Jock Scott has a slightly more surreal memory of one of the Brixton gigs. 'I remember seeing the *Cut The Crap* group. Joe says to me later, "How was the gig?" I said it was just 'alright', but what really struck me about it was the way the stage was lit, because the lights were coming from behind, and it looked like . . . you know how Liverpool had won three European cups? That's what it looked like, because Sheppard and the other guys have all got big ears, that all stick out like that.' It must say something if Jock's enduring memory of this group was the new boys' ears.

On the personal front, Joe had experienced two extremes of emotion early in the year. First, Gaby gave birth to a baby daughter, who they named Jazz Domino after Charlie Parker – the heroin-addicted saxophone genius – and Joe's favourite Van Morrison song.

But after this happiness, tragedy struck in early March when Joe's father, Ron Mellor, died. Although he had kept in touch with his parents over the years, Joe had not been close to either of them.

The birth of his daughter and the death of his father in such a short space of time forced the 31-year-old Strummer to start thinking about his life. It was maybe then that being an angry young punk rocker started to sit uncomfortably on Joe's shoulders.

All this was further compounded a couple of months later when his mother, Anna, was diagnosed with cancer.

Although I wanted nothing to do with Joe's Punk Rock Revival Roadshow, the split had brought me back in contact with Mick – who I spoke to on the phone and visited at his current abode in Colville Gardens, by Powis Square. When Mick got sacked I felt both sorry for him and outraged at the callous, Rhodes-ian way it was undertaken.

When I went round to his flat, I was struck by his good humour and optimism. This was not a broken man in need of help, although he said he appreciated the support. Mick started with his usual practice of playing me the latest hot new imported twelve-inches. I remember one groove in particular, because I spent an afternoon tracking it down later that year when I went to New York for the first time. It was called 'I'd Like To' by Feel; upbeat, classy boogie – the hybrid of disco and electro, which was blossoming out of New York at the time. It was obvious that Mick still had his dancing shoes on.

He was equally enthusiastic about the group he was putting together. I cast my mind back to when Mick got thrown out of Violent Luck, who'd come to nothing. He went on to form The Clash. Similarly, within days of being kicked out of The Clash, Mick started work on writing new songs and gathering a group.

He'd done some live mixing for Sigue Sigue Sputnik – Tony James' audacious new cyberpunk-influenced outfit – and played on an album for General Public, a band that featured former members of The Beat. But, most of the time, Mick was getting back to his old self, writing songs and recruiting musicians. His enthusiasm had returned and, what's more, he didn't have Bernie Rhodes trying to dictate his every move, unlike Joe.

At the time, Robin Banks was Mick's neighbour and saw a lot of him. I have this vague recollection of Robin telling me back then about the new group Mick was putting together and that he was helping out with the words. 'We lived opposite each other in Colville Gardens and used to hang out of the window and wave at each other! When he got kicked out that came out of nowhere but he just threw himself straight into music. He took acting lessons, but that didn't last long. We went to football a lot to see Queens Park Rangers. Then I went to Brighton for a week, didn't drink at all, and wrote some lyrics for him. Mick was really pleased and went and put it all together.'

Mick could easily have gone solo at this point. He'd already more than proved that he could deliver complete albums, as well as tracks where The Clash had served as more of a backing group, such as 'Stay Free' or 'Train In Vain'. But he wanted to form a band again. Mick will always love the feeling of being in a group.

'The best way to travel, without a doubt, is with a group of you because you have each other to share the experience,' he says. 'It's much more fun. I don't know what it's like but a solo artist can't have as much fun as a band. You don't get to reach that point that you do with a band, or get to that point that we got to with the bands that we were inspired by. The Clash catered to the imagination and made people think, "Wow," what you can possibly do.'

Sometime in late 1983, Mick took Robin's lyrics into a Notting Hill studio and added some music with the new band he was putting together. 'We were called Total Risk Action Company,' laughs Mick. 'The A Team were pretty big at the time, I seem to remember.'

On bass there was Leo Williams, who I'd managed when he was in Basement 5. Saxophone came courtesy of 'a Canadian basketball champion called John Boy'. On drums was Topper Headon. If you're talking about Great Lost Clash Albums, what has become known as the 'TRAC Tape' is the real lost treasure. The missing link between 'Rat Patrol From Fort Bragg' and Big Audio Dynamite. 'At the time, Mick looked upon it as a rehearsal really,' says Robin. 'He calls it "The Lost Album".'

Mick is firmly in control here but, maybe surprisingly, eschews hip-hop experimentation in favour of a kind of fluid funk, which sounds totally organic with its jazzy undertones. Topper's inimitable grooves propel the sparse guitar and dominant

The sleeve to the 1987 double album bootleg of Big Audio Dynamite's November 1985 London gig. L-R Greg Roberts, Leo Williams, Mick Jones, Don Letts, Dan Donovan.

sax, while Mick sings with stark passion. There's hardly any other overdubs. Titles include 'Hiroshima', 'Interaction', 'Napoleon of Notting Hill' and the first version of 'The Bottom Line', which would become the first single when the group mutated into BAD. At this stage, it was sung lower and more resembled the stripped-down remix Rick Rubin later turned in.

Robin wrote it as a spur for Mick – 'When you reach the bottom line/The only thing to do is climb.' I must admit it's quite stunning to hear Mick set free and running loose with no pressure. The groove and gazelle-like guitar are given free rein and the vocals are pure, let-it-out soul.

'Napoleon Of Notting Hill' is described by Robin as Mick's 'How Do You Sleep' – the venomous put-down Lennon wrote about McCartney after the Beatles split. Mick wrote these words, and sings them as an emotional ballad. There's a reference to getting 'your backroom boys to work on your schemes'. The song never saw the light of day, but sounds like it was a necessary exorcism of past demons so Mick could move on.

Unfortunately, there was still the matter of Topper's habit. Pete Townshend, who'd recently got over his own addiction, paid for Topper to have the same black box treatment that had worked for both him and Eric Clapton. When this didn't work, Mick made him try the electro-acupuncture cure that had worked for Keith Richards. That didn't work either. Mick tried to restrict money from him but he just found others ways to get it.

Topper lasted until late spring. ' I was in the first line-up of BAD but I fucked it up because of the gear. I fucked that up because I just couldn't stop doing it. Then I was going to play with Joe and I fucked that up. Then Paul's band Havana 3AM and I fucked that up. I fucked them *all* up.'

After Topper and Mick parted company, Mick chose to drop his claim to the Clash name and free up the royalties so that he could buy equipment for his new group. Hence Topper received his money for the last two Clash albums and 'Rock The Casbah'. No prizes for guessing what he did with that.

The inevitable disaster happened when Topper was found concussed with a broken ankle after falling through the skylight of a motorcycle showroom. He managed to get off with a police caution. To this day, he hasn't got a clue what he was doing up there in the first place or why he was trying to break in. The accident necessitated a stint in hospital, which saw him temporarily get off smack.

When he came out, he became the first of The Clash to release a solo record – a cover of Gene Krupa's 'Drumming Man', which also featured the three Barnacle brothers from Dover and Mickey Gallagher. He got a deal with Mercury and recorded an album at Wessex with former Clash engineer Jerry Green producing. With the addition of session pros like Jimmy Helms, Bobby Tench and Van Morrison's bass player Jerome Rimson, they recorded an album of soul, R&B and jazz, which attracted some positive reviews.

Mick continued building his band. Don Letts came on board and injected a large chunk of its unique flavour. Since the sacking debacle, he'd become close to Mick, who listened to his suggestions and visions. Don was a punk rock messenger in that he understood cultures and how to turn rebellion into positive action. He had been with Mick during his New York renaissance and had also his head blown sideways by hip-hop's impact. Even though he didn't play an instrument, Don added to the multi-media flavour of the new group, brought in the mastermix-style sound effects and started toasting alongside Mick's vocals. To replace Topper, they recruited drummer Greg Roberts through a *Melody Maker* ad.

As with The Clash, Mick was surrounding himself with strong characters who create a resounding impact. After toying with calling the new group Real Westway (after Real Madrid), Mick finally settled on the no-nonsense and memorable Big Audio Dynamite. Or BAD. Meaning good. Very good.

Meanwhile, the bogus Clash took off for another US jaunt that started in Knoxville, Tennessee on 27 March and ran for over 40 dates until the end of May. Ironically, given that Joe was now professing to hate America, the trek was longer than any US tours undertaken by the old group.

Minus Mick and Topper, the band was less of a draw. At the University of Oregon gig on 27 May, the promoters lost 'a bundle' when less than 2500 turned out in an arena that comfortably seated 8500. As poor ticket sales became a pattern, it became obvious that the curiosity factor and nostalgia angle were wearing thin. Or as Suicide's Alan Vega had predicted after Mick's sacking, 'The audience for their politics and their ideals just won't be there in the States without a guitar hero to watch.'

Joe's misery was compounded by having to leave Britain so soon after his father dying, his mother falling ill, and Jazz Domino arriving.

Once the band returned to the UK in June, the first steps were taken on the convoluted journey that would culminate in the odious *Cut The Crap*. This involved the new boys, sometimes Paul and rarely Joe, holed up in the Lucky Eight trying to work up songs using tapes of Strummer chord patterns. The official line was that Joe was at home writing, but, was actually spending time with his sick mother, who started chemotherapy treatment later in the year. Ironically, Joe was writing his new riffs over a drum machine – a technique he'd criticised Mick for using during the *Combat Rock* demos.

The new Clash had picked the wrong time for inaction, as the country was being torn asunder by Margaret Thatcher's oppressive right-wing government.

Unemployment was at record levels, with whole communities thrown onto the dole as pits and factories were closed down as part of the Tories' ongoing campaign to destroy trade unionism. In Spring 1984, the miners went on strike and a veritable white riot was going on as pickets battled police and squaddies.

Seemingly oblivious, the band spent most of the summer on holiday. They resurfaced in September to play a short series of Italian festivals, the first of which was organised by the Italian Communist Party, in memorial to their former National Secretary, Enrico Berlinguer, who had died three months earlier.

The band's next UK shows took place on 6 and 7 December at Brixton Academy, in aid of the miners strike. Although this was a bit of a late gesture, the gigs went under the banner of 'Scargill's Christmas Party', in reference to the National Union of Mineworkers leader. Here they debuted three new songs – 'North And South', which was about the UK's widening geographical divide, 'Dirty Punk' and 'Fingerpoppin'', which were basically punk-by-numbers.

Work on the album also started that month. For some reason, Bernie had booked a studio in Munich. 'I think Bernie decided to work in Munich because it was away from the studio grapevine,' Joe later told the *Joe Strummer Resource* web-site. 'We can see signs of nerves showing here. He's always loved a cheap deal, and I think he got one on this studio in Munich. So he just flew people over there . . . He probably flew Pete over for a week hanging about. Really, it was more like Bernie marshalling his pieces, and using them against each other or one by one in order not to have his authority challenged.'

After telling the new boys to stay at home, Bernie laid down backing tracks with Joe. He had taken Mick's seat to the extent that he directed proceedings – rather in the fashion of his old mate Malcolm McLaren on his *Duck Rock* hip-hop project – which saw McLaren get other people to do the work while he took the bulk of the credit. Session man Michael Faye did the programming, while a bloke credited as Herman (Young Wagner) added layers of synthesiser.

The already-written tracks lined up for the album included 'Dictator', 'Three Card Trick', 'Are You Ready For War?' (retitled 'Are You Red . . . y?'), 'This Is England', 'North And South', 'We Are The Clash', 'Dirty Punk' and 'Fingerpoppin''. Newly written tracks included 'Movers And Shakers', 'Play To Win', 'Cool Under Heat' and 'Life Is Wild'. Former Blockhead Norman Watt-Roy played most of the bass, with Paul only appearing on a couple of songs. According to Robin Banks, this was nothing new, as Norman contributed much of the bass to *Sandinista!*

Paul explained his absence in 2003 when *GQ* magazine asked him what his worst Clash record was. '*Cut The Crap*. It had the potential to be quite a good record but Bernie got too involved. If I had known that was going to happen, I would have stayed and seen it through. I thought I was doing the honourable thing by staying away, telling Joe to see his vision through.'

Considering that the original aim of this new band was to return to the early Clash principles of integrity and unity, this recording was more fragmented than any Clash album had ever been. It was as if Bernie was taking Joe's songs and realising his own vision. Maybe as a concession to the original ideals, Bernie allowed the five-piece to come in and play together on two more tracks – 'Do It Now' and 'Sex Mad War' (retitled 'Sex Mad Roar'). This was the only time they were all in the studio together.

The standard of the songs, even Joe's lyrics, is abysmal. Rather than slaughter the lot, let's take one as an example – 'Movers And Shakers'. Whereas 'Clampdown' and 'The Magnificent Seven' decried the dead-end drudgery of conveyor belt labour, here Joe was urging people to throw themselves into crap jobs. He praises the guy washing cars at traffic junctions – 'This man earns 'cos it's understood/Times are bad and he's

Cut The Crap – *The new Clash's death rattle was released in November 1985.*

making good.' Maybe Joe was harking back to his ukulele days, as the effect is like an unfunny take on George Formby's 'When I'm Cleaning Windows'. Basically, the whole song rewrites Tory enforcer Norman Tebbit's notorious 'on yer bike' rant.

As the sessions progressed, Joe got more depressed and disillusioned and finally walked out. 'I started thinking, this is all my fault, letting this thing happen. Firstly, letting Bernie manipulate me into getting rid of Mick – which Mick helped by being the grumpiest sod you've ever seen in your life, permanently. Then the actual recording process became more and more horrible as I'd realised what I'd done.' Mixing was handled by Bernie and Joe was mortified when he heard the finished product, which CBS were obliged to release because they'd paid Bernie an advance for it.

A more memorable Strummer move came on 1 May 1985, when he took the group on a seventeen-day busking tour around the UK. The quintet, who all left home with a tenner, hitch-hiked from city to city, met up at a pre-determined site and proceeded to thrash out an acoustic barrage of covers and Clash songs. Passers by rubbed their eyes as Strummer and company whacked out such classics as the Monkees' 'Steppin' Stone' (as covered by the Pistols), Gene Vincent's 'Be-Bop-A-Lula' and some from the new album. Returning to his busking roots was Joe's way of bringing things down to earth after the appalling experience of making *Cut The Crap*.

The busking tour started in Sunderland and saw the quintet playing everywhere from shopping centres to under canal bridges. They entertained the queue at an Alarm gig – a considerable irony, as The Alarm had ineptly lifted their entire musical blueprint and band-of-the-people stance from mid-period Clash. Also, Joe had been less than kind to them in interviews.

The group lived on the change they made and, reversing proceedings of old, slept on fans' floors. Other cities the tour visited included York, Nottingham and Leeds. On 14 May, the played an acoustic set in one of the upstairs rooms at Edinburgh's Coasters disco.

Simon Trakmarx, of punk website *Trakmarx*, was another who refused to have anything to do with the new Clash, but recalls a mate of his waking up in his Leeds home to the sound of the group played outside his bedroom window. 'He was a guy called Olly Little, who was a bit fed-up, he woke up and it was like, "Fuck me, it's Joe Strummer!" He leaned out the window and offered them a cup of tea, so they came in and sat around for a bit.'

For many Clash fans, the busking tour provided their only positive memory of the post-Mick line-up. It might have been a publicity stunt, but it carried a deeper relevance for Joe. Here he could pay homage to his roots and remind himself why he started in the first place. Joe hated the new album and its mismatched walls of synths and terrace chants. As he heard *Cut The Crap* for the first time, Joe realised what he'd done. The busking tour would turn out to be the new Clash's live farewell to the British public.

They did play three European festivals that summer – Denmark's Roskilde on 29 June, Finland's Rockscene festival on 13 July and Athens, Greece, on 27 August. These paid well and were studded with big names of the day, such as Paul Young, Depeche Mode, The Cure and Paul Weller's Style Council. The new Clash had started off with around 40 per cent of their set being comprised of new material – this had now been whittled down to just 'Three Card Trick'. There was a press conference in Denmark where the group, led by an increasingly desperate looking Kosmo, failed miserably to drum up some Us Festival-style havoc.

In Athens, 200 anarchists tried to bust their way in and a near-riot was caused in the 60,000-strong crowd by Culture Club, as the Greek audience struggled to cope with Boy George's gender bending. After the gig, Joe reprised his Paris runner and disappeared to Spain, where he sat, 'sobbing under a palm tree,' as he realised The Clash was all over.

Meanwhile, Bernie continued to mix the album in a London studio with two engineers.

'This Is England' was released on 12 October and reached Number 24. The flip was 'Do it Now', while the twelve-inch also carried 'Sex Mad Roar'. 'This Is England' was about the only realistic candidate for a single on the whole sorry album.

Most reviews were fairly favourable, apart from a massive panning from *NME's* Gavin Martin who wrote, 'Strummer's rant bears all the signs of agit-rocker well into advanced senility: voice rambling and cracking over syn-drums flutter, football chants and ugly guitar grunge.' *Uncut's* Rob Hughes later called it, 'the Jones-less Clash's last great roar, in which Strummer seethes and writhes over a guttural guitar scrawl.'

Mick's departure hadn't entirely turned the light out on Joe's talent. Certainly, it had been misdirected by Bernie's brainwashing, but 'This Is England' is a good song with some nice Joe-isms like, 'I got my motorcycle jacket, but I'm walking all the time.' Imagine what it would have sounded like with Mick at the controls . . .

On 19 October, the *NME* carried a rather bizarre Clash Communiqué from Bernie and Kosmo. 'As legal difficulties over the name The Clash have forced the band off the road, the group known as The Clash hope to play some shows in the UK and Europe before the end of 1985. The long-awaited album will be released in early November, and The Clash will start touring under a temporary name until this dispute is resolved.' The story also reported rumours that Joe and Paul would reunite with Mick and Topper.

This was strange. For a start, Mick had relaxed his claim to the name the previous year when it was obvious that he wouldn't be forming a band with Topper. Also, he had Big Audio Dynamite so why would be want to keep the Clash title? Also, if there was a problem with the name, how could the new line-up have released 'This Is England' as The Clash?

What had happened was that, while in Spain, Joe decided that he couldn't carry on with this group. He returned to the UK after the single was released and called the rest of the band around to Lancaster Road. Here he announced that he was leaving both Bernie and the new Clash. Joe and Paul agreed to pay them off.

Joe felt genuinely sorry for his 'new platoon', as he told *NME*'s Sean O'Hagan in 1988. 'I think about those guys sometimes and hope it didn't fuck up their lives too much, because they were good people in a no-win situation.'

In the October 1999 issue of *Mojo*, Nick Sheppard talked about the last Athens gig in Pat Gilbert's Clash overview. 'I knew then the whole thing was going down the tubes because of the atmosphere between Joe and Bernie. Just before we went on stage, Joe gave Bernie a look of pure contempt . . . I'm not sure what had been said exactly. I knew then it was over. I think Joe realised it was a mistake to have got rid of Mick. It was like, "Oh fuck! I've dropped the plate." The next thing I knew Joe had buggered off to Spain for a month. Bernie was tearing his hair out, phoning me every morning.'

In 2000, Joe told *Record Collector*'s Sean Egan that Bernie had persisted in trying to keep the Clash name afloat by trying to audition a replacement singer to tour behind the new album. He adds that about two or three auditions took place with Paul and Kosmo. This one does beggar belief, especially on Paul's part.

Cut The Crap was finally released in early November and provided a definitive demonstration that The Clash minus Mick were indeed, crap. The disc came wrapped in a dire punk-by-numbers sleeve, which Joe had nothing to do with: some guy with a Mohican and one of Bernie's 'communiqués' for liner notes. 'RADICAL change begins on the STREET!! So if you're looking for some ACTION . . . CUT THE CRAP and Get OUT there!'

Whereas 'Pepe Unidos' had appeared on earlier Clash records as a kind of production pseudonym for Joe and Paul, Bernie credited the new album to 'Jose Unidos' – probably so it would look like another pseudonym for Strummer. 'It wouldn't have been so bad if Bernie had got the blame, but this was unbearable,' Joe

New Model Clash; Paul, Pete Howard, Joe, Vince White, Nick Sheppard.

told Gavin Martin in 1986.

The blame for the whole sorry debacle of *Cut The Crap* lies firmly with Bernie Rhodes who, having coerced Joe into nudging Mick out of the group, slipped into the driving seat. He then proceeded to smother the album in ill-conceived peripherals such as drum machines, backing vocals and incongruous synthesisers. Joe's writing had suffered. He was still being prodded to 'write about things you know,' but, in his unhappy and guilt-ridden frame of mind, could only manage a series of vapid 'punk' slogans.

Tragically, The Clash had turned into a Ramones-style punk cartoon, but without Da Brudders' great songs and the all-important sense of humour. On this album, The Clash didn't exist as a band any more. It was a Bernie Rhodes vanity album.

Unsurprisingly, *Cut The Crap* got panned. Slaughtered. *NME*'s Mat Snow likened the songs to Sham 69 and slammed the often-indecipherable, naff lyrics – 'Where's his knack for a potently well-turned phrase?' Over at *Melody Maker*, Adam Sweeting went off the deep end. 'It's crap!' he stormed, 'And it doesn't cut it. Football chants, noises of heavy meals being regurgitated over pavements and carpets and a mix that Moulinex would be ashamed of. Who the hell does Joe Strummer think he is? *Cut The Crap* is a bedlam of horrible noises, uneasy bedfellows and ships colliding in the night.'

Sounds' Jack Barron defied comprehension to stand alone, awarding the LP four and a half stars. 'The Clash don't miss Mick Jones, and the band have finally emerged to lucidly stitch their love of ethnic musics with gut-level rock.' Rather puzzlingly, Barron wrote, 'Joe Strummer has never been a poet,' although he gets it right for this album when he says, 'he deals in propaganda with broad slashes of filmic imagery.'

The album made Number sixteen in the UK – purely on the back of the band's name – but barely managed to scrape into the US Top 100, peaking at Number 88.

The *NME* of 23 November finally reported the split. A Rhodes-Vinyl statement (under Joe's name) stated that Strummer and Simonon would continue as The Clash and release a single called 'Shouting Street'. Joe's tribute to Portobello Road might have been the last thing he wrote for The Clash, but it wouldn't see the light of day until his first solo album in 1989.

'Joe said, "I've got this song, 'Shouting Street', let's work on that, and I said, "Fine," but I didn't get another call,' recalled Paul. 'I think Joe wanted to avoid any confrontation, which didn't bother me. I wasn't looking at my watch.'

Meanwhile, Mick had continued developing Big Audio Dynamite. In early 1985, they supported U2, who had always acknowledged their Clash influence, on some European and American dates. 'They were generous to BAD,' Mick told Gavin Martin, who was now at the *Daily Mirror*. 'But I used to sit backstage at some places in America thinking what might have been. It was pretty hard to take.'

In the spring, BAD started recording their first album at Sarm West – the former Basing Street Studios where The Clash had recorded *Give 'Em Enough Rope*. Here they laid down their riotous hybrid of rock 'n' roll, dub and hip-hop, with samples running amok and Mick's subject matter grounded firmly back in London.

In September 1985 they released their debut single, 'The Bottom Line', which didn't chart but pricked up a lot of ears with its sheer newness. After the tired, confused death throes of the new Clash, it was like a blast of fresh air. Mick extended his hip-hop fixation when Rick Rubin, the kid who'd started the huge Def Jam label with Russell Simmons, remixed it for the States and put it on his label, which had recently become an offshoot of Sony.

The group's first album, *This Is Big Audio Dynamite*, was released a week after *Cut The Crap* and got infinitely better reviews. A week later came the announcement of the Clash split.

Within a year of sacking Mick, Joe had realised what a mistake he'd made in choosing to go with Bernie. With the new album an unmitigated disaster and the bogus Clash gone, Joe now decided he had to find Mick and persuade him to reform.

Joe tracked Mick down to the Bahamas, where he was on holiday and doing some work with Talking Heads spin-off, the Tom Tom Club 'This was the first time that I'd gone to Nassau in the Bahamas,' recalls Mick. 'I'd just finished the first Big Audio Dynamite album, and Joe came over and rode round the island on a bicycle for two days looking for me. Finally he found me, and he said, "C'mon, let's get it back together again." And I'd just done the first BAD album, and I said, "No, I've just done this record, come and have a listen to it." So we went over to Compass Point Studio's special listening room.

'I came in really excited about it. I said, "What did you think?" Joe just said, "I've never heard such a load of old shit in my life!" He didn't mean it. He just wanted me to get the group back together again.'

Only Joe could weigh in like that, although he did apologise for sacking Mick and acknowledged what a disaster the bogus Clash had been. But Mick had just spent over two years picking himself up, forming his new group and creating their first album. He'd accepted Joe's apology, but wouldn't ditch his new band. 'He just laughed at me,' said Joe later, who shouldn't have been suprised at this reaction. But, although Mick felt vindicated, he would always say that he got no great satisfaction out of seeing the way that Bernie had stitched Joe up.

As the two camps' careers went in diametrically opposite directions, BAD made their major live headlining debut at London's Town & Country Club on 28 November. Me and the same crew from Aylesbury who used to follow The Clash went along. There was an aura around BAD that filled me with the same excitement that I'd got from The Clash in 1976, although they were poles apart, musically.

This was different because it was a British adaptation of the new music coming from America's dance underground (which I'd become obsessed with because of The Clash). They were *fresh*. Mick could easily have played his Clash songs, like 'Train in Vain' or' Should I Stay Or Should I Go?', but chose to move on. Instead they encored with an inspired cover of Prince's '1999', which had actually been suggested by Joe.

BAD's gigs became massive celebrations of the groove and sonic innovation. Subsequent singles like 'E=MC2' and 'Medicine Show' remain classics of their time. When I was living in New York City, I saw just how readily BAD had been embraced by the hip dance crowd. Supporting were a bunch of upstarts called the Beastie Boys.

I'd initially gone to New York to visit my son, who was only a year old but had been taken away by his mother. Mick's then-partner, Daisy, had given birth to a daughter called Lauren in 1984, so he knew what I was going through. 'Go and see your son,' said Mick as he sorted out a plane ticket. It remains one of the loveliest things anyone has ever done for me, as I was able to be with my son during those crucial years. Thank you again, Mick.

The Clash split had a profound effect on Joe. 'I had to disassemble myself and put the pieces back together,' he reflected on Channel 4's *Wired* in 1988. 'I felt completely destroyed by that experience. I'd lost my parents, my group. You want to think about things. You become a different person.'

Joe told the *San Antonio Current* that he wished they'd jacked it in after *Combat Rock*. 'But then again, you can't have it the way you want it really. You've got to accept the way it was. And that's what happened. But, yeah, that would have been a sweeter way to end.'

So The Clash was no more, although to many fans they hadn't existed since Mick got the push. What a hole they left, and what a fucking waste. They could have done so much more with the talent at their disposal. The memories of The Clash with Mick Jones acting as Joe's perfect foil alongside Paul and Topper are unique and timeless.

A live reunion might have dumped a tin of black paint over the original motives and later achievements of one of the greatest rock 'n' roll bands ever. On the other hand, with the staggering musical progression the group achieved in their seven years of glory, the prospect of the classic lineup messing about in the studio again would have been truly fascinating. The wrong move would have been to revisit the final year of the Clash and turn their rebellion into money.

But in late 1985, Joe was alone. Mick was starting to set the roof on fire with BAD, Topper was lost to his habit, and Paul was embarking on a new career in painting. Joe was now consigned to the wilderness. Apart from losing his father, Joe had lost his band. It would take him a long time to fully get over it.

Joe himself summed it up during a drinking session after The Clash split with his old mate Allan Jones, which the future *Uncut* editor quoted in his obituary for Joe. 'I fucked it up so badly. I listened to all the wrong people, did all the wrong things. One of the greatest bands ever, you know, and it all got totally fucked up. I'll always regret it, always.'

I also bumped into a remorseful Joe in the pub around this time. It was a Sunday afternoon session at the Warwick Castle on Portobello Road. He was full of regret. 'I really stabbed Mick in the back,' he whispered, although he stood by his dislike of Mick's behaviour. But Joe now firmly blamed Bernie for instigating the split and hated what he and Kosmo did to The Clash. Now Joe's attitude was that, as with Topper, the problem could have probably been solved in-house, like a normal family row. A long break might have saved The Clash. Cutting off two limbs certainly didn't. 'It was just awful with Bernie,' he said. 'Destroyed me and our group.'

My memory of this particular meeting nearly twenty years ago is slightly blurred. I think I was with Jock and he doesn't remember either. But talk did inevitably turn to The Clash. One moment stands out, amidst the general guffaws and reminiscing about trouser requirements, gaffer tape sessions, sandwich rituals and berserk gigs. Joe grinned. A massive, lighting-up-time *smile*.

Then a laugh and a shake of his head. 'That was fucking great, wasn't it?'

CHAPTER SEVENTEEN
THE UNHAPPY WANDERER

That's the phrase I used to chuckle at and say, Joe Strummer: The Wilderness Years!
You can hear it on some cheap TV show in the middle of the night on cable!
– Joe Strummer

And so began what Joe would later call 'the wilderness years'. The period between The Clash splitting and the gradual formation of the Mescaleros in 1999 would see him flitting from project to project that, although occasionally great and always interesting, lacked the focus and profile that he'd previously enjoyed.

Having been fleeced of self-confidence and left high, dry and bandless by Bernie, Joe greeted 1986 in a well of depression. He became a familiar, rather forlorn, figure traversing the bars and pubs of Notting Hill.

'Round the corner from the Warwick Castle, there was a little Portuguese guy running a coffee bar,' recalls Jock Scott, who lived in the area at the time. 'Joe used to go in there first thing in the morning, nine or ten o'clock. He'd go down Portobello and you knew you could catch him in this little coffee place. The guy was selling just coffee and sandwiches. He was a nice man who had a bottle of brandy under the bar.'

Joe's meanderings inadvertently led him to the next stage of his career. For the first time, it wouldn't involve him playing rock 'n' roll to foaming punters. Just before Christmas, he sneaked into an end-of-shoot party at a Portobello canal basin bar for Alex Cox's new film, which told the story of doomed lovers Sid Vicious and Nancy Spungen. Cox buttonholed Joe in the gents' toilets for a theme song for the film, which was to be called *Love Kills*.

Joe was initially reticent. Those who had known and liked Sid were wary of such projects, especially in the wake of appalling records like the *Sid Sings* LP. But Joe saw a rough cut and relented. He came up with 'Love Kills', a song that took the form of a dialogue between Sid and the cop arresting him for Nancy's murder.

In a gesture of reconciliation, Joe invited Mick to play on this, and another new song called 'Dum Dum Club'. Mick agreed and also produced the two tracks – partly because his old mare Glen Matlock was playing on the remakes of old Sex Pistols songs. Joe also came up with some background music, which he couldn't be credited for because his CBS contract wouldn't let him submit more than two tracks to a soundtrack if they didn't release it.

During this period, Joe became a father for the second time when Gaby gave birth to their second daughter. Once again, the couple dipped into their musical influences to come up with the name Lola Maybelline, which nodded to the Kinks and Chuck Berry.

Joe on the set of Alex Cox's shambolic western Straight To Hell *in 1986.*   261

Less happily, on 25 April, Joe was arrested while driving at high speed up Kensington Park Road at four in the morning. He was found to be well over the alcohol limit, banned from driving for eighteen months and fined £200.

Meanwhile, Mick's Big Audio Dynamite was continuing to thrive and had gained an enthusiastic following. They'd gained a synth player when Dan Donovan, the son of sixties photographer Terence – who'd taken the cover photo for the album – joined up.

In April, their second single, 'E=MC2', was released. This remains my favourite BAD song – uplifting, melodic and up there with any of Mick's late-period Clash rockers. His production, which saw the tune littered with samples from Donald Cammell and Nic Roeg's hallucinogenic gangster masterpiece, *Performance*, was startling and futuristic. If Joe had taken big but misplaced steps toward domestic themes with his bogus version of The Clash, Mick homed in on the essence of London with resounding success.

Many were shocked to see Mick and the boys playing the song on *Top of the Pops*, but I'd always felt that The Clash's stand against doing this came from Joe anyway. As a result, the single rose to Number Eleven on the chart. This beat The Clash's highest placing with 'Bankrobber', and illustrated the sort of sucesss they could have enjoyed if they'd relaxed their embargo.

BAD's debut album, *This Is Big Audio Dynamite,* reached Number 27 and remained on the chart for 27 weeks, scoring gold disc status in the process. The band's second single was a funky spaghetti Western hip-hop epic, 'Medicine Show'. This was released in June and got to Number 29. Old rifts seemed to be healing when Joe and Paul showed up in Don's gun-toting video dressed as Southern US cops. It would have been a full-on Clash reunion, but Topper was too caught up in his own pursuits to make it. The still on the back of the sleeve shows a suitably portly and sweaty Joe looking a dead ringer for Rod Steiger in *In The Heat Of The Night.*

This renewed bonhomie between old Clash members less than three years after the split showed just how simply all that ugliness and unhappiness could have been avoided. You don't lose close mates that easily – unless outside forces intervene and succeed in destabilising the relationship.

Joe must have felt some additional pangs of regret when BAD headlined a free concert on Clapham Common, following a march in support of the newly formed Artists Against Apartheid organization. I went on the march and arrived at a scene not unlike Victoria Park eight years earlier – even down to BAD going on so late that they had to truncate their set. The Clash would have loved it.

'Love Kills' saw the light of day in late July. The film's title had been changed to *Sid and Nancy,* which meant that Joe's song had nothing in the movie to pin it to. It was released as a single by CBS who had the rights to release Joe's contributions as singles while the album came out on MCA. It came with a little-seen video from Alex Cox, which was shot at Tabernas, near Almeria, Spain – Sergio Leone Spaghetti Western territory.

NME's resident angry young punk, Steven Wells, huffily called the simple but contagious rocker, 'weak and pitiful'. It only reached Number 69 in the charts, but would receive a new lease of life in 1989 when it appeared on the soundtrack to *Wired*, the bio-pic of *Blues Brothers* star John Belushi.

During the summer, Big Audio Dynamite started recording their second album at Trident Studios, in St Anne's Court, Soho. This was the same place where I'd witnessed Mott the Hoople finish their swansong, 'Saturday Gigs', in 1974. Joe popped into the sessions on Mick's 31st birthday after bumping into Don Letts in the street, and never looked back. He remained at the studio until recording was finished, working the round-the-clock sessions and sleeping under the grand piano.

Although Joe didn't sing or play on the album, he ended up co-producing it with Mick, and also co-wrote five tracks, either with Mick or other members of the band. In an odd twist, reminiscent of Mick's supposed stipulation for *Combat Rock*, Joe insisted that the album be mixed in New York. While it's possible that Joe was trying to give Mick a subtle taste of his own medicine, it's more likely that he was trying to make amends by suggesting a venue that his old partner loved. Once again, this proved a long and costly process, which saw Joe pushing himself to the limit and practically moving into the studio for three weeks.

Joe also suggested the album's title, *No.10 Upping Street* – a hip alternative to the Prime Minister's residence. My impression at the time was of two mates, now free from pressure and outside interference, having fun and making some rather good music. Even the most casual onlooker couldn't help but notice that Joe and Mick were working together a lot more closely than on their last ventures with The Clash.

Joe co-wrote five tracks: 'Beyond The Pale', where his message was, 'Immigration built the nation'. 'Limbo The Law', a latin/hip-hop/rock mutation that explores gangsters and movies; 'V. Thirteen', which would later be a single, cinematically deals with a dark future peppered with 'rockheads', but finding hope in the DJ; 'Ticket' again tackles immigration, but from Don and Leo's Jamaican perspective. 'Sightsee MC!' was a total cruncher, bringing together rock-hard beats and rap in the Def Jam style that was sweeping the hip clubs courtesy of Rick Rubin and his Beastie Boys. The song is like a guided tour around the real London, with its post-pub brawls, gay meat-racks and riot-damaged tower blocks. It ends the album as one of the best examples of what Mick was trying to do with BAD.

Although musically different, it's also the closest to what Joe and Mick were doing when they started The Clash and wrote songs like '1977'. Some have suggested that this is what The Clash might have sounded like on the follow-up to *Combat Rock*, but the input of Don and the other members cannot be underestimated.

After the album had been completed, Mick got to meet his all-time hero, Keith Richards, when he was on holiday in Jamaica with Don. 'Me and Don were sitting on the beach and suddenly Keith just appeared and ambled up, looking like a pirate king with a big knife in his belt. He invited us over to his place and he's got all his rasta guys there. We did a bit of jamming. While we were there Chuck Berry came to the place, but he was very quiet and just sat in the corner.'

The reason for Chuck's presence was that Keith was about to embark on his pet project, *Hail! Hail! Rock 'n' Roll* film about Berry. How did Mick feel about meeting Keith at last? 'Like in *Wayne's World* where they're going, "We're not worthy"!' He says

Mick and friend wait for Primal Scream to arrive at Vice Versa studios, under the Westway, 1994.

he didn't mention the classroom fight where he stood up for Bo Diddley against Robin!

In September 2004, I asked Mick if BAD had been a conscious effort to merge rock and dance styles. 'Definitely,' he agreed, but added modestly that he didn't necessarily think he'd managed it. 'It's very difficult to try and cross over dance music with rock music. Many people have tried and many have failed. It might be like a long term thing.'

No. 10 Upping Street was released in late October but got lukewarm reviews, although it did make Number Eleven in the UK album charts. At the time I was living in New York City (thanks to Mick), so I didn't know that the singles 'V. Thirteen', 'Sightsee MC!' and the rousing Eddie Cochran/hip-hop call-to-arms, 'C'mon Every Beatbox', hadn't really troubled the UK chart. I just heard them played in New York clubs, as Mick ensured that the remixes still resonated with the dubbed-up groove-power then prevalent in the city. When a BAD track got selected as a single, Mick – ever abreast of dance music's tides – stripped it down, stretched the instrumental sections and applied the advanced dub techniques which were coming in from Chicago as the acid house scene gained momentum.

Ultimately, it had been great to see Mick and Joe working together again. Of course, while promoting the album, Mick had to field the inevitable questions about Joe joining BAD or the possibility of The Clash now reforming. He did say that he would be helping Joe write songs for a solo album he was planning, which Strummer said he wanted to make as raw and primitive as possible. This didn't happen, because Joe got involved in film projects and Mick was tied up with touring *Upping Street*. Also, looking at the paths the two artists followed later, it's apparent that musically, they were heading in totally different directions.

Joe got on the BAD-wagon in order to work with the old mate he'd so badly dissed. Comparing the naked soul and rootsy global-music palette of Joe's later solo outings with the way Mick subsequently embraced acid house, it's obvious that, although the pair could get on again personally, they were set on exploring vastly different creative paths.

The Clash had come to mean musical innovation with social comment and that now lived on in Big Audio Dynamite. The spirit of punk was alive, not in three-chord thrashes with slogans shouted over the top, but applying the DIY ethic to new technology like samplers and drum machines. Hip-hop and acid house showed that anyone could go in the bedroom with a basic recording setup and produce results that could go on to sell thousands on the underground market. These were the principles of 1977 ten years down the line.

As a vehicle for social comment, hip-hop had burst out of the block parties onto the world stage via groundbreaking aural activists like Public Enemy – who cited The Clash as a major influence. Bernie later claimed to *NME*'s Stewart Ballie that he'd been instrumental in the formation of the Def Jam label with Russell Simmons and Rick Rubin. He also claimed to have a hand in the making of Public Enemy's seismic *Yo! Bum Rush The Show* album.

I interviewed Rick and Russell in London in 1985, DJ-ed with Rubin at the label's launch party in the UK around that time, and became mates with the fledgling Beastie Boys. After I moved to New York in 1986, I became a regular at the Def Jam offices and Rick Rubin's apartment. Although he was said to be living in New York at the time, there was no sign of Bernie.

By 1987, Joe's creative urges were drawn to the film world, initially through his Alex Cox connection. After *Sid and Nancy*, Cox's next film was going to be *Walker*, a black comedy about vile mid-nineteenth century US colonist William Walker, who took a posse of mercenaries called the Immortals and invaded Nicaragua in 1855. He set himself up as a dictator and Cox identified parallels with Ronald Reagan's administration, which was then operating in the same region. Joe was similarly aware of Reagan's rampant imperialism and enthusiastically signed up for the film.

Before filming got underway, Joe took part in a spring benefit for the Sandinistas, which Cox had organised at Brixton's Fridge with former Roxy promoter Andy Czezowski. Also appearing were Elvis Costello and The Pogues. *Sid and Nancy* producer Eric Feller thought that it would be a great idea to take the lineup on a tour of Nicaragua, and film it. When the necessary financial backing failed to happen, Fuller and Cox decided to make a movie with the same lineup. This would become *Straight To Hell*.

Alex, Joe and writer Dick Rude conceived the idea of a vulgar spaghetti western-type affair during a drunken night at the Cannes Film Festival. Unlike many schemes born out of piss-ups, this one actually materialised and was shot over three weeks with a budget of £900,000 from Island Pictures, who were attracted by the lineup. The participants, who were on a profit-share deal, relocated to Almeria, Spain, where Alex shot Joe's 'Love Kills' video. Apart from Joe, who flew there on 6 August after getting back from BAD mixing sessions in New York, *Straight To Hell* featured Costello, The Pogues, a cameo from director Jim Jarmusch, and Xander Schloss, ex-guitarist from LA punk band the Circle Jerks. It also included an appearance from the future Mrs. Cobain, Courtney Love, who'd ended up with a small part in *Sid and Nancy* after auditioning for the lead female role.

The story concerned the exploits of three inept and perma-pissed hitmen, and Velma, their pregnant trailer-trash female accomplice (Courtney). Joe played a hitman called Simms – 'a dirty rat, a poseur who knows his guns but when he comes to getting it right he's pretty damn useless,' he told *NME*'s Lucy O'Brien, who was covering the shoot. Joe took his part seriously by wearing the same clothes for the duration and, following Cox's habit of sleeping on set, kipped in an old car. He even went out drinking in local bars wearing his gun and holster. Joe's fingers had to be taped up because they were so raw from practising his gun technique. Eventually, he gets shot by Velma.

After witnessing Joe shoot Shane McGowan, Lucy asked him how it felt to be slinging a gun. 'Good', replied Joe. 'I'm only telling the truth. It's hard to resist a gun. Hold it. Aim it at someone's head and pull the trigger.' She also asked him about acting. 'It's all timing. Obviously music helps because you got timing and singing.'

At this time, Joe had definitely caught the acting bug, as he told *Q*'s Simon Banner. 'It's what I want to do, to be an actor. Not an ac-*tor*, though. I'm not going to go to drama school. I've discovered that there's a lot more to acting than just learning the lines. I've had an intense life, so I've got a lot of experience to draw on.'

Alex Cox told Lucy O'Brien, 'I wanted Strummer and The Pogues because they're all really charismatic, great faces and natural actors.'

Of course, there would be a soundtrack. While in Almeria, Joe, Xander, and Michael Sandoval wrote 'Salsa Y Ketchup', about Schloss's character's hot-dog stand, Disco Wiener Haven. Back in London, Joe, Costello and the Pogues all wrote songs, while Joe suggested Shane's crew cover 'Danny Boy'. Joe supplied the two songs he was allowed – 'Ambush At Mystery Rock' and a ballad called 'Evil Darling', which only appeared on the soundtrack album. He also provided some uncredited background music. The film and soundtrack both bombed, although I'm not surprised about the album, which was released on Stiff Records offshoot Hell and was near-impossible to find.

Joe slipped in another movie late that year, when he took the bit part of a rocking security guard called Mario in *Candy Mountain*, a rock 'n' roll road movie set in Canada. Joe's involvement came about through the film's co-director, Rudy Wurlitzer, who was also writing the script for the upcoming *Walker*. His previous work included scripting *Pat Garrett and Billy The Kid*, a favourite of Joe's with its soundtrack by Bob Dylan. The film also featured Tom Waits, Dr John and David Johansen, but sank into obscurity after getting limited UK distribution in 1989.

In December, Anna Mellor lost her battle with cancer. After years of distancing himself from his parents, Joe had at least got close to her in the period before her death.

In January 1987, shooting started on *Walker*. The budget was nearly $6,000,000 and location work in the Nicaraguan city of Granada lasted over eight weeks. Apart from lead roles Ed Harris and Marlee Martin, the cast was bolstered by Cox's usual crew, including Dick Rude, Pogue Spider Stacey and Xander Schloss. Joe played the mercenaries' hirsute dishwasher, Faucet, who also gets shot by a woman.

Robin Banks was now living in Stockholm, Sweden. While visiting London, he thought he'd pop around and see Joe. 'I knocked on the door of the house in Lancaster Road and someone answered the door – this bloke with long hair and a beard. I said, "Is Joe there?" He said, "I am Joe, you cunt!" He was doing *Walker* at the time.'

Despite hurling himself into his roles – as Robin discovered – Joe's enthusiasm for the thespian life was rapidly cooling. 'This is the beginning of the end. It's too difficult,' he told *NME*'s Graham Fuller. 'I'm trying to play down the acting bit at the moment,' Joe confessed to Ted Mico of *Melody Maker*. 'My secret ambitions may be another matter, but I don't want to set myself up by saying I want to be a great actor. Pop stars have a lot to live down in that field.'

Joe revealed the cause of these doubts in *NME* when he said, 'I don't know what to do for myself. I don't know whether to go back to rocking or not.' Most people I met who'd also encountered Joe in the pubs around Portobello Road said the same thing – he was lost without The Clash.

In the absence of any clear direction, Joe kept busy. Inspired by Dylan's work on *Pat Garrett and Billy The Kid*, he asked Alex Cox if he could do the whole score for *Walker*. Cox agreed and Joe brought a little Casio synth, a cheap guitar and a four-track tape recorder to use on location. He approached the project with the same 'method' approach he employed for his acting – soaking up the atmosphere of the film and his surroundings into his compositions. Joe then set about banging down

'I am Joe, you cunt!' – Joe on the set of Walker, *1987.*

the roughest musical sketches onto tape.

In the end, fourteen tracks were selected from Joe's 'method composing' sessions. You could call it his first solo album, as recording commenced after shooting was complete at Russian Hill Recording Studios in San Francisco. Joe hired a gang of Bay Area session men, augmented by Xander on guitar and Dick Bright helping him with string and horn arrangements. The one Strummer vocal that made the movie was 'The Unknown Immortal', while two others – 'Tropic Of No Return' and 'Tenessee Rain' – surfaced on the soundtrack. This came out on Virgin's Movie Music offshoot, so CBS restricted Joe to three vocals.

The *Walker* soundtrack was released in February 1988 to much acclaim – even from the previously highly critical Gavin Martin, who awarded it eight out of ten in *NME*, and wrote, 'You may be a little stunned and staggered at first (I was) to find the man with the demon bark and three chord bite has composed every note here. But from lustrous samba percussion, through flamenco horns and country inflections, it's all gorgeously effective and superbly detailed.'

Clash veteran Charles Shaar Murray, who was now writing for *Q*, gave it four out of five and commented on 'a remarkably elegant and loose-limbed and accomplished set of ersatz Latin themes spiked with delicate country touches . . . If the movie turns out to be utter rubbish, it certainly won't be Joe Strummer's fault.'

This praise provided Joe with a much-needed boost, even if the soundtrack failed to break out of that notoriously insular market. 'I remember having a bit of a chuckle 'cos the press had written me off after the *Cut The Crap* debacle,' said Joe on the *Joe Strummer Resource* website. 'The reviews were incredibly, reluctantly good . . . It is a good record. No-one's ever heard it, but never mind.'

The film itself wouldn't be released until the following year and suffered from going against the grain of what was considered 'commercial' in US cinemas. The political parallels with the Reagan administration were putting Alex in a similar kind of anti-establishment bracket that had sometimes hampered The Clash when it came to getting over to mainstream American audiences. *Walker* only received limited distribution in the UK when it was finally released in March 1989.

The summer of 1987 saw Joe back in the UK. He played on a version of 'London Calling' with The Pogues for Irish radio programme *The Session*, which led to him being asked to fill in for sick guitarist Phil Chevron on the band's November US tour.

Joe enjoyed the low-profile approach, standing at the back while concentrating on getting his rhythm parts right. He even stepped up to the mic for two Clash songs – 'London Calling' and 'I Fought The Law'. The tour finished up in Britain in late December, with Joe being asked back the following March to play the group's annual St Patrick's Day knees-up at Kentish Town's Town & Country Club, which was later released on video.

Having taken over CBS In 1988, Sony decided to cash on the band's back catalogue by releasing a Clash retrospective album. Originally called *Revolution Rock* but optimistically retitled *The Story Of The Clash, Volume One*, the 28-track double set was compiled by Mick and released in March. It would climb to Number Seven in the UK charts, and was preceded by 'I Fought The Law' being re-released as a single in February and making Number 29. In late April, it was followed by 'London Calling', which got to Number 46. The album was released in the US in June.

The Story Of The Clash made no attempt to tell its tale chronologically, being more of a damned good representation of The Clash's diverse back catalogue. For example, the first CD kicks off with 'The Magnificent Seven' and finishes with 'Bankrobber', with the earliest track being 'I Fought The Law'. The second disc starts with 'White Man' and brings in the first album's highlights. In no particular order, the set would probably be more suitably titled *The Best Of The Clash*, but it serves as an evocative collection. Tellingly, it contains nothing beyond *Combat Rock*.

Joe contributed sleeve notes under the pseudonym Albert Transom – 'band valet'. He roughly sums up the Clash story with a surrealistic twist and, perhaps hopefully, left the door open by concluding, 'If I had to sum it up, I'd say we played every gig on the face of the earth and that's what it's all about . . . I've just heard they'll give me some room on Vol. 2 so maybe I will be able to tell the bits I've had to skip or leave out.'

'It's a great story,' said *Melody Maker*'s Paul Mathur, while Elliott Murphy of *Rolling Stone* wrote, 'The story of The Clash is a story that ended too soon . . . The Clash's brand of rock, while commercially accessible, was truly revolutionary . . . We need this band more than we did then.'

Irrespective of the nostalgic clamour, the rest of The Clash were active enough to rule out any hope of a reunion anytime soon.

BAD recorded their third album during early 1988. *Tighten Up Volume 88* was released in June and, although Joe wasn't involved, some Clash input was present in the form of Paul's sleeve painting of a blues dance by Trellick Tower, the monolithic high-rise at the top end of Harrow Road. The album reached Number 33 in the UK.

Paul had been painting since The Clash split, but exercised a desire to play music again in late 1987 when he teamed up with former Whirlwind singer Nigel Dixon to form Havana 3AM. The pair went to the Texas border to ride Harley Davidsons and, after a road trip that roped in ex-Sex Pistol Steve Jones and an ever-growing wild bunch, ended up in Los Angeles. Here they recruited guitarist Gary Myrick and played some gigs in Texas and California. Paul and Steve Jones even found themselves jamming in the studio at Bob Dylan's request. The results appeared on a track on his *Down In The Groove* album. But Paul soon tired of the LA lifestyle and returned to painting in London.

In January 1989, Paul and Topper were going to form a band together but heroin tried to join that one too. I later heard that Topper had been playing bongos with acid-house hoodlums Flowered Up and may have been about to join them. This connection came about through their manager being Terry McQuade, the young skinhead who'd claimed to be Joe's cousin in *Rude Boy*.

Havana 3AM were sporadically active, supporting BAD on their autumn 1989 tour and finally released their first and only album in February 1991. Paul then returned to painting full-time. Sadly, Nigel Dixon succumbed to cancer in 1993.

Topper was still on the slippery slope. Now back in his hometown of Dover, he

The Story of The Clash Volume 1 – *An optimistically titled collection that showcased the band's unique diversity.*

was sentenced to fifteen months jail for supplying heroin, after a drug buddy overdosed around his house. 'I only gave him a bit,' he protested. Topper served ten months and went back on smack when he came out in September 1988.

At this point, Kosmo came back on the scene. After the bogus band had split, he'd moved to New York and seemed to turn over a new leaf away from Rhodes. Kosmo was one of the main instigators in the removal of Topper and Mick, and also a major reason for Johnny Green departing the ranks. But Johnny regained some respect for Kosmo in the late eighties when he tried to help Topper out of the black hole he'd dug himself into.

'Topper told me in depth that in the late eighties and early nineties, Kosmo sorted him out. He put him in rehab at The Priory, tried to sort out his debts – which were about £750,000 – and generally stood by him. He didn't need to do that. When I saw him at Joe's funeral, I had to say, "I thought you were a cunt, but from what Topper told me maybe I've been a bit harsh on you."'

Meanwhile, Joe had started working on his next soundtrack – a film called *Permanent Record*, directed by Marisa Silver. It starred Keanu Reeves in a story about the impact of a Midwestern schoolboy's suicide on his classmates. At that time, teenage suicide was a sensitive topic in the US, being particularly rife in Midwestern small towns. It was also a subject that had been close to Joe's heart after the death of his brother. He was moved enough to take it on.

To record the soundtrack at Baby O studio in Los Angeles, Joe put together a band, which he called The Latino Rockabilly War. Xander Schloss played guitar, joined by Willie MacNeil from the Untouchables on drums, jazzman Jim Donica on bass, Tupelo Joe Altruda on guitar and keyboards, with local Latin musicians Poncho Sanchez and Ramon Vanda beefing up the percussion.

Joe extended his interest in splicing together diverse genres and, having already joined Latin and rock 'n' roll rhythms at the hip, revisited the style of second-line gumbo-funk – as practised by New Orleans bands like the amazing Meters – which he'd dabbled in on 'Julie's Been Working For The Drug Squad'. This group was a skin-tight funk ensemble playing with an underlying Latin jerk in the groove. Clipped and syncopated, the style could easily slide into Joe's canon. Add the fact that Joe was now itching to play rock 'n' roll with a band again and it was apparent that another intriguing, cross-cultural Strummer stew was cooking.

Helpfully, the usual contractual restrictions were avoided because the soundtrack was being released on Epic, Joe's US label. The Latinos recorded a welter of material for the movie. Four out of the six vocal tracks Joe recorded made it to the film and the soundtrack LP – 'Trash City', 'Baby The Trans', 'Nefertiti Rock', 'Nothin' 'Bout Nothin'', plus the instrumental theme song, 'Permanent Record'. One of the unused vocal tracks – 'Cholo Vest' – would eventually surface as the B-side to Joe's October 1989 single, 'Island Hopping'. It contained the line, 'Nobody really, really thinks about you when you're gone.'

In June 1988, Epic released 'Trash City' as a UK single. 'Resurrection bloooooooody Joe!' bellowed *NME*. 'There might not be a riot goin' on, but there sure as hell is a small hooley a-rockin'! Nobody makes the pulse race better.' The album followed in mid-July and prodded the same organ's Stuart Bailie to write, 'Joe is pushing off on his solo adventures with an increasing sense of purpose.' Stuart mentioned the Latin influences, but added that Joe had moved on from using them for 'melancholy atmospherics' and into 'an upbeat basement rattle'. The tracks that had been used were the rough 'n' ready rockers, while the slower outings didn't make it. The latter was the area where Joe had tried to push his musical boat into fresh waters. But he was rocking again, even if he did dismiss the album as 'a knock off job' in a 2000 interview with *Record Collector*.

When *Permanent Record* came out in the US, it touched a nerve and was a success – unlike in the UK, where the subject matter was too remote for British audiences.

When in London, Joe spent much of his time in the pubs around Portobello Road. Jock Scott fondly remembers seeing him regularly. 'I was always drinking at the Warwick Castle. When Joe was in town, he would go in there for a pint and a game of pool and a chat with the boys. This was before they even had afternoon hours, before they changed the law. In fact, they changed the law the day we were in the pub! It was like ten to three and the barman said, "Drink up now!" We said, "Fuck off! It's now illegal to do that because they've changed the law!"

'There was about five of us, and Joe was there. We staged a sit-in. We said, "We're not fucking having this!" We leapt the bar and started pulling pints, saying, "We're not going anywhere." Seamus, the landlord, saw that it was getting beyond his control, so he just locked the door and said, "You're the ones who are providing me with my income, so you are the ones who will have the benefit of this new law." So there was an afternoon lock-in. It was a fantastic session. We were all singing Clash songs with harmonies and that. We thought, when the legality of the country changes in your favour, you must stand up for your rights. Joe was very much in favour of that.'

Joe decided to keep the Latino Rockabilly War going with the same line-up and, after playing a series of benefit gigs throughout June, agreed to play a one-off benefit for Class War, an East London-based squatters' organisation.

The gig never happened, but Joe decided to support the anarchist Class War by going out on tour for a month from mid-July under the banner Rock Against The Rich. *NME*'s Danny Kelly pointed out that this enemy could now be considered to

Joe backstage at Liverpool on the Rock the Rich tour, July 1988.

include the former Clash mainstay. Joe replied, 'The issue isn't how well off or otherwise Joe Strummer is. They just needed some kind of front man.' He maintained that he was doing the tour primarily to raise cash for the local organisations who needed it, as well as a matter of human rights. Cynics reckoned it was another of Joe's misguided political gestures.

Talking again to *NME*, who were always ready to shoot Joe down just for wearing the wrong t-shirt, he reasoned to Stuart Maconie, 'After so long away, I just couldn't go out again to the heartland of Britain simply for the money. I didn't want anything like a Joe Strummer star trip. There had to be another reason.'

Everyone was happy to see Joe back on stage, especially not pretending to be The Clash. He favoured Clash covers like 'Police And Thieves' and 'I Fought The Law' over originals, but also threw in 'Love Kills', some of the *Permanent Record* soundtrack, 'Keys To Your Heart' and even a couple of Pogues tunes. It was somewhat puzzling, though, that he wasn't playing songs he'd co-written with Mick for The Clash, but did tackle 'V. Thirteen' and 'Sightsee MC!'

Joe invited Jock on the tour as MC. 'We did a mad tour on the bus – what a carry on that was! It was a real Portobello Road thing, tied in with Bash The Rich, whatever it was. Joe was coming in the pub all the time. He said, "Look, we're gonna do some gigs – we wanna kill the rich!" There was a reggae band and a local band in every town, and Joe agreed to do it with the Latino Rockabilly War. He said, "We will need a compere." So I got roped in.'

Jock's first gig was in Glasgow, where the entourage was booked into a temperance hotel, sparking outrage in the touring party. 'Glasgow is the home of boozing,' fumed Jock. 'You've got to get pissed to get in sync with the locals!' For the occasion, Jock wore his tartan suit and a big gold chain – 'We were like the rich guys.' The next gig was in Edinburgh, Jock's hometown.

'I got to the gig. Nothing was happening. No sign of the band. I went to the dressing room and I couldn't get the door open. Eventually, I got it open, and it's fucking Strummer lying on the floor. He's got his Crombie coat on top of him and his grey hat, and he's out. Sparko. Sleeping, catching up. Because we'd done quite a wild journey from Glasgow to Edinburgh on this mad bus with this fourteen-piece reggae band and gave people a lift. As many people as you can get on this bus.

'I liked that about Joe. Get to the gig, do the soundcheck and then I'll have a sleep and then I'll wake up and then we'll do the gig. He was a trouper.'

Joe's time away and the UK's changing musical climate – by now the weeklies were gripped by the acid house explosion rocking the nation – meant that he was no longer front page news. Joe knew this, as he said to *NME*'s Sean O'Hagan, 'Things move on. I don't mind stepping back. I *know* I'm a good writer, a good musician and I know that, these days, I'm a page twenty guy. It's cool.' Which is exactly where the *NME*'s editorial wags placed the story.

Having got any gigging urges out of his system for the time being, Joe returned to acting. He was offered a role in Jim Jarmusch's *Mystery Train*, which featured a story and setting that Joe couldn't refuse. Set in Memphis, the portmanteau movie recounted three interwoven tales with Elvis Presley as the common theme. Joe played an English rocker called Johnny who was nicknamed Elvis.

Jarmusch was another guerilla director like Alex Cox. He'd enjoyed success with *Down By Law* and also liked to work with a small squad of like-minded people. *Down By Law* had featured Tom Waits, and the rumpled genius now provided the DJ narrative for *Mystery Train*. Joe filmed his parts at night, alongside ghoulish blues legend Screamin' Jay Hawkins, who'd once toured with The Clash.

'The kick was that it was August, I don't know who arranged that, but it was all night shoots so breakfast was about 9pm and work through the night till about 6am,' Joe told Howard Petruziello of *The Music Monitor*. 'So I was able to get all around Memphis and saw, touched, did everything. Sun studios, the whole works . . . That cruddy cheap paintboard. It's amazing, that's where he did "That's Alright". That's where rock and roll was born. It's beyond belief.'

Mystery Train would be released to great acclaim in the UK in December 1989 – but without a Strummer soundtrack, as that was handled by Jarmusch's regular music man, John Lurie. Despite the positive experience, Joe still felt that music was his true vocation. He told *NME*'s Stuart Maconie that films were 'not important to me. Making records is what matters. And if you're going to do that properly, you don't have time to piss about in any other medium.'

I was still living in New York in 1988. In the two years I'd lived there I'd lost touch with most of my old Clash mates, partly because I'd become a little too immersed in some of the City's darker aspects. I always saw BAD when they came to town, and it was great to catch up with Mick. Then they stopped coming. It was only when I returned to the UK in mid-1990 that I found out that Mick had almost died two years earlier.

Before BAD's July-August UK tour, his four-year-old daughter Lauren had gone down with chicken pox. In the last week of the tour, Mick fell ill too, except it affected his throat and lungs. He was rushed to St Mary's Hospital, Paddington, where it turned into pneumonia. Mick ended up in intensive care where he was in a coma for over two weeks. For eight hours he was on the verge of death.

Happily, Mick pulled through, but then caught a hospital bug and was put in the AIDS ward. He suffered nerve damage and had to have speech therapy to learn how to talk again. It would be another nine months before he fully recovered.

More particularly sad news came in the form of the death of Mick's grandmother, Stella, in March 1989. Stella had basically brought Mick up and I know he thought the world of her. A lovely lady, Mick would dedicate the next BAD album, *Megatop Phoenix*, to her (as well as thanking an army of staff from St Mary's).

Mick's illness had ruled out any plans to collaborate with Joe on the solo album he'd started planning after shooting finished on *Mystery Train*. Strummer relocated to Baby O studios in LA and started by forming a group for the project, as the previous line-up had disbanded after the tour.

Schloss and MacNeil remained, with Lonnie Marshall joining on bass. Joe wanted the ultra-basic live approach again, even down to using the sixties ingredients like valve amps and open microphones capturing everything going at the same time. Only vocals and guitars were overdubbed.

For some reason, the results wouldn't see the light of day for nearly a year. (In that time, CBS re-released the entire Clash back catalogue on mid-priced CD.) The album was called *Earthquake Weather*, its title inspired by tremors that rocked LA a couple of times during recording. The music mingled tough, stomping rockers like 'Boogie With Your Children' with spacey reggae and mellow Latin noodling. The album's highlights were 'Shouting Street' – the last song Joe wrote for the new Clash in 1985 – and 'Leopardskin And Limousines'.

The cover showed a fully-clothed Joe standing on the diving board of an LA swimming pool clutching his faithful Telecaster. The *NME* review was quite nasty, with Andrew Collins citing, 'a minefield of duff moments' and accusing Joe of 'being soppy in his old age . . . When he sounds hard, he can pull freight trains with his teeth, but when weaknesses like his penchant for weedy Latino tinkling come to the fore, it's all a bit of a comedown.' Joe's lyrics were branded, 'a poor Xerox of Tom Waits'. Ouch.

Joe told BBC 2 music show *Rapido* that he wanted, 'to grow up with my audience. I don't expect to be getting through to the younger pop crowd. I learned that from Paul Simon' – a reference to the former Simon and Garfunkel singer, who'd matured his sound via a worldly palette of influences on his acclaimed *Gracelands* album. You might have expected this kind of global plunder from the amount of travel Joe had been doing, especially given his past preoccupation with the plight of oppressed peoples.

Listening to *Earthquake Weather* now, it's fairly apparent that Joe had yet to find his feet in making 'grown up' albums. Many of the lyrics have to be gleaned from the song sheet because they're so low in the mix. Joe later admitted that the reason for this was he still hadn't fully regained the confidence that had taken such a bashing in the latter days of The Clash. And yeah, his growl sometimes does resemble that of Tom Waits, in places. Titles like 'Jewellers And Bums' and 'Dizzy's Goatee' (a reference to jazz legend Dizzy Gillespie) are definitely Waitsian. Nothing wrong with that, but it would take another decade for Joe's world-view and Strummer-drive to fully come into their own when he formed the Mescaleros.

The album only made Number 58 before dropping from sight, and failed to chart in the US. Joe spent the last three months of 1989 touring Europe and America. He later described it as, 'a vicious tour', and wondered why he'd bothered, as the jaunt left him £24,000 in debt.

When the tour hit New York City on 11 November, Joe had a moment of clarity that would determine his life for the next few years. 'I think this is when I decided to quit,' he told the *San Antonio Current* in late 2001. 'We were playing away across the States and really sweating it out every night . . . Then, when we hit New York City, a guy came into the dressing room after the show – we were sitting there, gasping for breath – and he said, "Hey Joe, I'm sorry but I've got to tell you that I went to Tower Records in Greenwich Village to buy the record and they didn't have a copy." . . . I just realised that if I couldn't even get my record into Tower Records in Greenwich Village the very night that the tour hit New York – never mind Poughkeepsie or Oswego – I thought, "Well, you better retire yourself boy!"'

Joe also explained that the death of his parents and his new responsibilities as a father had given him cause to reassess his priorities. 'Suddenly you're holding a lot of things on your shoulders and you've got to ride with it.'

If Joe's first solo album took the retro-path he hankered for and bombed, Mick was pointed fast forward at the future – until he lost his band again. After recuperating from his recent brush with death, he'd hitched up with Bill Price again at the Kinks' Konk Studios to make BAD's fourth album, *Megatop Phoenix*. Its predecessor had seemed to be treading water somewhat, but this reverberated with Mick's newfound love of acid house, some wonderfully melodic songs and a stoned sense of humour. It was almost like a continuous New York mastermix radio show with snatches of hip-hop nuggets and silly samples linking tracks.

The dance groove underpinned Mick's lyrics, which tackled issues relevant to the UK at this time – like acid house culture on 'House Arrest'. Joe's album had been far removed from London in terms of location, style and subject matter, whereas BAD were referencing the biggest musical phenomenon to sweep the nation's youth since punk rock.

Acid house saw thousands of people getting together and dancing in fields and clubs until dawn on ecstasy while loving every minute of it and each other. The police, establishment and tabloids hated this evil, drug-fuelled new craze like nothing since punk rock. They shut down raves, busted participants and were supported by a damning sensationalist narrative from the media. *NME*'s James Brown was dead right when he said *Megatop Phoenix* was the closest thing to capturing the mood of the times since *The Clash*.

Acid house was just as big a social revolution as punk. Although starting with a stream of groundbreaking and gloriously innovative records from Chicago and Detroit, the UK took to its anything-goes philosophy and carried it. Once past the initial upswing and silly cash-in phase, dance music grew into the biggest youth-orientated market in Britain, while the underground threw up startling, cutting edge variations.

The music continued punk's ethos of DIY recording and releasing records, rejuvenated groups brought together by punk – like Primal Scream – and spawned artists such as the Chemical Brothers who would go on to play a major role on the world stage long after the ecstasy had worn off. These groups often cited The Clash as their seminal jumping-off point.

Dance music went on to sustain itself through a multitude of developments. The genre's most recent success story has been The Streets, which sees Mike Skinner marrying slice-of-life commentaries to dance grooves. Mick Jones, whose musical visions shaped the sound of The Clash, was gripped in the late eighties, but still managed to infuse the groove with his original rock 'n' roll spirit and wry observations about life.

Megatop Phoenix made Number 26 in the UK and 85 in the US. It came as some surprise at the start of 1990 when Don, Leo and Greg left Mick to form their own outfit called Screaming Target (after the Big Youth album).

In late '90, I interviewed the new group for British black music weekly, *Echoes*. Don explained how they needed to make their own mark out of Mick's shadow and he was tired of feeling that he 'always ended getting the Ringo song'.

'A lot of bands break up for musical differences,' he added. 'For me it was cultural differences. I basically had to write songs Mick could sing as a white man. There's a lot we shared as human beings, then there was a whole spectrum that Mick couldn't understand, which was how I felt as a black man. I had to spread my wings. It's not a bad thing. It's all part of our growth. Speaking as a black man, I felt I had a lot stifled up inside that I wanted to get out. I was culturally stifled.'

Around this time Mick broke up with Daisy too. Both Mick and Joe must've been glad to see the back of the 1980's.

In November 1989, *Rolling Stone's* editors picked their top 100 albums of the decade. *London Calling* came in first. The nineties arrived with further speculation about a Clash reunion – based on the simple deduction that Joe's album had bombed, Mick had no group, Paul's band was totally low-profile and Topper's *Waking Up* solo album hadn't done the business.

As a result of acid house, Norman Cook had left jangly indie band the Housemartins and embarked on a career as a dance music DJ/producer that would see him rise to become the genre's most well known celebrity as Fatboy Slim. Cook was also a massive Clash fan – he'd appeared on the mid-eighties Channel 4 music show *The Tube* scratching the intro to 'Clash City Rockers'. In February 1990 he released 'Dub Be Good To Me', a forerunner of the dance bootleg craze which saw bedroom producers making new mutants out of disparate songs. He mated the groove and bassline from 'Guns Of Brixton' with the vocal from SOS Band's 'Just Be Good To Me' under the name Beats International, and scored a number one hit.

Although Cook would later say he took the bassline from an old ska record, the tune further cemented The Clash into the public consciousness. Paul Simonon retaliated by getting dance DJ Jeremy Healey to remix 'Guns Of Brixton', which was released in June 1990 as 'Return To Brixton'. This made Number 57 in Britain.

Meanwhile, Joe carried on his low-profile movie appearances. In Spring 1990, he made a cameo as a pub singer in Finnish director Aki Kaurismaki's black comedy *I Hired A Contract Killer*. Kaurismaki was a mate of Jim Jarmusch's – hence Joe's involvement – and had made his name the previous year with *Leningrad Cowboys Go America*. There wasn't a soundtrack, but Joe contributed two moody ballads to the film – 'Burning Lights' and 'Afro-Cuban Be-Bop'. These went under the tag 'Joe Strummer and the Astro-Physicians', even though, some congas aside, it was an entirely solo effort.

In the summer of 1990, Pogues frontman Shane McGowan was cutting a dangerous figure around London, to the point where few producers would touch the band because of his drugs and booze-fuelled unpredictability. So The Pogues asked Joe to produce their next album, *Hell's Ditch*. He rose to the occasion, living out his eternal admiration for Guy Stevens, introducing his Spanish influences and looming larger than life in the studio.

Wearing a straw hat, Joe manically extracted killer performances from the group and earned the nickname Strumboli. 'What I learned was to use whatever it takes, whether it's being polite and gentle or angry,' Joe told *Q*. 'The Pogues understand the emotional level's got to be up there.' Joe's first major solo production job was released in September to great acclaim, typified by David Quantick's nine out of ten in *NME*.

Once again picking himself up after being deserted by his band, Mick formed Big Audio Dynamite 2, using young Notting Hill musicians Nick Hawkins (guitar), Gary Stonadge (bass) and former Sigue Sigue Sputnik drummer Chris Kavanagh. Dan Donovan was also initially involved before defecting to Screaming Target.

Their first outing was one of Mick's criminally overlooked masterworks. 'Free' was commissioned for the soundtrack of a dodgy American movie called *Flashback* and was issued as a US promo single in the hope that it would take off in the clubs. Although this didn't happen, I played it to death when I got it in New York. I could relate to the optimism-out-of-desolation in the lyrics, having just lost my own house and family.

Mick was now writing about himself and declaring his inner strength when he sang the defiant chorus. 'I'll keep it up till I'm free, or I won't have nothing at all.' Mick's intensely personal lyrics are delivered over a sensitively melodic backdrop which rides the funky dance beat but threads together a jigsaw of the Stones' 'Sympathy For The Devil', melancholy guitars and electro stabs. To my mind, it's up there with his great Clash songs.

BAD 2 made their live debut at the Town & Country Club's fifth birthday bash on 10 August at north London's Alexandra Palace. Opening up were New York's hip Deee-lite and it was good to see Mick back in action again. He also supplied guitar and backing vocals on a single by Aztec Camera's Roddy Frame called 'Good Morning Britain', which was released in September and made Number nineteen in the charts.

The band then released a limited pressing album called *Kool-Aid*, which entered into the acid house spirit by looking like an underground white label. It featured more painfully personal songs and Mick would later remix and rejig it for release as *The Globe*.

Whereas Joe was striving for something he couldn't quite nail down after the demise of The Clash, Mick had been through the mill too but was determined to come out fighting. 'If I had my time again, I would do it all the same,' he sang on 'Rush'. Although the songs on *Kool-Aid* still boasted an acid house beat and sensibility with titles like 'On One', Mick was starting to tire of the scene's relentless party mentality. He appreciated the wider scale implications of the acid house movement, but still needed his music to say something more than 'let's party'.

Q's Ian McMillan described the album as 'a refreshing auditory experience . . . Perhaps the only common denominator is, oddly, The Clash: there are echoes of, in particular, *London Calling* all over this album.'

There wouldn't be another album bearing the Joe Strummer name until 1999. This was partly because of the contractual straitjacket that Joe found himself subject to. 'I'm a lazy sod is the truth,' he explained to *Punk* magazine's Judy McGuire in 1999. 'I did have a stumble in the business end of things; I had to wait out a contract, which took some years. So there was no way forward for a while . . . Part of me felt it was time to shut up for a bit. And then other parts felt let someone else have a go. I had this business contract thing which blocked me up for a while, so it was kind of good because I needed a break. And also, I wanted to see my kids grow up.'

Joe had planned to start recording a second solo album at the beginning of 1991, but Sony were against it because it would trigger the next stage of his contract. 'They thought there was going to be huge returns so they offer you huge advances to make the records.' But *Earthquake Weather* bombed. 'So Sony thought, we can't let this bloke make another record because the wording of the contract was that as soon as I started a session they had to write me an enormous advance cheque. And they knew they weren't gonna see any of it. Why not throw 200 grand out the window, why don't you?'

On the *Strummersite*, Joe reckoned that The Clash had been taken advantage of business-wise in their early days. 'It's really like child abuse. They know that you're young, keen and stupid. They really take advantage of that . . . They'll do anything to get a record out there. They're trading on your keenness, your eagerness.'

'I bored them out of it,' he said of the record company to *The Big Takeover*. 'Yeah, I shut down production! I had the same contract as George Michael. I watched him get slaughtered in the court, yeah? And I thought every point he was making was valid, and they just smashed him down anyway. There ain't no justice in England . . . I just had to shut down, which is why I haven't made any records in nine and a half years, because I just had to bore them out.'

In other words, Joe went on strike – 'There you go, that's just what I did . . . Taking ten years to get a piece of paper out of an office! You gotta have patience, and you gotta keep in a good mood.'

That 'piece of paper', which Joe's new manager Tim Clarke got out of Sony in the late nineties, would mean Joe could make solo deals elsewhere, while Sony had the rights if the miracle of a Clash reunion came to pass. These hopes were given a shock boost by what happened next.

The Clash never did adverts. They'd been asked many times but turned them down as a matter of policy. However, when Levi's asked to use 'Should I Stay Or Should I

The re-released Should I Stay Or Should I Go *– The Clash's only Number One single came six years after the band had split.*

Go', the group left the decision to Mick. He reasoned that everyone wore Levi's, the very trousers of rock 'n' roll. Plus the wedge did come in handy. Get your music in a TV advert and you've got a guaranteed hit.

So, ironically, the only Number One hit of The Clash's career came posthumously after 'Should I Stay Or Should I Go' was released as a single on 2 March 1991, accompanied by a video of the group performing the song at Shea Stadium. As BAD were still signed to Sony, Mick was able to place BAD's 'Rush' on the B-side.

Of course, by allowing this The Clash set themselves up as sitting ducks for lemon-faced detractors. But The Clash were no more. They'd spunked money and been ripped off something rotten in the past, so why the hell not enjoy some kind of payback? And if it gave Mick's new band a leg-up in the process even better. Obviously, the last count rankled a bit with the others, but there was a certain buzz about The Clash finally getting to Number One and any arguments about the consistency of the band's manifesto were history.

Ten years later, Joe gave permission for Jaguar to use 'London Calling' for a car advert in the US. He was philosophical when the *Strummersite* asked him about it. 'Yeah, I agreed to that. We get hundreds of requests for that and turn 'em all down. But I just thought, "Jaguar, yeah." If you're in a group and you make it together, then everyone deserves something. Especially more than twenty years after the fact. It just seems churlish for a writer to refuse to have their music used on an advert and so I figured out, only advertise the things you think are cool.'

Joe told *NME*'s Stuart Bailie that he was fixing the fuel pump of his faithful 1955 Morris Minor when somebody stopped by with the news that The Clash were

Number One. 'It's kinda weird that you didn't have to lift a finger. It wasn't as if you were at the height of your touring and all that hard work, and you'd feel, "Ah, *we did it!*" It took a trouser advert to take it there, and it was very peculiar.'

Sony saw a golden goose and re-released *The Story Of The Clash, Volume One*, which went to Number Thirteen. Then they followed the single with another reissue of 'Rock the Casbah' on 13 April. This got to Number Fifteen. Then Sony had another go with 'London Calling', now for the third time round. This only reached 64. 'I Fought The Law' and 'Train In Vain' would follow but didn't chart. *Combat Rock* was also re-released in May. Additionally, Don Letts' Clash promotional videos were compiled into the *This Is Video Clash* collection.

Add to that another UK only compilation called *The Singles* and you have the sound of udders being milked dry. That one got to Number 68 in 1991.

If The Clash had *really* wanted to cash in, they would have reformed then. A lot of bands would have done. *NME* reported a rumour that The Clash had been offered ten million pounds for a one-off US tour. As time went on, speculation drove the figure ever upward. In 1993, the *Daily Star*'s pop columnist Rick Sky announced that The Clash were reforming for $50 million! But there were always too many factors against this. These included Mick's preoccupation with BAD, Paul's genuine lack of enthusiasm, Topper's condition and Joe's other projects.

For Joe and Mick, reforming The Clash would be admission that their subsequent projects hadn't worked. That wouldn't bother Mick so much because he'd had no choice but to go it alone. Joe, on the other hand, hadn't been able to make the post-Mick Clash work.

In 2000, He told *Record Collector*'s Sean Egan that a proposal for a reunion had come in 1991 from Mick's manager, Gary Kurfirst. 'I didn't want Mick's manager to manage The Clash', said Joe. This was understandable, but Joe's next comment beggared belief; 'I'm terribly loyal in a stupid way and I knew that the best combination was Strummer-Headon-Simonon-Jones on the floor and Bernie Rhodes managing it. I'd got Bernie back in when we were faltering somewhere in the middle period to manage us for the two final years of glory.' Mick and Topper might have been forgiven for not wanting to go that way, especially as Bernie had instigated their departures from The Clash in the first place.

In September 1991, the uncontrollable Shane was asked to leave The Pogues – three days before they were due to start a six-month world tour. Who you gonna call? Joe agreed to take his place and used his acting skills to trot out their repertoire, while slipping in 'London Calling' and 'I Fought The Law', plus more Clash tunes as the tour progressed.

Joe himself underwent a big personal change in 1992. After a roller-coaster career, he wanted to get closer to his family. He took Gaby and the girls on holiday to Andalucia, which had been the home of Richard Dudanski and wife Esperanca for years. Joe loved the friendliness of the locals and laidback way of life, so the Spanish holiday became an annual event in the Strummer calendar.

Then Joe moved out of London, to a farm in the village of Newton Stacey, near

Andover, Hants. This was an attempt to knit the family together. Joe was still spending a lot of time in the Warwick Castle, which was hardly conducive to marital harmony. Maybe country life would herald a new start for Joe, his career, his relationship with Gaby and the kids. 'Joe just said he needed to get the kids out of London,' recalls Johnny Green.

Joe installed a home studio at the farm and tried to teach himself how to use the developing technology. He started working on the soundtrack to a movie called *When Pigs Fly*, which was being directed by Jim Jarmusch's girlfriend Sara Driver. Joe ended up contributing eight tracks, including the theme music and one intriguingly called 'Storm In A D-Cup'. The film was released in the US in 1993 but there was no soundtrack album and it failed to make an impact.

I got a big surprise when I took my son to see the 1994 film adaptation of classic kids' cartoon, *The Flintstones* – BAD 2 had turned in a cover version of Tommy Steele's early British rock 'n' roll hit, 'Rock With The Caveman'. In September 2004, Mick selected the original for a *Radio Clash* compilation CD of the band's influences, which was given away with *Mojo*.

Joe spent most of 1993 trying to settle down with the family at the farm, but split up with Gaby in early 1994 when the relationship failed to work out. Subsequently, he moved back to London.

In December 1993, *Q* published a feature which simply asked, 'The Big Question: Should The Clash Re-form?' and asked a celeb-slanted cross-section this much-discussed poser. The answers were interesting. Against were names like Sting, John Peel, Vic Reeves, the Manic Street Preachers and Bernie Rhodes, who declared that it would only be a good idea if he were involved. Bernie then went in for one of his grand claims, 'I wrote the lyrics to the first album that made Joe come across as a "spokesman for a generation", as they say, and he hasn't done anything since because I wasn't there.' Tony James thought they should, 'because attitude lasts forever,' while Muff Winwood – then head of Sony – obviously thought it would be a mighty fine idea. Maybe Don Letts hit the nail on the head when he simply said, 'Every generation needs its own soundtrack.'

On 16 April 1994, Joe gave his first live performance since his dates with the Pogues. This took place in Prague for a Rock For Refugees benefit gig in aid of people escaping the former Yugoslavia. He jammed with a local band called Dirty Pictures, playing Clash songs.

But his return to London saw no immediate end to that lonely tunnel. Then the light at the end grew brighter. Joe's life was going to be changed again – by love and . . . acid house.

CHAPTER EIGHTEEN

THE STRUMMER OF LOVE

I wanna live, and I wanna dance awhile – Joe Strummer, 'X-Ray Style'

During the first half of the nineties, Joe was like a headless chicken, lurching from project to project but never quite coming home to roost. Poor sales of *Earthquake Weather* propelled him toward film projects that, though often critically acclaimed, seemed doomed for obscurity. Ever since Joe fell under Bernie's influence and dismantled The Clash, he'd felt terrible guilt and tried to blank it out by taking every film or soundtrack that was offered to him. He got through the tough years by beating himself up for what had gone wrong with The Clash. Although he still acknowledged that Mick had been near impossible to work with during the final phase of their partnership, Joe never stopped punishing himself for the group's demise.

'Long as I kept my mind,' he told *Punk* magazine's Judy McGuire in 1999. 'It helps because I like to smoke weed . . . It was almost like my Prozac . . . I knew if I could keep my mind more or less sane, not get bitter . . . I knew it would be living death to do that so I just tried to blame everything on myself, which is probably very appropriate . . . That's how I maintained my sanity – giving it to myself hard.'

In June 1994, Sony released the *Clash on Broadway* triple-CD retrospective, which was put together by Kosmo. It was the usual mix of singles, album highlights, B-sides and, most interestingly, some never-before-released tracks – 'Every Little Bit Hurts', 'One Emotion', 'Midnight To Stevens', plus a live version of 'Lightning Strikes (Not Once But Twice)'. It wasn't cheap – the age of the six quid Clash album was definitely over – but was essential to Clash completists just for these tracks. This makes it all the more inexplicable why other desirable items, such as *Combat Rock* leftovers, like 'The Beautiful People', 'Kill Time' and the outrageous 'Walk Evil Talk', weren't also included. The booklet's fun too but, in the light of other bands' subsequent retrospectives and Mick's discovery of the Vanilla Tapes, it is obvious that the definitive Clash collection is still to be compiled.

During the same year, Mick became mates with Primal Scream – rock 'n' roll's wild bunch who'd reared out of their indie beginnings with the groundbreaking *Screamadelica* album. As their tour DJ from 1994 onwards, I hadn't been so closely involved with a band since my days with The Clash. I also remixed a couple of Primal Scream's singles – in a little studio tucked under the Westway, where the group would come to jam on songs for their next album. This Clash connection didn't go unnoticed as the Scream were avid fans. I felt that the group was carrying on The Clash tradition in their attitude and constant foraging for new sounds to convey their hallucinogenic hedonism.

Joe at the San Diego Hootenanny Festival – as The Mescaleros took shape, Joe increasingly embraced outdoor events.

On 9 April, the Scream were playing an historic double-header with George Clinton's P-Funk Allstars at Brixton Academy. Backstage, I introduced singer Bobby Gillespie to Mick. In late August, the Scream headlined the last night of the Reading Festival and I was delighted when Mick turned up in the backstage caravan. A lot of reminiscing went down, before he got up to play on 'Loaded' and a storming version of 'Jail Guitar Doors' for the encore. 'Mr. Mick Jones,' announced singer Bobby Gillespie, with beaming pride.

Not long after, I was remixing their next single, 'Jailbird', at the studio, so we invited Mick, who only lived up the road. He arrived and jamming commenced, degenerating into an early hours trawl through classics such as the Stones' 'Wild Horses', James Carr's 'Dark End Of The Street' and 'Jail Guitar Doors', which Gillespie had down word perfect, even down to the 'fuck 'em!' What a buzz!

In November, Mick's band – now simply Big Audio – released an album called *Higher Plane*. Mick paid homage to his 'hood with 'Harrow Road' and also included a song written for his ten-year-old daughter Lauren, 'Light Up My Life'. In the UK, there was a twelve-inch promo of the self-explanatory 'Looking For A Song', which dealt with writer's block. It would be Mick's last album with Sony, who let him go after it failed to chart.

Around this time, Joe embarked upon a relationship with Lucinda Henderson, who everyone knew as Luce. She was ten years younger than Joe and the daughter of an architect. Luce was divorced, with a four-year-old daughter called Eliza.

When in London, Joe rented Paul Simonon's basement but, in early 1995, Joe, Luce and Eliza moved to Ivy Cottage in Heckfield, near Basingstoke. It was here that Joe adopted an old woodshed in the garden and set about turning it into his studio. Eventually, he had it upgraded to 24-track status. Imaginatively, he called it 'The Woodshed'.

Johnny Green visited a few times. 'It was a nice old house, a bit rundown. Down there you got the feeling that Joe was flexing his muscles. He had a little recording room in the old pork smoking shed, where they used to hang the pigs. It was tiny but he kept all his mementos from the Clash days there too. Joe couldn't throw anything away and just kept it all in boxes. I saw his trilby from the *London Calling* era sitting on top of a box covered in spiders' webs. It was a really strange place but a fucking great house, which used to be owned by the Rothschilds.

'There was this big tree in the garden with a pulley on it for the kids. I was standing there looking at it one day and Joe came up and put his arm around me and said, "Johnny, if I ever try and reform The Clash you come down here and hang me from that tree."'

Around the time Joe met Luce, he heard via Rick Rubin that Johnny Cash was looking for songs to cover for the *American Recordings* album that would go on to revitalise his career. Fired up, Joe sat down and wrote 'The Road To Rock 'n' Roll' and sent it to The Man In Black. It didn't get used but later, when Joe went to see Johnny play at a Hollywood Boulevard club, Rick introduced the pair. 'Rick whispered in his ear, "That's the guy who wrote that 'Road To Rock 'n' Roll' song," Joe told Howard Petruziello. 'Johnny turned around and looked at me and leaned right over – you know he's a really big guy – and said, "You know you really confused me with that song, boy!" I just went, "Uhhhhhhhhh!" I would have loved to have sat down and talked to him about it.

'Then I realised that this is a great tune. I used it on a personal note, to woo my wife! My first marriage had split up and I met another girl and to prove I wasn't a complete idiot I played her that tune. So it's kind of our song, if you know what I mean.'

Not only was 'The Road To Rock 'n' Roll' the song which allowed Joe to meet Johnny Cash and win his future wife's heart, it turned out to be the first song he wrote for what would become *Rock Art and The X-Ray Style*, his first proper album in ten years.

Parenting at the piano – Joe and step-daughter Eliza.

As a wooing troubadour, Joe was a resounding success. On 31 May 1995, he and Luce were married at Kensington and Chelsea Register Office. The witnesses included the prolific designer Josh Cheuse, who'd put together the *Clash on Broadway* sleeve, and Tricia Ronane, formerly BAD's PR, who was now Paul's mis-sus and looked after affairs relating to the old Clash. On the marriage certificate, Joe cited his occupation as 'producer'.

1995 saw the publication of the first proper biography of The Clash – *The Last Gang In Town*, by Marcus Gray. Although undeniably well researched, Gray's sanctimonious tome spends most of its time trying to shoot down everything the group did. Nobody had ever met this bloke, although Johnny Green tells a story about how the author tried to get Joe's input for the revised edition. 'He must've followed us to a bar and then waited outside. He didn't have the bottle to actually approach Joe. Instead he left his phone number under the windscreen wiper of Joe's car. We came back from the bar and Joe saw the note. "What a tosser," he said, and threw it away.'

In the mid-nineties, Joe felt that he needed something to focus on in order to get back on the creative track. In 1995, this came in the unlikely forms of the rave drug, ecstasy, and Richard Norris – half of one of the early nineties' hottest dance production teams, The Grid. Richard and partner Dave Ball, formerly Marc

Almond's Soft Cell sidekick, came out of the acid house explosion and took dance music into the charts with contagious stormers like 'Swamp Thing' and 'Diablo'.

Richard spent eighteen months working, hanging out and witnessing an ever-more revitalised Joe get back in the swing of things. He also helped introduce Joe to the joys of big gatherings and techno music, which, with their aforementioned DIY ethic and attitude, were similar to punk. Previously, dance music had been against all that Joe stood for – music made by machines. The dismissive 'faceless techno bollocks' barb was such common currency that it had become a t-shirt. But soon after, Joe even started DJ-ing at raves and clubs, either in the back room or between headliners. His selection covered his favourite styles, including reggae, world music and classic rock 'n' roll.

The Clash were approached to reform for that year's Lollapalooza shindig with a rumoured $5,000,000 on the table. Mick's manager Gary Kurfirst was up for it, but Paul was more concerned with his painting as he could now command up to three grand for each piece, while Joe demurred because Topper still wasn't in the clear. Mick and Joe even paid for another stint in rehab.

The following year, Mick would content himself by recording a new BAD album called *Entering A New Ride*, complete with new member Rankin' Roger from The Beat. They encountered a hitch when Radioactive refused to release it, but the album would eventually surface via the net. The BAD Sound System came into play, with the group's DJs playing at club nights where Mick sometimes got on the mic as MC.

At the end of June, Joe set out on a jamboree that would go on for months and change his life. Driving his old Cadillac, accompanied by Luce, he went to the Glastonbury Festival. Here, along with broadcaster Keith Allen (who'd been working for the ICA the night The Clash played there in 1976), Joe started his now-legendary annual campfire sessions that became known as Strummerville.

They printed up t-shirts carrying the name that would stick with Joe on his further travels. Joe, Luce and Keith were quickly joined by a bunch of reprobates with names like 'Magic' Martin and the infamous 'Dodgy' Roger Goodman. Totally entering into the festival spirit, Joe tried ecstasy for the first time, courtesy of the latter. And loved it.

'We got the idea to set up Strummerville around the campfire,' explains Roger, who had travelled on to the WOMAD festival with Joe. 'There was me, Joe, Damien Hirst, Keith Allen and Chrissie Hynde. I was trying to push Joe forward into this thing where we could all be involved. We were all just sitting about, smoking and we did some of this drug that was going about called GHB. It was disgusting. I found out later that it was what they used for cleaning kitchen equipment. Very dangerous, like poisoning your body. The trouble is we must've drunk about a hundred bottles before we found that out. It just monged you out and put you to sleep.

'In the early hours, Keith Allen went off in Joe's jeep to get a Hammond organ, for some reason. He came back with it on the roof when the dawn was coming up! So we found a wire from one of the kitchen units and plugged it in. Keith started playing that fugue – you know, the 'Phantom of the Opera' – right in the middle of a field. That woke everybody up!

Joe at the Real World Recording week. (Left): Eliza, Lucinda, Joe and Roger Goodman. (Right): Peter Gabriel, Roger, Lucinda and Joe.

'That's where Joe took his first pill. His revelation was, "Now I know what Mick was all about with Big Audio Dynamite. Now I know why he likes all that stupid dance music." It was like an epiphany for him. We consumed tons of them that week. We didn't come down for days.'

Joe didn't want the party to stop, so the posse then made its way to the annual WOMAD festival at Reading, where Joe used his name to blag his way backstage. Here he got talking to Gary Dyson from world music-techno outfit Azukx, who was planning to move on to Peter Gabriel's Real World studios at Box, near Bath, after the festival. The Real World Recording Week started on 22 July, and involved 90 or so artists collaborating, using the eleven rooms in the studio to see what happened.

'We got on really well,' recalls Gary. 'I phoned to see if it would be okay to bring Joe along. He did have a bit of an entourage with him. It was messy, but it wasn't bad. He was really on one! He'd just discovered ecstasy, so he knew the score. Roger had a field day! He was really into Joe so he was on cloud nine – and making sure everyone else was too. A lovely guy.'

'We camped outside the front gate,' remembers Roger, 'and the studio staff . . . their backs were really up. The only chilled person there was Peter Gabriel. He said, "I love the anarchy you've created in my camp and the way that you're scaring everybody."'

Richard Norris recalls that Mike, the studio manager, was a bit wary of Joe's crew, initially thinking they were gatecrashing for a rave. But Joe met up with Peter Gabriel, who was cool. 'They weren't really invited to Real World, but in typical Joe fashion, he got there and decided, "Right, we're gonna set up camp." Joe would take over an area, very much in the spirit of his Glastonbury camp. So many times studios would get turned into bizarre Moroccan tents. There'd always be millions of flags.'

Richard had taken part in Real World Recording Week in 1991, with The Grid. In 1995, Richard wasn't invited as a producer but Alex from The Grid camp was working there, so he went along.

'It was a family atmosphere at that studio. You went down and were treated like a long lost old mate. So I just went down to check it out. I was sitting in the sunshine outside this amazing studio in an old mill, and I heard this voice saying, "Can anyone programme this drum machine?" It was Joe. So I said, "I'll do that for ya," and he gave me this weird old drum box and I started doing some techno beats. So I just started programming this machine for Joe . . . They didn't have any equipment or production sorted out, so we just went round borrowing eight-tracks and bits and pieces and just started recording – Joe with his shaker, singing, then some sort of troupe from Bangladesh in the corner playing bongos, Vernon Reid from Living Colour doing a bit of guitar . . . So it kind of took off from there really.'

Joe and his loved-up crew of nutters didn't stop the party the whole time they were there. 'They nearly threw us off the site,' says Gary. 'All night we'd be playing drums and banging away, with Richard making wobbly noises on his synths. Joe was there just egging everybody on. He was totally in his element.'

September 2001's *Mojo* reported a particularly funny incident from the never-ending party. Joe was asked if he wanted to jam with a venerable Arab musician. He agreed enthusiastically, but wondered if he'd heard right when told they would be playing in the nude. Joe

Rockin' in the Real World, July 1995.

duly turned up at the studio, shuffled about outside before stripping down with only his guitar to preserve his modesty. Walking in, he was taken aback to find everyone dressed.

'I thought we were supposed to be nude,' blurted a bemused Strummer. 'I think there's been some mistake,' said the Arab musician, and held up his Middle Eastern lute. 'I play an oud.'

'After that WOMAD thing we hit it off and continued having a party for the rest of the year!' laughs Gary, a man you could safely say was touched by the hand of Joe. Gary had a family bust up after WOMAD. 'It was fucking messy. Joe got me at the end of all that. I said to him, "It's a pity you didn't meet me two years ago."'

Gary was not a Clash fan before he met Joe – 'that probably made it easier' – but had encountered Luce years before when he used to clean her car in West London. He says that he feels honoured to have been with Joe at the time when his life turned around. 'He wasn't doing anything, but this inspired him to get going. He found his love of life again. It was a fantastic time. I didn't really know much about Joe Strummer before I met Joe Strummer. I met him on very equal ground. It was a pleasure for me to work with him. Joe was an incredibly intelligent man with a certain wisdom. He was always interested in people. He always wanted to know about people. He was always interested in you. That's what was really nice about him. I don't think I ever heard him talk about himself.'

After the Real World experience, the party convened back to Joe's house, now with Richard Norris in tow. Roger was sent back to London to get more supplies. 'Then I realised I hadn't had any kip for five days. I was exhausted. At this point, nothing could keep me up, so I gouched out in the garden. Pockets and Joe took me in and put me on the couch. They started undressing me, but I was still half-awake, and I could only think, "They're trying to shag me!" I told Joe the next day and he laughed until he cried. He said, "Maybe Pockets but not me!"'

Joe's festival bender continued when our intrepid revellers decided to invade Glasgow's T-In-The-Park festival. Black Grape were headlining on the Sunday, but the party, which had swelled to over 30, arrived on the Thursday. After setting up camp and inaugurating the proceedings in suitably excessive fashion, Joe sent Roger to get the passes on Friday morning – '34 people on Black Grape's guest list, please'. Not possible. He was told he'd have to wait until the Grape arrived on Sunday.

Returning to base with the bad news, Joe said, 'Roger, you're the only person who can do this." He went back, charmed his way to a gold stage pass and, pretending he was Black Grape's tour manager, typed out the names of all 34 guests. This was accepted as the Grape's guest list and everybody got in.

Roger printed up limited t-shirts to mark Joe's '95 festival blowout with slogans such as 'Strummerville – planning permission has now started', 'Strummerville – planning permission has been granted', 'Get Real, World! Come to the city that never sleeps' and 'Don't live in the past, think of the future'. On the back they said,

'Technoganic Tour – Glastonbury-WOMAD-Real World-T in the Park.'

As the summer wore on, Joe and Richard continued to hang out, go to clubs and raves and started working together. This came about when The Grid went to Spain to shoot the video for what would turn out to be their last single, 'Diablo' – which I remixed. Joe loved Spain so they agreed to meet him there. The party raved on.

'We did this mad all-nighter with these kind of cyber-punks called the Turbo Unit, who were living in the hills above Malaga. They had these flatbed fire engines and put raves on. We were in a dust bowl all night and, again, it turned into a bit of a situation. We'd just got the first Black Grape album and we were just coming up when we were listening to it. It was a fantastic night. But the *NME* got wind that Joe was there and that he was doing something with The Grid, so they flew over. I think Joe got wind of it because the next day he left. I don't think he wanted to do an interview with them. But that was the night that we decided to do something together.'

During this period, I was DJ-ing at a big north London club called The Rocket, scene of many a messy techno all-nighter. At the time, I DJ-ed every week at dance clubs around the world – pounding, hedonistic mayhem all the way. Halfway through my set some familiar figures ambled onto the stage. I recognised Richard Norris, who introduced me to Black Grape frontman Shaun Ryder. Then I did a double take when the other guy greeted me with a loud cry of 'Needsy!' It was Joe, who I hadn't seen for about fifteen years! He was having a whale of a time and was just as surprised to see me in this situation.

Over the bellowing cacophony, we caught up with current activities and Joe said how much he was into the new electronic dance music. We didn't really mention The Clash, although there may have been a spot of 'budgies-on-stilts' style banter. It was great to see him and we vowed to hook up, maybe even do some work together. But, at the time, I was impossibly busy and Joe was consumed with fresh ideas and projects. Now, of course, I wish I'd found a spare day and taken up Joe's invitation to come down to Somerset for the day.

Keith Allen, who'd written the lyrics for New Order's 1990 World Cup anthem 'World In Motion', was pulling together a football single for the 1996 European Championship, along with Black Grape. They were slated to be working with producer Danny Saber, but he couldn't make it, so Shaun asked Joe – a Chelsea supporter – and Richard if they'd help out.

'Me and Joe just sat up all night creating this riff which was like, "Come and have a go if you think you're hard enough!", explained Richard Norris. 'I belted it out really, really loud. At around ten o'clock, my girlfriend Liz went out to Metalheadz [Goldie's drum 'n' bass club]. She came back and we were still at it. Joe had his typical enthusiasm, going, "Come on! Let's get this going, let's get it to really work!" We went to Shaun's hotel at about ten o'clock to try and get him to come back to my house. It took until about two o'clock, but we got him back, and put him in a seat in the corner, which he managed to break, and just cranked it up really loud. Joe was vibing around the room with a bottle of brandy in his hand. The neighbours came down from upstairs, totally irate. "What are you doing at this time of the morning?" And Joe just answered the door and said, "It's for England!"

'I had a great time. I remember Joe, typically, would be in the middle of the room just writing with pages of lyrics everywhere. One of the other guys from Black Grape walked in and said, "What the fuck are you doing?" Another night I remember I'd gone to bed and Joe and Shaun just stayed up all night ranting at each other. Just coming down in the morning and seeing Shaun's eyes and his face. He went, "Where were you, man?" He was just really vibed up in the way that only Joe could do to people.'

Apart from Joe's title, 'England's Irie' featured his lyrics and vocals. Richard handled the remixes and there was a bombastic video too. The single was released in June and made number six in the charts. Joe even relaxed the old ban to make his *Top of the Pops* debut – twenty years to the month since The Clash did their first gig.

Richard and Joe decided to knock some of their 'mad festival jams' into songs. Joe and Richard had an artist friend called Robert Gordon McKarg III, who called himself The King Of The Cut-outs and used massive woodcuts as his medium. Robert was putting together an album called *Sandpaper Blues*, which roped together a selection of disparate artists to each record their own tune with the same title as the album. Others among the host of names included former MC5 guitarist Wayne Kramer, Wilko Johnson, blues veteran John Mayall and ex-Lone Justice chanteuse Maria McKee.

Joe, Richard and Gary Dyson went into London's Orinoco Studios, off the Old Kent Road – Joe singing, Gary chanting and Norro programming, with Ian Tregonning handling the recording. Joe's lyrical take on 'Sandpaper Blues', which he'd subtitled 'Another Fine Piece of Madera', was that putting food on the table meant doing a good job. There's an infectious hook over a funky Columbian-influenced groove, with Joe sounding totally relaxed in such warm surroundings. The track appeared on the limited edition, sandpaper-sleeved CD under the name Radar.

'It kind of snowballed from there really,' says Richard. 'When I was working with him he hadn't really done any stuff for a while. The thing I did with him was the bridge to actually get him back on stage and finding, "Yeah, I really wanna get a band, I really wanna tour." When I was working with him it wasn't that easy initially because he was pretty self-conscious and his confidence wasn't as high as it could've been. It took quite a lot of effort.'

He never tried to rest on his laurels, I ventured, noticing that Richard was talking about Joe in the present tense.

'No, exactly, it's not really in his nature. He was wanting to push it and when he was recording he was always very self-critical. He'd really beat himself up about it if it didn't go right. I just remember being in the smallest room at Orinoco – the Toyshop. Joe would be putting down a guitar and he might as well have been at Shea Stadium. Blanng!! It was fantastic. The spirit was always there.'

The duo recorded reams of material, much of which Richard still keeps in a cardboard box scrawled with Joe's handwriting. Richard describes the whole scenario as, 'Beautiful chaos. There was no management, no record company – there was just us with a new vision, a new idea, trying to do something new that hadn't really been done and was limited by technology. Sometimes the technology was great and it really worked, and sometimes it was a real drag.

'One bit I remember was, we were in Orinoco in the little studio. The Beastie Boys were doing a big Dali Lama gig and they were trying really hard to get The Clash to play that. The Beastie Boys would come on the phone when we were recording and it would be, "Joe, can you turn it down, it's the Dali Llama calling!"'

During these sessions Masatoshi Nagase, a Japanese actor who was in *Mystery Train*, gave Joe some money to fund a collaborative project. With this budget, Joe and Richard went in the studio and started work.

'We'd write a track a day,' recounts Richard. 'I'd be programming really hard and Joe would be playing the guitar and then at the end of every day we'd be getting it all together. We'd go, "Great, this is the track for Nagase," but then every day the same thing would happen and Joe would just go, "No, this is too good for Nagase," so we ended up creating nearly half an album of "too good for Nagase" tracks. We had a lot of material then.'

Another song, 'Yalla Yalla', became the first Mescaleros single. This time the mood was dubby North African-flavoured funk – 'Yalla Yalla' is Arab for 'come on' – Joe's favourite phrase in later life. They also recorded an early version of 'The Road To Rock 'n' Roll'.

'Diggin' The New' was another Nagase track that would find its way onto the first Mescaleros album. 'The whole spirit of the song and the lyrics were very much about Joe not really getting it about techno and dance music for years,' says Richard. 'Oh, took me a long time to get it/You gotta live in this world, go diggin' the new,' sings Joe.

'That was the situation, I think, because Joe thought of it as machine music and very faceless, but once he got into the whole spirit of it and the scene and going out to festivals and stuff, he really got into it. He thought nothing of driving 200 miles to go and see Leftfield playing.

'On "Diggin' The New" the lyrics are very much his starting to get into that festival thing, and starting to get into the dance thing. Probably realising that there was a lot of crossover and a lot of respect from people from the dance end, like [Andrew] Weatherall and myself. I took Joe out to the Heavenly Social once. We went to a lot of stuff. I took Joe to Metalheadz a load of times – the loudest, noisiest, most airless place. It was really good fun going down there. We went to loads of Black Grape gigs and festivals.

'My take on it all now, which was probably the downfall of my collaboration with Joe, was I really wasn't thinking of it as a Joe Strummer project. I was really into this idea that we were gonna create this punk rock-acid house monster together. It wasn't proper acid house. It was more the idea of trying to mix it up. It was a band. We came up with different band names. It was called Radar at one point, then Machine. Damien Hirst thought it should be called Middlesex, because Joe had this track called "Diggin' The New", and the chorus was, "Boy, tran or girl."

'The problem was, we were trying to create a band involving Joe, but it was a new identity, a new man thing, which was obviously quite a tall order really. We were never going to top The Clash! We did a load of tracks and we were talking to different people, including Simon Fuller's 19 organisation.'

Toward the end of 1995, Joe found time to go into the studio with bucolic crusties the Levellers, who he had met on his festival travels. Joe supplied piano on a track called 'Just The One', which made Number Twelve in the UK singles chart when it was released in December.

Earlier that year, Mick's band had returned to being called Big Audio Dynamite and released an album called *F-Punk* on Radioactive Records, which was also home to Black Grape. The album title was a play on George Clinton's sprawling P-Funk organisation, and served as a suitable description of Mick's continuing mission to fuse dance and punk strains. Once he'd got into the harsh urban rattle of drum 'n' bass, Mick's lyrics continued to become more personal than ever. The album was hard to obtain and didn't chart. Strange to think that both Joe and Mick were getting into drum 'n' bass at the same time. The mind boggles at what they might have turned out together.

In early 1996, Joe was asked to do the soundtrack for a film called *Grosse Point Blank*. It had been co-written by actor John Cusack, who played a hitman alongside Dan Ackroyd. The film, which also starred Minnie Driver, was a kind of black romantic comedy, is set amidst a high school reunion. There's a welter of 1980s hits, including 'Armagideon Time' with Joe's background music plugging the gaps.

'John Cusack was a big fan of The Clash and really wanted Joe to get involved,' explained Richard. 'So Joe went over and did that. I got a call about two days after he got there. "Norro!" He always called me Norro, because you have to have a nickname with Joe. "You've got to get on the next plane because we've got a great studio in this house where we're staying and you can come over and record all the stuff, and do all the tracks for the album for the soundtrack." So I literally got the next plane out and took all the demos, backing tracks – all the stuff we'd done basically. We were just going to add to that and do lots more. But when we got there I started banging away with an insane, fast, quasi-drum 'n' bass kind of nightmare record with sirens on it and mad, over-the-top drum programming. That was called "Come On". It didn't really gel.

'We were going out all the time. Round to Rick Rubin's, Oliver Stone, the Red Hot Chili Peppers, who we'd met when I put their gig on over here through Joe, Axl Rose . . . it was continual partying. He was obviously looked on as rock royalty over there.'

After ten years of low esteem, low-key projects – in fact, general lowness – Joe felt good to be the centre of attention again. He slipped effortlessly into the 'rock royalty' niche and partied hard with LA's glitterati. Although he never lost his essential individuality, humour and zest, this was a far cry from sitting in the Woodshed trying to regain the confidence to launch himself back into high-profile activity.

Joe's relationship with Rick Rubin was cemented on that trip. 'It was very much me and Joe going around his house, getting a big ghetto blaster and putting the Meters on and sitting round the pool with Rick Rubin saying, "Yeah, you should be making records like this,"' recalls Richard. 'But it didn't pan out because for the film we had a different agenda at that point. It didn't really work out in the studio. In the end we basically used all the backing tracks we'd done for the earlier stuff, just demos. We just put all that into the film. Me and Joe just fell out, basically. The whole scenario just wasn't working out. Joe wouldn't come into the studio to record.'

Later, Richard said the split occurred after he went out to dinner with a movie agent 'who was a lunatic who went on coke binges and started arguments'. The guy later spoke to Joe and credited Richard with some less than complimentary words about him.

'I think it was just being in LA and having this very different scenario from when we were mucking about in Ladbroke Grove,' reasons Richard. 'It just put a different perspective on everything and it didn't really pan out. It was great hanging out, but I kind of went home under a black cloud. And that was it. We didn't work after that. It was really sad. Quite emotional, basically.

'I got paid really well. A lot of the stuff went into the movie. It just said "Music by Joe Strummer". I didn't get a credit or anything, but it was an amazing experience. Finishing the tracks on the Friday, then we had to take it up to the guy splicing it into the movie, then go and see the preview on the Monday with the cast.

'We had some good times. We hooked up with Black Grape there. They were doing the first night of their American tour in Acapulco, so we drove down. Just [me and Joe] and a couple of Black Grape roadies in the car. Getting stopped at the border, but Joe just talked to them in Spanish and got us through. We were probably the only people getting pulled going *into* Mexico. Allegedly there were certain things in our mouths at the time.

'Black Grape were playing this fantastic, 200-people tiny little bar. A chaotic gig, but just brilliant fun just being in Mexico with him. It had taken no time getting from LA to Mexico, but getting back took us hours and hours. Just Joe and Lucinda in the front and me and Shaun Ryder in the back. We had this massive ghetto blaster just pumping out really loud hip-hop, and Shaun just going, "The vibe! The vibe!" for six hours.'

This adventure conjures up images of recreational abuse. Joe appeared to be drinking quite heavily at this time. Black Grape, in typically gung-ho fashion, became enamoured with the mega-powerful PCP – Angel Dust – when they were out there.

'Well, you can't deny that the sessions that we had weren't sessions,' says Richard. 'Some of the time it did get problematic. I'd be in there all day doing the programming and Joe would come in at ten. We'd get right on it and he'd start doing the vocal about twelve. You just had to catch the point before he was a bit fucked, which was definitely down to a confidence thing that was emerging. He was getting more and more confident. He was getting back into it.

'When we'd be working in the studio and we'd been at it all day and it had got to four or five in the morning and I was really tired, he'd be going, "Come on, let's do more more more!". I'd be really near to absolute burnout point, but he'd push and then it'd be a good, positive thing. But then he'd write me a note afterwards, "Thanks Norro, for fucking pushing it to the edge." He'd always write something positive afterwards. He was definitely a nighttime person. He would start late and go on all night. That'd be his thing.

'I think some of the things we were doing definitely sparked his enthusiasm to get back and do it live. When we were working together there were loads of weird things we were gonna possibly do. We were going to produce Morrissey at one point. We went and got picked up by the record company to see Morrissey supporting David Bowie. It was like, Joe's gonna produce Morrissey, I was going to be the co-ordinator with him. We were meant to meet Morrissey after the gig, and waited to meet him, and it turned out he was too shy to meet us.

'We really fell out for a bit, but not for long. Six months later we were still mates. Every gig that I went along to and Joe knew I was there, he'd always dedicate "Yalla Yalla" to me, and he would still say that the mix we did was the best one. Every time I saw him he'd go, "Got to release that one, Norro, it's the best one!"

'The Mescaleros eventually took quite a lot of the stuff that we did and remixed it. It was a difficult time for me. The Grid had split and the thing with Joe hadn't really worked out, but I wouldn't have changed it for the world. It was just a gargantuan task we were setting ourselves. But you've gotta have a go, as Joe would say. I think if it hadn't been for this bizarre culture mish mash that we were trying to get he would never have done the Mescaleros. I think it was the bridge to that.'

Joe would later talk about working with Richard as a doomed experiment that got him working again. 'Because he was coming from acid house and I was coming from punk, we had to bridge a lot of ideological gaps,' he told *Record Collector*'s Sean Egan in 2000. 'We both fought our corners very hard, and in the end we fell out.'

Richard kept up his involvement with the outer limits of electronic music by forming a band called the Droyds and starting a label called God Made Me Hardcore. One of his signings was me and my girlfriend's group, Bunnymad 69. Now Richard and Dave are working together again as The Grid and Norro is getting round to wading through the hours of material he produced with Joe. He still has boxes filled with cassettes marked up in Joe's handwriting, while the first Mescaleros album (which would evolve from all this) still carried the Mark of Norro.

With Richard gone, Joe stayed on in LA. He co-wrote and played on a couple of tracks with former Stray Cat Brian Setzer. 'Ghost Radio' and 'Sammy Davis City' would appear in April 1996 on Setzer's *Guitar Slinger* album.

Next, Joe made contact with a face from the past – Rat Scabies, drummer with The Damned, who'd been punk rock's answer to Keith Moon. Any rivalry between the class of '76 was long forgotten by now as Joe and Rat hitched up and made plans to form a band, start a record label and explore the world of dance music together.

In 1976, The Damned were almost outcasts for getting the first UK punk single and album in the shops and also being utterly destructive chaos-mongers. But Rat doesn't see the fact that he was hanging with one of his major rivals from twenty years before as anything to do with mellowing with age.

'No, I don't think it's that at all,' he reasoned in the back of Simon Trakmarx's car as we made our way to the Joe Strummer exhibition in September 2004. 'People have just learned how to bury their deep hatred and loathing for each other and realised that life's too short. The Damned, certainly, were easily wound up. I think we should've known better really, taking perhaps a more provocative stance perhaps than was necessary.'

Speaking of his relationship with Joe, Rat recalls, 'Every now and again we'd see each other at mutual friends' birthday parties and stuff, and the occasional Christmas card.'

I hadn't seen Rat since the late seventies, when *Zigzag* wasn't his favourite publication at all. Now he's a magnificently entertaining fellow, who obviously had a lot of time for Joe. He'd been in LA with the intention of licensing a Damned album and ran into Joe at a Ministry show at the Palladium. The gig was also attended by wheelchair-bound sixties acid guru Timothy Leary.

'I saw Joe by the bar so I went over and we chatted. I said, "Look, it's Timothy Leary." Joe said, "We've gotta go and meet him! He's gonna be dead soon." We went back to the dressing room and met Timothy Leary, had a jolly good time, then all went back to [Ministry mainstay] Al Jourgensen's hotel.'

Next day, Joe asked Rat if he had a kit and wanted to play drums with him. 'So that was it. Joe used to write over everything. He had this big thing on the wall. He got up and said, "It's our love of perma-culture that brings us together." When he found out I was into the same sort of thinking, we found it a lot easier to talk about other things.

'There was the question of whether Joe's guitar should be cleaned up and made to work properly, like all the other Fender Telecasters. Of course, Joe didn't want any of those things. He didn't even have a case for that guitar. There's a really good reason in Joe's logic, which worked out really well, because if he had a case he had to check it in as a bag and he was so worried that something terrible would happen to his guitar, or it'd be stolen by a baggage handler. If he didn't have a case nobody could argue with it and he could put it above his seat.'

Joe and Richard had recorded some *Grosse Point Blank* material at Westlake Studios in Santa Monica – another of Joe's prime blags, in the grand tradition of the *Cost Of Living* EP coming off the back of the *Rude Boy* overdubbing sessions. 'It was the best studio in the fucking world,' declares Rat. 'That was where we worked. I was in there for three straight months. I do remember Luce saying that Joe had already been in the studio doing some stuff, sleeping under the piano and things. Joe decided to hang out and stay where he was.'

Rat brought in bass player Segs, who'd been in dubwise punk outfit the Ruts and now worked with dance titans the Chemical Brothers. Various sessions hatched under that roof, including another soundtrack that floundered but enabled Joe and Rat to explore other projects, like their band, which they called Electric Doghouse. Joe still had his dance music bug and spent a lot of time recording Rat to make beats. From what Rat says, it sounds like they were touching on drum 'n' bass.

'We put in about eighteen hours a day in the studio,' recalls Rat. 'We just kept on working, kept on churning it out, reels and reels of it. It was all about making really fast loops up. That's kind of what me and Joe were looking for.'

Subsequently, Joe fell in with local producer and label boss Jason Rothberg, who became one of his drinking partners and acted as a kind of unofficial manager until 1999. He was putting together a compilation album in aid of the Human Rights Action Centre and, with LA engineer John X Volaitis, Joe, Rat and Segs hammered out a psychedelic-tinged outing called 'Generations'. The song would lend its name to the album, *Generations 1: A Punk Look At Human Rights*, when it appeared the following year.

'We had one day to record it,' Joe told Todd Martens of the *Daily Trojan*. 'I didn't really have time to think about what kind of direction that tune would be. I just wrote it and we burned it out.' He added that they also had to race against the clock because Segs had to catch a plane back to London – to the extent that his cab driver was waiting in the control room.

John X christened the group Electric Doghouse – 'because we were always in the doghouse,' Joe told Todd Martens. 'I know, it's

Welcome to Strummerville – 'Magic' Martin, Joe and Rat Scabies with the squatting Roger Goodman in 1995.

kind of a limp joke, but then I bought a book for one of my kids and it was all about a dog going out at night and going to this club for dogs. Say you go to sleep and you think your pet's asleep in its basket and this owner decides to follow his dog and the dog goes out wearing shades, drinks all night and has a party. In the book the club was called the Electric Dog House!'

The band also recorded 'War Cry', which Joe had written with Norro. The track eventually popped up on a sequel called *More Grosse Point Blank*.

Throughout these sessions, Joe and Rat stayed in a plush house high in the Beverley Hills, while Joe drove around in his '55 Cadillac – complete with a bullet hole acquired over Christmas. 'It had been shot!' laughs Rat. 'He'd left it in a car park over Christmas and he came back and somebody had shot his car.'

As Rat recalls, 'One of the best parties we had was at that house. We lived at the top of this hill and Elle McPherson lived next door, about twenty yards away. The handbrake went on Joe's Caddy so it went back and hit all her walling. That car was like a fucking tank. We came out and we were all horrified. Harry Dean Stanton was there, Danny Saber, all these proper fucking Hollywood celebs and then suddenly we've all got to go out and rebuild this brick wall so Elle McPherson doesn't notice. They kept threatening to chuck us out of the estate because of all the noise. And

Joe's got all these flags up everywhere and camouflage netting on the balcony.

'That was the first thing that we did when we went into Westlake studio. Me and Joe were sitting there, and he said, "What can we do to decorate?" And there were no plants in there, so we went round and we took every single plant in the building, from every other studio, wherever we could find anything green, and we just put it in our room. Then Joe got the netting up over the piano, then all the flags went up. They had to come and ask for some of the plants back but we wouldn't give 'em over.

'Joe had this great sense of humour. He had a brilliant knack of being able to change an atmosphere. He'd just come in and everyone would be really pissed off about something. He'd just crack a couple of jokes. I don't know how, he'd just turn it on, so then everybody would feel better.

'We'd sit there with some wine and after a couple of glasses I always used to start to fall asleep and every time I'd nod out Joe'd try and steal the spliff from my fingers. It was a game we had. Every time he nearly got it I knew it was time for bed. I'd be nodding and I'd feel the spliff just being gently tugged.

'We met up with Shaun Ryder in LA while we were there. He's really funny. I was amazed at what a charming bloke he was. He was a real charmer and he was real witty and entertaining. Black Grape were really happening and the connection there was Danny Sabre. On those sessions we had every producer in LA come through the door. Joe was being very heavily courted at the time because the CBS deal was just coming to an end. Mostly Joe was rude to 'em. They'd come in and try and do something and Joe'd just go "No".

Joe and Rat were getting along so well that they planned to start a record label in LA over the Christmas 1995 holiday period. The pair would alternate between London and LA. The idea stalled when Joe and Luce decided that for family reasons, it would be better to return to the UK as a permanent base. Joe was having a cracking time with the Rat pack but, through Luce, he had gained a stepdaughter with Eliza. After what happened with Gaby, he was making the right move.

'We went, "Oh well, we'll go back to London and see what happens,"' says Rat. 'As we'd gone on it became more and more obvious that we weren't really getting to where we wanted to be with it. So we came back to London and Segs had this idea that we were gonna start working with Steve Dub Jones, who does the Chemical Brothers. We were gonna get Dubby on the firm with the tapes that we'd got. Most of it just lay on the shelf in the studio. Jason Rothberg's says he's got most of them back now. He got 'em out the studio and he's got the rights to it. Now Joe's popped his clogs everyone's going, "Ooh, they should come out." And they weren't *that* great. Some of it was brilliant. But it was all . . . stoner. But then, some of it could compete with anything.'

In the spring of 1996, Joe finally returned home from his LA adventure. He recorded a track on a Rykodisc tribute album to Beat figurehead Jack Kerouac, who'd been one of his heroes at school. Joe provided backing music for Jack reading his 'MacDougal Street Blues' in a fifties nightclub. Ensconced in the Woodshed, Norro worked the beatbox, while Joe played guitar, bass and synth over an old drum pattern of Norro's. There was a slight problem in that a tape of Frank Sinatra could be heard filtering through from the next room, 'So I had to invent this crazed backing part,' he told Todd Martens. 'Every time Frank Sinatra would pop his head around the door, I'd have to cruise over the top of it.' The album, *Kerouac – Kicks Joy Darkness,* which also featured artists like Patti Smith, Michael Stipe and John Cale, would be released in April 1997.

In mid-1996, Joe began work on another film, which he'd initially been asked to do in 1994 but had taken two years to come to fruition. Joe took a leading role in *Docteur Chance,* under the supervision of French director Francois-Jacques Ossang. Joe's character was a guy called Vince Taylor – which was also the name of the rock 'n' roller who wrote 'Brand New Cadillac'. They spent three months filming in the Atacama Desert, Chile. Joe contributed a song, 'Victory Lane', to the soundtrack, which was only released in France under the alternate title, 'Messagero Killer Boy'.

The film debuted at the following year's London Film Festival, with Joe and Ossang attending the premiere and staging a press conference. Joe later told *Punk*'s Judy McGuire, 'After the film – there's about a thousand people in the house – me and Ossang got up and on the stage and they opened the floor to questions. The whole audience sat there like that [Joe sits completely still and silent] . . . Not daring to move a muscle. 'Cause no one could understand what the fuck had just gone on . . . not a man or woman spoke. And me and Ossang were standing there. And they went, "So perhaps you could tell us what the film's about." I had no fucking idea what the film was about!'

1997 saw Joe alternating between Los Angeles and the UK, where he was trying to put an album together using material recorded with Norro and songs he'd produced with former Grid percussionist Pablo Cook. They sent one, 'Living In The Flood', to reggae legend Horace Andy, who took it as the title track to the album he released in 1999. Joe once again teamed up with Brian Setzer for a song he'd written about his Cadillac, 'Who Would Love This Car But Me?' This would appear on Brian Setzer's *Ignition* album in 2001.

When he spoke to Todd Martens, Joe quashed rumours that he'd recorded an entire album under the Strummerville banner then trashed it. He added that, apart from the Norro and Cook songs, his album would include material recorded with the Electric Doghouse, and maybe Brian Setzer. 'I've been doing all these various projects and there's quite a lot of things bubbling in the sea around me.'

One of the first things Joe came up with for the album was its title – *Rock Art and The X-Ray Style.* After the crash of Machine/Radar, Joe was feeling down and 'in the doldrums'. He popped next door to see 'Pockets', his 'crazy neighbour', to cheer himself up, and while there picked up an old book on anthropology. One of the chapters was called 'Rock Art and the X-Ray Style' – in reference to the way Australian aboriginals painted animals on rocks with their bones showing.

'I went, "That's it!" and from that moment it was on,' Joe told Howard Petruziello. 'Can you imagine if you have a bunch of songs floating around, but then you get a title for the work you feel more focused, you have something to aim at. It holds it all together.'

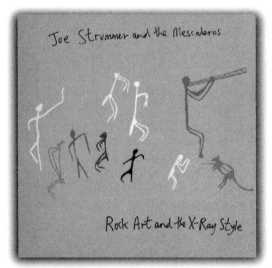

Damien Hirst's aboriginal-inspired cover art for Joe and the Mescaleros 1999 debut album, Rock Art And The X-Ray Style.

'It's funny,' says Rat Scabies. 'I was going through some stuff I've got from Joe . . . If he had an idea for a name for a group, he'd just scribble it down to see how it looked. "X-Ray" was one of the names he wanted to use. I've just got this written on a book of matches.'

Joe's neighbour, Pockets, would later play an important part in maintaining Joe's legacy by helping stage the *Joe Strummer – Past, Present and Future* exhibition. Johnny says he made a living making candles, while Rat Scabies describes him as, 'the nearest thing Joe ever had to a tour manager.'

Meanwhile, Johnny Green had been busy writing *A Riot of Our Own*, his ripping account about his experiences with The Clash. If anyone ever got close to the group it was Johnny, and he captures the mayhem of that time perfectly.

'When I decided to do my book, I went to each of them, except Topper, and said, "I'm gonna do a book based on my memories of it all. I'm not asking permission, I'm letting you know what I'm doing." Paul said, "I'm not helping." Mick was great; he made me a cup of tea. I rang Joe and he rang me back and said, "Come on down." So I went for a couple of days down to this cottage he was renting and he said, "I'll do a foreword for you." So he wrote a foreword and faxed it to me.'

When Johnny got the first copies of his *A Riot of Our Own* in 1997, he took them along to The Clash's annual business meeting. He left copies of the book and returned later. 'None of the band had looked at it, but Luce was there and she was reading it. She came over to Joe, who was making a rum punch, ruffled his hair and said, "My hero." I was quite easy on him. I wasn't easy on Mick. Paul wouldn't look at it.'

Johnny also remembers an occasion when Joe had builders in to do up his house. 'They asked if he was a rock star or something. So Joe went into town, bought some copies of the book, signed them and gave one each to the builders.'

Joe's campfire was one of the highlights of the 1997 Glastonbury Festival. This kind of chilled out scene would have been unthinkable during the hippy-hating heyday of The Clash.

I played at Glastonbury that year, DJ-ing before Primal Scream came on. It was the proverbial mudbath. The heavens had opened, and as our coach crawled in, the site resembled a battlefield. Sodden punters trudged through the deep mud and did their best to keep up the festival's traditionally warm vibe. This was proving decidedly difficult under the torrential rain, hurricane gales and First World War conditions.

'We ain't beaten, man – we will beat this deluge,' declared Joe through the Thursday afternoon's driving rain. He then rallied his troops and started the campfire. Booze flowed and people came and went, joining in with the element-defying spirit. Songs were sang and jokes told, presided over by Joe, who never left his position for the whole three days. His good humour bolstered everyone's spirits and the event passed into legend to be repeated at subsequent festivals. Joe also DJ-ed at the festival.

A couple of journalists from *Select* magazine encountered Joe at the campfire, who was in element-defying mood. 'These are abysmal conditions . . . But as long as we get this fire going, we can somehow operate . . . We have to be able to do this. We will beat this quagmire! Without doubt!'

When *Q* published a special Glastonbury issue after the 2003 festival, they devoted a page to 'Joe the Lion' and his campfire. Keith Allen recalled, 'The camp became a very spiritual thing for him, he loved it – if he'd had his own way he'd have lived outdoors. I know it makes him sound like an old druid, but he was very in tune with the earth . . . He was a magical man – I still think he's here somewhere. Joe's camp . . . was just a wonderful place to go, and everyone was welcome. He was just the kindest, most concerned, genuine person you could meet.'

Further adverse weather conditions blew up for Joe in August when he went to Japan to DJ at the massive annual Fuji Rock festival. The event, which is held in the shadow of the famous Mount Fuji, had to be cut short because of an impending typhoon.

Towards the end of 1997, Jason Rothberg put together a Clash tribute album called *Burning London,* in aid of children's charities. A wide spectrum of artists which included Moby, Ice Cube, No Doubt and Rancid tackled Clash songs – all approved by Joe, who contributed sleeve notes. Paul did the cover artwork, while Topper played on the Afghan Whigs' version of 'Lost In The Supermarket'. Unsurprisingly, reunion-hungry Sony stepped in and released the LP later that year.

Early in 1998, Joe recorded an album's worth of material with former Happy Mondays' funky dancer, Bez, who'd left Black Grape in 1995 over financial issues. Recording in his home studio, Joe even managed to get Bez singing. Maybe that was one of the reasons they couldn't get a record deal!

By the spring, Joe and family moved to 'Yalway', a large manor house in Broomfield, near Bridgwater in Somerset. He settled in well and loved to walk his dogs in the surrounding countryside.

That summer, Rick Rubin asked Joe if he would contribute to Chef Aid – a joke benefit organised in support of the loverman school cook played by Isaac Hayes in the demented cartoon series *South Park.* With Rick producing, Joe had a band that included big Clash fan, Tom Morello of Rage Against The Machine. The track, 'It's A Rockin' World', appeared on the album that following November. Joe also got to appear in animated form on the TV show, making up spontaneous dialogue and recording it at Real World.

Sony announced that The Clash would be releasing a live album in 1999 after Joe had unearthed a tape of one of the Shea Stadium gigs when moving. Inevitably, this sparked further reunion rumours, but Joe was determined to make his own album. Mick and Bill Price started putting together the live album, sifting through reams of tape for likely candidates. Joe chose to leave them to it, as he couldn't 'stand going back to the past'.

In August, Joe was asked to present a month-long series of weekly shows on the BBC World Service, appropriately titled *London Calling*. This was the station that Joe had first heard when a child overseas. He rose to the occasion, playing a mixture of his favourite reggae, world music and rock 'n' roll.

For that summer's World Cup in France, Keith Allen again struck gold with another football song. Under the name Fat Les, he cooked up the singalong knees-up that was 'Vindaloo' with Blur's Alex James and artist Damien Hirst in tow. The track made Number One, and was enough to send Keith back in the studio later that year to record a Christmas novelty song, 'Naughty Christmas (Goblin In The Office)'. This time Joe came along to the Real World session. The single only reached Number 21 but the session provided an unexpected dividend, as Joe struck up an immediate bond with Antony Genn, who had played with Pulp and once danced starkers onstage with Elastica at the Reading Festival. Since the demise of Machine, Joe had been anxiously searching for a new collaborator.

'Oh yeah, I didn't really know what to do,' he told Howard Petruziello. 'See, I'm really a lyric man. I mean, I can write songs, like I wrote "London Calling" or "X-Ray Style", but I think it's really good when you get two heads on it, like Rogers and Hammerstein, Lieber and Stoller, Strummer and Jones . . . You have to have it equal.' Joe goes on to describe how he'd seen Genn around London doing sessions. 'I knew that he had the best musical head in town. I bumped into him at one of these sessions and he said to me, "You're Joe Strummer, you should be making a record!" I said, "I know, you wanna get on it?" Within a week we were in a studio knocking out *Rock Art And The X-Ray Style*.'

Still short of a record deal for his new material, Joe signed up with Simon Moran's SMJ management in early 1999. Having successfully 'bored them out', Joe finally got out from under the Sony deal and was allowed to pursue solo projects elsewhere. But, his contract still said that if he recorded anything with Mick or Paul it would be classed as Clash activity and belong to Sony. In America, they went with Hellcat, an offshoot of the independent Epitaph. This came about through Jason Rothberg, who organised the *Generations* album. He introduced Joe to Hellcat owner Tim Armstrong, who was also leader of Clash-worshipping punk outfit Rancid and leapt at the chance to do a Strummer record.

However, whereas the US proved to be no problem, the UK showed total indifference to Joe's demos. It took some wildly successful shows in Paris and Hamburg to convince Mercury Records, that Joe should have his own label, which he called Casbah Records. The deals were short term. In other words, Joe had to prove himself.

As Real World was occupied, time was booked at Battery Studios, Willesden, North London. The sessions started on 14 February – the date that Joe would subsequently give as the start date of the band he would name the Mescaleros.

With Joe and Antony at the core, Pablo Cook survived from Machine to provide percussion, while Martin Slattery – at a loose end after Black Grape called it a day – came in on keyboards, sax, guitar and anything else that he picked up. In 1998, Martin had been in a band called Bond. After he met Joe and fell into the Mescaleros, Martin quickly earned himself the ultimate Strummer compliment of a nickname in 'El Slatto'. He would become one of Joe's main musical collaborators, along with Scott Shields – who Martin had met when both were in Bond. A multi-instrumentalist, Scott had started his career with five years in Scottish rock band Gun, and played bass when Martin nabbed him for the Mescaleros. The pair became indispensable to Joe, to the extent that Luce trusted them with completing the band's *Streetcore* album after Joe's death.

Drumming was shared between Pablo, Ged Lynch from the Grape, then Steve 'Smiley' Barnard, who'd been playing with Robbie Williams, and had played on 'Forbidden City', joined the touring line-up. Recording sessions commenced in earnest and another seven finished tracks were added to the three Norro songs. The only compulsory break came every day at six o'clock when Joe watched his favourite TV programme – *The Simpsons*. 'I'm kind of Homer, you know!', he laughed.

Starting with a show at Sheffield's Leadmill on 29 May, Joe and the Mescaleros embarked on a month-long series of UK dates and European festival appearances. At the end of June they went to the US for six gigs, before returning to Britain for the T In The Park Festival on 11 July. The band then headed back to continental Europe, via the Fuji Festival, for a series of outdoor shows that took them through until 4 September.

The thinking behind these gigs was to test the water with the new band. The gigs were intimate clubs, while the lucrative festival spots were on the middle of the bill. Although the group featured some of their new songs, Joe couldn't escape the fact that, for a lot of the audience, it was the first time they'd seen a former Clash member in action. Some had only just been born when the band split up. Hence Joe felt obliged to play the back catalogue, homing in on his favourites like 'White Man', 'Bankrobber' and 'Straight To Hell' and even going back as far as 'London's Burning.' For the first time since The Clash, Joe actually felt he was in a group again and enjoyed performing the old songs.

In August, *Q*'s readers voted Joe Number 24 in their '100 Greatest Stars Of The 20th Century' poll – not bad for a man who hadn't done anything high-profile in over ten years. The accompanying blurb said, 'The Clash were the only punk band that really mattered and were their generation's Beatles with Strummer as Lennon to Mick Jones' McCartney. With political insight . . . and the sus to embrace reggae, Strummer bled on his Fender Telecaster and morphed from revolutionary into beat auteur into mohican guerilla.'

Accompanied by the entire Clash back catalogue on remastered CD, the band's live album, *From Here To Eternity*, was finally released on 4 October and reached Number Thirteen in the UK (It didn't chart in the US). The title came from Fred Zinneman's classic war movie set in the US barracks at Honolulu before the bombing of Pearl Harbour. It had already been namechecked in 'The Right Profile' as Montgomery Clift was one of the stars. The LP's Westway by night cover was designed by Paul.

Of the seventeen tracks, eleven date from 1980 onwards – mostly from a gig that year at Boston's Orpheum. Three of the tracks were intended for the ill-fated *Rude Boy* soundtrack, which explains why the sleeve states that 'some instrumental over-dubs' had been added to them, 'to repair technical deficiencies on the original live recordings.' There's nothing from *Give 'Em Enough Rope* or *Cut The Crap*.

During the Mescaleros' November 1999 US tour, Joe confessed that he hadn't even heard the album, 'Are you kidding? . . . I need some time to stop and think and then stick it on. I can't judge it or play it now on a bus or on a plane, in a lobby or at a gig, in the dressing room, wherever we are. It ain't right to hear it. I want to really hear it. You can imagine, it's personal to me. It may be insane, but that's just the way I am.'

To coincide with the release of *From Here To Eternity*, BBC2 showed Don Letts' *Westway To The World* documentary, which achieved the mighty feat of summing up the essence of The Clash, combining the sheer excitement of his old footage while the band and those close to them recounted the whole amazing story.

Topper's declaration that he'd probably do the same again if he had the chance is one of the film's most touching moments – especially as he still looked stoned and fragile. 'I'm an addict, I was still using then so I look a bit gaunt,' he admits. The previous year Topper had suffered a near-fatal car crash and, once again, used the hospital stint to try and get off smack. He used his share of the advance from the live album to buy a house in a village near Dover, away from temptation. Even then it would take another five years for Topper to finally win his battle.

The Clash's profile was at its highest since 'Should I Stay Or Should I Go' hit Number One. But there was absolutely no hope of any reunion. Joe's focus was fixed on the Mescaleros.

First 'Yalla Yalla' was released as a single. It came with a 'live summer '99' version of 'The X-Ray Style', an intimate bongo-pattering acoustic slowie, plus a non-album slab of near-freeform space blues in 'Time And The Tide'. Joe also got his wish and included Norro's 'King Dub', which stretches and skews 'Yalla Yalla' to the outer limits of sonic space. The single didn't chart but announced that Strummer was back, to a lot of people's pleasure, and certainly set the warm, low-key tone for the album.

Rock Art and The X-Ray Style was released on Casbah through Mercury Records on 18 October. Joe deliberately kept the length to around 50 minutes, in homage to the traditional maximum for a vinyl pressing. The cover was designed by Damien Hirst, using the cave paintings mentioned in the title – which Joe would say were done 60,000 years ago, 'beyond history. Cool, isn't it?'

It didn't so much kick the door down and holler, 'I'm back!', but eased in as a mature reflection while looking to the future. It saw Joe taking stock, set against an acoustically dominated backdrop with shades of the world music he'd picked up on a few years before. The mood was decidedly mellow and positive. Joe might have become enamoured with rave culture and the power of dance music, but that did-n't mean he leapt straight on a loved-up smiley bandwagon of cold-crushing techno beats. If anything, the album was the calmest thing he'd ever done.

X-Ray Style kicks off with 'Tony Adams', a breezy reggae-flavoured outing that features a riff which somehow recalls 10cc's 'Dreadlock Holiday'. The lyrics are

Left: Paul Simonon's Westway cover to the Clash's 1999 live album. Right: Don Letts' magnificent Westway To The World *documentary.*

apocalyptic in a 'London Calling' style as they describe the power and electric atmosphere of a full-blown rave. Lines like, 'stroboscopic snowflakes fell from the stratosphere' and 'waiting for the rays of the morning sun' hit a chord with anyone who's ever experienced a belting all-nighter.

Tony Adams – who is he? Joe explained it to Howard Petruziello. 'Tony Adams is an English football player who was the captain of the national team . . . This guy is tall, he stands in the back, he doesn't say nothin', he's noble, he's got an interesting history, he's dated Caprice, he's fought drink addiction, he's written an autobiography, he plays the piano and I wanted to celebrate him because he's one of the unsung heroes, not the flashy striker who gets the goals, but more like an oak tree.'

The warm world music blanket of 'Sandpaper Blues' follows, before the pattering 'X-Ray Style', which boasts the particularly poignant line, 'I wanna live, and I wanna dance awhile.' This one made *Uncut* Clash aficionado Simon Goddard's ten best list in the magazine's tribute to Joe. He called it, 'devastatingly beautiful . . . Strummer the survivor sings from the heart.'

'Techno D-Day' and its crashing chords is another of Joe's rave adventures, this time based on an event he visited in Cornwall. He managed to write about rave culture in the same way he described life around Portobello Road or in a Mexican desert. At that time, there hadn't really been anyone trying to comment on the social aspects of the dance revolution – except for Mick ten years before. Ultimately, dance music's biggest influence on Mick was in the social possibilities of such huge trouble-free celebrations and the aural trailblazing of the new breed of producers and DJs.

What Joe might not have realised was how big an influence The Clash had been on many of the first wave of UK dance producers. Andrew Weatherall has repeatedly voiced this very point, and I recall a very stupid after-club session at the home of one of Slam, the Glasgow DJ-producers who have risen to become one of dance music's biggest and most respected forces. Hours earlier, Stuart McMillan, Orde Meikle and their manager Dave Clarke had been providing a delirious night at their eponymous club in the city centre. Now they were cavorting around the room playing air guitar to 'Complete Control'.

When I told them I was writing this book, Dave sent me the following message: 'Without Joe Strummer and what he said and meant and stood for there would be no Slam. We were taught more by Joe through his interviews and lyrics and personality than we were at school and our ethos as Slam is about trying to empower others to do the same and follow their dreams with a conscience.'

I'd often drop Clash tracks when I was DJ-ing, and got positively encouraged to do this when I warmed up for Prodigy on their 1996 European tour. As the Essex firm became one of the biggest bands in the world, they were always keen to corner me for Clash stories. When Joe went to raves he was greeted like royalty. The same had gone for Mick. To a kid who wasn't even born when The Clash appeared, dance music was as big a revolution as punk rock. To some ex-punk rockers, dance music had the same impact they remembered in 1977. In an understated way, *Rock Art and The X-Ray Style* saw Joe still serving as some kind of spokesman for a new generation.

The second side of the album – or the last half of the CD – is a gentle, chilled out glide. No balls-out rockers, mainly slow-paced songs with evocative lyrics and accompaniments that often verge on the beautiful.

'Nitcomb', despite its unattractive title, is a quite poignant ballad based on Antony's highly sensitive music. It's Joe's declaration of defiance, meaning it'll take one of those narrow-toothed combing devices used to get bugs out of kids' hair to get rid of him. It also contains the line, 'I'm standing at the sale of the shoes of bankrupt men/I just had to buy a pair of shoes that life can live again' – which Joe would later say was totally autobiographical.

'Diggin' The New' was next, then 'Forbidden City' – one of the first songs to be written but last to be recorded. Joe was inspired by the events in Tiananmen Square and deals with the last vestiges of communism in China, again lamenting the plight of the people. The music comes on like a skanking take on sixties Latin-tinged doo-wop groups like the Drifters.

'Yalla Yalla' makes a welcome appearance, before the album comes to rest with the gorgeously melodic dub ballad 'Willesden To Cricklewood'. The end of the journey and, though slow and quite melancholy, a final celebration. This is Joe once again writing about his surroundings – in this case, multi-ethnic Willesden High Street.

The album was greeted with the most acclaim Joe had got from the press in a long time. *Uncut's* five-star review was enough to merit a sticker on the CD case. '. . . triumphant return by former Clash legend . . . an album brimming with hope and optimism, that looks forward both musically and lyrically . . . mesmerising.'

Q called the album, 'a joy: prime Clash dubbery . . . worth spending time and money.' Former *NME* editor Neil Spencer enthused that Joe was, 'a man at ease with himself and his fellow citizens – at least, those of them with heart, a quality splendidly conspicuous on *Rock Art And The X-Ray Style.*'

'It was kind of like being new,' Joe told the *San Antonio Current* in 2001. 'No spotlight on you, nobody wanted to know you – you're kind of free to operate . . . I kept that experience of *Earthquake Weather* as a template of how hard it is in the world when you've not got your hit group with you or the crest of the youth wave you were riding has crashed on the shore. It's sink or swim time . . . I just wanted to get to the point where the label, Hellcat, was willing to make another record.'

On the same day the album was released, Joe and the boys started a nine-date UK tour, before starting a month-long US jaunt on 1 November. It was like Joe was making up for all that lost time. The set consisted of a large chunk of the new album, plus some of Joe's Clash faves, including 'White Man', 'Rock The Casbah', 'Straight To Hell', 'Bankrobber' and the ever-present 'London's Burning' as the closer.

Joe's willingness to play Clash numbers live was quite surprising in the light of his ambivalent attitude to the live album. But it seems that, even if he couldn't handle hearing The Clash do them, he certainly hadn't fallen out with the songs themselves. This was not a feeling shared by Mick though – in all the incarnations of BAD, and now Carbon/Silicon, I've never heard him play one Clash song.

'I wanna play the songs,' explained Joe. 'You see, it suddenly occurred to me that the songs aren't just stuff that's written on a bit of paper or put on a record. What if a song is like a person? Like a song might have some sort of . . . kinetic energy of a kind that we can't, that we haven't managed to quantify or identify . . . I feel that they demand to be played. And I'm more than happy to play them, 'cause they're really well-made songs.'

By now, Joe seemed to have made some kind of peace with what happened with The Clash, although talk to anyone who knew him and they'll say that he never fully got over the part he was coerced into playing in their demise. As he asserted on *Westway To The World*, 'I still wouldn't change anything about the Clash experience at all. It's all part and parcel to me; the glory, the meeting the people, the rocking the houses all over the US – that is part and parcel of taking no royalties on *Sandinista!*, getting a knock on *London Calling*. That is all part of one thing in life. It was an amazing thing.'

Joe got some idea of the public affection for him when he got hooked up to the internet at home. It was another new thing that he had to come to terms with and learn from scratch, like the home studio, or even the CD player – once he could bring himself to accept music that wasn't presented on vinyl. Joe had to get Luce to work the computer, but was bowled over when they turned up Josh Cheuse's *Strummerville* website and found 40,000 hits. After hearing about how great nu-punk baby bands like Blink 182 were from his girls, Joe could now get a firsthand impression of just how much he meant in the scheme of things.

At last Joe Strummer was back – on his own terms and enjoying the lack of pressure. After the 'wilderness years' of the nineties, Joe could approach the 21st century with a new focus, a proper band and his most acclaimed music since the heyday of The Clash.

CHAPTER NINETEEN
TUBAS IN THE SUN

Joe was a nice man, a good man, and a good musician – Johnny Cash

Joe greeted the 21st century in appropriate fashion – fronting a full-tilt rock 'n' roll band. On 6 January he started a month long Australasian tour with the first of three dates in Japan. This was followed by a series of dates in New Zealand and Australia, the bulk of which were as part of the Big Day Out roadshow.

On 27 March, Ian Dury died from cancer of the liver at the age of 57. All four former Clash members were particularly saddened by the news. They had become close to Ian while Blackhill managed both bands, and Blockheads such as Mickey Gallagher and Norman Watt-Roy had regularly guested on Clash tracks. Like Joe, Ian had become one of rock's foremost wordsmiths.

A week later, Joe played at the Poetry Olympics Party at the Royal Festival Hall in London. It was organised by beat generation poet and organiser Michael Horowitz, who had put on Allen Ginsburg at the Royal Albert Hall in 1965. Joe had struck up a friendship with Horowitz at the Poetry Olympics itself the previous October. Backed by Pablo Cook and Tymon Dogg, Joe played 'Island Hopping' – the sailor's tale from *Earthquake Weather* – 'Junco Partner' and 'London's Burning'.

Playing as a trio, with minimal instrumentation, gave Joe considerable inspiration – 'That really gave me the feeling of "This is the way to go,"' he told *livedaily.com*'s Colin Devenish in August 2001. 'Sometimes you get tired of the big guitars and the walloping drums and all that stuff. It can get boring. I was looking for a break in the weather, or some ways to change things up a bit. And doing that beatnik Poetry Olympics evening gave us the feeling to go onto this record and try a little bit of groping around, whether we kept to it or not.'

On 6 May, Joe and the Mescaleros played Brixton Academy. Mick went along with Robin Banks, who remembers Mick's reaction to the proliferation of old Clash songs. 'Mick got drunk and, when they did the Clash songs, he said, "They're using all my arrangements!" he wasn't really pissed off. It's just when he gets pissed he remembers how great he is, and he did all those arrangements, for everything.'

That summer, the Mescaleros played more festivals, including the V2000 events at Hylands Park, Chelmsford on 19 August, and Weston Park, Staffordshire, the following day. After these dates, Antony Genn quit the band, leaving Joe without a musical partner again – although his old mucker Tymon now joined up as a full-time Mescalero.

Joe's enthusiastic endorsement of all things outdoor bore literal fruit when he hitched up with the Future Forests organisation, whose mission is to protect the earth's climate. They do this by contacting companies and giving them the opportunity to combat the amount of carbon dioxide they produce by tree planting and introducing more environmentally friendly technology. Joe's love of nature had developed from living in the country and the Glastonbury campfires and he wanted to do something to protect them.

Future Forests' website says that Joe's, 'inspiration and energy backstage at Glastonbury 1996 was the spark that got Future Forests going.' Joe is quoted as saying, 'Bands must be contributing to global warming by their buses, equipment trucks and the diesel used to power the stages. Can you imagine how much CO2 the pressing and the distribution of a CD creates? What shall we do about it?'

Next on Joe's agenda was a second Mescaleros album. What would become *Global A Go-Go* started life with five trial days at Battery Studios. In the absence of Antony Genn, production duties fell to Joe, Martin Slattery and Scott Shields. Richard Flack, who had become an invaluable part of the set up, engineered. This combination worked, as the sessions took the form of jams with Joe improvising over the top. The only track he went in with ready-written was 'Bummed Out City', which, 'was triggered by having a row with my wife.'

In October, Joe was honoured with a *Q* Inspiration award. To celebrate, the Mescaleros played a gig at the 100 Club on 27 October. 'I am a man just about to leap off the top of a cliff into a forest of long-bladed knives,' a nervous Joe announced to a visiting *Q* reporter in the dressing room before showtime. The group started their set with five new songs they'd written that week in the studio, before moving on to a bevy of Clash faves, including 'London Calling', 'Rock The Casbah', 'White Man', 'I Fought The Law' and 'London's Burning'. The crowd went mad, with old punks in tears and one fat bloke being hurled on to the stage, where he remained deliriously semi-comatose.

'I thought he was dead,' laughed Joe afterwards. 'Just heat exhaustion, it turned out. It was a fantastic, fun occasion. Terrific. Straight out of the studio and "1-2-3-go!" It's lovely to be a human being again.'

Joe went to the *Q* ceremony with Keith Allen and received his award from Alex James of Blur. In his acceptance speech, Joe thanked his, 'compadres Mick, Paul and Topper.'

On 30 October, Joe must've felt some sense of *déjà vu*, as he embarked on ten-date stadium tour of the UK with The Who. It wound up at Wembley Arena on 16 November, after which, Joe sacked drummer Steve 'Smiley' Barnard. When it came to ejecting musicians, Joe still had his ruthless streak. 'Smiley' was sacked with a simple late night phone call. No explanation or anything. I can't find anyone who knows the reason why. Steve went on to form a band called one*iota.

The album sessions started in earnest at Battery toward the end of 2000. The way *Global A Go-Go* was created is reminiscent of *Sandinista!* Martin or Scott would get a groove rolling, then Pablo and Richard would kick up a beat and add the instrumental topping. Joe would have a few pre-written lines, but preferred to go with the flow, often improvising on the spot. Recording would start early evening and go round the clock, sometimes running until lunchtime. Scott later talked to *Mojo's* Pat Gilbert about the intensity of the sessions. 'Man, I got seriously fucked up, I went mental. Joe was in his element, so full of energy. He was inspiring everyone, coming in at 5am shouting, "I love that guitar! It's fucking great!"'

'Everyone co-wrote this record,' Joe told Colin Devenish. 'That's the best bit about us, is that we don't know what we're doing, so it allows us to sort of give birth to itself somehow.'

Joe is simply credited as providing vocals for *Global A Go-Go*, while songwriting on most of the tracks is attributed to Strummer/Slattery/Shields/Cook and Dogg. 'You've got to let the music people do the music. I really feel my strongest quadrant would be lyric-writing, because I can't play the guitar for fuck . . . You might as well get the experts to hone in and bring their expertise to bear on the final thing, instead of hogging it all for yourself.'

The diverse range of musical styles evident on the album was unplanned. It simply developed through the band's combination of organic creativity and collective blissful ignorance. Joe had no intention of making a Joe Strummer solo album and found it easy to blend the different inputs into a cohesive whole.

'We're too stupid to realise we have to be coherent,' he told David Peisner of the *San Antonio Current* in late 2001. 'That's our saving grace really, because you do what you feel and you hope it works . . . I don't think it's worth approaching anything with a grand design, 'cause then you can't let things happen. You've got to let things happen somehow, to get things really natural and grooving.'

Joe agreed that working with the Mescaleros was, 'very similar to Clash sessions, because the Mescaleros like to work with the vibe, like The Clash did . . . And both The Clash and the Mescaleros were really long-distance session rats, as I call it. A session might go eighteen hours and you kind of get somewhere in that time . . . It's kind of like being in a spaceship.'

What Joe didn't tell the rest of the band was that he was constantly fighting a financial battle to keep the studio clock ticking. At this time, the Mescaleros were surviving primarily on gig money, not having the support of a big record company. Joe often worried that they'd be thrown out at any moment, but he managed to wing it for the best part of three months, until the album was finished in February. Mercury wouldn't take up the option but Hellcat did – hence the sleeve thanks, 'for not quitting out on us.'

On 24 May, The Clash received the 2001 Ivor Novello Award for their 'Outstanding Contribution To British Music'. The ceremony at London's Grosvenor House Hotel was attended by Mick, Paul and Topper, who were joined by Johnny Green. The disaster-prone Topper was on crutches, having broken his leg in a pub fight. 'With the Clash, there's always an element of comedy,' Joe told the *Dallas Observer*'s Robert Wilonsky. 'When they went, "Ladies and gentlemen, The Clash! And will someone help them up onstage?" I loved that bit.' Receiving the award from Pete Townshend, Joe said, 'This is for Guy Stevens. Rock the Casbah!'

The occasion was particularly significant as it brought the classic line-up together in the same room for the first time in eighteen years. Also, as it would sadly turn out, the last. Topper describes the day as, 'Lovely. The first time we'd been together

Together again for the last time – Paul, Joe, Topper and Mick at the Ivor Novello Awards, May 2001.

for all those years. We spent the first ten minutes apologising to each other and then we all laughed and realised that back then we were all young and headstrong. We were also totally different personalities. Now we were all a bit older and wiser. It was great. A lot of hatchets got buried that day.'

'That was the real Clash reunion,' says Johnny. 'That was the only time they were all together for donkey's years. It was just very sweet and affectionate. They did all just sit there and say sorry, at first. A bit coy, and very, very funny. They're so serious in the pictures, but people forget how funny they were together.'

'Johnny Appleseed' was released as a single in early July. The lyrics concern the exploitation of workers, with lines such as, 'If you're after getting the honey/then you don't go killing all the bees'. It starts low-key, with Tymon's fiddle, and gradually rises to an anthemic crescendo. It was an obvious choice for a single. The video showed Joe and the boys busking on the streets – a constantly recurring theme in Joe's life.

Global A Go-Go was released on 16 July 2001. The album again featured ten tracks. Josh Cheuse's sleeve plants the band name and photos on customised disposable lighters. Inside there's a fantastically atmospheric shot of Joe singing in the studio. Richard Norris has this on his wall at home, it was taken during the 'Yalla Yalla' session and he's standing to the right of Joe.

'Johnny Appleseed' sets the mood for the album, as it takes off on a fascinating journey through Joe's consciousness, as his lyrics stream out in the form of asides, ad-libs and complex lyrical patterns. The world music influence is still there in some of the melodies and rhythms, but the mood is more acoustic, stripped down, and folky. Joe's delivery is reminiscent of sixties protest singers, while the predominant instruments are Tymon's violin, acoustic guitars, harmonica and a fair smattering of bongos.

There's plenty of space for Joe to stretch out and the album often veers from moving to exhilarating in the space of a few bars. That's the fun of it. Joe's vocal acrobatics, lyrical flights and downhome-yet-surreal space blues-scapes are evocative of Captain Beefheart's early stuff.

As with *Rock Art and The X-Ray Style*, the new album starts raucous and electric and gradually winds down into more chilled out mood. 'Cool 'N' Out' starts with some Link Wray style guitar twangs before upping gear into a supercharged Latin-flavoured rocker washed in psychedelic dub effects. 'And punk rock's what it's all about', sings Joe in the middle of what's basically an anti-war song. The title track – a tribute to Joe's beloved BBC World Service – is a riot of noise and colour that also features a surprise background bellow from Who frontman Roger Daltrey.

'Bhindi Bhagee' has an African flavoured melody, over which Joe semi-speaks lyrics detailing the variety of ethnic gastronomic delights to be found along Willesden High Road. These act as a springboard to a smorgasbord of global music. 'Gamma Ray' – a gutteral dub slinker with a touch of space shuffle – begins in a Chinese takeaway and ends up name-checking Cher and Creation Records founder Alan McGee.

The folk-blues influence is to the fore on 'Mega Bottle Ride', another surreal romp that recalls mid-sixties Dylan in its surreal imagery of '4-D tequila' and 'dancing to Fifth Dimension in the discosphere'.

'Shaktar Donetsk' is another psychedelic blues ballad with an aching vocal. Spacily acoustic with Tymon hovering in the ether, it's another distinct nod to the early seventies. Joe was inspired to write the words after reading about a truckload of fifty-eight Chinese immigrants who suffocated in a truck bound for Britain. Joe's lyrics recount the tale of a Ukrainian exile from the former Yugoslavia. The title refers to one of the Ukraine's biggest football teams, whose scarf he wears – 'the banner of freedom'. 'Mondo Bongo' is a mellow number, with a summery bongo patter, and finds Joe in Latino language-twist mode.

'Bummed Out City' is Joe's most personal lyric on the album, being prompted by an argument with Lucinda. 'And it was me, drove off the off ramp/It was me, I admit I had the map', Joe admits as he ends up in Bummed Out City. Joe ends up pleading for 'your mercy and your pity'. This is an unashamed love song – done Strummer style – a delicate, acoustic plea, which is quite beautiful.

'At The Border, Guy' is one of the album's strongest tracks and its most upfront reggae outing. The song's humorous worldview rides a skipping seventies roots style rhythm with a bass riff not unlike Bob Marley's 'Lively Up Yourself', augmented by Augustus Pablo-style melodica.

Global A Go-Go demonstrated that the Mescaleros had developed and refined their own unique sound – an effortless hybrid of styles and strains, which transcended genre and simply celebrated a multitude of global sonic delights. But, although not averse to the odd psychedelic splash, most of the effect is achieved by valve amp rawness, acoustic timbre and subtly melodic embroidery.

The album goes out on a seventeen-minute instrumental version of the traditional Irish folk ballad 'Minstrel Boy' – the kind of song you're taught at school, but one that Joe had been toying with for years. Apart from the distracted mumbling of what is credited as 'off-stage voices' from Joe, the focus is on Tymon's violin and a wall of acoustic guitars and percussion. Scott is credited with, 'Just sat there, staring off into space'. The result is a poignant, hypnotic coda. The fullest realisation of Joe's Celtic roots and an audacious finale to another strong album.

The cover credits the great jazz-blues diva Nina Simone and Michael Horowitz for inspiration and is dedicated to Joey Ramone, the man who'd so influenced Joe during the early days of The Clash. Joey died from lymphatic cancer on Easter Sunday, 15 April 2001. From now on 'Blitzkreig Bop' – the song that Joe, Paul and Sid all honed their chops with – would be added to the Mescaleros live set (along with Iggy and the Stooges' '1969'). Everybody was sad about the death of such a gentle and influential punk pioneer.

Reviews were positive again. Pat Gilbert wrote in *Mojo*, 'Lyrically, he's still unbeatable . . . it's funny, idiosyncratic and proof that Joe has found a dignified career post-Clash.' *Q*'s Danny Eccleston wrote of an, 'internalist concept album' and, 'its intense heart-on-sleeve belief in racial harmony, social justice and rock 'n' roll.'

Joe believed that he'd finally made the record that Paul Simon told him would come one day when the pair met in 1994 – something that brought together everything he'd ever done into one great album. That was a pep talk that Joe always bore in mind as he embarked on the Mescaleros trail.

After *Global A Go-Go* was finished, Pablo left to join Moby's touring band. Luke Bullen came in on drums. He'd previously served four years with a band called Addict, before a brief stint in another named Zanderman. Simon Stafford from Sheffield, formerly of indie-poppers the Longpigs, joined on bass, allowing Scott Shields to switch to guitar. Thus the Mescaleros' final five-piece line-up was in place.

In June 2001, the Mescaleros toured the record stores of the UK, playing then signing autographs. As Joe put it, 'the full kebab.' They did some festivals, and visited the US again in July, including some dates supporting Brian Setzer, which saw Pablo temporarily rejoining the line-up. The group made several in-store appearances, notably on 24 July at New York's huge Tower Records – around the corner from Bond's. They also visited Toronto, Chicago and San Francisco, before landing in LA, where they holed up for a couple of weeks.

On 31 July, a *Rebel Noise* website correspondent known simply as 'Steve' interviewed Joe at the Chateau Marmont hotel. That same week in LA, Joe played gigs at the Greek Theatre and Viper Room, signed autographs at Tower Records and taped a session for cable channel VH-1. Joe reflected on what he now considered to be a rebirth. 'I do feel like a lucky son-of-a-gun, to be honest. I think it's really rare to get a second shot in the music business. I think I did it through a lot of hard work, and I was really fortunate to meet the right people . . . It's all quite good because it's like I'm beginning my career again, except at least I've already had the experience of going through it once.'

Joe Strummer in 2001 was the happiest he'd been since the making of *London Calling* more than twenty years earlier. Now he had two more dynamite albums to his name and a bunch of musicians he believed in. No wonder he did so many interviews at this time.

Joe's compulsive note making formed the basis of the sleeve of 'Johnny Appleseed', the first single from Global A Go-Go.

He was still at the Marmont when interviewed by Colin Devenish of the *livedaily* site. Joe described the tour as 'the world's first international in-store tour . . . If you can't get on the radio, you've got to pull something out of the bag. The only thing we could think of was . . . to try and do some in-stores, moving as fast as we could. We're gigging in-stores – we're not just standing around – and then afterwards we sign stuff.'

Colin asked Joe if he ever felt like he was in competition with his past. 'You've got to face up to your past. It can feel like a millstone in that situation, but mainly, I feel proud about it.'

Joe returned to the UK in September where he attended a launch party for *The Clash*, Bob Gruen's photo-history of the band. At the shindig, Joe ran into Barry 'Scratchy' Myers and asked him if he'd like to man the decks at some future gigs. 'The years just seemed to fall away,' recalls Barry, who said his sets consisted of, 'the music that turns me on – Marley, Columbian, good old rock 'n' roll. There'd be a lot of Primal Scream at Joe gigs. It was what I've essentially always played – the same mix, but brought up to date. People say that Joe embraced world music but that's a term I don't like. I mean, rock 'n' roll is world music. Everything comes from the world. I prefer the term "roots music."'

The band returned to the States for another tour on 4 October, which wound up at LA's Troubadour three weeks later. The band's itinerary on the eighteen-date jaunt was fairly gruelling, as the dates were mainly one-nighters. When a much-needed day off appeared on 17 October, Joe booked in a benefit show for Groundwork Aid – whose aim is to end world hunger. The concert was thousands of miles out of the tour route. 'That nearly killed everyone,' Joe told the *Strummersite*. 'Well I hope we did something for the cause.'

Joe Strummer and The Mescaleros.

However, Joe did get to sing 'London's Burning' in front of a sixty-foot flaming video screen. On 30 October, the Mescaleros started a five-date tour of Japan, before rounding of the year with a short string of UK shows and a trio of gigs in France and Greece.

In December, Joe and the band recorded a vocal version of 'Minstrel Boy' for the soundtrack of *Black Hawk Down,* a Ridley Scott action film about US troops rescuing their stricken chopper squad comrades in Somalia. After the 11 September World Trade Centre atrocity, victims' families adopted 'Minstrel Boy' as something of a theme.

On 1 April 2002, in a move reminiscent of The Clash's Bond's residency, Joe played five nights at the 600-capacity St Ann's Warehouse in Brooklyn, New York.

During this US visit Joe got to realise a long held ambition by recording with Johnny Cash at Rick Rubin's house. Joe had long been a fan of the legendary Man In Black, who sadly, would die himself the following year. Cash had risen from dirt-poor origins in Arkansas to become one of the new blood disruptors of country music in the mid-fifties. He sang about life, death, hope and religion in that inimitable voice, championing workers on the railroads and gaining a massive following in the prisons. During the early part of his life, Cash fought addictions and career slumps, but saw his profile rejuvenated in 1994 when he hitched up with Mick's old mate Rick Rubin for the *American Recordings* series. He was the original rebel and voice of the underdog.

Rick told Pat Gilbert how Joe always came around his house when he was in LA, 'because he thought it had the best pool.' When Joe discovered that Johnny was recording there he came every day, taking it in silently 'like a student' as Cash recorded his vocals in the booth. 'Did Johnny know who he was? No, but we soon enlightened him.'

Strummer and Cash duetted on Bob Marley's 'Redemption Song', which eventually appeared on Johnny's five CD *Unearthed* collection of out-takes and material he recorded in his final year. Rick also produced two songs with Joe alone – another version of 'Redemption Song' and 'Long Shadow'. The latter was another song that Joe had written for Johnny – scribbling the lyrics on a pizza box and paper towel. Cash didn't use this one either, but Joe recorded it himself in Rick's garage on a little tape recorder, after firing himself up in his car with his Columbian dance music tape. 'That was Joe; everything he did was unique and special,' said Rick.

2002 was designated as the year that punk celebrated its Silver Jubilee, as the Queen notched up a 'golden' half century. Personally, I would've picked 1976 as the year that punk rock broke through, but the benchmark here was the 25th anniversary of the Pistols' 'God Save The Queen'.

The Pistols themselves celebrated with another well-paid reunion, which failed to spark the interest garnered by their *Filthy Lucre* tour of six years earlier. When I spoke to John Lydon at that time, he said, 'It's my Jubilee too!' The Pistols' London show was at Crystal Palace National Sports Centre – a godforsaken location with dodgy sound and half-capacity crowd. I remember being thankful that it wasn't The Clash up there.

During the week of the Queen's Golden Jubilee celebrations, I DJ-ed at promoter Sean McClusky's 'Sonic Mook Future Rock 'n' Roll Festival' at the ICA. Fourth on the bill was a new band called The Libertines. That was more like the spirit of punk. I couldn't help but cast my mind back to the same stage over twenty-six years earlier.

Joe played no part in these retrospective celebrations, instead opting to appear at London's annual Fleadh festival, in Finsbury Park – an annual celebration of 'roots' music. The Mescaleros continued gigging through the summer, including three Hootenanny Festivals in California during the first week of July.

In August, Mick started producing *Up The Bracket*, East London band The Libertines' first album. He'd heard about them, checked them out and agreed to do it after being impressed by what he'd seen and heard. *NME* made it a lead news story, with Mick commenting, 'They're a London rock 'n' roll group, which obviously appeals to me . . . They do remind me of The Clash a little bit. There are the same elements, you know, four guys in the band, the tunes are really good, you can't help but get sucked in.'

Singer/guitarist Carl Barât said, 'I don't really know much about The Clash. But he told me what he and Joe Strummer were like together. It sounded like a parallel of me and Pete [Doherty], so it all felt perfect.'

Unfortunately, you would also have to bring Topper into the equation as drug abuse played a part in Pete being thrown out of the band during 2003. He later returned, but was thrown out again subsequent to recording their eponymous second album in 2004.

On *Up The Bracket*, Mick went for a production that was 'rough and raw and raucous and exciting' – rather like the first Clash album. The album proved a massive success, with the *NME*'s blanket coverage of the band mirroring that accorded The Clash twenty-five years earlier.

'It's like The Clash in the way it's the four guys that make the thing and not just any one individual,' declares Mick. 'The other guys in The Libertines [bassist John Hassall and drummer Gary Powell] are not much talked about. He's a great bass player and they're both very talented musicians. They're a great rhythm section and they play their part to the full but they get no credit whatsoever.'

Around this time, Mick also started working on his own new project with old mucker Tony James. Initially called James-Jones, they would later mutate into Carbon/Silicon and become the latest step in Mick's crusade to forge new hybrids from rock and dance music.

Earlier in the year, I'd spent an evening with Mick for the first time since the Primal Scream sessions in 1994. That isn't the first time I'd actually *seen* him. 2001 was my own 'lost year' with booze the culprit. I'd bumped into Mick at a couple of parties but don't remember a thing. My girlfriend, Michelle, later told me how Mick looked after her when I vanished during a party for some other punk book. 'You were on the ground!' Mick chortled.

On the evening in question Mick and me went along to a gig by Liverpool tribute band, Radio Clash. I'd always been wary of such groups, and so had Mick. But I'd been booked to DJ and phoned Mick up to invite him. 'I dunno, I might get bothered,' he said. But, after I'd played my set at the little Shoreditch club, I ran into him at the bar. Mick had decided to come and had a whale of a time. The band were pretty good, faithfully reproducing the more punky Clash classics, even if the 'Mick' was a diminutive ginger guy in army uniform!

Mick was smiling all night and shocked the band, who didn't know he was coming, by standing right up front. Afterwards, he even joined me in coming backstage to say hello to the group. It was great to see Mick again and we promised to keep in touch.

As 2002 wore on, Joe pursued several outside projects, in addition to preparing the next Mescaleros album. He created the Long Beach Dub All Stars to record a version of Jimmy Cliff's 'The Harder They Come' for *Free the West Memphis 3* – a benefit album in aid of three heavy metal fans wrongfully imprisoned in 1993 for an allegedly 'Satanic' child murder. He co-wrote a song called 'Gypsy Girl' with Cerys Mathews of Catatonia, which eventually appeared on her *Cockahoop* album in May 2003. Joe also teamed up with Jools Holland and his Rhythm & Blues Orchestra on his song, 'The Return Of The Blues Cowboy', which appeared on the *Small World, Big Band* album.

On 21 August, Joe celebrated his 50th birthday at Richard Dudanski's place in Andalucia, Spain, accompanied by his family. The date was also near to the anniversary of the death of Federico Garcia Lorca, the much-revered Spanish poet and playwright whose name I'd first encountered on account of Tim Buckley's *Lorca* album. He'd been shot nearby by fascists before the Spanish Civil War and was a big hero of Joe's, who'd mentioned him on 'Spanish Bombs'.

In late September, the Mescaleros were back in Japan, playing the Asagiri Jam festival and Tokyo's Liquid Rooms. During the encore, they played a song called 'Sam Po Suru' – in Japanese!

Subsequently, the Mescaleros started rehearsing for their upcoming UK tour. Joe was again asked what kept him going, this time by the *Strummersite*. 'Mackerel and rice,' he replied. 'Enthusiasm. Cynicism can age a person. It's a negative energy. It can drain your energy supply . . . Like a creative idea or something that excites you. You've got to be able to keep seeing the possibilities, having new ideas . . . I like talking about how good things should be. I hate listening to other people's boring anecdotes.'

In November, The Clash were nominated and accepted for the Rock 'n' Roll Hall Of Fame, along with The Police and Elvis Costello. Richard Norris phoned to tell me the good news. We agreed that it would be a great idea to attend – especially as The Clash started talking about reforming for the occasion. No way did we want to miss out on probably the most craved reunion in rock 'n' roll history since the Beatles.

Joe was interviewed about it on MTV. 'I think we should play,' he said. 'It would be shitty and snotty not to.'

'We knew that the four of us would be flying to the States to be inducted and thought that it would be great to get up and do two or three numbers,' recalls Topper. 'That's as far as we got . . .'

When the news about the induction came through, Sony couldn't believe their luck and asked The Clash to select their favourite songs for a double CD collection that would be called *The Essential Clash*.

November also saw the Mescaleros set off on a UK tour under the banner Bringin' It All Back Home, after the Dylan song. The jaunt included a community benefit gig at the Palace in Bridgwater on 17 November. The money raised went to a new media centre called the Engine Room.

Band and crew travelled and slept on a large tour bus, with the gear on a trailer behind and Joe turning the upstairs front area into his lair. 'Joe took over the front bit, a couple of bunks,' recalled 'Scratchy' Myers. 'He'd have all his shit laid out. Joe would need to go off and be on his own. He had to have his space. It wasn't like Joe was cracking the whip or anything, but it was *Joe Strummer* and The Mescaleros. It wasn't The Clash. I would say the Mescaleros were more than a backing band, but it wasn't a group in the same way that The Clash were. Joe was the boss and paying everybody, but he certainly wasn't Mr Unapproachable.

'What I liked about being on the bus was it was a different way of doing it. It changed the time around a bit. You'd sleep on the bus as it drove to the next place. I liked waking up about eleven or twelve in a new place. I spoke to Joe about it on the last morning in Liverpool and said, "It's great, innit?" He just smiled and said, "Yeah". Some people took it better than others, but I was determined to have a good time and so was Joe. it was wonderful being back on the road with Joe. Just all too short.'

There were two records that Joe would ask Barry to play either before he came on or, as the last record of the night after the band. Joe's favourite was 'Le Minuet' by the brilliant reggae/jazz guitarist Ernest Ranglin, which Joe described as, 'Like bathing in the cool water of a fragrant ocean.' The other was Dr Alimantado's 'Born For A Purpose', a classic late seventies roots anthem.

Barry reckons the Mescaleros were heading towards a harder rock 'n' roll feel after the 'unplugged' flavour of the previous line-up. 'Joe's influences were as broad as the Atlantic Ocean and the Seven Seas, but he was still a rock 'n' roller and a punk rocker. That's what I liked about the last incarnation of the Mescaleros.'

The 15 November concert at Acton Town Hall was the undoubted highlight of the tour. This gig entered into Clash legend as the night Mick and Joe stood side by side on stage again for the first time in nineteen years.

Considering the tragedy that would take place just over a month later, the enormity of what happened in the little hall that night is quite staggering and, like so much of The Clash's legend, would assume a significance far beyond that which anyone involved at the time realised.

The gig was in aid of the Fire Brigades Union, who were striking over the government's refusal to negotiate a pay rise after wages had failed to keep up with inflation. The claim for a 40 per cent increase was submitted in Spring 2002. Finally, in November, the fire-fighters commenced strike action for the first time since 1977.

FBU convenor Geoff Martin had caught Joe and the Mescaleros at that June's annual Fleadh concert in North London. He struck on the idea that, with the Union in dire need of funds to support any action, maybe the Mescaleros might help their cause. Joe immediately agreed to include a benefit in his upcoming Autumn tour. The Acton gig raised £10,000 for the FBU's hardship fund, with extra income coming from sales of a book put together about the event called *The Last Night London Burned.* The small publication, which includes photos by Pennie Smith, Jill Furmanovsky and Grant Fleming, pays tribute to Joe and recalls that special night.

The set they played ran as 'Shaktar Donetsk', 'Bhindi Bhagee', 'Rudie Can't Fail', 'Tony Adams', 'White Man', 'Mega Bottle Ride', 'Get Down Moses', 'Police And Thieves', 'Cool 'n' Out', 'Police On My Back', 'Johnny Appleseed', 'Coma Girl' and 'I Fought The Law'.

The encores took Joe completely by surprise as, halfway through 'Bankrobber', he was joined by Mick Jones, who just sauntered on and plugged into the same amp. It was the kind of moment that onlookers now talk about with misty eyes.

In September 2004, I asked Mick if he'd felt physically compelled to get up there and share a stage with his old sparring partner for the first time in nineteen years.

'A little bit. Not exactly physically, but I just felt compelled to go up there. It was halfway or a third of the way through 'Bankrobber'. He was just there playing and I ended up on stage with him, which I felt totally compelled to do. It wasn't planned in any way.'

So Joe didn't have a clue that was going to happen?

'Not at all.'

Was he shocked?

'Joe was happily surprised. He shouted out when he saw me, "Play guitar now!" Just like that, and then the next number was . . . he wouldn't say what it was. He just said, "You know it". And he went into the A position, like this [mimes chord] and it was, "1, 2, 3, 4 – [Sings] WHITE RIOT! And he didn't let me know that we were playing it. Then we did 'London's Burning.'

'It was great. He was being driven home and the guy who was driving him said, "Well, what did you think when Mick got up on stage?" And Joe went, "Bloody cheek!" [Laughs] But he was just joking. As it turned out, that was going to be our last show, rather than some white shirt, black tie event. If it was going to be anything it was going to be something like the old days really. It reminded me of one of those old town hall gigs with union banners and everything.'

Robin Banks told me another story about the car ride home after the Acton gig. 'During the ride

Produced to raise funds for the Fire Brigades Union Hardship Fund, The Last Night London Burned *provides an evocative account of Joe and Mick's final gig together.*

home, Joe was really quiet. Luce said, "What's the matter? Is it something to do with playing with Mick?" He just said, "It's fucking amazing." It was totally unusual.'

Mick added that, after Joe's failed attempt to persuade him to reform The Clash when he tracked Mick down in the Bahamas, 'there were other times we were gonna get the group back together again. But then he'd go, "Maybe we shouldn't bother." Once we were sitting in [London venue] the Union Chapel many years later and there'd been some talk about it. But he tried to bring in some manager, some manicured manager – a bloke I'd never even met. So I didn't want to. Everybody was in fancy dress and we were sitting together in these pews at the Union Chapel at some dance event and he said, "So, it doesn't look like we're gonna do it then". And I said to him, "Yeah, perhaps we shouldn't bother," and that's the last time we ever talked about it, until right up until the very end when we thought we may possibly play for the Hall of Fame. But Paul didn't wanna do it, Topper was sort of up for it . . . but it didn't work out that way.'

Geoff Martin wrote in *The Last Night London Burned*, 'These guys may have been offered millions to play together by the big corporations and here they are, for the fire-fighters, playing through the same amplifier. The boys from the garage are back in town.

'Joe Strummer came into our lives as he left it. Standing up for the underdog against the machine and doing it with a fire and a passion that I've never seen anyone else come near. We'll miss him badly but we'll keep the spirit alive by stepping up the struggle. The fire-fighters' battle for a decent, living wage is as good a place as any to start.' And then he quotes, 'No man born with a living soul can be working for the clampdown.'

Ironically, Joe and the Mescaleros had been asked to write a new theme tune for *London's Burning*, the popular UK TV show about the realities of life in the fire brigade. Joe was going to write a new song but pulled out because, 'the TV people were very punchy and aggressive,' the song would have been heavily edited and 'the money was shit.'

Joe's last ever gig was actually a week later at Liverpool University, where he encored with '(White Man) In Hammersmith Palais' – a rare placing for the song in Joe's set list. The tour confirmed that the Mescaleros had turned into a euphoric and powerful live prospect. It all boded so well for the upcoming album, not to mention the possibilities that Joe and Mick playing together again might have unleashed.

Of course, the FBU benefit added further fuel to the growing flames of speculation about a reunion. An interesting postscript was that Mani, the former Stone Roses bass-player who now pumps the funk with Primal Scream, got a call from Joe, shortly before he died, asking if he'd be interested in playing bass for The Clash.

The Madchester legend recalls, 'Joe phoned me when I was on the tour bus in Edinburgh and said, "I don't want to cause any kerfuffle in the Scream but Paul's got rheumatoid arthritis and doesn't want to play the Hall of Fame show. Would you be interested in playing bass for us?" Well, of course I was! Then Joe died. But I came that close to playing in The Clash! A lifetime ambition, Needsy, but it sadly wasn't to be . . .'

Johnny Green confirmed this, saying, 'One of the reasons Joe asked Mani was to give Paul, who wasn't that bothered, a kick up the arse and also to have a fall-back.'

Johnny also recalled that the band weren't impressed that it cost $2,500 a ticket for the event. It was decided that the group would indeed play – but at another, yet-to-be-arranged venue. 'They planned to come out onstage and start playing, then announce, "If you wanna see any more it's free,"' says Johnny. 'Then they were gonna walk out the back door and go to another hall where the real gear had been set up and play there for nothing.' Even in 2003, The Clash couldn't resist one last bold statement.

In December, the Mescaleros went back in the studio to work on their third album – this time the residential Rockfield in Monmouthshire. Not wishing to break with tradition, Joe set up camp in the studio, working all night. He even had a spliff bunker-style space in the live room, which doubled as a vocal booth.

U2's Bono contacted Joe about helping write a song for an African AIDS Awareness concert, which was planned to be held in February 2003 and hosted by

Nelson Mandela. He got as far as writing some words for a song that would be called '48864', after Mandela's prison number.

Furthering his involvement with Future Forests, Joe initiated the planting of a new forest on the shores of Loch Bracadale, at Orbost on the Isle of Skye. He wanted to counter the carbon monoxide it took to manufacture his CDs. This was also a direct link with his ancestors, being close to his mother's family home. Overshadowed by the imposing McLeod's Table, Joe's forest also acts as a haven for wildlife and created local jobs. Joe's example as the first CarbonNeutral artist, as the *futureforests.com* website puts it, attracted support for the cause from fellow artists like Pink Floyd, Coldplay, Foo Fighters, David Gray and Massive Attack.

After Joe's death, the project continued to expand and, by September 2003, Future Forests put the tree count at nearly 2,500. There's a special section of the forest called Rebel's Wood, where the public can dedicate a sapling, set up as a permanent memorial to Joe.

Sadly, the following year it would also go by the name of the Joe Strummer Memorial Forest.

CHAPTER TWENTY

THE FUTURE
IS UNWRITTEN

Everywhere Joe went, people would always go, 'Wotcha Joe'. That was the beauty.
He had that marvellous common touch. It was a universal thing very few people
have. That was the marvellous consistency he had. He was prepared to go the
extra mile. – Robin Banks

I remember the day of 23 December, 2002 all too well. It was the day that I found out that Joe Strummer had died. The run-up to Christmas – shopping frenzy, matey piss-ups, kids getting all excited . . . then that terrible announcement on the news. I first saw it when the sound was off on the TV. A photo of Joe, then a clip of 'London Calling'. An immediate feeling of split-second curiosity, then a rapidly growing panic. Why else would Joe be on the national news?

They said that Joe had died of a sudden heart attack, the day before. Words can't explain the dive-bomb sensation in my own heart. Countless memories of the man, both onstage and personal, came flooding back. The trouser incident, being gaffer-taped up for the world premiere of *London Calling*, my teddy boy hair-style, the cry of the wildebeest, the Reverend Joe Sandwich . . . also some of the most devastating live shows I'd ever seen. Me and my girlfriend played 'Bankrobber' and 'White Man' and cried.

This indeed cast a long shadow over Christmas. The worst kind of black cloud. Total loss and grief. I tried to ring Mick, but he'd already gone to Broomfield to comfort Joe's family. I rang Don Letts and Richard Norris on Christmas Day and they were both in shock. At that time, I was yet to be reunited with Topper, Robin Crocker, Johnny Green, Scratchy and the other old Clash mates I would re-encounter while doing this book. Joe's death was one of those things that refused to sink in as cold fact.

It transpired that Joe, who had been preparing for Christmas with Luce and the kids, had taken his dog for a walk in the early afternoon of 22 December. He returned, went in the kitchen, sat down in a chair and passed out. First Luce, then neighbour Michael Carvill, tried to revive him, but when the paramedics arrived, Joe was pronounced dead at the scene.

The following day, the West Somerset Coroner confirmed that Joe had died of sudden cardiac arrest due to artheroma – a weak wall in the coronary artery that could've gone at any time. Part of the reason we were all so shocked was that Joe only ever subscribed to the wild rock 'n' roll lifestyle in small doses. He'd never succumbed to full-blown addictions to any form of drugs or alcohol, although of course he'd had his brushes with everything. He'd never shot up, ravaged his immune system to total

'Strummer was a poet. He moved people in a political way because he was
totally in tune with what was going on in the world' – *Joe Ely*

325

debilitation with cocaine, succumbed to heroin's fateful lure or taken alcoholism to the point of pitiful daily dependency. I kept thinking, 'It should've been me," because I've been guilty of all those crimes against the human body.

'A friend of Lucinda's called me in the afternoon,' recalled Mick. 'I didn't know this person at the time. I didn't know if it was completely true but then I found out it was. It was quite soon after . . . It must've been a couple of hours or so. It was a terrible shock.

'I went down there the next day in the morning, because all the people would be calling. I would know all the people from the Clash part of Joe's life so I went up to take the calls. I had to help with all the calls, which was massive. Joe had many groups of people where he had friends.'

Joe's official website issued a simple statement: 'Joe Strummer died yesterday. Our condolences to Luce and the kids, family and friends.' The online condolence book on the *Strummernews* site immediately got 24,000 entries from around the world.

Mick's statement to the public simply said, 'Our friend and compadre is gone. God bless you, Joe.' He was first to express a musical tribute by releasing an already-written song called 'Sound Of The Joe' online.

The first people that Mick contacted with the tragic news were the remaining Clash members. The day Joe died, Topper was playing a gig with a local blues band at a Dover pub called the Dublin Castle. Johnny Green, who lives up the road in Whitstable, was along for moral support.

'That night had been great,' recalls Johnny. 'Topper was wonderful, playing these old blues numbers. But Mick was ringing and I knew something had gone off the way Topper just threw the phone across the room. I watched him when he was on the phone. His legs buckled into the carpet. I knew it was Mick. Of all the people who could have rang, it was Mick who got through.

'We'd been so euphoric because Topper had played so well. We just sat there for three hours while I fielded all the calls. The phones went berserk. Paul Simonon, Kosmo . . . I managed to stop all the press calls. There was this deep feeling of numbness. Topper had played a great gig and was really pleased with himself and then that. Then the world went mad. Suddenly we were leapfrogged back to the down years.'

'There were all these messages from Mick saying to phone him urgently,' recalls Topper. 'I thought, "I'll phone after the gig." It's a good job I did. Mick just said, "Joe's dead". I just couldn't believe it, I felt terrible.'

Topper, who was still trying to shake the heroin monkey off his back at that time, adds, 'I thought if anyone should've been dead in The Clash, it should've been me. I'd only seen Joe a month earlier at Shepherds Bush Empire. It was such a shock. I can still hardly believe he's gone.'

'Unreal,' continues Johnny. 'I couldn't quite take it on board. Me and Topper looked at each other and said, "It should have been us.' It really should've been me.' The next day, Channel Four sent a film crew to interview Johnny at home. Although he only appeared in the report for a few seconds, the interview formed the basis of John Snow's report.

Robin Banks was at a mate's flat when someone staggered in and announced, 'I just heard on the radio Joe Strummer is dead.' It was a totally nonchalant remark,' recalls Robin. 'I just went down the phone box and phoned Mick and Miranda [Mick's girlfriend] said he'd already gone down to Broomfield to be with Luce. So I phoned Topper. He was in shock. I just couldn't believe it.'

Jock Scott saw it on a newspaper rack. 'I went, "Fuckin' hell."'

Barry Myers was sitting at home and got a call from Simon Stafford. 'It's indescribable to this day. It still doesn't make sense. We're getting on for two years now and everybody just says the same thing – I still really miss him.'

Sitting in a Notting Hill pub with Mick, I found it quite strange and emotional to hear him talking about Joe's death and the last time he saw him. But there is no doubt about the fact that any past differences were long gone. By December 2002, Mick and Joe were mates again.

'I saw him the Friday before he died, actually,' remembers Mick. 'It's funny, because I was in the Groucho Club. I was upstairs and there was some do on downstairs. Keith Allen came up and said, "Did you know Joe's downstairs?" I rushed downstairs and he was totally . . . not crowded or anything, he was just there. There we spent the rest of the evening. We ended up just talking about stuff.'

The duo was joined by actor and comedian Nigel Planer – best known as Neil the hippy from The Young Ones. 'We just had a really nice conversation. We talked about life and stuff. We just had a really nice conversation.'

Johnny's last memory of Joe is from the final Mescaleros tour. 'I walked with Joe in the drizzle on Hastings sea front about three weeks before he died. We walked and talked about the old days . . . My favourite memory is just driving at night, staring at the road, with Joe sat next to me with his arm round me, whispering. When you were talking with Strummer he made you feel like you were the most important person in his life. He could really zero in on you. I saw The Clash quite a lot and I never tired of watching him centre mic. It was always fresh, new and exciting, dynamic every time. I never saw him coast it.'

So why Joe? A man who burned with so much intensity had to live with constant stress. Even though his life and career seemed to be getting happier and more fulfilled as the 21st century got underway, Joe had spent much of the ten years between the demise of The Clash and formation of the Mescaleros depressed and stressed.

He blamed himself for the dissolution of The Clash through firing Topper and Mick, and suffered that guilt until he died. But even then, and as he found his feet again with the Mescaleros, Joe lived life with full-on enthusiasm and passion. He thrived at night, outlasting men half his age, fuelled by red wine and weed. He had fun but was always concerned for those around him. Joe's heart was so huge that it couldn't fail to have been under pressure supporting such an all-embracing life force.

Even though I hadn't seen much of Joe during the nineties, I still felt like I'd lost a great friend. I knew music had lost one of its true maverick geniuses in this everquesting creative dynamo. Also, Joe was a truly good bloke. As the years went on and new generations discovered The Clash, Joe became an articulate, sharp and dryly-humorous expounder of his strong personal theories and philosophies. Ironically, his basic ideology was founded on the original hippy principles of peace, love and understanding. But with Joe it was real and grounded.

Joe truly cared about his fellow human beings, his planet and his music. Adhering to punk's basic ethic of constant change, he'd grown old gracefully and remained true to his principles. Now he could record with Johnny Cash, while forging forward with the Mescaleros. He could go to a rave then organise a three-day camp-fire singalong at Glastonbury, which left such a mark that the organisers would erect a permanent monument at the site in Joe's memory. Meanwhile, his former band found itself eulogised into a legend that transcended any other artists, apart from Elvis, Beatles and the Rolling Stones.

On 30 December, Joe was cremated at a private ceremony at the West London, Crematorium, Harrow Road. This was attended by his family and the surviving members of The Clash, the Mescaleros, as well as friends such as Johnny Green, Robin Banks, Pennie Smith, Barry Myers, Keith Allen, Don Letts, Glen Matlock, Rat Scabies, Jim Jarmusch, Bez, Chrissie Hynde, Patti Palladin and a welter of people just showing their respect like Norman Cook, TV host Mark Lamarr and Bob Morris representing Primal Scream.

Joe Ely, who had kept in touch with Joe over the years, flew in from Texas. He'd managed to grab the last seat on the plane and was sporting a permanent limp from an accident with a wall. Kosmo turned up in a flash late-fifties car – 'A bit ostentatious, I thought,' says Johnny. I was gutted that family commitments and logistical problems prevented my own attending. I sat and played his records and raised several glasses.

In the pouring rain, the cortege passed the Elgin pub, where Joe had kick-started his musical career with the 101'ers. Paul Simonon led the procession with lone piper Alan Wilson playing 'The Minstrel Boy'. The coffin, which was draped with the MacKenzie tartan, was festooned with a Stetson hat and stickers saying, 'Vinyl Rules' and 'Question Authority. Ask Me Anything'.

During the service, Joe's favourites from his own songs were played, including 'White Man', 'From Willesden To Cricklewood' and a new one inspired by his daughter called 'Coma Girl'. Keith Allen read the lyrics Joe had just finished for Bono's Nelson Mandela project, and Joe's cousin Anna Gillies read out 'Hallaig' by Gaelic bard Sorely MacLean.

Everyone filed out to the unlikely strains of Lee Marvin's drunken cowboy musical gem, 'Wand'rin' Star', from *Paint Your Wagon*. Shit, I remember singing this as a party piece on Clash tours but this was the last place I expected it to pop up . . . or maybe not. The words take on a new poignancy in the light of the occasion. 'Do I know where hell is? Hell is in hello/Heaven is goodbye forever, it's time for me to go'. There, indeed, was not a dry eye in the house.

The only embarrassing moment was a pissed Courtney Love turning up late and hurling herself on the coffin. After the service, the wake was held at the Paradise Club in Harrow Road.

"It was like *This Is Your Life*", says Johnny Green. Another of those Clash on-the-road jokes was launching into impersonations of the show's former host, Irishman Eamonn Andrews. 'You thought you came here tonight to meet a friend but we're here for the death of Joe Strummer!' Trying to uphold the spirit of Joe's customary good humour was one way we could deal with our feelings of utter loss.

'I hadn't seen everyone getting on so well for years,' said Johnny. 'It was the most time they'd spent with each other since the days of The Clash. Joe was on particularly fine form.' Like everyone else who knew Joe, the shock and the sadness never goes. 'If anything I miss him *more* now,' said Don Letts a few months later.

Just before he died, Richard Norris sent Joe some music after the two of them discussed working together again. Richard was the first person I rang when I heard that Joe had died and he sounded devastated.

'I missed the funeral and I was really, really gutted,' he said later. 'After he died I just felt awful for a very long time. Apart from my father dying I hadn't had anyone very close to me die and no-one that I've collaborated with on a very close level musically. It really did shake me up for a long time.

'I went down to see Lucinda and planted a load of trees in the garden. It was really weird because, with all the people that I've met through Joe at the festivals and stuff like this, we were all mucking in and shouting, putting the trees together, and you just think . . . the one person that you can just hear going, "Come on, get your finger out!" Joe's most endearing quality would be just spirit. I can still hear him going, "Come on Norro! Let's do it, we've gotta do this!" It was just passionate that would sometimes come out in anger and passionate that would sometimes come out in soul.

'So I came back that night pretty stoned and went to bed, and I just heard him in my head, and he was shouting at me. It woke me up. He was shouting at me really loudly, "Norro, Norro! You must remember Ray Romero! Make sure you remember Ray Romero! It's important!" It was loud enough to get me out of my bed. So I got up and wrote it on the jotter. I didn't know what the fuck he was on about, but he turned out to be some kind of bongo player, which is quite fitting really.

Indeed he was. The fierce Puerto Rican kingpin of the Latin bongo hootenanny was foremost in his field, playing alongside such greats as Tito Puente and Ray Barretto. The Spanish connection coming through again.

'I couldn't speak to anyone when Joe died,' recalls Jock Scott. 'I was the same when Ian Dury died. I was very upset. He was a wonderful friend and, on the day of Joe's funeral, my phone never stopped ringing – people going, "Where's the funeral?" I said, "I've got no fucking idea." I'm not very good at funerals. I don't really care if I'm there. I stayed at home and had a few beers and a few spliffs and played his music. I don't have to crash in there, like Kurt Cobain's wife and throw myself on the coffin. I hate funerals. I know you should grit your teeth, take a valium and show your respects. I don't like going because I don't like seeing all the other people there looking guilty and that fucking carry on. I agree with Francis Bacon – when I die, shove me in a black plastic bag and throw me in the street and let them take me away with all the rubbish.'

Robin Banks commented, 'The main thing I felt was important about Joe was he had this enormous amount of compassion for other people. I thought initially a lot of that was just a pose. I was totally wrong. It wasn't a pose at all. He really related to other people. He cared about people. He cared about the big issues and the small issues. That's the best thing you can say about Joe. His musical taste was so catholic. His attitude to life and to people is reflected in his musical spectrum. He would never dismiss anything. He was open-minded.'

'He made the effort,' adds Jock. 'What you've got to remember and admire about him is with the position he was in. Look at how little Peter Doherty is failing to cope with it at the moment. You've got an idea, you do a band together, you do a few gigs. There's a scene kicking off and you're part of it. I thought Joe handled it very well, to the point where he could still walk the streets. Occasionally a couple of Japanese people might come up and go a bit berserk. He always handled it very well. There was never this sort of Mick Jagger carry on. "We're the Rolling Stones and we're on another level." He made the effort. A lot of them don't bother and that's why they go off into a tailspin.

'Every time I'm in a sort of tepee situation with a bonfire, I always think of Joe. When I see a natural fire on the open air, that's Joe. Guy Fawkes Night, especially.'

'Looking back at that time I spent with Joe, it helped me put a lot of things in perspective,' says Barry Myers. 'I wouldn't trade the time I spent with him in the last year of his life for anything. I do feel his spirit's still there driving a lot of us. He's in here with us and it's down to all of us to keep it going. It's wonderful the way people have come together; friendships are being made across different areas of Joe's life. He's still doing that. It's a case of we've got to work a bit harder now. He didn't want just sycophants around him. He took a lot of people on board with broken wings, but you always felt that he wanted those birds to fly. He believed in those people that he had around him. That was one of his special qualities.'

'If there was an epitaph for Joe it would be, say you were a complete stranger and you never knew him, he would make you feel the most welcome person around his campfire,' declared Roger Goodman. 'He'd find you a pillow and a blanket. That speaks for itself. No matter how out of it he was, I never once saw Joe lose his temper.' He added, 'And if you're going to write anything about Joe, it's got to be funny!'

Mick simply said, 'I cherish the time we had together, rather than regret the time we may have lost.'

Rarely has the passing of a musician been greeted with such an overwhelming outpouring of grief. If it seemed like while no one had a bad word to say about Joe when he was alive – eventually – his death opened the floodgates as tributes and praise flooded in, many from those who'd slagged him off in the past. This acclaim included the remaining members of The Clash, who saw themselves consistently held up as 'the greatest rock 'n' roll band of all time'.

Most of the newspaper and TV tributes came from journalists who'd been writing for, or aspiring to write for, the music papers when The Clash were in their prime. Several had slagged them off. Now Joe was, 'the voice of a generation'.

The Independent put him on the front page with former *NME* scribe and *Loaded* founder James Brown writing, 'Strummer was everything a rebel rock star should really be . . . Strummer had integrity, romance, looked great and was a brilliant sloganeer.' There was also a sensitive tribute from Chris Salewicz, who started writing a biography. *The Sun* called him 'the voice of a generation'. *The Daily Mail* said he shook 'the very foundations of rock music.' *The Times's* David Sinclair wrote, 'He was one of the great English rock stars, bold and influential beyond reckoning.' Andrew Perry of the *Daily Telegraph*, wrote, 'He was a lovely bloke, a man of the people, still angry at the world's injustices, but gentle, humble and heroic to the last.' Veteran Clash critic Gavin Martin, who got to know Joe later in his life, described him as, 'A proud punk rebel with a big, soft heart.' The *Daily Star* cited it the 'saddest death of the year.'

Tony Parsons was now writing for the *Daily Mirror*, and had made up with Joe after bumping into him at a Soho Club earlier that year. It was Tone's anti-Clash jibes that helped drive Joe out of his home at Sebastian Conran's, and he'd ferociously dismissed The Clash in *The Boy Looked At Johnny*. Now he admitted that Joe was, 'a brilliant musician, a beautiful man and a charismatic artist,' and that The Clash, 'changed lives. They certainly changed mine.'

The *NME* – who had initially supported, then slagged The Clash in the seventies – devoted much of their first post-Christmas issue to 'A true rock rebel.' Their initial obituary read: 'To put it simply, Joe Strummer was the political face of punk and in the late-'70s with The Clash produced three classic albums that are still seen – including by the cream of the new rock bands – as the most influential ever made.'

In the late eighties, Joe had accepted that he was destined to remain on page twenty of the paper, but now he was on page one, with eight further pages of news, history and tributes – including the largest one by editor Steve Sutherland, who I first met in the early eighties when he was a cub reporter procuring some Dutch courage in the pub next door to the Lyceum where The Clash were playing.

A touching tribute came from former *NME* writer Stuart Bailie, who'd met Joe on several occasions. 'Joe lived his life like he was in the coolest movie. He always dressed the part, and he held the smartest poses, even when the cameras weren't around. Best of all though, was the way that he spoke. Slow and musical, drawling from the back of his throat like Marlon Brando or maybe Clint Eastwood. His style was certainly coloured by Dylan's mid-60s persona, when words were mangled to wonderfully poetic effect. And behind all those fragments was the freewheeling character of Jack Kerouac . . . Adios Joe, you lived a significant life.'

Meanwhile, the paper sported a plethora of tributes from the stars, including Manic Street Preacher Nicky Wire, Glen Matlock, Pete Shelley of the Buzzcocks, Steve Jones and Bono. Johnny Ramone, a massive influence on Joe, spoke of his respect for The Clash, 'They were unique because, here they are, breaking up at the peak of their popularity, and having plenty of offers to come back and not doing it. While other bands always come back for the money, they had a belief in what they were doing.'

Sadly, Johnny Ramone would die from prostate cancer in September 2004.

Bob Geldof was dragged in as friend and contemporary, deftly managing to place himself in the same league as The Clash, when his old band had always been viewed as opportunist crap and he'd not been slow to put Joe down in the past. However, Sir Bob acknowledged that he had warmed to Joe over the years and admitted that, 'He was a clear contemporary and we were rivals. I believed we had to get inside the pop culture. He believed you should always stay outside and hurl things at it. We had endless arguments about it. As we all got older I realised what a nice person he was.'

Heavy metal bible *Kerrang!* described Joe as 'the greatest punk rocker of them all'. Ben Myers' four-page tribute said, 'Of all the punks, Strummer had aged the least and seemed the least likely to pass away so soon.'

Pennie Smith – whose photographs played a pivotal role in establishing the Clash's unique visual identity – popped up in new magazine *Word,* recalling that Joe was, 'always scribbling or reading, always asking or telling . . . Joe had a lot of living up to do, but to himself, not to any peer group.'

Even the Mayor of London, Ken Livingstone, whose name bore the prefix 'Red' when the Clash were going and he was attempting to defend London from rampant Thatcherism, praised the fact that Joe, 'wasn't afraid to voice his beliefs,' adding, 'Music has lost one of its true rebels.'

In *Uncut,* Joe's old mate Allan Jones wrote a moving tribute, calling his death, 'a temptation to celebrate him as the last of his kind – the rock 'n' roll rebel outlaw, fearless, outspoken, an emblem of rugged hope in a festering world . . . He cared enough to care, said what he thought should be said, and did what he thought should be done. He embraced the not always fashionable notion that music could mean something; make a difference, which it sometimes can . . . He believed.'

I'm glad Allan said this. No amount of mendacious dismissal of 'The Clash Myth' can change the fact that to many people, Joe was a genuine and abiding influence. He changed lives and attitude – even in the latter days by imbuing people who hardly knew him with his indefinable spirit. As Jock puts it, 'That's up there separate from Joe now. I remember all that carry on with Sid – "Sid lives" and all that. But there is the Joe Strummer mentality. Young kids who never had any experience of him feel that.'

And so the tributes kept flooding in. Too many to list here and all variations on a theme. How Joe and The Clash had changed their young lives and the man was an inspiration. Those who'd been fortunate to encounter Joe spoke about the personal qualities that have repeatedly been cited – care, consideration, passion and talent. If it hasn't been said, I want to add humour and mischief. From lyrical asides to buying Batman suits for dogs, he loved to laugh and feel the connecting strength of people having a warm knees-up. It speaks volumes for the man that most of the Strummer/Clash-related events and rendezvous I've encountered while doing this book have been accompanied by broad smiles and gales of laughter.

The tributes showed little sign of abating as 2003 motored on. First, The Clash were presented with the Godlike Genius award at *NME*'s annual prize giving. Mick, Paul and Topper were presented with the trophy by Primal Scream's Bobby Gillespie and model Kate Moss. Twenty-five years earlier, Bobby had been first motivated to start a band after witnessing a Clash gig in Glasgow. 'After that I never had a career plan, it just seems to keep happening,' he said.

Mick first met the teenage Bobby in Glasgow when he'd just had his life changed by seeing The Clash. 'That was the night they hauled Joe in,' remembers Mick. 'We were running back to the hotel through the streets of Glasgow because we were gonna get busted by the police. Bobby was one of the young kids running with us. Joe was held overnight in the cells and all the guys in there were fans of the Clash. They were all singing, "I don't wanna be the prisoner."'

In February, Don Letts' *Westway To The World* documentary was awarded a well-deserved Grammy. 'London Calling' marked a rare exception to a normal Clash rule when it popped up in *Die Another Day*, the new James Bond film. That month, Billy Bragg played some gigs under the 'Strumming For England' banner, in aid of Oxfam and the FBU. Barry 'Scratchy' Myers DJ-ed in New York at some tribute parties, where they showed some footage that Joe had permitted veteran Portobello Road figure Joly to film of the Mescaleros' Brooklyn residency in April 2002. Joly used to run the Better Badges shop in Portobello Road, had a hand in the Fifth Column shop but relocated to the US in the eighties. He'd always kept in touch with Joe and continues to fly the flag via his contributions to the *Strummernews* website.

Even the people of Bridgwater mourned Joe's passing. 'I used to see Joe around the pubs in the High Street,' recalls Kevin Heaphy, a local quantity surveyor who has all the Clash's records and saw them live in 1976. 'He was well liked but people respected his privacy. There were a few tears shed in Bridgwater when Joe died.'

At the Grammy awards ceremony on 6 March, a supergroup consisting of Elvis Costello, Bruce Springsteen, Miami Steve van Zandt and Foo Fighter Dave Grohl played 'London's Calling' in front of a huge blow-up photo of Joe.

On 10 March, The Clash were inducted into the Rock 'n' Roll Hall Of Fame at New York's Waldorf-Astoria hotel, represented by Mick, Paul, Johnny and Kosmo. The award was presented by U2's the Edge and Tom Morello. Mick accepted it, 'on behalf of all the garage bands.' There was no way they could entertain going on with a Joe stand-in so fellow award-winners the Police took their spot instead.

'It was very emotional being in New York for the Hall Of Fame,' Paul later told upmarket lads mag *GQ*. 'It was weird all of us being on that table together and especially because of Joe not being there, and of course after about ten minutes, there's nobody on the table, 'cos we're all in the toilets having a cigarette.'

Topper bottled out at the last minute, despite the efforts of Johnny, who'd organised his birth certificate and passport, got him a ticket and arrived to take him to the airport. 'He just said, "I'm not going,"' recalls Johnny. 'His bag was packed and he was sitting there with his dad. No one was really clear about the whole Clash thing for a long time. Just when Topper was starting to make sense of it all, this [Joe's death] happened. He just said, "That's enough. Joe ain't gonna be there. What's the point of going?" Also, he doesn't like tempting situations where everyone's drinking, and he also doesn't like flying. So he just didn't go.'

According to Robin, a medium in America is convinced that Joe went too – 'She says she saw Joe on stage when Mick collected his award.' The woman contacted Luce to tell her. Well, you wouldn't have expected Joe to miss an occasion like that.

Left: After his untimely death, Joe's family and friends established Strummerville – a charity aimed at providing young musicians with resources and support. Right: Curated by artist Gordon McHarg, the Joe Strummer: Past, Present & Future *exhibition celebrated Joe's life.*

Later the same month, Sony released the forty-one track double CD, *The Essential Clash,* which was followed in May with a similarly titled DVD of the videos, which included the *Hell W10* short. The album was dedicated to Joe and spanned their whole career with the emphasis on the first album and *London Calling.* A nice, reconciliatory gesture was closing the album with 'This Is England'.

On 19 April, Mark Lamarr presented an hour-long Strummer special on Radio One. Shortly after, Richard Dudanski organised a 101'ers reunion in honour of Joe at Notting Hill's Tabernacle. That year's Glastonbury Festival honoured its favourite son on 27 June with a Strummer tribute on the Left Field stage. Don Letts and Dan Donovan DJ-ed as the Dub Cartel and *The Last Night London Burned* – a film of the FBU gig – was shown for the first time. A single stone monument was unveiled on the festival site as a permanent tribute.

During the spring, Luce and some of Joe's mates launched Strummerville – The Joe Strummer Foundation For New Music. Their aim is to, 'provide benefits to individuals, groups and organisations to enable the production of music by creative young people who would otherwise be prevented from doing so simply because they lack the necessary funds. Our aim is to have creative workspaces called Strummerville in key locations around the world.'

When what would have been Joe's 51st birthday came around on 21 August, a special tribute event was held at New York's Knitting Factory club, with proceeds going to the Strummerville foundation. Over in Granada, Richard Dudanski organised a gig in an open museum on top of a hill in the gypsy quarter of Sacramonte. Joe used to trawl the bars and loved the atmosphere. The concert featured three bands connected to local band 091, who Joe had produced, plus 'Los Amigos de Joe Strummer', a loose ensemble including Mick, Tymon, Richard and the Pogues' Jem Finer. They played a set consisting of 101'ers and Clash songs, plus some covers, finishing up with a lengthy rendition of 'Gloria' – just like the 101'ers used to.

Pat Gilbert, one of the writers who caught The Clash's essence and wasn't afraid to trumpet it, covered the event for *Mojo* and said, 'It's a magical occasion, full of pathos, chaos and passionate rock 'n' roll. But, as the party under the stars winds up at dawn, the abiding sense is a kind of disbelief that we are all here in the first place. Joe Strummer not with us any more? The whole thing seems unreal.'

In October, *GQ* gave The Clash the Outstanding Achievement award in their Men Of The Year honours (previous winners include Bowie, McCartney and Michael Caine). Chosen by the readers, they were honoured simply for being 'the greatest rock band ever.' The accompanying feature depicted Mick and Paul as unlikely models for some highly expensive clobber by the likes of Prada, Gucci and Crombie. A far cry from applying a coat of emulsion to an Oxfam shop shirt!

Dylan Jones, who described Joe as, 'a manic, pompadoured troubadour with sloganeering Tourettes' asked Mick and Paul why The Clash's time had come right now?

'I think in a way the story wrote itself and it went right through to the end when Joe went,' said Mick. 'We were thinking of maybe playing the Rock 'n' Roll Hall Of Fame but it wasn't to be, and in the end it probably was right. There was a big carrot dangling there, and the lira was interesting, but . . .'

'But maybe also with Joe leaving us, in that sense that says that's it,' surmised Paul.

'That's it, the end of it', said Mick.

In January 2003, Luce gave her blessing to Martin Slattery and Scott Shields to finish off the album they'd started with Joe in the month before his death. The duo utilised Joe's detailed notes about how he wanted the songs to sound and simply finished them up, rather than make any major changes. The vocals were used as outlines that the completed songs were constructed around.

Joe's final album, Streetcore, *was released to widespread critical acclaim in October 2003.*

After having its originally scheduled release date put back from May, *Streetcore* was released in October. The album emerged as the strongest, most bittersweet epitaph Joe could've wished for. He would have been proud of the way Martin and Scott took the songs they'd been working on and, with the utmost sensitivity and respect, brought them home. With Lucinda's blessing and presence, the love for Joe shines through everything from the cover, strewn with his notes and musings, to the last aching note of the closing 'Silver And Gold'.

Streetcore's cover notes read, 'Deepest love to Lucinda, thanks for keeping Joe's faith in us. Joe . . . we miss you!' Luce herself lists a wide variety of friends and people who helped, including Joe's close friend Dave 'Pockets' Girvan, Johnny Green, Mick and Damien Hirst. 'And finally I would like to thank Joe who gave, showed and taught me everything I love and value today.'

'Coma Girl' appeared as a pre-album trailer on 6 October. It also opens the album. Joe sounds full of life and energy as he sings about a festival, which, with its mentions of moving through the stages and, 'Somebody was wailing off their head', had to be Glastonbury.

Jean Encoule of punk website *Trakmarx* gave the album a beautifully spot-on write-up and called 'Coma Girl', 'the most complete and affecting single to bear Joe's name since "Trash City". A stomping, mid-paced, archetypal stonker that encapsulates everything perfect, poetic and poignant about the Mescaleros evolution . . . Gone are the folky world music inflections of *Global A Go-Go* – this is punk rock 'n' roll via '(White Man) In Hammersmith Palais' – and all the more sturdy for it . . . surely he's never sounded as full of confidence, commitment and self-belief?'

'Get Down Moses' again hinges on a reggae undertow, but is hard-edged and assured. Just how good and sympathetic to Joe's approach the Mescaleros were becoming is evident here. They sounded like a band, instead of Joe plus mates and backing musicians. The words see Joe urging modern society to shape up. 'We gotta use this time before the next earthquake.'

'Long Shadow' was the second song that Joe wrote for Johnny Cash, who had died on 12 September 2003. This was another tremendous loss, which seemed to bear some kind of spiritual connection with Joe's passing as the pair had only come together in what turned out to be their last months on Earth.

Joe had much in common with Johnny Cash, apart from the fact that he was one of the few artists to whom Strummer submitted songs. Johnny was a true rebel and man of the people – championing causes, occasionally raising political hell by making his feelings known about war and the plight of Native Americans and becoming a Glastonbury hero after his mighty solo performance there in 1994. Johnny Cash spoke from the heart and was a timeless hero to many.

As he did with Johnny Cash, Rick Rubin projected Joe's vocals against the barest setting to bring home the depth and resonance of his lyrics and delivery. Just Joe and the acoustic guitar of LA musician Smokey Hornel.

'Long Shadow' comes on like Woody Guthrie or early Dylan, with Joe sounding upfront and commanding like he'd never been heard before. This undeniable tearjerker is indicative of Joe coming to terms to himself and his past. In light of his death, you could even read them as his last words to the world. 'You cast a long shadow/And that is your testament. 'He signs off, 'And somewhere in my soul, there's always rock and roll', and lets out a valedictory 'Yeah!' in case there's any doubts.

'Arms Aloft' unveils a snarlingly bombastic chorus that recalls the Beatles via Liam Gallagher. It still manages to leap from raucous rock 'n' roll to moments of softer sensitivity with the nudge of a black Telecaster. Joe's title utilises a phrase often used in rave culture to describe those hands-in-the-air moments of communal ecstasy, even if it's an ode to his favourite gig situations. 'Let a million mirror balls beam,' while, 'The spirit is our gasoline.' Aberdeen Football Club later installed the song as their new anthem. 'Punk Great Is Pitch Perfect' trumpeted a *Daily Record* headline.

The full band ballad 'Ramshackle Day Parade' is another highlight. It opens with beautifully melancholy keyboards and glides into a heavily overdubbed chorus. Here's some proof of how tuned into the Strummer sensibility Slattery and Shields were as this was obviously grafted on later and perfectly compliment's Joe's impassioned vocal.

'Redemption Song' comes next. This was the Bob Marley song that made me cry when *he* died and the last song of the set he played at Crystal Palace Bowl in July 1980. Joe delivers another spiritual connection with just an acoustic guitar for company. His voice drops from its usual soulful howl or manic bark to a rich, upfront delivery that brims with optimism and assurance. The self-confidence that was eroded when Bernie destroyed The Clash is back, strengthened by a new maturity which, would've augured so well for things to come. On the cover Joe dedicates the song to Captain Beefheart.

The song was released as a posthumous single on 15 December. At the New York video shoot a month before, a large graffiti wall mural had been dedicated to Joe's memory.

'Hey, hey, hey, it's the acid test/Got a busy day, I'm wearing a vest', declares Joe as a smile-inducing intro to 'All In A Day'. Another chunky, electric riff-rocker that drives home the difference between this album and its mellower predecessor. The energy level borders on the demented but the bridge makes you sit bolt upright as the song evokes late period Clash.

'Burning Streets' is a cinematic mid-tempo excursion that provides further evidence of the no-holds-barred acrobatic approach Joe was taking to his vocals. He's pouring the lot into this and you can imagine the veins standing out on his neck. 'Musically as expansive as the Mescaleros have gotten yet,' wrote Jean Encoule.

'Now we'd like to let rip, on a whole different tip', announces Joe with over the BBC World Service's 'London calling' clarion call. This introduces 'Midnight Jam', a smoky instrumental that evokes the spirit of *Sandinista!* – in that expands, explores and sets up an intoxicating foray into mood music.

'Silver & Gold' is Joe's last song on his last album. It's one of the few realisations of Joe's interest in New Orleans music.

Cheers! Joe Strummer 1952-2002.

It's saying something that, of all the tracks on *Streetcore*, it's the one to bring a tear to the eye. Joe begs forgiveness for the things he's done that, 'I know is wrong.' It finishes up, 'I'm gonna see all the city lights, and do everything silver and gold/I got to hurry up before I grow too old.'

Jean summed it up neatly when he wrote, 'Joe Strummer has left the building and the Mescaleros have no option but to follow – and that's a crying shame. I hope all you subsequent generations have someone equal to Joe Strummer to call your own . . . Someone who will fuck it all up and live through it to earn your forgiveness. Someone who will turn left when everyone else is turning right.'

Reviewing *Streetcore*, *Rolling Stone*'s Milo Miles wrote, 'Because his restless, barbed self will never be back to shake us awake, it's almost more fun to hear Strummer spill his subconscious in numbers such as 'Ramshackle Day Parade' (Marilyn Manson meets William Burroughs meets U-Roy) than to partake in the sturdy romance-adventure yarn 'Coma Girl'.' He adds that the ballads, like 'Silver And Gold' and 'Long Shadow' 'give you an honest-to-goodness pang.'

When *Uncut*'s Sean Egan asked Joe shortly before his death when it struck him that he'd recorded something 'so timeless and enduring' with the first Clash album, he was typically effacing. 'I'm still waiting for that feeling. You stand inside your own work and it's not easy to see it from outside. You've got to be harsh in judging your own work in order to avoid becoming soft.

'Smug self-satisfaction, that's not a thing to wallow in if you're active. Maybe that's kind of rocking chair stuff, but I'm always banging. There's been some brilliant rock 'n' roll records made in the past fifty years. You've got to try and top them.'

With *Streetcore*, Joe showed that he could still comfortably jostle with those great records and make his own mark again. It's the best epitaph of all because it's Joe doing his music and was planned as a start, rather than a swansong. From a purely selfish viewpoint, I wonder what kind of diamond would've followed this one?

Joe Strummer died when he was experiencing a rare level of personal happiness, respect from his peers, and was gripped by an unstoppable creative surge. In doing so, he could close the book on The Clash. In 1981, Joe scrawled 'The Future Is Unwritten' in one of his many notebooks. It took him another twenty years to open a new volume. Myth had given way to real life, which was cruelly taken away.

There's an indefinable but contagious spirit flying around right now, which seems to make the many people who knew Joe feel galvanised and all the better for being touched by him at some point. This is being passed on to those who are only just getting to know him now. There had never been and never will be another group like The Clash, and Joe was a beautiful one-off.

I'm just glad I experienced a pinch of this magic and hope I've passed some of it on. How I miss the man with the gaffer tape and the massive heart – but, as Johnny Green said, what a life!

EPILOGUE

Now that's over, sit down - whether it be in your Spliff Bunker or by your camp-fire - open a bottle, and stick on your chosen soundtrack. I hope this book said something about a man called Joe and a group called The Clash.

Joe Strummer casts a long shadow that seems to get longer every day. The same goes for The Clash. In 2004, while I was writing all this, not a week seemed to go by without some kind of media appearance, event or personal reunion occurring. On 3 July, I celebrated my 50th birthday by going to see Mick's new band Carbon/Silicon in London - a week after he'd celebrated his 49th. Here I found myself DJ-ing for half an hour before they went on. Then a week later Michelle turned thirty so we had a joint party in a Shoreditch hostelry called SMERSH. We liked this bar so, when it came around to Joe's birthday on 20 August, held a party to raise a few glasses in his direction while me and Richard Norris played Strummer-related music all night. 'Here's to Joe, we know you're here!' toasted Jock.

A major event was the *Joe Strummer - Past, Present And Future* exhibition. Under the Strummerville banner, it was held at the London Print Studio between 4-18 September – marking the 30th anniversary of the first Charlie Pigdog club night at the Chippenham.

On show was a fascinating collection of scribblings, drawings, lyrics and set lists, which had been sorted out from Joe's huge stash of plastic bags and boxes by the redoubtable Pockets. There were also some arresting photos, including some from former 101'er Jules Yewdall, who was one of the organisers along with Joe's artist mate Gordon McHarg. Both still live in the area where Joe squatted during the seventies and are members of the Walterton and Elgin Community Homes organisation.

'Joe kept everything,' Gordon told *The Independent*. 'His archiving was unbelievable. He was constantly note taking, although he didn't always have a notebook but wrote on whatever he could find. But no one has seen any of this stuff.' He reveals that Joe snipped out every bit of press he got during 1975-1977 and put it in a scrapbook.

'It will bring the spirit of Joe Strummer into the present and back to the area that meant so much to him,' said Debs Bourner, community services manager at WECH. 'This tribute is coming from the residents, who wanted to do something that had more longevity and impact than just a blue plaque on a wall,' she told *The Guardian*. She added that she's been trying to get the words 'Joe Strummer Was Here' built into the brickwork on the site of the old 101 Walterton Road squat.

At the exhibition launch party I saw people I hadn't seen since the Clash days. Travelling to the junket with Simon Trakmarx and Michelle, we picked up Rat Scabies. The Clash/Damned punk wars were a thing of the past as he spoke warmly about Joe. On arrival, I walked straight into former Basement 5/BAD bass player Leo Williams, who now works with Mick. I spotted Roger Goodman standing outside the door, then caught sight of a familiar figure fluttering like a moth behind a puzzled spectator – it was the first time I'd seen Johnny Green for over twenty years.

Mick turned up and didn't lose the massive grin on his face all evening. Robin Banks pointed out the cute Japanese fan letters. Richard Norris was taken by the

The iconic Joe from the cover of his 1989 album, Earthquake Weather.

circle of Joe's old typewriters set around the mock campfire. Other old faces included Barry Myers, Chris Salewicz, Annie Nightingale and Keith Allen. The atmosphere was warm, touching and inspiring. Joe's favourite rum punch was dynamite!

I spoke to Topper the day before the party and he wasn't planning to go, despite Johnny's offer of a lift. 'I just don't need it at the moment,' he reasoned. 'It's too close to home. I don't want to be reminded because I still miss Joe.'

The following month, Mick and Paul appeared on BBC2's *Later . . . With Jools Holland* to promote the *London Calling* reissue. Memorably, the host asked the duo if there was there was any chance of a 'Clash reformation'. 'Not completely,' replied Paul. 'We might do a duet,' suggested Mick.

Joe's name has recently popped up in the most unlikely places – like the BBC's *Restoration* series in July 2004. The show was a kind of architectural beauty contest, where viewers got to vote for the building that they felt was most deserving of restoration funds. The Strummerville charity had acquired and wanted to do up Castle House in Bridgwater – the first totally concrete structure in the UK. Strummerville plan to convert it into a music centre for disadvantaged kids, but years of neglect and vandalism mean a hefty cash injection is required.

The building made runner-up in the South-West heat of the final. To celebrate, Strummerville held a street party outside Castle House, which the BBC filmed for the programme. There was Mick playing 'Rock The Casbah' with Badly Drawn Boy and friends. Afterwards, a group of revellers retired to Yalway and the party continued until the next day.

From a personal perspective, this sense of reunion has grown to delightful proportions during the course of writing this book. It was great to talk to Topper again. He's been clean since early this year and is working hard to stay that way, going to Alcoholics Anonymous meetings and playing with a local blues band. We've even talked about making some music together.

'People say, "I bet you find living in Dover boring after The Clash," but it's nice and safe,' he says. 'It might be dull and boring, but it's for me. When I go to meetings I'm forty-nine and I'm always the oldest one in the room. Not many of those fuckers make it to forty-nine.'

Then, of course, there's Mick, whose presence always hovered over this project. He was the member of The Clash that I first got close to, hung out with for seven years and then kept in touch with after his sacking. Our respective commitments meant that we didn't see each other so much as time went on. For much of 2004, Mick was wrapped up in producing the second Libertines album. When he wasn't doing that, he had Carbon/Silicon gigs, Queens Park Rangers games and the small matter of a newborn baby called Eva – his second with girlfriend Miranda.

Finally, with the help of the gnu-like Banksy, we arranged a time and a place to meet up. One-thirty in the Prince Albert on Notting Hill Gate. Johnny laughed when I told him, recalling Mick's notorious lateness in The Clash. But on the dot of one-thirty, in walked Mick.

On the train up from Aylesbury, I remembered all the times with Mick from

1976 round at Wilmcote House, through the historic recording sessions and unforgettable scenes on all the Clash tours, then the mad fun of Big Audio Dynamite. I also recalled all the things he'd done to help me in the past, from producing and playing on my group's single, to paying for me to see my son in New York. It was indeed lovely to see him in a relaxed situation. As the conversation progressed, he loosened up and reminded me of the fresh-faced rocker I'd first interviewed twenty-eight years earlier. When Robin turned up the mood got even lighter and talk turned to wildebeests, for some reason.

'First thing you've got to know, Kris, is I don't remember a thing!' was Mick's opening gambit. Like everyone else from that time, Mick's specific memories of the Clash days are vague. It all happened so fast and the only person who turned out to be taking notes was Joe, although luckily Robin and I had recorded much of it for *Zigzag*. A mention of the Night Of The Sandwich draws a laugh from Mick, 'I vaguely remember some kind of ritual.'

Mick remembers the Mott The Hoople days with affection. When I mention that we probably first encountered each other at a London College of Printing gig in 1973, Robin says that he was a student there after getting thrown out of school. Mick says that his daughter Lauren, who would now be around twenty, goes there now.

It's touching to see Mick and Robin acting the goat together, jostling, cackling and remembering dodgy teachers like a pair of reprobates. In that respect, they're still forever two mischievous kids who live for music. Remember, this pair became mates after fighting over who was best, Chuck Berry or Bo Diddley.

'Mick seems at peace with himself these days,' says Topper. I agree. It's the most chilled I've seen him. Mick grew up addicted to music and media. It took him a while to appreciate the fact that he was now bigger than a lot of his idols. If you tell him that The Clash have more of a legend than his beloved Mott, he'll still look in disbelief. But I think it's finally sunk in.

He is happy that he was good friends with Joe in the years before his death, but admits that it took him years to get over being kicked out of The Clash. Mick is a survivor. As Johnny says, 'tough as old boots that Jonesy.' 2004 was a particularly good year for Mick – not only because of the acclaim given to *London Calling* and the maiden voyages of Carbon/Silicon, but because he found his name on the cover of a number one album with the hottest band to come out of London in years. *The Libertines* was the most talked about record of the year, shot to number one and earned Mick *Q* magazine's Producer of the Year award. Apart from being fresh, raw and unnervingly melodic, the inter-band tensions and drug problems have prodded many to compare them to The Clash.

When I asked him about The Libertines, Mick explained, 'These days there isn't much that excites my heart. The excitable spark that you get when you see a band like that. The rest don't have that. It's something that you can't really put your finger on but they have that.'

With Clash and Libs duties out of the way, Mick now wants to concentrate on Carbon/Silicon, who blew my head off when I caught them at Milton Keynes on their first tour in June 2004. I must have been gibbering in a similar fashion to that first time I saw The Clash up the road in Leighton Buzzard in October 1976. But they were a totally exciting experience. Another old mate was there – I hadn't seen Tony James since the mid-eighties when he led Sigue Sigue Sputnik. Now he was finally sharing a stage with Mick – thirty years after the London SS.

Opening with a song called 'Why Do Men Fight?', the group tore through a brazen stew of Mick's inimitably melodic songs, bluesy funk and a startling injection of dance grooves, which are thrown in from a laptop computer. At one point, Underworld's 'Born Slippy' came pounding out of the speakers. It was like a non-stop party. Afterwards I told Mick that the way in which the band's groove never stopped reminded me of Ike Turner's Kings of Rhythm at some futuristic juke joint. As the rhythm continued to sink its teeth into the floor, the sonic scenery never stopped changing.

The encore was a bit of a moment. 'This one's for Joe Strummer,' announced Mick. 'I know he's here somewhere.' Then it was straight into the simple but deadly stop-start riff of 'Spoonful', the Howlin' Wolf blues classic made famous by Eric Clapton's Cream in the late sixties. 'It was the first song I ever learnt – it's so easy! Robin showed me that.'

'Come and see us, we're getting better now,' says Mick three months later. 'We're still developing really. We're going to play a few more dates while we figure it out.'

Mick said he wants to tone down the dance-samples and emphasise the human element.

'We're gonna do that but it's more real now - more emotional impact. Before we were playing along with the loops and now we're playing with each other, more songs than the extra stuff. It's more like playing together like a real band now than it was. So it's good in a way that we haven't gone totally public. We're just gonna build it up slowly while we work it out. If we get these things right it's gonna be really good. It's good anyway but it'll be *really* good then.

'It's funny, because when I was talking earlier about how we were doing dance music and mixing it with rock . . . no one has done it. BAD did it to a certain extent, but no one's really cracked the code. I feel we might just crack the code this time, if we hold our nerve. It'll be like dance music but it'll be played by real people, forefronting the human element.'

The fact that he's still aspiring to some goal could sum the man up. Having defined punk rock with The Clash and set the benchmark for white dance music experiments, Mick still reckons he's on a quest to do the same thing he was managing quite awesomely a quarter of a century earlier.

After that highly enjoyable couple of hours, Robin and I bowled over to the West End to try and seek out Johnny Green at an *Exile On Main Street* photo exhibition. Guffawing like water buffalos and agreeing that it felt like 1977 was only last week.

It's taken me a whole book to say what I feel about Joe Strummer and The Clash. But I had to do it. It was the only way I could let out the curious mix of loss and celebration that lodges in the place where Joe Strummer always hit you – the heart. Some of the best times of my life were spent with this man and the group he was in. Between 1976 and 1983, The Clash were like a family, with Joe at the head of the household. The Clash were my life. But then you've probably realised that by now.

Never in my wildest dreams could I have imagined what would happen to the three young men I sat with in that dingy Camden Town boozer nearly thirty years ago. Or that the bloke under the table tugging my trouser leg wouldn't be with us anymore. While writing this, I felt the tears welling up several times as a particularly striking memory pops out of the mental toaster. Other times I laughed my antlers off. Now I'm wrapping up I feel a curious sense of elation that all this happened. Sometimes it felt like Joe was doing a Ray Romero routine, shouting, 'Come on Needsy!'

I still get the same rush of euphoria and shooting tingles down the spine when I watch old footage of The Clash. I get the same feeling listening to 'Long Shadow'. Of course, Joe had his faults and fucked up, but I didn't come here to try and taint his memory with grimy revelations, debunking of myths and cheap shots. I've tried to tell it how it was. So I'm here to shout 'Viva Strummer!' and 'Up The Clash!' in the loudest voice I can muster, and bollocks to the rest.

Johnny Green ushered me in and now he's going to usher me out, with something he said when representing Joe in *Clash* magazine's special on the group in September. Asked why there has never been another band like The Clash, he said, 'Because they never gave short change and they never cut corners. They went for everything full tilt openly and honestly and they meant what they said.'

This is for Joe so we'll go out on a high and leave the last word to the man himself in 2002. 'Punk was an attitude, not a music or a fashion. If I see a situation I'll fucking cut right to the heart of it. That's a punk attitude and I've got it inbred.'

Just as I was winding up this book, I heard that John Peel had died of a heart attack while on holiday in Peru.

'Uncle John' wasn't just the only Radio One DJ who'd play The Clash's records during their early days. His shows, initially on the pirate Radio London, then Radio One, were avidly consumed by Joe, Mick, myself and millions of others who grew up listening to the great man. He was still flying the flag for new and obscure musical delights at the time of his death.

I got to know John when his late producer John Walters contributed a regular column to *Zigzag*. Peely was always accommodating and tremendous company. He loved The Clash, even if they did mess up their one and only Peel Session. '(White Man) In Hammersmith Palais' figured at Number 5 in his all-time Festive Fifty.

John even played the Vice Creems single – followed by the quip, 'I wouldn't give up the typewriter just yet, Kris!'

He'll be missed immeasurably.

Kris Needs, October 2004

SELECTED DISCOGRAPHY

The 101'ers

Singles
Keys To Your Heart/Five Star Rock 'n' Roll Petrol [Chiswick, 1976]
Sweet Revenge/Rabies (From The Dogs Of Love) [Chiswick, 1981]

Albums
Elgin Avenue Breakdown [Andalucia, 1981]
Letsgetabitrockin'/Silent Telephone/Monkey Business/Shake Your Hips/Junco Partner/Don't Let Go/Motor Boys Motor/Sweety of the St Moritz/Surf City/Keys To Your Heart/Sweet Revenge/Gloria

The Clash

UK Singles [All released on CBS]
White Riot/1977 [7", 18 Mar 1977]
Remote Control/London's Burning (Live) [7", 13 May 1977]
Complete Control/City of the Dead [7", 23 Sept 1977]
Clash City Rockers/Jail Guitar Doors [7", 17 Feb 1978]
(White Man) In Hammersmith Palais/The Prisoner [7", 16 June 1978]
Tommy Gun/1-2 Crush On You [7", 24 Nov 1978]
English Civil War/Pressure Drop [7", 23 Feb 1979]
The Cost Of Living EP
I Fought The Law/Groovy Times/Gates of The West/Capital Radio [7", 5 May 1979]
London Calling/Armagideon Time [7" 7 Dec 1979]
London Calling/Armagideon Time/Justice Tonight/Kick It Over [12", 11 Jan 1980]
Bankrobber/Rockers Galore...UK Tour [7", 8 Aug 1980]
The Call Up/Stop The World [7", 28 Nov 1980]
Hitsville UK/Radio One [7", 16 Jan 1981]
The Magnificent Seven/The Magnificent Dance [7", 10 Apr 1981]
The Magnificent Seven/The Magnificent Dance [12", 24 Apr 1981]
This Is Radio Clash/Radio Clash [7", 20 Nov 1981]
This Is Radio Clash/Radio Clash/Radio

5/Radio 6 [12", 4 Dec 1981]
Know Your Rights/First Night Back In London [7", 23 Apr 1982]
Rock The Casbah/Long Time Jerk [7", 11 Jun 1982]
Rock The Casbah/Mustapha Dance [12", 18 Jun 1982]
Should I Stay Or Should I Go/Straight To Hell [7" 17 Sept 1982]
Should I Stay Or Should I Go/Straight To Hell [12" 17 Sept 1982]
This Is England/Do It Now [7" 30 Sept 1985]
This Is England/Do It Now/Sex Mad Roar [12" 30 Sept 1985]

US Singles [All released on Epic]
I Fought The Law/[White Man] In Hammersmith Palais [7", Jul 1979]
Hitsville UK/Police On My Back [7", Feb 1981]
The Magnificent Dance/The Magnificent Seven/The Cool Out/The Call Up [12", Mar 1981]
This Is Radio Clash/Radio Clash/Outside Broadcast/Radio 5 [12", Nov 1981]
Should I Stay Or Should I Go/Inoculated City [7", Jun 1982]
Should I Stay Or Should I Go/Cool Confusion [7", Jun 1982]
Should I Stay Or Should I Go/First Night Back In London [7", Jul 1982]
Rock the Casbah/Long Time Jerk [7", Oct 1982]
Rock The Casbah/Mustapha Dance [12", October 1982]
This Is England/Do It Now [7", Nov 1985]

Other Singles
Capital Radio/Listen/Tony Parsons Interview [NME 7", 8 Apr 1977]
Rudie Can't Fail/Bankrobber/Rockers Galore...UK Tour [CBS NL 7", Jun 1980]
Train In Vain/Bankrobber/Rockers Galore...UK Tour [CBS NL 12", Jun 1980]

UK Albums
The Clash [CBS, 8 Apr 1977]
Janie Jones/Remote Control/I'm So Bored With The USA/White Riot/Hate & War; What's My Name/Deny; London's Burning/Career

Opportunities/Cheat/
Protex Blue; Police & Thieves/48
Hours/Garageland.

Give 'Em Enough Rope [CBS, 10 Nov
1978]
*Safe European Home/English Civil
War/Tommy Gun/Julie's Been Working For
The Drug Squad/Last Gang In Town/Guns
On The Roof/Drug Stabbing Time/Stay
Free/Cheapskates/All The Young Punks (New
Boots And Contracts)*

London Calling [CBS, 14 Dec 1979]
*London Calling/Brand New Cadillac/
Jimmy Jazz/Hateful/Rudie Can't Fail/
Spanish Bombs/The Right Profile/Lost In The
Supermarket/Clampdown/The Guns Of
Brixton/Wrong 'Em Boyo/ Death Or
Glory/Koka Kola/The Card Cheat/Lovers
Rock; Four Horsemen/I'm Not Down/
Revolution Rock/Train In Vain*

Sandinista! [CBS, 12 Dec 1980]
*The Magnificent Seven/Hitsville UK/
Junco Partner/Ivan Meets GI Joe/The
Leader/Something About England/Rebel
Waltz/Look Here/The Crooked Beat/
Somebody Got Murdered/One More Time (+
Dub)/Lightning Strikes (Not Once But
Twice)/Up In Heaven (Not Only
Here)/Corner Soul/Let's Go Crazy/If Music
Could Talk/The Sound Of The Sinners/Police
On My Back/Midnight Log/The
Equaliser/The Call Up/
Washington Bullets/Lose This Skin/
Charlie Don't Surf/Mensforth Hill/Junkie
Slip/Kingston Advice/The Street Parade/
Version City/Living In Fame/Silicone On
Sapphire/Version Pardner/Career
Opportunities/Shepherds Delight*

Combat Rock [CBS, 14 May 1982]
*Know Your Rights/Car Jamming/Should I
Stay Or Should I Go/Rock The Casbah/
Red Angel Dragnet/Straight To Hell/
Overpowered By Funk/Atom Tan/Sean
Flynn/Ghetto Defendant/Inoculated City/
Death Is A Star*

Cut The Crap [CBS, 12 Nov 1985]
*Dictator/Dirty Punk/We Are The Clash/
Are You Red...y/Cool Under Heat/Movers And*

Shakers/This Is England/Three Card
Trick/Play To Win/Fingerpoppin'/North And
South/Life Is Wild

From Here To Eternity [Live album;
Columbia, 4 Oct 1999]
*Complete Control/London's Burning/
What's My Name/Clash City Rockers/
Career Opportunities/(White Man) In
Hammersmith Palais/Capital Radio/City of
the Dead/I Fought The Law/London
Calling/Armagideon Time/Train In Vain/
The Guns of Brixton/The Magnificent
Seven/Know Your Rights/Should I Stay Or
Should I Go/Straight To Hell*

US Albums
Give 'Em Enough Rope [Epic, Nov 1978]
As UK edition

The Clash [Epic, June 1979]
*Clash City Rockers/I'm So Bored With The
USA/Remote Control/Complete Control/White
Riot/(White Man) In Hammersmith
Palais/London's Burning/I Fought The
Law/Janie Jones/Career Opportunities/What's
My Name/Hate & War/Police & Thieves/Jail
Guitar Doors/Garageland*
Initial copies came with a free 7" single;
Gates To The West/Groovy Times

London Calling [Epic, Jan 1980]
As UK edition

Black Market Clash [Epic 10", Nov 1980]
*Capital Radio One/The Prisoner/
Pressure Drop/Cheat/City Of The Dead/Time
Is Tight/Bankrobber/Robber Dub/Armagideon
Time/Justice Tonight/Kick it Over*

Sandinista! [Epic, Jan 1981]
As UK edition

Combat Rock [Epic, May 1982]
As UK edition

Cut The Crap [Epic, Nov 1985]
As UK edition

From Here To Eternity [Live album;
Columbia, Oct 1999]
As UK edition

Compilations and Reissues

The Story of The Clash Volume One
[Columbia UK, Mar 1988]
*The Magnificent Seven/Rock The
Casbah/Should I Stay Or Should I Go/
Straight To Hell/Armagideon Time/
Clampdown/Train in Vain/Guns Of Brixton/I
Fought The Law/Somebody Got
Murdered/Lost In The Supermarket/
Bankrobber/(White Man) In Hammersmith
Palais/London's Burning/Janie Jones/Tommy
Gun/Complete Control/Capital Radio/White
Riot/Career Opportunities/Clash City
Rockers/Safe European Home/Stay
Free/London Calling/Spanish Bombs/English
Civil War/Police & Thieves*

The Singles Collection [Columbia UK,
Nov 1991]
*White Riot/Remote Control/Complete
Control/Clash City Rockers/(White Man) In
Hammersmith Palais/Tommy Gun/English
Civil War/I Fought The Law/London
Calling/Train In Vain/Bankrobber/The Call
Up/Hitsville UK/The Maginificent Seven/This
Is Radio Clash/Know Your Rights/Rock The
Casbah/Should I Stay Or Should I Go*

The Clash On Broadway [Columbia UK,
Nov 1991]
*Janie Jones [demo]/Career Opportunities
[demo]/White Riot/1977/I'm So Bored/ With
The USA/Hate & War/What's My
Name/Deny/London's Burning/Protex
Blue/Police & Thieves/48 Hours/Cheat/
Garageland/Capital Radio One/Complete
Control/Clash City Rockers/City of The
Dead/Jail Guitar Doors/The Prisoner/(White
Man) In Hammersmith Palais/Pressure
Drop/1-2 Crush on You/English Civil War
[live]/I Fought The Law [live]/Safe European
Home/Tommy Gun/Julie's Been Working For
The Drug Squad/Stay Free/One Emotion/
Groovy Times/Gates Of The West/Armagideon
Time/London Calling/Brand New
Cadillac/Rudie Can't Fail/The Guns Of
Brixton/Spanish Bombs/Lost in The
Supermarket/The Right Profile/The Card
Cheat/Death Or Glory/Clampdown/Train In
Vain/Bankrobber/Police On My Back/The
Magnificent Seven/The Leader/The Call
Up/Somebody Got Murdered/Washington
Bullets/Broadway/Lightning Strikes [Not Once*

*But Twice]/Every Little Bit Hurts; Stop The
World/Midnight To Stevens/This Is Radio
Clash/Cool Confusion/Red Angel
Dragnet/Ghetto Defendant/Rock The
Casbah/Should I Stay Or Should I
Go/Straight To Hell/Street Parade*

Super Black Market Clash [Columbia, Nov
1993]
*1977/Protex Blue/Deny/Cheat/48
Hours/Listen/Jail Guitar Doors/The City Of
The Dead/The Prisoner/Pressure Drop/1-2
Crush On You/Groovy Times/Gates Of The
West/Capital Radio Two/Time Is Tight/Justice
Tonight/Kick it Over/Bankrobber/Robber
Dub/Stop The World/The Cool Out/First
Night Back In London/Long Time Jerk/Cool
Confusion/The Magnificent Seven/This Is
Radio Clash/Mustapha Dance*

The Essential Clash [Columbia, Mar 2003]
*White Riot/1977/London's Burning/Complete
Control/Clash City Rockers/I'm So Bored With
The USA/Career Opportunities/Hate &
War/Cheat/Police & Thieves/Janie
Jones/Garageland/Capital Radio One/(White
Man) In Hammersmith Palais/English Civil
War/Tommy Gun/Safe European Home/Julie's
Been Working For The Drug Squad/Stay
Free/Groovy Times/I Fought The Law/
London Calling/Guns Of Brixton/
Clampdown/Rudie Can't Fail/Lost In The
Supermarket/Jimmy Jazz/Train In Vain/
Bankrobber/Magnificent Seven/Ivan Meets GI
Joe/Stop The World/Somebody Got
Murdered/The Street Parade/Broadway/Radio
Clash/Ghetto Defendant/Rock The
Casbah/Straight To Hell/Should I Stay Or
Should I Go/This Is England*

London Calling 25th Anniversary Edition
[Columbia, Sept 2004]
3 Disc Set:
Disc 1: as original album
Disc 2: *The Vanilla Tapes*
*Hateful/Rudie Can't Fail/Paul's Tune/I'm Not
Down/Four Horsemen/Koka Kola, Advertising
& Cocaine/Death Or Glory/Lover's
Rock/Lonesome Me/The Police Walked In 4
Jazz/Lost In The Supermarket/Up-
Toon/Walking The Slidewalk/Where You
Gonna Go (Soweto)/The Man In Me/Remote
Control/Working And Waiting/Heart &*

Mind/Brand New Cadillac/London
Calling/Revolution Rock
Disc 3: *The Last Testament – The Making of
London Calling* DVD

Clash related projects
Singles
The Vice Creems – *Danger Love/Like A
Tiger* [7", Zigzag Records, 1978]
Tymon Dog – *Lose This Skin/Indestructible*
[7", Ghost Dance, 1981]
Ellen Foley – *The Shuttered Palace/Beautiful
Waste of Time* [7", Epic, 1981]
Ellen Foley – *Torchlight/A Game of Man*
[7", Epic, 1981]
Futura 2000 – *The Escapades of Futura
2000* [12", Celluloid, 1982]
Janie Jones & The Lash – *House of The Ju-
Ju Queen/Sex Machine* [7", Big Beat, 1983]

Albums
Ellen Foley – **Spirit of St Louis** [Epic, Mar
1981]
*The Shuttered Palace/Torchlight/Beautiful
Waste Of Time/The Death Of The
Psychoanalyst Of Salvador Dali/MPH/My
Legionnaire/Theatre Of Cruelty/How Glad I
Am/Phases Of Travel/Game Of A
Man/Indestructible/In The Killing Hour*

Joe Strummer

Singles
Love Kills/Dum Dum Club [7", Epic, Jun
1986]
**Trash City/Theme From Permanent
Record** [7", Epic, Jun 1988] with The
Latino Rockabilly War
Gangsterville/Jewellers And Bums [7",
Epic, Aug 1989] with The Latino
Rockabilly War
Island Hopping/15th Brigade [7", Epic,
Oct 1989] with The Latino Rockabilly War
**Island Hopping/Cholo Vest/Mango
Street/Baby O'Boogie** [12", Epic, Oct
1989] with The Latino Rockabilly War

Albums
Earthquake Weather [Epic, Sep 1989]
*Dizzy's Goatee/Gangsterville/King of the
Bayou/Sikorsky Parts/Boogie With Your
Children/Slant Six/Island Hopping/
Leopardskin Limousines/Jewellers And*

Bums/Highway One Zero Street/Passport To
Detroit/Shouting Street/Ride Your
Donkey/Sleepwalk* with The Latino
Rockabilly War

Joe Strummer & The Mescaleros

Singles
**Yalla Yalla (album version)/The X-Ray
Style (Live)/Yalla Yalla (Norro's King
Dub)/The Time And The Tide** [7",UK;
Casbah/Mercury, US; Hellcat, Oct 1999]
Johnny Appleseed/At The Border, Guy
[7", Hellcat, Oct 1999]
Coma Girl/Blitzkrieg Bop (Live) [7",
Hellcat, Jun 2003]
**Redemption Song/Arms Aloft/Junco
Partner** (Live) [7", Hellcat, Dec 2003]

Albums
Rock Art & The X-Ray Style [UK;
Casbah/Mercury, US; Hellcat, Oct 1999]
*Tony Adams/Sandpaper Blues/X-Ray
Style/Techno D-Day/The Road To Rock 'n'
Roll/Nitcomb/Diggin' The New/Forbidden
City/Yalla Yalla/Willesden To Cricklewood*

Global A Go-Go [Hellcat, Jul 2002]
*Johnny Appleseed/Cool 'N' Out/Global A Go-
Go/Bhindi Bhagee/Gamma Ray/Mega Bottle
Ride/Shaktar Donetsk/Bummed Out City/At
The Border, Guy/Minstrel Boy*

Streetcore [Hellcat, Oct 2003]
*Coma Girl/Get Down Moses/Long
Shadow/Arms Aloft/Ramshackle Day
Parade/Redemption Song/All In A
Day/Burnin' Streets/Midnight Jam/Silver And
Gold*

Acknowledgements

Writing this book has been an unmitigated pleasure. Not only because it gave me an excuse to relive a string of pricelessly groovy times and revisit favourite records. It also brought me back in contact with some old mates I didn't think I'd ever see again, who in turn played a great part in the book's inception. I started getting in touch with characters from my Clash past, many of whom I hadn't seen for over twenty years.

First came Robin Banks, Mick's school accomplice and my best mate/partner-in-crime in The Clash glory years. It felt like 1977 again as we talked every day, although Robin set the template for everyone else when he admitted it was all, 'a bit of a blur'. But he has been an invaluable inspiration and I can't thank him enough for his insights [even if he does have the testicles of a giraffe instead of ears].

Then it was Johnny Green, the bisonic man who kept The Clash on the road, before becoming road manager for the band I managed with more riotous results. Johnny's recollections and observations, injected with the spirit of Foghorn Leghorn, were crucial and I'm so glad we're back in touch. Both wanted to write forewords.

Like Johnny said about Joe's funeral, this was starting to feel like *This Is Your Life*. Thanks to these two, I hooked up with Topper Headon - again for the first time in over twenty years. Now finally sorted out from the problems that have plagued his past, Topper was totally honest and made the effort.

Mick Jones started all this and his spirit hovered mothlike over this book's creation as the memories came flooding back. He took time out to talk in a hectic schedule and I thank him for that. The man's a genius and, according to Paul, a Thompson's gazelle. Don Letts filmed it all and helped elevate Mick out of his post-Clash shockwave period with BAD. The Clash were part of his multi-cultural mission and his *Dread Meets Hip Hop Downtown* compilation was my soundtrack while writing this. Thanks to Don for the support and permission to use the *Westway To The World* material.

Richard Norris helped wrench Joe out of his nineties wilderness and restore his burning edge, paving the way to the Mescaleros. Thanks to Richard for the story of Strummer's return and the early encouragement.

Jock Scott - much-loved member of the Clash crew since the late seventies and master of the extended anecdote - rode again. Cheers, Jock. 'Dodgy' Roger Goodman was close to Joe from the infamous ecstasy epiphany of mid-'95 and he continues to carry on the Strummer philosophy on life. His tales and photos proved invaluable.

Special merit award to my editor Dick Porter, who chewed it up and spat it out with aplomb and sensitivity to the mighty task at hand. The midwife who delivered my baby! Once again I wrote too much but Dick's sympathy to the cause and sense of humour turned out to be a magic ingredient.

FML Management - David & Joseph Stopps, Sara, Nicky and Jeanette - for letting me use their facilities (and also putting on The Clash in Aylesbury those times!).

And finally, Michelle Long, my long-suffering partner. We got engaged while I was doing this! Unfortunately for my beloved, I came right off the back of doing a Keith Richards epic and straight into this. Suddenly, she's got to put up with blokes phoning up pretending to be different forms of Serengetti wildlife. Michelle thinks doing this book has turned me into a better person. Certainly a happier one, but most of the credit goes to her. As ever, I love you.

Strummer/Clash-related shouts go out to: Steve 'Roadent' Connelly; Barry 'the Baker' Auguste; Luce & Joe's extended family; Barry 'Scratchy' Myers; Paul & Tricia Simonon; Pennie Smith; Tony James; Rat Scabies; Leo Williams; Gary Dyson; Richard Dudanski; Rick Rubin; the Mescaleros; Pockets; Pat Gilbert & Mickey Foote.

Of course, this book is dedicated to Joe's immortal memory, but also R.I.P. Guy Stevens, Stella Marcus, David Needs, Ian Dury, Johnny Cash, Johnny Thunders, Jerry Nolan & the three brothers Ramone.

Now the roll-call: My long-lost son Daniel Lee Needs; my mum Joan Needs; The kids - Abbey, Chloe, Jamie & Ellie Long; Julia & Adrian Needs & their families; Julie & Alan Long; Aaron, Chris & Julian Liberator, Guy 'The Geezer' McAffer; Paul Kirwan and the boys at the Record & Tape Exchange, London; Robin Pike; Irvine Welsh & Beth; Bob Morris; Dave Clarke, Stuart McMillan, Orde Meikle, Jim Hutchison & Soma; Alan, Jackie & Paul Clayton; Keith Richards; Martin Duffy, Della & Louie; Gary 'Mani' Mounfield & Imelda; Bobby Gillespie & family; Andrew Innes, Alison, Eva & Sid; Robert Young, Jane & family; Everyone else at Scream Central; Grant Fleming; Graham Gillespie, Titch, Bob & the Queens mob; Ivor Wilkins; Dave Beer & the Basics family; Andrew Weatherall & Keith Tenniswood; Jim Fyffe; Simon Edwards; Prodigy; John Peel; Annie Nightingale; Kiss & WBLS, New York City; Ronnie Wood & the Faces; John & Norah Lydon; The Slits; Alan McGee & Kate; Grant Fleming; Mike Dowse; Siobhan Fahey & Wildcat Will; Dean & Heather Thatcher; Rob Callaghan, Angie, Rob Savage, Roots, Joolz, Ronnie, Warren Smith, Squiffy, John Fez & the Breakin' Even crew, Reading; Carl Loben & DJ Mag; Nick Darby & Update; Martin & Hannah, plus Louie @ Revolution Records, Aylesbury; Alan & SMERSH bar; Jonas Stone; Vernon; Bernie, Sam & Charlotte; El Strongo & Mel; Jodie & Steve; Cherry & Jack, LA; Nicky; Stuey & Linda; Nigel the herbsman; Kelly Mullis; Jodie & Steve; Phil & Sara Silcock; Cherry & Jack, LA; Steve Mirkin, LA; Marc & Nancy Mikulich; Parker & Mary-Beth DuLaney; Ian Hunter & Mott; My long-haired friends Caramella, Tinkabell, Harry & Misty; Foghorn Leghorn & the wildebeests of Serengetti for inspiration.

Additonal thanks to Sandra Wake, Terry Porter, Louise and Rebecca at Plexus for putting up with another epic.

Also my appreciation to various publications who - for better or worse! - have written about Joe and The Clash, including *Sniffin' Glue, NME, Uncut, Mojo, Q, and Clash*. Clash-wise scribes: Mark Perry, Charles Shaar Murray, Allan Jones, Simon Goddard, Chris Sandwich, Gavin Martin, Nick Kent and Simon Harper. Will *Zigzag* rise again?

Many thanks to Simon and his wonderful *Trakmarx* website for flying the flag.

Lastly, if you're in the crowd tonight, have a drink on me.

Thanks to the following photographers, magazines, publications and photographic agencies: Adrian Boot/Sony Music; Paul Slattery/Retna; John Tiberi/Redferns; Richard Mann/Retna; Joe Stevenson/Retna; Erica Echenberg; Ray Stevenson/Retna; Jonh Ingham; Sheila Rock; Stevenson; Annette Weatherman; Caroline Coon/Camera Press; Lynn Goldsmith/Corbis; Jon Hammer/Getty; Roger Ressmeyer/Corbis; Pennie Smith/Sony Music; Paul Slattery/Sony Music; Virginia Turbett/Redferns; Dennis O'Regan/Corbis; Ebet Roberts/Redferns; Kees Tabak/Retna; Walter McBride/Retna; Neal Preston/Corbis; Mike Laye/Corbis; Adrian Boot/Retna; Daniel Lainé/Corbis; Jim Sharpe/Redferns; Roger Goodman; Anthony Saint James/Retna; Dave Hogan/Getty; Anthony Pidgeon/Retna. Also thanks to Carl Loben of *DJ* magazine, Simon (Suburban Kid) and special thanks to Roger Goodman for all his Joe photographs and memorabilia. All other images, photographs and ephemera courtesy of Kris Needs, *Zigzag, New York Rocker, Flexipop!*, and (CBS) Sony music. Cover image courtesy of CBS.

It has not been possible in all cases to trace the copyright sources, and the publishers would be glad to hear from any unacknowledged copyright holders.